**Rediscovering the American Midwest**

Series Editors: Jon K. Lauck and Patricia Oman

The Midwestern Moment                   Jon K. Lauck, ed.
The Forgotten World of Early Twentieth-Century
Midwestern Regionalism, 1880–1940

The American Midwest in a Scattering Time      Sara Kosiba, ed.
How Modernism Met Midwestern Culture

Pieces of the Heartland                     Andy Oler, ed.
Representing Midwestern Places

# The Midwestern Moment

To Ellis W. Hawley, Kansan

# The Midwestern Moment

The Forgotten World of Early Twentieth-Century Midwestern Regionalism, 1880–1940

Edited by
Jon K. Lauck

Hastings College Press | Hastings, Nebraska

© 2017 by Hastings College Press

All rights reserved. No part of this book may be used or reproduced in any manner whatsoever without permission from the publisher, except in the case of brief quotations embodied in critical articles and reviews.

**Copy Editors**
Bruce Batterson
Emily Bennett
Kaitlin Grode

**Book Design**
Patricia Oman

**Paperback**   ISBN-10: 1942885504    ISBN-13: 978-1-942885-50-4

**Hardback**   ISBN-10: 1942885490    ISBN-13: 978-1-942885-49-8

Manufactured in the United States of America.

Text is printed on acid-free, chlorine-free paper.

# Contents

| | | |
|---|---|---|
| Jon K. Lauck | Introduction<br>Mapping the Contours of the Midwestern Moment | ix |
| Elizabeth Raymond | Creating the Heartland<br>The Midwest Emerges in American Culture | 1 |
| Robert Loerzel | "People are getting tired of Broadway and Fifth Avenue"<br>The Origins of the Society of Midland Authors | 19 |
| Jeremy Beer | Midlander<br>Booth Tarkington's Defense of the Midwest | 35 |
| Harl A. Dalstrom | "Let us write like inspired artists and sell like shrewd Yankees"<br>Bess Streeter Aldrich's Early-Twentieth-Century Middle West | 55 |
| Cherie Dargan | The Realistic Regionalism of Iowa's Ruth Suckow | 71 |
| Zachary Michael Jack | The Curious Case of Jay G. Sigmund<br>The Midwest's Most Rooted Regionalist? | 87 |
| Michael J. Pfeifer | A Symphonic Midwest<br>The Minneapolis Symphony Orchestra and Regionalist Identity, 1903–1922 | 101 |
| Paul Emory Putz | The Homer of Middle-Western America<br>Walt Mason's Syndicated Midwestern Poetry | 113 |

| John E. Hallwas | Village Realism but No Revolt<br>Frazier Hunt's *Sycamore Bend* | 129 |
| John E. Miller | South Dakota Artist Harvey Dunn<br>Expressing Midwestern Regional Values<br>and Identity on Canvas | 143 |
| Kimberly K. Porter | The Most Talked-About Personality<br>in the Middle West<br>Henry Field's Struggle to Maintain the<br>Midwestern Ideal on Iowa Radio | 161 |
| Allan C. Carlson | "Flee to the Fields"<br>Midwestern Catholicism and the Last<br>Agrarian Crusade, 1920–1941 | 185 |
| Michael C. Steiner | The Midwestern Mind of Jane Addams<br>Cultural Pluralism and the Rural Roots of<br>an Urban Idea | 207 |
| Philip A. Greasley | The Rise of the Midwest, the Chicago<br>Renaissance, and the Quest for<br>National Recognition | 229 |
| Jon K. Lauck | Typecast Rebels<br>The Strange Careers of *Winesburg, Ohio*<br>and *Main Street* | 247 |
| Tom Perrin | Edited for the Old Lady in Dubuque<br>The Middlebrow Literature of the Midwest | 265 |
| Contributors | | 281 |

Jon K. Lauck | Introduction

Mapping the Contours of the Midwestern Moment

Prior to the mid-nineteenth century, much of what is now the American Midwest was still considered "the West" or the "the Great West." A large part of the region was still a transition zone and its people migratory and in motion, and it often served as a short-term destination and then a departure point for many Americans.[1] By the Civil War era, however, the Midwest began to take a more fully developed and permanent form. The politics of opposition to the Kansas-Nebraska Act galvanized the region, and when the Civil War came the Midwest landed solidly in the camp of the North, which was led by a consciously regionalist president from Illinois. The catastrophic war hardened the regional lines between the Midwest and the South.[2] This became the vital phase of midwestern regional identity formation.

What followed was a surge of regionalist energy in the Midwest. During the latter third of the nineteenth century, Midwesterners began to forge a strong regional culture and find voices to speak for the region, a cultural flowering made possible by the growing prominence of the Midwest in the nation at large.[3] In the wake of northern victory in the Civil War, the Midwest was the ascendant and victorious region that had supplied the industrial might, agrarian bounty, and soldiers needed for victory. Six of the seven presidents elected after the Civil War were Midwesterners, and they often waved the regionalist/anti-southern bloody shirt during their campaigns. Midwestern farmers enjoyed the fruits of bountiful soils, steel rails spread out and united the region, and industrialists tapped the region's forests and ores, the profits from which they used to build homes on Summit Avenue in St. Paul and on Chicago's Gold Coast and to fund the region's cultural infrastructure.[4] In Chicago, to take an obvious example, cultural institutions flourished, as Philip A. Greasley notes in this volume: the Field Museum (1893), the Art Institute of Chicago (1879), the Auditorium Building (1889),

Orchestra Hall (1904), the University of Chicago (1890), the Armour Institute (1890), the John Crerar Library (1894), the Newberry Library (1887), and the Chicago Public Library (1873) were all built during this era. This is also the era when the terms *Middle West* and *Midwest* became common.[5] In 1900, a historian declared that the Midwest "yields to no region in the world in interest, in romance, and in promise for the future. Here, if anywhere, is the real America—the field, the theater, and the basis of the civilization of the Western World."[6] The Midwestern Moment had arrived. Later, after a small burst of activity during the 1930s, these regionalist energies dissipated and the Midwest was too often neglected as "fly-over country"—but that is a story for another day and future books.

Our purpose here is to explore the contours of the Midwestern Moment in its various manifestations and, we hope, to help outline a research agenda for future historians. One logical first step is to trace the origins of the process by which the American Midwest came to be identified as the American heartland, the center of the nation, a place of bucolic beauty and agrarian idealism. In her contribution to this volume, Elizabeth Raymond, who has been thinking about this matter for a couple decades, explains the earliest understandings of the Midwest and how views of the Midwest evolved over time but still remained associated with a particular set of reassuring cultural images, mostly rural, often related to corn. The midwestern agricultural heartland, despite several periods of pain and economic stress and much socio-economic change since the era of the Midwestern Moment, still remains, Raymond explains, a "national source of psychic as well as visual relief" (13).

Another natural place to begin to understand the Midwestern Moment is Chicago, the unofficial capital of the Midwest, where regional enthusiasms ran strong in the late nineteenth century. In addition to the cultural institution-building noted above, intellectuals and writers in Chicago during this era were looking to formalize their work and the efforts of others around the region. They wanted a space to talk and share their work and invite in traveling writers and lecturers. As Robert Loerzel explains, they were "getting tired of Broadway and Fifth Avenue in their literature" and were frustrated by the "constant drain of talent which New York was taking" from the Midwest (23). As a result, in 1907, they formed the Attic Club, which then became the Cliff Dwellers club in Chicago, after a novel of the same name by Henry Blake Fuller.[7] In 1915, many of the same people formed the Society of Midland Authors, which created a cultural space for an emerging group of midwestern writers from the SMA's self-designated territory of Illinois, Indiana, Iowa, Kansas, Michigan, Minnesota, Missouri, Nebraska, North Dakota, Ohio, South Dakota, and Wisconsin. The SMA still meets every spring in Chicago.

Within the Society of Midland Authors there existed a tension between an older generation of midwestern writers and intellectuals and an emerging group of midwestern modernists, the latter of which are more often remembered today. But during the early stages of the Midwestern Moment the high ground was held by a more traditional group of regionalist writers perhaps best symbolized by Booth Tarkington of Indiana. During the late nineteenth and early twentieth centuries, Tarkington was wildly popular and a nationally known writer and widely recognized voice of the Midwest. In his chapter, Jeremy Beer explains Tarkington's one-time prominence, his forgotten complexity, and how Tarkington resisted the forces that sought to erase him from our cultural memory.

Several midwestern regionalist writers, seldom remembered today, followed in the wake of Tarkington. Beth Streeter Aldrich, as Harl Dalstrom explains, moved from Iowa to Nebraska and began writing novels and stories about the rural and small-town Midwest. Aldrich rebuffed those who thought the Midwest was not worth writing about and her novels sold well. Her novel *A White Bird Flying* garnered the third highest sales in the country in 1931 behind Pearl S. Buck's *The Good Earth* and Willa Cather's *Shadows on the Rock*. The short stories of Iowa's Ruth Suckow also captured the day-to-day rhythms of the rural Midwest, as did her novel *The Folks* (1934), a Literary Guild selection in 1934, as Cherie Dargan explains in her chapter. Another Iowan, Jay G. Sigmund, remains even more obscure than Suckow, perhaps because he rooted himself in eastern Iowa and did not indulge the literary circuit as much as Suckow did, as Zachary Michael Jack explains here. But Sigmund was recognized by the literary greats during the decades of the Midwestern Moment and his stories and poetry are perhaps the most faithful to the mission of rendering the essential tempo and truths of midwestern life.

The literary work of Tarkington, Aldrich, Suckow, and Sigmund was complemented by other forms of midwestern regionalism that simultaneously emerged in the realms of music, newspapers, art, and radio. To break its cultural dependence on the East, midwestern civic leaders began to organize their own symphony orchestras in cities such as Detroit (1887), Chicago (1891), and Cincinnati (1895). In his chapter, Michael J. Pfeifer tells the story of the Minneapolis Symphony, which was organized in 1903. The Minneapolis Symphony traveled all around the Midwest and brought music to many of the region's smaller cities and generally succeeded in "reversing the eastern hegemony that had long characterized the country's classical musical scene" (108).

Word of the travels of the Minneapolis Symphony spread by way of the Midwest's thick constellation of newspapers, which were essential to the civic life of the region and which often carried news of the work of regionalist writers or their work itself. Paul Emory Putz, in his chapter, examines the life of Walt Mason, the "Homer" of the midwestern country town. Mason, who was a Nebraskan, gained prominence from 1909 to 1920 when he went to work at William Allen White's *Emporia Gazette* in Kansas. His homespun poems and columns promoting the work ethic, country life, and baseball made him a prominent regionalist voice, particularly when his work became syndicated and ran in newspapers all over the Midwest. The Illinois newspaperman Frazier Hunt also spoke for the region, as John E. Hallwas chronicles in this volume. Even though he left his Alexis, Illinois, newspaper to move to New York and become a foreign correspondent, Hunt was so impressed with his years as a country editor that he wrote a novel that challenged the images of small towns supposedly purveyed by Sinclair Lewis's *Main Street*. Set in 1922, Hunt's *Sycamore Bend* relays the story of the small-town editor Will Hadley at the *Sycamore Bend Sentinel* and portrays the communal charms of small-town life in rural Illinois. The novel mocks those who ridicule small towns as "only for second-raters—the left-overs—the people who didn't have enough ambition to move out of their tracks" (132).

A country editor in the mold of William Allen White and Frazier Hunt was also crucial to the long-term preservation of some iconic regionalist art from the Midwest from this era. Aubrey Sherwood of the *De Smet News* in De Smet, South Dakota, began beating the drum for the assembly and preservation of the rural midwestern paintings of Harvey Dunn, who, as John E. Miller explains here, belongs in the same category as the iconic midwestern artists Thomas Hart Benton, Grant Wood, and John Steuart Curry.[8] After some training at South Dakota Agricultural

Jon K. Lauck    xiii

College (later South Dakota State University) and a move to Chicago in 1902 for more study, Dunn became a nationally known illustrator for major magazines while still traveling home to South Dakota to collect the thoughts that would ultimately become four dozen paintings that depict life in the rural Midwest.

Outside of the realms of art, music, and literature—and surely the hottest new medium of the era of the Midwestern Moment—was radio. In her chapter, Kimberly K. Porter examines the life of midwestern radio pioneer Henry Field, who took his Iowa seed business to new heights by dabbling in radio station programming in Omaha and then, in 1924, by launching KFNF, his own station. KFNF catered to his rural, midwestern audience by focusing on seeds, soil, and farming, by playing gospel tunes such as "Shall We Gather at the River" and "Pass Me Not Gentle Savior," and by scoffing at cultural elites and jazz music.

By catering to rural Midwesterners, Henry Field's radio station tapped into the richness of the midwestern agrarian tradition that gave rise to the powerful imagery of the region that Elizabeth Raymond explores in her chapter. After the 1920 census, however, when it was reported that the nation had become more urban than rural, many commentators worried about the diminishment of the American agrarian tradition. During this era midwestern Catholic leaders, following on the work of the largely Protestant Country Life Commission, began to articulate these concerns with added vigor. They launched, as Allan C. Carlson explains in his chapter, the "last agrarian crusade" to preserve the old midwestern rural order and resist the rise of urban influences.

While midwestern agrarian sentiments and Henry Field's rural regionalism were buttressed by the heavily churched countryside and emerging radio networks, the power of the urban Midwest grew unabated and it also generated new and varied forms of regionalist work. When pursuing her settlement house agenda in Chicago, Jane Addams drew upon her small-town experiences growing up in Cedarville, Illinois, as Michael C. Steiner explains in his chapter. Addams's childhood in diverse but peaceful Cedarville inspired her advocacy of a new model of urban pluralism designed to meet the needs of the modern city. Chicago was also an important location for the emergence of a new midwestern and modernist literature. As Greasley explains, an older, more traditional midwestern regionalist literature became overshadowed by the second generation of the Chicago Renaissance, which Bernard Duffey called "the Liberation" and which was led by "liberated intellectual bohemians" such as Sherwood Anderson.[9] At the same time, as I attempt to demonstrate in my chapter, Anderson operated on multiple levels. The work of Anderson and Lewis, to whom Anderson is often linked, can be too narrowly interpreted as merely a "revolt from the village" when it is often more finely balanced, more sympathetic to the Midwest, and more closely linked to traditional midwestern regionalists such as Ruth Suckow than is commonly remembered. In additional challenges to definitions of midwestern literature of the interwar years as rural and traditional, Tom Perrin explores a contrasting "middlebrow" strain, and Greasley deftly describes the writers of the second generation of the Chicago Renaissance. The emergence of important African American writers in Chicago, including Richard Wright and Gwendolyn Brooks, is also discussed by Greasley.

There is much to be said, in short, about the forgotten and misunderstood and complicated voices of the Midwestern Moment and much more to be learned. We hope that this volume will prompt more discussion and more research about the Midwest during this era and other time periods and further contribute to the upsurge in work on the Midwest in recent years.[10] The details and nuances of the Midwestern Moment have only been scratched, it seems, and far too few of its varied voices heard from in recent decades. The work of Walt Mason, Frazier Hunt, and Henry Field, for example, was completely new to me when this project began. With the rise of digitization and the opening of vast new quantities of data from older midwestern newspapers and archives, future graduate students could surely find more of the Midwest's forgotten voices on their way to dissertations and books on the Midwestern Moment. It also seems to be time for a substantive treatment of the prehistory of the Midwestern Moment, or an examination of the Civil War era and the process of midwestern identity formation.

Whatever direction future research takes, its circulation will be dependent on interested publishers. With that in mind, I want to extend my heartiest thanks to Patricia Oman, the tireless director of Hastings College Press, who believed in this project from the start. This collection is the first in the Rediscovering the American Midwest series and will soon be one of many new works about the Midwest published by Hastings College Press.

## Notes

1. David M. Wrobel, *Global West, American Frontier: Travel, Empire, and Exceptionalism from Manifest Destiny to the Great Depression* (Albuquerque: University of New Mexico Press, 2013).
2. Christopher Phillips, *The Rivers Ran Backward: The Civil War and the Remaking of the American Middle Border* (New York: Oxford University Press, 2016).
3. Michael C. Steiner, "Regionalist Thought in the Midwest," paper presented at the First Annual Midwestern History Conference, Grand Valley State University, Grand Rapids, Michigan, April 2015; Benjamin T. Spencer, "Regionalism in American Literature," in Merrill Jensen (ed.), *Regionalism in America* (Madison, University of Wisconsin Press, 1951), 231–38; Jon K. Lauck, *From Warm Center to Ragged Edge: The Erosion of Midwestern Literary and Historical Regionalism, 1920–1965* (Iowa City: University of Iowa Press, 2017), 1–4.
4. Jon K. Lauck, "Why the Midwest Matters," *Midwest Quarterly* 54.2 (Winter 2013), 165–85.
5. James R. Shortridge, *The Middle West: Its Meaning in American Culture* (Lawrence: University Press of Kansas, 1989).
6. Albert Bushnell Hart, "The Future of the Mississippi Valley," *Harper's Magazine* 101 (February 1900), 413. On the region's prominence during this era, see also Cameron Blevins, "Space, Nation, and the Triumph of Region: A View of the World from Houston," *Journal of American History* 101.1 (June 2014), 129.
7. Bernard R. Bowron, Jr., *Henry B. Fuller of Chicago: The Ordeal of a Genteel Realist in Ungenteel America* (Westport, CT: Greenwood Press, 1974).
8. Sherwood also promoted the work of De Smet's Laura Ingalls Wilder, who is a well-remembered voice from the Midwestern Moment. See John E. Miller, *Laura Ingalls Wilder's Little Town: Where History and Literature Meet* (Lawrence: University Press of Kansas, 1994).
9. Bernard Duffey, *The Chicago Renaissance in American Letters: A Critical History* (East Lansing: Michigan State College Press, 1954), 131.
10. Jon K. Lauck, "The Origins and Progress of the Midwestern History Association, 2013–2016," *Studies in Midwestern History* 2.11 (October 2016), 139–49; Jon K. Lauck, *The Lost Region: Toward a Revival of Midwestern History* (Iowa City, University of Iowa Press, 2013).

Elizabeth Raymond | Creating the Heartland
 | The Midwest Emerges in
 | American Culture

In a 1976 article entitled "How the Middle West Became America's Heartland," historian Martin Ridge points to what now seems an eternal verity of the U.S. landscape. Ridge observes in passing that "the visual image of the American farm is neither the cotton field nor the vineyard, but the corn and wheat fields of the Middle West." Schematic pictorial maps confirm his claim, with corn stalks, hogs, and shocks of wheat routinely serving to evoke the Middle West. In a country that sings about its beauty in terms of spacious skies and amber waves of grain, there is perhaps nothing remarkable about this. Yet the association is hardly inevitable. After all, as historian Jon Teaford points out, "the production of motor vehicles was a midwestern industry as characteristic of the heartland as the planting of corn."[1]

But it is corn that prevails in popular regional imagery. BBC journalist Alistair Cooke observed the phenomenon when he toured the United States in the early 1940s. Cooke traveled throughout the country to document the impact of World War II for English readers. He visited cities and war plants but also inspected ranches and all manner of farms. Well acquainted with the range and variety of American agriculture, Cooke noted that the midwestern model was its predominant representation. When "foreign economists, agricultural writers, special investigators and newspapermen gravitate to study 'the American farmer,'" he wrote, they inevitably came to Iowa:

> Why he should be sought here is probably an intriguing study in itself.... I would agree with the Western wheat and livestock farmer that because the Department of Agriculture is staffed by Midwesterners, Washington and the newspapers and their readers unwittingly accept the small diversified-crop farm as "typical" of the country.[2]

While the nature and scale of midwestern farming has changed considerably since Cooke's travels, the region's popular association with agriculture and rural ways of life has not.

Depictions of midwestern rural landscape as both universally characteristic of the region and also normative for the nation have been noted by numerous scholars and they figure prominently in creating the Midwestern Moment that is the subject of this volume. In this essay I briefly trace the emergence of this iconic midwestern heartland as a monoculture of neat row crops displaced the original oceanic tall-grass prairies. Although by no means universally characteristic of the landscape in the region, the corn fields of the country's temperate interior have come to be understood and represented as quintessentially midwestern and thus, by extension, American. As Douglas Reichert Powell notes, "a region is not a thing so much as a cultural history, an ongoing rhetorical and poetical construction." This essay explores that historical process of rhetorical and poetical construction as it applies to the Middle West and especially to the fertile, agricultural center portion that came to be popularly known as "the Corn Belt."[3]

These "typical" midwestern corn landscapes were physically constructed by generations of farm families who worked hard to graft the rectangular survey onto the formerly boundless prairies in the form of section line roads and tidy geometrical fields.[4] Simultaneously these new landscapes were culturally imbued with meanings in a continuing historical process of interaction between people and place. Literary and artistic representations were as important as the physical transformations in creating this symbolic landscape. The regional revivalism of the early twentieth century played an instrumental part in crystalizing the association between the region and its major crop. By the mid-twentieth century the transformed prairie landscape of the Middle West had come to be the widely accepted symbol of the American agricultural heartland.

---

Physical and cultural definitions of the region are notoriously various. Debates about its boundaries can be heated. While the U.S. Census Bureau carves out an expansive twelve-state region that it neutrally labels "North Central," geographer James Shortridge has pointed out that the Middle West's precise location and extent varied through the nineteenth century, never conforming neatly with state boundaries. Indeed in 1935 ambitious New Deal planners from the National Resources Board devised an intriguing series of detailed national maps, each of which depicted a distinct set of regional subdivisions as determined by variables such as soil type, mineral resources, metropolitan regions, political affiliation, or "socio-economic homogeneity." Their extensive cartographic efforts culminated in a proposal to designate a series of environmentally rational regions "based upon composite planning problems." The Midwest they defined looks substantially like one recently featured in a *New York Times* article that attempted to map the American heartland. That map defined the Midwest in terms of areas where a high percentage of residents professed loyalty to baseball teams in the central division.[5] Opinions about what is and is not midwestern still diverge in the twenty-first century, but Shortridge's late-twentieth-century consensus view of its location covered a region roughly coterminous with the pre-settlement tall-grass prairie, where native grasses were plentiful and well-watered, and grew to a height of six to eight feet. This area—centered on Iowa and Illinois, but extending east into western Ohio and west to include the well-watered eastern portions of Kansas, Nebraska, and the Dakotas—is characterized by flat, open, relatively featureless terrain, and is devoted even in the twenty-first century primarily to agricultural uses, especially the cultivation of wheat, soybeans, and corn. It is the latter, in particular, that has come to characterize the region symbolically, sometimes to the dismay of its citizens, at other times with their active collusion. Although cities and industry contain the population and dominate the economy, farms remain central to popular perception and representation of "the Corn Belt." Its relentlessly rectilinear landscape of family farmsteads surrounded by large, flat fields is familiar even to those who may never have set foot in the Midwest. The symbolic ear of corn is the visual icon of "flyover country."[6]

Originally covered by a carpet of grasses and forbs that was extended, if not produced, by Native American burning, the midwestern prairies confounded early Euroamerican observers. They recorded its peculiar effect in terms similar to those employed by Paul Gruchow when describing the Cayler Prairie in northwestern Iowa: "There is no place to hide on the Cayler. This was the feature of the prairie landscape that overwhelmed so many pioneers, the realization that it was so exposed, so naked. There was something relentless about the scale of it."[7] Stephen Kearney, for instance, crossing Iowa from Omaha to Minneapolis in 1820, evinced no high hopes for the country he encountered:

> A very great portion of the country in the neighborhood of our route could be of no other object (at any time) to our govn't in the acquisition of it, than the expulsion of the savages from it ... for the disadvantages [lack of timber and water] will forever prevent its supporting more than a thinly scattered population.[8]

Explorer Joseph Nicollet was similarly unimpressed when he reported on the James River country in Dakota in 1839. Among the records of his trip was a recipe for an "effervescent draught" of tartaric acid and bicarbonate of soda, which he prescribed to members of his party in order to relieve the listlessness induced by prolonged exposure to monotonous prairie scenery.[9] In the midst of the oceanic openness of unfenced and undrained grasslands, both observers and inhabitants were challenged to construct a place more human in scale. They did so in several discrete phases, both physical and conceptual, to produce the now familiar midwestern Corn Belt.

As travelers and tourists followed in the wake of early explorers, accounts of the prairie landscape multiplied. One early English visitor, W. Faux, writing in 1819, deplored the Illinois landscape he encountered: "I hate the prairies, all of them; insomuch that I would not have any of them of a gift [sic], if I must be compelled to live on them." In time, however, Faux and other critics were countered by a growing body of prairie enthusiasts, travelers who created paeans to the landscape's grandeur and extent, the mysteries of its origins, the beauty of its flowers, and—a particularly common theme—its uncanny resemblance to settled English countryside.[10] The region became exotic. Scottish adventurer Laurence Oliphant in 1855 acclaimed the "wonderful combination of civilisation and barbarism" he found on the newly settled prairies of Minnesota; while American John Van Tramp concluded authoritatively that the Illinois prairies were fully the equal of the country's most acclaimed and venerable scenic wonder, Niagara Falls:

Though Illinois, in her physical outline, presents to the traveler but few very bold and striking features, she is by no means void of objects of interest to the student of nature. Her expanded prairies, decked in their holiday array that outvies "Solomon in all his glory," besides their landscape beauty, inspire a feeling of sublimity, from their vastness, like unto that experienced by a first view of old ocean; and perhaps no natural object in our country—not even excepting the classic Niagara—would more fix the admiration of a visitor from the Old World, than a view of the Grand Prairie in its summer attire.[11]

Collectively these early accounts stimulated a "prairie craze," a popular convention of prairie viewing that remained a strong force until the late nineteenth century. Well-instructed visitors such as Margaret Fuller visited the region to see its natural splendors, wrote about what they saw, and thereby made the Midwest into a significant tourist attraction as well as a settlement destination. Land agents and travel writers alike conspired to render the new landscape enticing to an expanding reading public. Their settlement guides and travel accounts referred to the region as the "Great West" and taught at least two generations of readers to regard it as both unique and instructive. Prairie landscape became one of the nation's nineteenth-century natural wonders, one part of the sublime landscape that intellectuals promoted as a both a factor distinguishing the United States from Europe and one that would ensure its national preeminence.[12] Devotees of this tradition of scenic veneration displayed their sophistication through the aesthetic appreciation of the prairie landscape. When he visited the United States, in 1842, Charles Dickens asked specifically to be taken to see a prairie. While contemporary American tourists might be hard pressed to see its appeal, travelers like William Ferguson, in 1856, could exclaim about the landscape without the slightest hint of irony: "A western prairie! a dream realised!" Almost twenty years later, Grace Greenwood was similarly moved. In an image that confounds the modern scenic aesthetic, she inquired: "If a cornfield of several thousand acres is not 'a symbol of the infinite,' I should like to know what is."[13]

As transportation improved and settlers domesticated the tallgrass prairies, the focus of romantic tourism moved still further west, to the more dramatic expanses of California and the Rocky Mountains. In the prairie Midwest, by contrast, fences, drainage tile, railroads, and section line roads replaced waving grasses to create an agricultural landscape that gradually took on a new identity as just one among many distinct western districts. No longer *the* west, and certainly not the Great West of early nineteenth-century fame, the region slowly emerged in a more mundane form as the nation's diminished "middle" West.[14]

New chronicles recorded the changes. In this second phase of its historical identity, from approximately 1860 to 1890 (later in more western areas), the emerging region was enthusiastically hailed as the quintessential embodiment of America's agrarian destiny. The midwestern agricultural landscape was recorded and celebrated in the maps, county atlases, and local histories of the mid-nineteenth century and later in numerous memoirs, diaries, and journals of what came to be known as the pioneer period. Eventually it found its way into the popular press. In these multiplying texts a regional mythology of environmental triumph and transformation was first produced.[15]

Here, the perspective was internal, as residents recorded their pride in having physically recast the trackless prairies to make them into productive farms. When Norwegian immigrant and later judge Andreas Ueland summarized the process retrospectively, in his 1929 autobiography, for example, his sense of personal achievement was palpable:

> I see farms to the right and left with comfortable dwellings and big, red barns, sheltered in groves of planted trees.... I pass through towns with fine buildings for dwellings and business. I reflect that when there wasn't yet a wagon road where I now ride in a Pullman, Norwegian and Swedish immigrants came here in canvas-covered wagons pulled by oxen, and where they found no human trace on the ground they unhitched, built log or sod houses for shelter, and out of the wilderness made what I now see.

The judge interpreted the productive Minnesota landscape as a valuable human creation, not a space for exalted contemplation of nature's beauty. Himself intimately involved in the transformation, Ueland knew well the emotional and physical cost of those farms and railroads. He was proud of effacing the prairies and making the land productive.[16]

Ueland's quiet meditation on Minnesota abundance summons up an alternative narrative of midwestern landscape. Writer Hamlin Garland summarized the mechanics with an elegant metaphor in *A Son of the Middle Border:* "Day by day the settlement thickened. Section by section the prairie was blackened by the plow," culminating in "land [that] needed only to be tickled with a hoe to laugh into harvest." But less articulate witnesses also rejoiced in the agricultural abundance they helped to produce. In 1848 an anonymous Illinois farmer praised the fertility of the prairie when comparing his new situation to his previous home: "In Ohio a feller has to fight hard for every inch o' ground he gets, and when the ground is once cleared off, it can't begin to compare with this soil, all clear and slick to your hand." So, too, did other proud nineteenth-century prairie farmers who left no written records of their lives, but paid to record their accomplishments for their peers and posterity in the farmstead engravings that illustrated the ubiquitous county atlases of the period. Their homely pride in the bounteous new environment they had composed out of raw land fairly leaped from the pages.[17]

Glorification of early agricultural struggles is a central feature of later midwestern novels like Ole Rølvaag's *Giants in the Earth* (1927) or Willa Cather's *O Pioneers!* (1913), but it appears first in a more mundane setting, in the hundreds of county atlases and histories issued in the Midwest in the last third of the nineteenth century. There the prairie was characteristically depicted as an obstacle, and its residents as brave pioneers, laboring to produce farmland. One 1872 Illinois account summarized the positive changes they effected: "The villages have sprung up as it were in a day.... The stately thickets have grown to luxuriant forests, from which the deer have fled, and what was then a paradise to the eye has become the fruitful garden of the world." The Corn Belt was by the late nineteenth century emerging into local legend, if not yet national visibility.[18]

Midwestern residents understood that farmland was a creation. Illinois was not naturally "the Garden of the World." It had to be produced and maintained by hard labor, just as the native prairie before it was produced and maintained through the efforts of the indigenous tribes who burned it annually. Writers of myriad county histories stressed the backbreaking work, harsh climate, and constant natural disasters that formed a counterpoint to their hard-won accomplishments. The published volumes assured their readers that "few can form a correct idea of the hardship and inconvenience of settling a new country," while lovingly recounting the heroic sacrifices that prairie settlers made to produce their seemingly mundane geometric landscape of section line roads and half-section farmsteads.[19]

This second version of midwestern landscape enjoyed national prominence. William Warntz suggests that the Corn Belt was well defined, though still unnamed, by 1879. Its tremendous fertility and bounteous harvests were a recognized factor in world markets, and helped to create the regional metropolis of Chicago. In popular history, midwestern productivity became the normative American environmental mythology, underlying later, doomed attempts in more arid environments like the Nevada desert or Montana high plains to accomplish the same miracle of agricultural abundance on initially unpromising land. Eventually, however, urbanization and industrialization focused national attention elsewhere and the formerly miraculous fecundity of the prairie came to seem routine.[20]

This third phase in the construction of the Midwest as America's agricultural heartland had its roots in the late nineteenth century, as rural and urban distinctions gained new significance and visibility in U.S. society and regional literature emerged as a distinct genre. Earlier American scenic tastes had not distinguished meaningfully between natural and industrial wonders; tourists were instructed by guidebooks to seek out and appreciate both. America's fin-de-siècle intellectuals, however, preferred a wilderness aesthetic that extolled "nature" as a social and psychological restorative. In this context, the relentlessly agrarian landscape of the Corn Belt became routine, neither wild enough to suit newly fashionable scenic tastes nor sufficiently efficient and technological to inspire progressive engineers.[21]

In this third incarnation, "middle" became a newly pejorative term for the region, which emerged officially for the first time as "the Corn Belt" in 1910. The *Century Dictionary* then defined it as a region primarily devoted to the cultivation of corn and hogs, covering the state of Iowa and portions of Ohio, Indiana, Illinois, Missouri, Kansas, and Nebraska. Simultaneously the spread of consumer culture and the significant impact of industrialization and immigration in U.S. cities gave rise to a contemptuous dismissal of rural culture as smug, materially impoverished, socially backward, and intellectually confining.[22]

The literary manifestation of this development was the early twentieth century "revolt from the village" identified most prominently with Sinclair Lewis's 1920 novel *Main Street*, but incorporating as well other midwestern writers including Floyd Dell, Sherwood Anderson, Susan Glaspell, and George Cram Cook. For them, and in the national press as well, the Midwest no longer signified either national fulfillment or individual achievement. Carrying on the economic critique of writers like Hamlin Garland and Joseph Howe, later writers bitterly criticized the region's failed promise by exposing the blighted or circumscribed lives of its residents. Despite the efforts of midwestern intellectuals to foster a competing regional culture, the Corn Belt was dismissed by numerous commentators as deadeningly materialistic.[23]

Other texts echoed this change in the cultural valence of midwestern landscape. Early twentieth-century atlases were no longer exuberant visual records of expansive farmsteads and prize-winning livestock. Now merely sober maps of property ownership, some excluded even the names of those who merely rented land. Novels depicting the Dust Bowl years of the 1930s, like Josephine Johnson's *Now in November* (1934) or Frederick Manfred's *This Is the Year* (1947), no longer recounted stories of agricultural triumph. Instead they inventoried failures, portraying the emotional as well as economic costs of the collapsing grain markets of the 1920s and the subsequent environmental crisis of the Dust Bowl, as farms and hopes were lost to erosion and foreclosure.[24] In Manfred's novel, for example, protagonist Pier Frixen's efforts to make sense of the loss of his farm during the Depression are both heroic and tragic:

> [H]e had tried to catch his anchor into the soils, had tried to get his roots down so deep that neither the wind nor flood, heat nor cold, could ever tear him out again … and had failed. Did a man have to die before he became a part of the old lady earth? Did a man's land work easier after it had been sweetened with the dust of his blood and brains?

In a significant twist on the previous regional narrative of triumph, Frixen's ignorance of the land produces disaster. Manfred's message is clear: Mistreated prairie soil will not produce. The midwestern breadbasket has betrayed its optimistic creators. Instead of the heralded nineteenth-century agricultural utopia, their heirs produced only exhausted cropland and a culturally bankrupt society. A nation now enamored of newer wests learned to see the middle version as a cultural backwater and an agricultural blunder.

Manfred's was not an isolated motif. Impressive numbers of depression-era midwestern novels were published from the 1930s through the 1950s. Writers like Paul Corey, Holger Cahill, and Lois Hudson repudiated second-stage triumphalism in works that painfully enumerated the costs and consequences of creating the Corn Belt. In *Judd Rankin's Daughter* (1944) Susan Glaspell overtly addressed the injustices of early midwestern history when she noted, "the deep obligation to make a good life, as a great wrong had been done in getting this land." Collectively these novels chronicled the Corn Belt's tragic failures to live up to its early agricultural promise. Their critique was echoed by another generation of writers during the farm crisis of the 1980s, when numerous farmers lost their land in another wave of overextension and loss of faith in the agricultural promise of the Corn Belt. By 1988, for essayist Howard Kohn, fertile land no longer proclaimed the triumph of hard working owners: "The land mocks the farmer by outlasting him and outlasting his family, no matter the number of successive generations."[25]

General dismissal of midwestern prairie landscape as a disappointment was not uncontested, however. At the same time, in the early decades of the twentieth century, a group of regional writers, artists, and intellectuals rallied to advance an alternative regional analysis, giving rise to the Midwestern Moment the present volume explores in detail. E. Bradford Burns traces the process in Iowa, where he notes the formative influence of John T. Frederick's journal, *The Midland*, and argues that "intellectual and farmer alike understood that the soil shaped place and people. It constituted the seed from which regionalism sprang." Michael Steiner notes its connection with a broader national interest in regionalism created during the same years (from 1890 to 1920) that was spurred by "a remarkably varied group of self-conscious Midwesterners." The result in the Midwest was an outpouring of poetry, fiction, essays, paintings, and conferences devoted to a more nuanced assessment of midwestern culture, one that complicated the simplistic identification of the Midwest with prairie agriculture. Collectively these works offered an alternative to the cosmopolitan dismissal of the agrarian Corn Belt, as Midwesterners articulated and promulgated their own definitions of the region and its importance.[26]

Paradoxically, during the final decades of the twentieth century, even as agricultural production declined as a percentage of the national economy and family farms decreased in number during the farm crisis of the 1980s, the midwestern landscape enjoyed a renewal of its symbolic eminence. In movies like *Country* (1984) and *Field of Dreams* (1989) the region emerged again to national attention, this time as a kind of nostalgic historical icon, the visible incarnation of Jeffersonian agrarianism. Not only was the midwestern Corn Belt again depicted as quintessential American farmland, but it also solidified its claim to be the country's symbolic heartland. According to critic Barry Gross, the Midwest had now become the normative psychological standard by which the rest of the nation was measured and found wanting:

> The suspicion persists that what goes on at either coast is the extreme, the perverse and bizarre, the grotesque and the Gothic, unreal and worse, unAmerican. The belief persists that the middle represents the heart and the center, the norm against which the extreme East and the extreme West are measured as abnormal, aberrational.

Iowa native son Ronald Weber, a journalism professor, echoed the same comforting notion of the Corn Belt as the physical embodiment of pastoral idealism: "Iowa is like that for me, an attractive idea, an imaginative center crowded with memories, a landscape of unstartling beauty. There more than most places, a gentle balance seems to have been struck between God's bounty and man's hand." Even Weber admits, however, that, "returning, I'm never tempted to stay."[27] The contemporary Corn Belt is a good place to be from, perhaps, but not necessarily to be.

In the postindustrial United States, landscape architect Robert L. Thayer Jr. observes, "looking at rural landscapes is therapeutic compensation for the pressures of a technological world." In the national imaginary, Corn Belt farms have become picturesque, rather than working landscapes. Thus the *New York Times* regularly covers the Iowa State Fair—including the cow sculpture made entirely of butter—and notes that its agricultural exhibits are increasingly popular, because there is now nowhere else to see such things: "There's no 'grandfather's farm' any more." The contemporary midwestern landscape functions for vicarious visitors as a kind of national living history museum, a nostalgic place to see in operation those consensus values and craft skills deemed inappropriate or old-fashioned in modern, multicultural America. It is the symbolic national "farm" from which all our farm-to-table restaurants are supplied.[28]

The inherently conservative overtones of this heartland image are inescapable. Representation of the Midwest as the Corn Belt, the mythic family farm that scarcely exists in practice but that looms large in imagination, ignores the urban/suburban reality in which most Midwesterners actually live. It effaces the racial and ethnic diversity of the contemporary midwestern population just as the nineteenth-century environmental mythology of shaping "empty" prairie landscape concealed the displacement of aboriginal peoples from their land and homes. Consistent focus on rural landscape and culture to the exclusion of more populous midwestern cities allows this symbolic "whitening" to occur.

Ironically, the same region that once proudly trumpeted its status as a human creation now grows restive about the ambivalent environmental heritage of that achievement. After generations of work to drain wetlands and square the earth's curves in Iowa, efforts there now turn toward laborious restoration of the original prairie grassland. In the state in the United States where perhaps the most sweeping environmental alterations have taken place, tall-grass prairie enthusiasts fan out in cemeteries and railroad rights-of-way to gather seeds from relict native plants. Collectively, they seek redemption from the consequences of their forebears' environmental sins. The latter were scathingly catalogued by Jane Smiley in her 1991 novel *A Thousand Acres*, where she depicted the horrifying physical and psychological costs of the habits of environmental domination that produced Iowa's richest corn fields. The landscape legacy of the heartland, it turns out, is very mixed indeed.[29]

And yet, its national appeal continues. However unreal and irrelevant the Corn Belt image may seem in the postindustrial United States, it, too, is an important mythic relic, a national source of psychic as well as visual relief. Deservedly or not, the contemporary Midwest "is the region that defines itself most as nation and is accepted as such by other regions of the country," the place that reassures America by giving us Walt Disney and some notion of "normal" that is so pervasive as to resist—or perhaps to be requisite for—all attempts at subversion. Even the normally splenetic humorist Bill Bryson, touring the Midwest, finds himself reduced to cliché when confronted by the resonant landscape of the Corn Belt:

> It was wonderful to be back in the Midwest, with its rolling fields and rich black earth. After weeks in the empty West, the sudden lushness of the countryside was almost giddying.... Every farm looked tidy and fruitful. Every little town looked clean and friendly. I drove on spellbound, unable to get over how striking the landscape was. There was nothing much to it, just rolling fields, but every color was deep and vivid: the blue sky, the white clouds, the red barns, the chocolate soil. I felt as if I had never seen it before. I had no idea Iowa could be so beautiful.[30]

Grace Greenwood, who effusively heralded infinity in a corn field more than 100 years before, would have sympathized with Bryson's bemused surrender to the enveloping comforts of Iowa fields. Despite its varied reputation over decades, the imaginative lure of the Corn Belt landscape—and the region that produced it—proves remarkably enduring.

## Notes

1. This essay builds on but expands work initially published as "Middle Ground: Evolving Regional Images in the American Midwest," in Theo D'haen and Hans Bertha, eds., *Writing Nation and Writing Region in America* (Amsterdam: VU University Press, 1996). Martin Ridge, "How the Middle West Became America's Heartland," *Inland* 2 (1976): 19. Jon C. Teaford, *Cities of the Heartland: The Rise and Fall of the Industrial Midwest* (Bloomington: Indiana University Press, 1993), 104. See also John A. Jakle, "Images of Place: Symbolism and the Middle Western Metropolis," in Barry

Checkoway and Carl V. Patton, eds., *Metropolitan Midwest: Policy Problems and Prospects for Change* (Urbana: University of Illinois Press, 1985), 74–103.
2. Alistair Cooke, *The American Home Front 1941–42* (New York: Grove Press, 2006), 218–19.
3. Douglas Reichert Powell, *Critical Regionalism: Connecting Politics and Culture in the American Landscape* (Chapel Hill: University of North Carolina Press, 2007), 6.
4. The classic account is Hildegard Binder Johnson, *Order Upon the Land: The U.S. Rectangular Land Survey and the Upper Mississippi Country* (New York: Oxford University Press, 1976), but see also John C. Hudson, *Making the Corn Belt: A Geographical History of Middle-Western Agriculture* (Bloomington: Indiana University Press, 1994).
5. See James R. Shortridge, *The Middle West: Its Meaning in American Culture* (Lawrence: University Press of Kansas, 1989), for an illuminating series of maps depicting varying regional understandings of which states belonged in the Midwest. Iowa is the one universal inclusion. The New Deal regional maps can be found in the National Resources Committee's 1935 report, "Regional Factors in National Planning and Development" (Washington, DC: Government Printing Office). The proposed composite is on page 166. The *New York Times* took on the issue in an article titled "Where Is the Heartland: Mostly in Our Heads," where authors Emily Badger and Kevin Quealy acknowledged that "the interior ... has long been the hardest part of the country to map" (January 3, 2017: A3). For one state's ambivalence about its midwestern status, see Elizabeth Raymond "'Is Minnesota in the Midwest Yet?' Images of an Iconoclastic Midwestern State," *Midwestern Miscellany* 39 (Fall 2011): 64–79.
6. Aspects of this subject have received attention from numerous other scholars. In addition to Ridge, these include: Andrew R.L. Cayton and Peter S. Onuf, *The Midwest and the Nation: Rethinking the History of an American Region* (Bloomington: University of Indiana Press, 1990); the scholars collected by Cayton and Susan E. Gray in *The American Midwest: Essays on Regional History* (Bloomington, University of Indiana Press, 2001); Shortridge, *The Middle West*; Michael C. Steiner, "The Birth of the Midwest and the Rise of Regional Theory," in *Finding the Lost Region* (Lincoln: University of Nebraska Press, forthcoming); Robert Thacker, *The Great Prairie in Fact and Literary Imagination* (Albuquerque: University of New Mexico Press, 1989); Robert Wuthnow, *Remaking the Heartland: Middle America Since the 1950s* (Princeton: Princeton University Press, 2011). See also William Warntz, "An Historical Consideration of the Terms 'Corn' and 'Corn Belt' in the United States," *Agricultural History* 31 (1957): 40–45.
7. Paul Gruchow, *Journal of a Prairie Year* (Minneapolis: University of Minnesota Press, 1985), 21–22. Similar observations were evocatively recorded by many midwestern novelists, notably Ole Rølvaag in *Giants in*

*the Earth* (1929) and Willa Cather in *O Pioneers!* (1913). For a history of prairie perception and modification, including the role of Native Americans in maintaining it, see Hugh Prince, *Wetlands of the American Midwest: A Historical Geography of Changing Attitudes* (Chicago: University of Chicago Press, 1997).

8. Stephen Kearney, "An Expedition Across Iowa in 1820," *Annals of Iowa*, 3rd series, 10 (January, April 1912): 357.
9. Nicolett is quoted in Lloyd McFarling, ed., *Exploring the Northern Plains, 1804–1976* (Caldwell, ID: Caxton Printers, 1955), 183.
10. W. Faux, *Memorable Days in America: Being a Journal of a Tour to the United States, Principally Undertaken to Ascertain, By Positive Evidence, the Condition and Prospects of British Emigrants; Including Accounts of Mr. Birkbeck's Settlement in the Illinois* (London: W. Simpkin & R. Marshall, 1823) 221, 221–22. The tone for these accounts was set by English speculator Morris Birkbeck, whose 1818 *Notes on a Journey in America* was written to promote his Illinois prairie settlement (and to whose optimistic claims Faux was responding). Although American farmers traditionally judged land according to the kinds of trees it supported, geographer Douglas R. McManis concludes that the story of settlers avoiding prairies in the belief that they were barren is not true. McManis suggests that absence of appropriate technology (John Deere's 1837 steel plow) and justifiable fears about the unhealthiness of wet prairies slowed settlement of those areas, but that settlers moved rapidly onto dry prairies (*The Initial Evaluation and Utilization of the Illinois Prairies, 1815–1840* [Dept. of Geography Research Paper #94, Chicago: University of Chicago, 1964]). For nineteenth-century systems of judging land, see John R. Stilgoe, *Common Landscape of America, 1580–1845* (New Haven: Yale University Press, 1982).
11. Laurence Oliphant, *Minnesota and the Far West* (Edinburgh: William Blackwood & Sons, 1855), 257; John Van Tramp, *Prairie and Rocky Mountain Adventures, or Life in the West* (Columbus, OH: Segner & Condit, 1867), 471–72. For European and American responses to prairie landscape, see Thacker, *Great Prairie* and Raymond, "Down to Earth: Sense of Place in Prairie Midwestern Literature," PhD dissertation, University of Pennsylvania, 1979. The environmental experiences of indigenous peoples, although equally relevant to a history of evolving prairie midwestern images, are more difficult to recover. Obviously the prairies were not alien to these long-time tribal residents, whose environmental practices helped actively to produce the landscape regarded by Euroamericans as "natural." Accounts of their experiences, however, were scarce. For two suggestive perspectives, see Simon Pokagon, *The Red Men's Greeting* (Hartford, MI: C.H. Engle, 1893), Ayer Collection, Newberry Library; and *Standard Atlas of Peoria City and County* [IL] (Chicago: Ogle & Co., 1896).
12. For the nationalistic implications of landscape appreciation see Anne F. Hyde, *An American Vision: Far Western Landscape and National Culture,*

*1820–1920* (New York: NYU Press, 1990) and Marguerite Shaffer, *See America First: Tourism and National Identity, 1880–1940* (Washington: Smithsonian Institution Press, 2001).

13. William Ferguson, *America by River and Rail; or, Notes by the Way on the New World and Its People* (London: James Nisbet & Co., 1856), 335; Grace Greenwood, *New Life in New Lands: Notes of Travel* (New York: J.B. Ford & Co., 1873), 12.
14. Shortridge says the term Middle West was first used in roughly its contemporary sense by Frederick Jackson Turner in an 1896 article for *Atlantic Monthly*, though commentators had been searching for an appropriate regional label for some time previous. Michael Steiner makes the important point that absence of the defining label does not necessarily imply lack of a coherent regional self-consciousness (Steiner, "The Birth of the Midwest and the Rise of Regional Theory").
15. For this agrarianism, see Stilgoe, *Common Landscape of America*, esp. 202–203. Henry Nash Smith's classic discussion of the origins and implications of American agrarian triumphalism in *Virgin Land* (Cambridge: Harvard, 1950) is still worthwhile.
16. Andreas Ueland, *Recollections of an Immigrant* (NY: Minton, Balch & Co., 1929), 261.
17. Hamlin Garland, *A Son of the Middle Border* (Boston: Grosset & Dunlap, 1917), 144, 62; Ohio farmer quoted in John Regan, *The Emigrant's Guide to the Western States of America* (Edinburgh, Oliver & Boyd, 2nd ed. [c. 1848]), 44. For the atlases, published from the 1860s throughout the century, see Michael P. Conzen, "The County Landownership Map in America, Its Commercial Development and Social Transformation 1814–1939," *Imago Mundi* 36 (1984): 9–31; and "Maps for the Masses: Alfred T. Andreas and the Midwestern County Atlas Trade," in Conzen, ed., *Chicago Mapmakers: Essays on the Rise of the City's Map Trade* (Chicago: Chicago Historical Society, 1984), 46–63. For agricultural abundance as the basis of prairie midwestern sense of place see Raymond, "Learning the Land: Sense of Place in Prairie Midwestern Writing," *MidAmerica*, 14 (1987), 28–41.
18. Combination Atlas Map of Lee County [Illinois] (Chicago: Everts, Baskin & Stewart, 1872), 5. For Corn Belt chronology, see William Warntz, "An Historical Consideration of the Terms 'Corn' and 'Corn Belt' in the United States," *Agricultural History* 31:1 (1957), 40–45.
19. Map of Bureau County, Illinois, With Sketches of Its Early Settlement (Chicago: N. Matson, 2nd ed., 1867), 10.
20. Warntz, "Historical Consideration"; William Cronon, *Nature's Metropolis: Chicago and the Great West* (New York: W.W. Norton & Co., 1991).
21. Richard Brodhead suggests that late-nineteenth-century regional literature was a form of mental tourism for acquisitive, educated elites in perpetual search of the "unmodernized picturesque" (*Cultures of Letters: Scenes of Reading and Writing in Nineteenth-Century America* [Chicago: University

of Chicago, 1993], 133). For the wilderness aesthetic, see Peter Schmitt, *Back to Nature: The Arcadian Myth in Urban America* (New York: Oxford University Press, 1969) and Roderick N. Nash, *Wilderness and the American Mind* (New Haven: Yale University Press, 3rd ed., 1982). Raymond Williams's analysis of the complex relationship between agrarian and urban culture and literature offers rich insights for the American context, although it is devoted to British literature (*The Country and the City* [New York: Oxford University Press, 1973]).

22. Warntz says the 1910 edition of the 1906 *Century Dictionary* was the first to use the term Corn-belt. For the emergence and political significance of opposition between rural and urban value systems, see Sarah Burns, *Pastoral Inventions* (Philadelphia: Temple University Press, 1990); and Don S. Kirschner, *City and Country: Rural Responses to Urbanization in the 1920s* (Westport, CT: Greenwood Press, 1978). Sally McMurry documents systematic attempts to improve rural housing in order, among other things, to make living conditions competitive with middle-class city life in *Families and Farmhouses in Nineteenth-Century America: Vernacular Design and Social Change* (New York: Oxford University Press, 1988).

23. In *Kinship with the Land: Regionalist Thought in Iowa, 1894–1942*, E. Bradford Burns portrays the alternative efforts of people in that state to maintain and disseminate a regional culture grounded in sensitivity to the agrarian landscape (Iowa City: University of Iowa Press, 1996). See Jon Lauck, "The Myth of the Midwestern 'Revolt from the Village'" for a nuanced account of the origins and intentions of Carl Van Doren's "revolt" critique of midwestern literature (*MidAmerica* XL [2013]: 39–85).

24. For the successive phases of the atlases, see Michael P. Conzen, "The County Landownership Map in America, Its Commercial Development and Social Transformation 1814–1939," *Imago Mundi* 36 (1984): 9–31. Frederick Manfred, *This Is the Year* (Garden City, NY: Doubleday, 1947); Josephine Johnson, *Now in November* (New York: Simon and Schuster, 1934).

25. Manfred, *This Is the Year*, 611; Susan Glaspell, *Judd Rankin's Daughter* (St. Paul: Webb Publishing Co., 1944, reprint University of New Mexico Press, 1976), 140; Kohn, *The Last Farmer: An American Memoir* (New York: Harper and Row, 1988), 269. Other novels recording the environmental and social costs of the Depression in the Midwest include Holger Cahill, *The Shadow of My Hand* (New York: Harcourt, Brace & Co., 1956); Paul Corey, *County Seat* (1941), *The Road Returns* (1940), *Three Miles Square* (1939) (all Indianapolis: Bobbs-Merrill); Lois Hudson, *The Bones of Plenty* (Boston: Little, Brown & Co., 1962). Roy W. Meyer, *The Midwestern Farm Novel in the Twentieth Century* (Lincoln: University of Nebraska Press, 1971) is an invaluable resource for its enumeration and analysis of the genre.

26. Burns, *Kinship*, 63; Steiner, "The Birth of the Midwest," 5.

27. Gross, "In Another Country: The Revolt From the Village," *MidAmerica* 4 (1977): 108; Weber, "My Middle West," *Notre Dame* 14 (1985): 29. The classic study of the idea of a middle ground in American culture is Leo Marx's *The Machine in the Garden: Technology and the Pastoral Ideal in America* (New York: Oxford University Press, 1964).
28. Thayer, "Pragmatism in Paradise: Technology and the American Landscape," *Landscape* 30 (1990): 5; "Iowa's Annual Fete for the Fat of the Land," *New York Times* August 12, 1996, A6. For an alternative interpretation of how midwestern fairs function for residents, see Leslie Prosterman, *Ordinary Life, Festival Days: Aesthetics in the Midwestern County Fair* (Washington: Smithsonian Institution Press, 1995).
29. For prairie restoration, see Dianne Blankenship, "Making Friends with Giants," in Cornelia F. Mutel and Mary Swander, eds., *Land of the Fragile Giants: Landscapes, Environments, and Peoples of the Loess Hills* (Iowa City: University of Iowa Press, 1994) and Richard Manning, *Grassland: The History, Biology, Politics, and Promise of the American Prairie* (New York: Viking Penguin, 1995).
30. David Marion Holman, *A Certain Slant of Light: Regionalism and the Form of Southern and Midwestern Fiction* (Baton Rouge: Louisiana State University Press, 1995), 17; Bill Bryson, *The Lost Continent: Travels in Small-Town America* (New York: Harper & Row, 1989), 285.

Robert Loerzel

"People are getting tired of Broadway and Fifth Avenue"

The Origins of the Society of Midland Authors

In 1914, Carl Sandburg called Chicago "Hog Butcher for the World." Edgar Lee Masters, a Chicago lawyer born in Kansas and raised in downstate Illinois, was giving voice to the common folk buried in a cemetery in a fictional town called Spoon River. Kansas newspaper editor William Allen White and Indiana poet James Whitcomb Riley had legions of fans. Looking across this literary landscape, one could see that the Midwest was teeming with creativity. When John M. Stahl surveyed the situation, he decided that the region's authors needed an organization. Stahl, an insurance company owner who had written novels and published magazines for farmers, noticed that New York, Boston, and other Eastern cities had more literary organizations and events than Chicago and the Midwest did. "It was rare that a foreign author of note came farther west than Niagara Falls," he observed.[1]

Stahl, who was born in 1860 in Mendon, Illinois, never achieved fame as an author, but he came up with the idea for the Society of Midland Authors, a regional organization still in operation more than a hundred years later.[2] In the early twentieth century, the SMA was one of several literary groups that brought Chicago's writers together in camaraderie and collaboration.[3]

In 1914, Stahl told fellow writers Mason Warner and Douglas Malloch about his idea. All three had been involved in the Writers' Guild of Chicago, a group that held monthly dinners, though some people quipped that it "had nothing to do with writing" and that "anyone who could sign a check could join."[4] Warner ran a Chicago advertising agency, and he would write travel books.[5] Malloch, a humorist and toastmaster hailed as the "Lumberman's Poet," edited the Chicago trade publication *American Lumberman*.[6] "We agreed," Stahl recalled, "that the first thing to do was to form an organization of the authors of Illinois, in which should predominate those authors who stood for decency and, of course, only those whose work had been recognized as highly meritorious; and, even more important, keep out those that had created the ill feeling toward and contempt of Chicago."[7] Stahl loathed the avant-garde and vulgar, like some of the writing in *The Little Review*, which Margaret Anderson had begun publishing in Chicago that same year. Stahl later praised her for publishing Sandburg, Sherwood Anderson, and Vachel Lindsay— "authors who had something worth while to say and they learned how to say it well"—but he complained that many of the other writers in her circle "gained a measure of notoriety in Chicago and brought discredit on not only that city, but on a wider territory. They wrote bizarre prose or poetry and larded it well with filth."[8]

Stahl wanted to see authors from the Midwest (or the Midland, as he called it) creating more wholesome literature about the places where they lived. "The Midland authors have not made their own country loved because they have not taken the characters or scenery that lay right at hand," he told the *Christian Science Monitor* in 1915. "You can pick up any hundred books produced by the Midland authors, and you will find less than five per cent have stayed at home in their stories. I believe in the West and its authors. They have not appreciated themselves. They will, however, gather strength by association."[9] This wasn't the first crusade in Stahl's life. Earlier, he'd been a leading voice for better roads and rural mail delivery. "Having the vision of getting the authors together was just one of his many constructive ideas which he put into action with Napoleonic strategy and energy," remarked playwright Alice Gerstenberg, who was among the writers Stahl recruited.[10] "None but a bold man would have sought to weld such individualistic—dare I say egotistic?—creatures as authors into a society of any sort," said one of the authors Stahl roped into his fledgling society, Hobart Chatfield Chatfield-Taylor. "Invitations were sent to Midwestern authors to come to Chicago for the purpose of breaking bread and uniting in the spirit of friendship and common bond. Some of them might have even met Stahl's rigid criteria for 'literary decency' and unabashed civic boosterism."[11]

Despite Stahl's hatred of modern literature, he invited one of the movement's leaders, Harriet Monroe, who'd started *Poetry: A Magazine of Verse* in 1912. Stahl admired and respected Monroe, but he knew that she considered him "hopeless" because he preferred Victorian literature and poetry that rhymed.[12] In March 1914, Monroe's magazine published Sandburg's "Chicago," which still defines the city in the public's mind today. "Harriet Monroe found in Sandburg's liberated, dissonant poetry—as well as that of Masters, Vachel Lindsay and many others—exactly the sort of unconventional work she wanted for her new journal," *Chicago Tribune Book World* editor John Blades wrote in a 1983 essay. Others in Monroe's era, including the editors of *The Dial*, a patrician literary journal published in Chicago, "disapproved of the spoken, proletarian cadence of Sandburg's poems, refusing even to acknowledge that they were poetry," Blades wrote. "Sandburg, Monroe and other Chicago novelists, poets and editors were at the vanguard of a revolt—a revolt both from rural values and from the genteel literary tradition that had prevailed in Chicago since the 1871 fire. At the time, they were considered vulgarians by the contemporary literary establishment," Blades explained.[13]

The group Stahl assembled included Hamlin Garland, a Wisconsin native celebrated for *Main-Travelled Roads*, an 1891 collection of short stories describing the hardships of life on the prairie. Garland had moved to Chicago in 1893, announcing soon afterward: "The rise of Chicago as a literary and art centre is a question only of time, and of a very short time." And he was determined to help make that happen: "This is where I belong, here in the great Midland metropolis," he wrote.[14] Chatfield-Taylor was another literary heavyweight in Stahl's group. "He was a cosmopolite, but strangely, a somewhat shy and diffident gentleman with whom conversation seemed a trifle remote," Gerstenberg observed.[15] Born into a wealthy family in Chicago, he'd added the second Chatfield to his name so he could inherit money from that side of his family.[16] He'd written novels, memoirs, and a biography of Molière, and he'd edited a literary journal called *America* in 1880s and 1890s. Chatfield-Taylor and his wife—Rose Farwell, daughter of former United States Senator Charles Benjamin Farwell[17]—were regulars at the Little Room, a gathering of artists and writers,[18] who usually convened in the Fine Arts Building on Michigan Avenue after Chicago Symphony Orchestra concerts. Early members of the SMA were also in the Little Room's "polite circle of bohemians," including Chatfield-Taylor, Monroe, and Garland, as well as sculptor Lorado Taft; Edith Wyatt, who dramatized middle-class family life in her novel *True Love*; and George Ade, a newspaper columnist originally from Indiana, famous for his *Fables in Slang*.[19]

In retrospect, it is clear that the literary energies of the Midlands were building, as was the momentum toward a new midwestern literary organization. "There were friendly groups of artists in Chicago at this time, and they were less divided by cliques and professional barriers and jealousies than in certain other cities," Monroe remembered. "We used to meet on Friday afternoons ... to talk and drink tea around the samovar, sometimes with a dash of rum to strengthen it, and every visitor who was anybody in any of the arts would be brought to the Little Room by some local confrere," she wrote, recalling that the group often staged "a hilarious play or costume party."[20] In 1907, Garland started a more formal arts group, the Attic Club, which was all-male at first—including men who hung out at the Little Room.[21] In 1909, the club changed its name to the Cliff Dwellers, taking the phrase from the title of a novel that Henry Blake Fuller had written about Chicago. Garland said he'd told Fuller: "We are building something in this Club which will be alive and jocund when you and I are gone, and I want its name to be characteristic of Chicago and a reminder of you and your first fictional study of Chicago life." Fuller unenthusiastically replied, "Nobody will want to be reminded of me."[22]

On March 1, 1914, *Poetry* hosted a banquet in honor of Irish poet William Butler Yeats. The guests included writers who would soon join the Society of Midland Authors, such as Lindsay, the "Prairie Troubadour" from Springfield, Illinois. In Yeats's speech that night, he praised Lindsay's poem "General Booth Enters into Heaven." "This poem is stripped bare of ornament; it has an earnest simplicity, a strange beauty," Yeats remarked. And then Lindsay performed a new poem called "The Congo" for the assembled literati. "Only a few of us had ever heard Lindsay recite his poems: the audience was quite carried away with his gusto," Monroe recalled.[23]

Lindsay had been tramping around the country, sleeping in barns and handing out sheets of his "Rhymes to Be Traded for Bread."[24] Garland described Lindsay as "rough-hewn," noting in 1914 that Lindsay was growing more confident. "I do not blame him for doubling up his fists," Garland wrote. "He has been forced to fight for every inch of his advance. 'Springfield still regards me as a "nut,"' he said."²⁵ When Lindsay accepted Monroe's invitation to attend the Yeats banquet, he had written to her from Springfield: "I am sorry you will have to pay my car-fare, but I am dead broke. Can't you advance me what the poems are worth that you have on hand?—I don't want to be an extra expense. My plan of life is very simple, you see—to live at home—on nothing. I only notice my empty purse when people ask me to go places."²⁶

The authors Stahl invited to discuss forming a new group gathered on November 28, 1914, at the Auditorium Hotel. "Feelings ran high about the constant drain of talent which New York was taking from us," Gerstenberg recalled in an unpublished memoir she wrote in the 1960s. "It was thought that some gatherings of home writers could promote mutual inspiration and a bond for remaining."²⁷ "This organization won't mean that editors are going to be flooded with stories written about Illinois," one attendee, Edwin Balmer, told the *Chicago Tribune*. "It's a wrong idea to suggest that Illinois writers write exclusively about Illinois. They ought not to, unless they have a good story about Illinois. But it is true that people are getting tired of Broadway and Fifth Avenue in their literature. Most of the Illinois people who make their living by writing write of the west."²⁸

Stahl was not able to attend the next meeting in December 1914 where Garland insisted that the group should include authors from a wider region rather than focusing strictly on Illinois. "The committee … was of the unanimous opinion that a distinctive literature was not a matter of State lines," according to the minutes. The committee voted to cover twelve states: Illinois, Indiana, Iowa, Kansas, Michigan, Minnesota, Missouri, Nebraska, North Dakota, Ohio, South Dakota, and Wisconsin.²⁹ According to the *Tribune*, the organizers wanted to include "those bubbling wells of literature, Indiana and Kansas"—especially White, the longtime editor of the *Emporia Gazette*, whose widely quoted editorials had earned him the nickname the "Sage of Emporia"; and Riley, the "Hoosier Poet" famous for "Little Orphant Annie" and "The Raggedy Man." The committee approved Garland's motion to call this new group the Society of Midland Authors, though Emerson Hough (whom Stahl described as "100% American") objected to the name. Hough, an Iowa native living in Chicago who wrote historical novels and westerns, thought "Midland" evoked England rather than America.³⁰

The minutes noted: "The committee feels that effort should be made to recognize and preserve the special midland quality, and that association and acquaintance will tend toward that end." The organizing committee defined the new society's mission: creating "a closer association among the writers of the Middle West, a stimulation of creative literary effort and the establishment of a library of books and manuscripts" by the region's authors.[31] On January 19, 1915, the *Christian Science Monitor* reported: "Besides the desire to foster the Midland in literature, the society has other aims—more intimate relationship between publishers, editors and among themselves—but the chronicling of the Midland will remain uppermost."[32]

And then Garland promptly did just the sort of thing the group was trying to discourage: he moved to New York in January 1915. Garland had been planning the change for months. His father had died, giving him less reason to remain in the Midwest. "I began at once to think very definitely of taking my family to New York City, where most of my literary friends lived and from which all my income was derived," he recalled. "It may be counted as a weakness, but I was no longer content to live the life of a literary pioneer." In his journal, Garland wrote that he'd felt "only half hearted" about his efforts to set up the Society of Midland Authors. "Fine and earnest as most of our Midland authors are, they form only a small nucleus in the midst of a ramshackle, ripping, roaring metropolis," he wrote. "Only the paragraphers, reporters, and poets of the daily press are able to survive in this bleak and noisy town."[33]

The Society of Midland Authors held its first meeting, voting itself into existence, on April 24, 1915, at the Auditorium Hotel.[34] Garland was back in town for a visit, and he gave a speech that night when the newborn society held a banquet.[35] His friends accused him of abandoning Chicago. "There was nothing for me to say in reply to this, for each time I return I feel more keenly than ever the fact that my life in Chicago is almost rural by contrast with my life in New York," Garland wrote. "My Chicago home is comfortable, my way of life peaceful and easy, but I am walking in a circle. I am making no progress. There are no surprises here, no stimulation to effort. If I were forced to live here I fear I should very soon cease to produce anything at all."[36]

But Garland stood up for the Midland in comments to a North Dakota newspaper covering the event, the *Bismarck Tribune*. "Practically all of the stuff written in recent years, which can classify as literature has been dripped or pounded out up in these old states of Illinois, Kansas, the Dakotas, Michigan, Ohio and Indiana," he said. "The stuff is printed in New York—but that is all."[37] Garland's autobiography, *A Son of the Middle Border*, was published in 1917, followed by a sequel, *A Daughter of the Middle Border*, which won the Pulitzer in 1922, but Stahl remarked: "He never should have emigrated to the East. Hamlin Garland has written best when he wrote of the West or with the West in his heart. He is of the West, no matter where he may live. I am bold to say that I think no one else has so well written of certain Midland people."[38]

The society chose James Whitcomb Riley as its first honorary president, but he was too ill to attend the society's events in Chicago; he died in 1916.[39] The SMA's first actual president was Chatfield-Taylor. "Few of the authors I have met are as interesting, instructive talkers as Chatfield-Taylor," Stahl commented. "Not many have traveled as extensively or observed as intelligently and diligently; not many have met as many eminent people—eminent in widely different fields; and he is full of positive opinions which he expresses in language equally positive, spiced with witticisms and kindly irony. He has all that is required of the captain of a football team; but he has a dislike, amounting to positive hatred, I am sure, of physical exertion. His ample face proclaims goodwill and hospitality; and he has enriched his life by having often at his board authors and painters and singers of note."[40]

The society's fifty-two charter members also included Edna Ferber, who would win a Pulitzer Prize for *So Big;* lawyer Clarence S. Darrow, who'd written *Farmington*, a novel of life in a small Ohio town; William Morton Payne, literary critic for *The Dial;* and Alice French of Davenport, Iowa, who wrote under the pen name Octave Thanet, using dialect in her sketches of Arkansas plantation life. Another founding member was British native Maurice Browne, who ran the Chicago Little Theatre—one of the first theaters anywhere to produce intellectual and experimental plays in a small space—in the Fine Arts Building. "At last Chicago possessed a focal point for the meeting of the creative talents," said Gerstenberg, who acted in Little Theatre shows.[41]

Other prominent authors soon joined the society: Jane Addams, founder of Chicago's Hull House, winner of the 1931 Nobel Peace Prize, and author of *Twenty Years at Hull-House;* Edgar Lee Masters, author of the influential poem cycle *Spoon River Anthology*, published in April 1915; George Barr McCutcheon of Indiana, author of the best-sellers *Graustark* and *Brewster's Millions*; his brother John T. McCutcheon, the "Dean of American Cartoonists"; and Ring Lardner, the sports journalist and author of *You Know Me Al*.[42] The SMA was surprisingly co-ed for the early twentieth century—201 men and 149 women are listed as members in society yearbooks from 1915 through 1943.[43]

Chatfield-Taylor hosted the Society of Midland Authors at Fairlawn, his estate in the leafy northern suburb of Lake Forest, on one June afternoon each year from 1915 to 1917.[44] The first outing included a polo game and a dramatic performance at the Aldis Playhouse, which was run by SMA member Mary Reynolds Aldis and her husband, Arthur.[45] "We all went to Lake Forest on the same train and I remember feeling shy and unacquainted until (fellow SMA members) Lillian Bell and Mary Donahey reached out their wings," Gerstenberg recalled. "I was impressed by the portrait-appearance of Rose Chatfield-Taylor as she graciously greeted us with a suave smile.... However she might have felt about entertaining this new band of writers Hobart had collected, she came along with the idea that he should fraternize."[46]

The Aldis Playhouse also staged an unusual one-act play by Gerstenberg on November 29 and 30, 1915.[47] *Overtones* featured characters saying their internal thoughts aloud. Two actresses played "cultured women," while two others played the "primitive selves" hidden inside those women.[48] Gerstenberg was in the cast, and Monroe was in the audience. "Harriet, small, thin, serious of face, dark eyes deep and sometimes softly yearning for human warmth as she slipped her arm around my waist," Gerstenberg recalled. "She could be caustic to the point of annihilation in speech, her standards were so definite." But Monroe was astonished by "the miracle" she had just seen.[49] In the January 1916 *Poetry* she reviewed *Overtones* as well as another play, Cloyd Head's *Grotesques*, which the Little Theatre had performed. "How did the Elizabethans feel when the young Shakespeare tried his first experiments on them ...?" Monroe wrote. "Did these people know what was happening? Was their little personal emotion, their pleasure of the moment seized and swept on into tireless spaces of wonder and joy? A little of this larger thrill shook me twice last month."[50]

The Society of Midland Authors was at the center of a great flourishing of theatrical arts, but the moment would pass. The Little Theatre struggled to make money, shutting down in 1917, just five years after it started. "It was Chicago's irretrievable loss when it folded," Gerstenberg wrote.⁵¹ Browne, the Little Theatre's mastermind, left Chicago and later achieved success on the stage in London. In 1918, the flu pandemic took the life of Chicago playwright Kenneth Sawyer Goodman, an SMA charter member. His parents, William and Erna Goodman, gave $250,000 to the Art Institute of Chicago to create a playhouse named after him—the Goodman Theatre, one of the nation's leading regional theaters.⁵² For her part, Gerstenberg stayed active in the SMA for nearly six decades. In 1971, when she was 85, she commented on how she had spent her career as a dramatist in Chicago, even though New York City was where most playwrights worked. "It was tough living in Chicago so far from the centre!" Gerstenberg wrote.⁵³

Typical SMA events included an annual dinner and regular luncheons featuring appearances by local and visiting authors. Chatfield-Taylor noted that "even authors, if they can be caught unawares and induced to unbend, like to play and make good cheer."⁵⁴ But good cheer did not always prevail. The ultrapatriotic Hough was the SMA's president from 1916 to 1918, as the United States went to war in Europe. Hough pushed for a change to the group's constitution to keep out any "alien enemy" or "person who has been known to express disrespect for the Government or the Institutions of the United States." What precisely happened with this proposal is unclear in surviving documents, but when the SMA published its next yearbook, the bylaws didn't include the provision.⁵⁵ Another SMA member, Darrow, denounced this type of Red Scare tactic. "No man can speak his convictions, no man can write them, and no man can print them with the fear of jail in his heart!" he said in a speech in Chicago in 1919.⁵⁶

It's hard to tell from the surviving records if there was any tension among the SMA's members over the content or style of their writings. But as Stahl made clear in his memoir, he clung to his close-minded concept of "decent" midwestern literature. He denounced another focal point of the Chicago literary scene, the Dil (or Dill) Pickle Club, calling it an example of "eruptive discharges" that were "offensive to good taste and literary decency."⁵⁷ And yet, other SMA members—Darrow, Lardner, and Sherwood Anderson—were among the speakers at this bohemian joint. The motto above its door at 18 Tooker Alley on the Near North Side proclaimed: "Step Down. Stoop Low. Leave Your Dignity Outside." Its manifesto stated: "We of the Dil Pickle believe in everything. We are radicals, pickpockets, second story men and thinkers. Some of us practice free love, and some, medicine. Most of us have gone through religion and have tired of it. Some of us have tired of our wives." ("Second-story men" was slang for burglars.) According to Thomas Dyja's 2013 book *The Third Coast*, "It was Chicago Dada, an intellectual free-for-all, part cabaret, part poetry slam, part performance art."[58]

In 1920, H.L. Mencken declared that Chicago was the literary capital of America. "The most important writing of recent years had … come from the big city in the middle of America's heartland," Mencken wrote in the *London Nation*. "In Chicago there is the mysterious something that makes for individuality, personality, charm; in Chicago a spirit broods upon the face of the waters.… there is an eagerness to hear and see, to experience and experiment. The town is colossally rich; it is ever changing; it yearns for distinction. The newcomers who pour in from the wheat-lands want more than mere money; they want free play for their prairie energy; they seek some imaginative equivalent for the stupendous activity that they were bred to. It is thus a superb market for merchants of the new."[59]

But shortly after Mencken's ode to Chicago, some believed that the literary scene began to fade. "The stampede to the east was alarmingly rapid," novelist Arthur Meeker Jr. would recall two decades later, when he was serving as SMA president. "Almost all our first rank writers found jobs (and flats) in New York, bought farms in Connecticut, or took one way tickets to Europe."[60] In spite of that exodus, many authors remained loyal to the Midland.

Two of Stahl's anecdotes about SMA events in the 1920s offer glimpses of how the group touched the lives of its members. One involves Sherwood Anderson, who was living in the southwest Chicago suburb of Palos Park, when he joined in 1922.[61] "He was a big, dreamy-eyed man with a sock of black hair straggling into his eyes—he looked as much like a gypsy rom as you'll often meet on Michigan Avenue," *Chicago Tribune* book critic and SMA member Fanny Butcher recalled. "He was more a struggling than a permanently arrived writer, however, when he lived here."[62] Anderson was reluctant as a public speaker, but an SMA event seemed to bring him out of his shell, according to Stahl. "Before the luncheon Sherwood Anderson came to me and insisted that I should not call on him to speak," Stahl wrote. "He declared emphatically that he could never think of three sentences to utter when he was on his feet before any audience, big or small, of any character. He was so earnest about it that I believed him. So I started the post-luncheon program by asking him to rise, saying that I would not call on him to speak, as he did not feel disposed to speak that day. I thought that I had done it all in masterly fashion and all he would have to do would be to make his pretty bow and smile idiotically, as prescribed for such occasions and the prescription nearly always followed. But Sherwood had changed his mind.... He rose slowly, with great dignity, and spoke for five minutes, and faultlessly. It was one of the best little luncheon talks I have ever heard. It was a gem."[63]

Stahl's other story from that era described a successful novelist encouraging a young girl with literary ambitions. Stahl introduced Masters's daughter, Marcia, to Zona Gale—a founding SMA member from Portage, Wisconsin, who'd written the best-selling *Miss Lulu Bett* and won a Pulitzer Prize for her stage adaptation of it. "I presented her to Miss Gale, making the inane remark that Marcia wished to be an author and had a long and rocky road ahead of her," Stahl recounted. "'But every step will be full of joy!' immediately exclaimed the famous author.... And she talked to the little girl in that kind way of which Zona Gale is the mistress, God bless her for her big, warm heart. I and Marcia will remember always, with a feeling too deep to be profaned with words, the few minutes she stood beside Zona Gale with Zona Gale's arm around her."[64] That girl grew up to be an author—writing poetry, poetry criticism, and journalism under the names Marcia Lee Masters and Marcia Masters Schmid. She joined the SMA and won two of the society's literary awards in the 1960s.[65]

SMA members scattered around the Midwest weren't able to attend events as often as their counterparts in Chicago, but some made the trip for special occasions. Alice French came from Iowa to speak at the SMA's annual dinners in 1915 and 1916, including a lecture on "Obsessions in Literature."[66] Poet Arthur Davison Ficke traveled to Chicago once in a while. "There were … great casualties among the ladies whenever Arthur Ficke arrived, the Adonis of Davenport, he was called," Fanny Butcher recalled. "He never lived here, so we didn't see him often, but hearts went not pit-a-pat but bumpety-bump when we did."[67] But in 1917, Lindsay sent his regrets from Springfield, when he was unable to attend an SMA outing to the Chatfield-Taylor estate. "I do not come to Chicago so very often and those delerious [sic] occasions are well pictured on my memory's canvas, so to speak," he wrote to Gerstenberg.[68] Novelist Margaret Hill McCarter lived in Topeka, Kansas—far from SMA gatherings in Chicago. But in 1925 she declared: "It has meant very much to me to be identified with the body."[69] She was replying to a question from SMA leaders, who'd asked the members if the society should continue to exist.[70] Letters poured in, most of them echoing Caroline Alden Huling, who wrote: "NEVER give up the ship."[71] Karleton Hackett, a member who lived in Chicago, remarked: "There are many of us who cannot attend the meetings—say once in a great while, yet it's a distinct spiritual comfort to know that the Society exists and that the meetings are being held."[72]

And so the SMA lived on. By 1931, it had begun a newsletter—a typewritten missive, usually a few pages long, reporting on news about its members. It helped authors scattered around the region to keep tabs on their colleagues.[73] And in 1940, the *Chicago Tribune* offered the SMA as evidence that the city's literary scene wasn't quite dead: "We thought that all the authors in this erstwhile literary capital of the nation ... had departed for Hollywood until we ran into a soiree of the Society of Midland Authors the other night. There were dozens of them, including the inevitable consorts."[74]

Like any literary group, the SMA faced the challenge of persuading writers—often perceived as solitary artists—that they should join an organization. "It is a distinct characteristic of the modern Chicago author that he (or she) is more or less a lone wolf," Meeker observed in a *Tribune* essay in 1941, when he was SMA president. "Gone is the convivial period when crowds of the town's brightest wits forgathered daily over a glass of beer.... Nowadays that has completely changed. Taking our cue from the prevailing apathy of our fellow citizens, we literati have learned to let one another peacefully alone."[75] And indeed, some writers are not joiners. Fuller never joined either the Society of Midland Authors or the club named for his novel *The Cliff-Dwellers*. And the documentation is unclear about exactly when Sandburg became an SMA member. Monroe invited him to join in 1921, but his name is absent from surviving SMA membership directories until 1962, late in his life.[76]

The Society of Midland Authors seemed to find a new sense of purpose after it began bestowing annual awards for the region's best books in 1957. The prizes have honored books on an immense range of topics, not just stories about the region. But Chicago and the Midwest inspired many of the SMA's most prominent award winners: Saul Bellow, Studs Terkel, Gwendolyn Brooks, Mike Royko, Jane Smiley, Dempsey Travis, Leon Forrest, William Maxwell, Louise Erdrich, Alex Kotlowitz, Aleksandar Hemon, and Stuart Dybek, to name a few.[77] When Marc Kelly Smith, founder of Chicago's Uptown Poetry Slam, emceed the SMA awards dinner in 2013, he gave a dramatic performance of Sandburg's poetry. "A tradition of the Midwest is that everyday people are really connected to literature," Smith remarked. "In the Midwest, we write about our place—it's not high-falutin', it's really down to earth."[78]

### Notes

1. John M. Stahl, *Growing with the West: The Story of a Busy, Quiet Life* (New York: Longmans, Green and Co., 1930), 421.
2. Alice Gerstenberg, "Come Back with Me," unpublished memoir, Chicago History Museum, MSS Lot G, 265.
3. Timothy B. Spears, "Literary Cultures," in *The Encyclopedia of Chicago*, ed. James R. Grossman, Ann Durking Keating, and Janice L. Reiff (Chicago: University of Chicago Press, 2004), 438.
4. Stahl, *Growing with the West*, 400; Fanny Butcher, "The Society of Midland Authors," a speech from September 27, 1962, printed in 1963–65 SMA Yearbook, Society of Midland Authors Collection, Special Collections, University of Illinois at Chicago Library, Supplement I Folder 5. The University of Illinois at Chicago Library's Special Collections maintains an extensive archive of Society of Midland Authors documents.
5. "Mason Warner Dead," *Chicago Tribune*, March 4, 1964.
6. "Poet of the Woods," *Pantagraph* (Bloomington, IL), December 30, 1919.
7. Stahl, *Growing with the West*, 422.
8. Ibid., 414–15.
9. *Christian Science Monitor*, Jan. 19, 1915, quoted in Stahl, 427.
10. Gerstenberg, "Come Back With Me," 265–66.
11. Hobart C. Chatfield-Taylor, "Historical Sketch," from SMA Yearbook for 1930 and other early years, SMA Collection, UIC, Folder 2.
12. Stahl, *Growing with the West*, 370.
13. John Blades, "Writers Captured the City's Lusty Voice," *Chicago Tribune*, January 30, 1983.

14. Donald L. Miller, *City of the Century: The Epic of Chicago and the Making of America* (New York: Simon & Schuster, 1996), 410–11.
15. Gerstenberg, "Come Back With Me," 266.
16. "Alphabet Stories: C—Hobart Chatfield-Taylor," Lake Forest-Lake Bluff Historical Society Newsletter, accessed May 25, 2016, http://www.lflbhistory.org/sites/default/files/pdfs/alpha-c.pdf.
17. Ibid.
18. Arthur Miller, "Lake Forest Country Places: Fairlawn, Part 2," Donnelley and Lee Library Archives and Special Collections at Lake Forest website, May 6, 1995, accessed May 25, 2016, http://www.lakeforest.edu/library/archives/lf-country-places/fair2.php.
19. Miller, *City of the Century*, 410.
20. Harriet Monroe, *A Poet's Life: Seventy Years in a Changing World* (New York: Macmillan, 1938), 197.
21. *The Cliff-Dwellers: An Account of Their Organization, the Dedication and Opening of Their Quarters, Constitution and By-Laws, Officers, Committees, and List of Members* (Chicago: 1910), 6.
22. Gary T. Johnson, "What a Global City Can Learn from The Cliff Dwellers—Past, Present and Future," November 27, 2007, address to the Cliff Dwellers, on Chicago History Museum website, accessed May 25, 2016, http://www.chicagohistory.org/documents/home/aboutus/from-the-president/speeches-and-articles/CHM-CliffDwellersCentenaryAddress.pdf.
23. Monroe, *A Poet's Life*, 339.
24. "Vachel Lindsay: 'Rhymes to Be Traded for Bread,'" Norris L. Brookens Library website, accessed May 14, 2016, https://library.uis.edu/archives/localHistory/lindsay/index.html.
25. Hamlin Garland, *My Friendly Contemporaries: A Literary Log* (New York: Macmillan, 1932), 17–18.
26. Monroe, *A Poet's Life*, 332–39.
27. Gerstenberg, "Come Back with Me," 264.
28. "Illini Authors Unite to Rival Hoosier Claims," *Chicago Tribune*, November 29, 1914.
29. December 9, 1914, meeting minutes, SMA Collection, UIC, Folder 48.
30. *Chicago Tribune*, April 25, 1915; Stahl, *Growing with the West*, 424; Butcher, "The Society of Midland Authors."
31. December 9, 1914, meeting minutes.
32. *Christian Science Monitor*, January 19, 1915, quoted in Stahl, *Growing with the West*, 427.
33. Garland, *My Friendly Contemporaries*, 24–32.
34. April 24, 1915, meeting minutes, SMA Collection, UIC, Folder 48.
35. *Chicago Examiner*, April 25, 1915.
36. Garland, *My Friendly Contemporaries*, 57.
37. *Bismarck* (ND) *Tribune*, May 16, 1915.
38. Stahl, *Growing with the West*, 371.

39. "Riley Thanks Authors for Distinction Given Him," *Chicago Tribune*, May 30, 1915.
40. Stahl, *Growing with the West*, 390–91.
41. Ibid., 425; Encyclopedia of Arkansas History & Culture website, accessed May 25, 2016, http://www.encyclopediaofarkansas.net/encyclopedia/entry-detail.aspx?entryID=1651; Gerstenberg, "Come Back With Me," 14.
42. Stahl, *Growing with the West*, 425–26; SMA Yearbooks, SMA Collection, UIC, Folder 2.
43. SMA Collection, UIC, Folder 2.
44. Miller, "Lake Forest Country Places: Fairlawn, Part 2."
45. "News of Chicago Society," *Chicago Tribune*, June 20, 1915.
46. Gerstenberg, "Come Back with Me," 268.
47. Ibid., 296.
48. Alice Gerstenberg, *Overtones* (New York: Doubleday, Page & Co., 1916), One-Act Plays website, accessed May 14, 2016, http://www.one-act-plays.com/dramas/overtones.html.
49. Gerstenberg, "Come Back with Me," 299–300.
50. Harriet Monroe, "Editorial Comment: 'Grotesques' and 'Overtones,'" *Poetry*, January 1916, 193.
51. Gerstenberg, "Come Back with Me," 15.
52. Goodman Theatre website, accessed June 1, 2016, http://www.goodmantheatre.org/90/index.php/kenneth-sawyer-goodman-and-his-legacy/.
53. Alice Gerstenberg to Russell P. MacFall, April 22, 1971, SMA Collection, UIC, Supplement I folder 2.
54. Chatfield-Taylor, "Historical Sketch."
55. H.C. Chatfield-Taylor, letter to SMA, July 24, 1918, SMA Collection, UIC, Folder 37; SMA letters to Ridgely Torrence, August 7, 1918, Folder 38; SMA 1919–1920 Yearbook, Folder 2.
56. John A. Farrell, *Clarence Darrow: Attorney for the Damned* (New York: Doubleday, 2011), 307.
57. Stahl, *Growing with the West*, 415.
58. Thomas Dyja, *The Third Coast: When Chicago Built the American Dream* (New York: Penguin Press, 2013), 54–55.
59. "Mr. Mencken's 'Chicagoiad,'" *The Literary Digest* 66, no. 1 (July 24, 1920): 29–30.
60. Arthur Meeker Jr., "Chicago's Role Appraised in Current Literary World," *Chicago Tribune*, December 7, 1941.
61. January 19, 1921, correspondence, SMA Collection, UIC, Folder 26; January 11, 1922, correspondence, SMA Collection, UIC, Folder 28.
62. Butcher, "The Society of Midland Authors."
63. Stahl, *Growing with the West*, 430–31.
64. Ibid., 433–34.

65. "Award Winners from Prior Years," Society of Midland Authors website, accessed May 25, 2016, http://midlandauthors.com/winners_past.html; Kenan Heise, "Marcia Schmid, Tribune Poetry Editor," *Chicago Tribune,* September 10, 1994.
66. SMA Collection, UIC, Folders 38 and 48.
67. Butcher, "The Society of Midland Authors."
68. Vachel Lindsay to Alice Gerstenberg, June 25, 1917, SMA Collection, UIC, Folder 38.
69. Dec. 13, 1925, letter, SMA Collection, UIC, Folder 27.
70. Nov. 27, 1925, letter, SMA Collection, UIC, Folder 25.
71. Dec. 3, 1925, letter, SMA Collection, UIC, Folder 27.
72. Dec. 2, 1925, letter, SMA Collection, UIC, Folder 27.
73. SMA Collection, UIC, Folder 51.
74. "A Line O' Type or Two," *Chicago Tribune,* Nov. 28, 1940.
75. Arthur Meeker Jr., "Chicago's Role Appraised in Current Literary World," *Chicago Tribune,* December 7, 1941.
76. SMA Collection, UIC, Folders 2 and 26.
77. Society of Midland Authors website, accessed June 1, 2016, http://midlandauthors.com/winners_past.html.
78. Ibid.

| Jeremy Beer | Midlander |
| --- | --- |
| | Booth Tarkington's Defense of the Midwest |

If the five decades spanning from 1890 to 1940 constituted a Midwestern Moment, then no author was more identified by his contemporaries with that moment than Newton Booth Tarkington. His defenders and critics agreed that Tarkington epitomized, for good or ill, midwestern literary regionalism prior to the rise of naturalism and modernism. "He is an Indianian first of all," wrote one observer, and Tarkington agreed: "I belong here, I am part of it, and it is part of me. I understand it and it understands me."[1] In the first two decades of the twentieth century, Tarkington's attitude toward his home region seemed like quite an advantage, "Indiana being so typical a state."[2] But to the next generation, Tarkington's close identification with the Midwest was precisely what made him passé.

So it has continued. Since his death in 1946, serious considerations of Booth Tarkington have been few, and those often hostile. While Tarkington's account of the social and aesthetic costs of industrial growth in the late nineteenth and early twentieth centuries has dated well, the literary guild has not in the interim become friendlier to traditionally inclined, patriotic WASPs, nor to authors whose styles and subject matters betray a pre-modernist orientation. Then too, as Gordon Hutner observes, literary historians have been for at least sixty years "vigorously antibourgeois."[3] Within the establishment, a writer such as Booth Tarkington—who claimed to be a Republican "very much as Ignatius Loyola was a Catholic"—has stood little chance of acceptance.[4]

As early as the publication of Sinclair Lewis's *Babbitt* in 1922, Tarkington knew he was standing against the prevailing winds. By the latter half of the 1920s his novels and other works were good-humoredly—almost *always* good-humoredly, Tarkington's unshakeable inclination toward geniality being one of the personality traits often held against him—scoring off artistic modernists and ideological enthusiasts. Tarkington, in other words, knew what the critics thought of him and what he represented, and he fired back. He took his position not only in defense of himself, but in defense of the characteristic values and beliefs of the place with which he strongly identified: the Midwest, or as Tarkington would have put it, the Midlands.

---

Born into a socially prominent Indianapolis family in 1869, Tarkington was named after his maternal uncle Newton Booth, governor of California from 1871 to 1875 and U.S. senator from 1875 to 1881. The Tarkingtons were members of the Indianapolis haute bourgeoisie, such as it was. President Benjamin Harrison and General Lew Wallace, author of *Ben Hur*, were family friends. When William Dean Howells came through on a lecture tour in 1899, the Tarkington family acted as his principal host, allowing Booth to get to know the man who would later become one of his champions.[5]

Despite their social status, the Tarkingtons were not wealthy. Financial support and, later, an inheritance from Uncle Newton allowed Booth Tarkington to do the things WASP young men were supposed to do: attend Exeter and Princeton, then return to the hometown to manage some property and take an active role in civic life (Tarkington served a term as an Indiana state representative from 1902 to 1904). To this respectable résumé Tarkington added an activity a little less respectable: writing fiction. For several years after he returned to Indianapolis from the East in 1893 he attempted to break into the magazines without success. Not until *The Gentleman from Indiana* was read by an enthusiastic Hamlin Garland at Doubleday did Tarkington find a publisher—and then he did so in a big way.

*The Gentleman from Indiana*, published in 1899, was a smashing success. It was followed by *Monsieur Beaucaire* (1900) and other period dramas. These novels made Tarkington famous, but it was not until he published *The Flirt* in 1913 that he—and his older friend James Whitcomb Riley, the Indiana poet—believed he had finally succeeded in shedding melodrama and sentimentality to achieve the realism preached by Howells and others.[6] (Strangely, Tarkington's critics often focus a good deal of their fire on *The Gentleman from Indiana*, which, while a pleasurable read, is arguably an item of late juvenilia in the context of the Tarkington corpus.) The works that, for a while, secured Tarkington's critical standing followed in short order: *The Turmoil* (1915), *The Magnificent Ambersons* (1918), and *Alice Adams* (1921). Before and after the publication of these works came dozens of other novels, plays, short stories, and essays. Few of his contemporaries churned out more words than did the steadily professional Tarkington.

Tarkington's writing also made him rich. Between 1902 and 1932, nine Tarkington works made the top ten in *Publisher's Weekly's* year-end lists of bestsellers. His biographer (there has only been one), James Woodress, estimated that at least five million copies of Tarkington's books were sold in the years prior to 1950—an era, he pointed out, prior to the issuance of cheap paperback editions.[7] Once his reputation was established in the early 1900s, Tarkington commanded large fees from magazines for the serialization of his novels, for short stories, for articles and memoirs—for virtually anything he wished to write. (For the 1930 serialization of the utterly forgotten *Mirthful Haven* in the *Saturday Evening Post* Tarkington received $60,000.)[8] And while his career as a playwright included many more failures than successes, Tarkington hit it big with plays like *The Man from Home*, *The Country Cousin*, and *Clarence* (which helped launch the career of Helen Hayes). By the Great Depression, Tarkington was so wealthy, and prices so low, that he was able to purchase works by Titian, Velázquez, Goya, Reynolds, and Gainsborough, most of which are today hung at the Indianapolis Museum of Art.[9]

This financial success did not—at first—come at the expense of Tarkington's reputation. William Dean Howells began to champion Tarkington after the publication of *The Turmoil* (1914). *The Magnificent Ambersons* won a Pulitzer in 1919; three years later, *Alice Adams* took home the prize. In 1921, *Publisher's Weekly* asked booksellers to name the most "significant" contemporary author: Tarkington came in first, ahead of Edith Wharton. The same year, Sinclair Lewis was telling his audiences, "When you are considering the clever unknown youngsters, don't ever suppose that because he sells so enormously, Booth Tarkington can't write better than any of them." Ellen Glasgow wrote Tarkington in admiration of *Alice Adams*: "You have achieved two things that I had believed almost impossible in American fiction—you have written of average people without becoming an average writer and you have treated the American girl without sentimentality."[10]

In 1922, *Literary Digest* named Tarkington America's greatest living author, and the *New York Times* put him on its list of the ten greatest living Americans. A decade later, in 1933, Tarkington received the National Institute of Arts and Letters Gold Medal, previously given only to Howells and Wharton, and in 1945 the American Academy of Letters honored him with its William Dean Howells Award, given just once every five years. Lewis wrote the award citation and was again gracious: "Mr. Tarkington ... has been one of the first, and he remains one of the chief, of all the discoverers of America in literature."[11]

Tarkington's best works retained influence for some time. Henry Steele Commager and Lewis Atherton, for example, both used *The Magnificent Ambersons* "as their point of reference in discussing the urbanization of the Midwest."[12] Likewise, as a "shrewd chronicler of the passing of the old order," Tarkington provided historical data for Theodore Dreiser biographer Richard Lingeman's *Small Town America*. And of course, Orson Welles's film version of *The Magnificent Ambersons*, despite the studio's mangling of the story, helped burnish Welles's reputation and was nominated for four Academy Awards.[13]

But in truth, by the time he was being honored by the American Academy of Letters in 1945 Tarkington's reputation in the literary world had been receding for some time. The rise of modernism—especially if we conceive the term broadly enough to include naturalism—had led to a radically different consensus on Tarkington than that which prevailed during his heyday. Writing in *The Nation* in 1921, Carl Van Doren inaugurated a tradition of dismissing Tarkington's importance. "Rarely has so persistent a reputation been so insecurely founded," Van Doren proclaimed (one wonders how "persistent" Tarkington's reputation could have been in 1921, when he had won his first major prize just two years earlier). Whenever Tarkington "comes to a crisis in the building of a plot or in the truthful representation of a character he sags down to the level of Indiana sentimentality." Note the use of Tarkington's home state as an adjectival sneer.[14]

In a verdict that would later be frequently cited, Vernon Parrington concluded in 1933 that Tarkington was "a perennial sophomore," a "purveyor of comfortable literature to middle-class America"—the America, in other words, of the Middle West.[15] Dreiser never directly criticized his fellow Hoosier in print, but he confided to friends that in his view Tarkington "does not know reality, does not know life, work, the average human being, or sex."[16] Willa Cather disdained Tarkington's "platitudes."[17] Ernest Hemingway, in comically Hemingway fashion, said that Tarkington "had the wrong dope, that fellow."[18]

These judgments won the day. The influential F.O. Matthiessen, affirming the truth of Parrington's view of Tarkington, claimed that the "limitation of Tarkington's pleasant 'neighborliness' is that it has little hard core of actuality."[19] Sinclair Lewis biographer Mark Schorer absolved Lewis from his public praise of Tarkington by noting "on Lewis's behalf that ... he did not admire Booth Tarkington ... so much as he did Dreiser, a less complacent Hoosier."[20] It is nevertheless at least a *little* surprising that today Tarkington is usually omitted from standard anthologies of American literature and studies of American realism. He merits no mention in *The Cambridge Companion to American Realism and Naturalism*. His name does not appear in the index of *The Cambridge Introduction to American Literary Realism*. He is not anthologized in *The Portable American Realism Reader*. He is not included in *Documents of American Realism and Naturalism*. The neglect is consistent.

---

The anthologists have taken their cues from more recent evaluations of Tarkington and his place in American, and especially midwestern, literature. Two of the more important of these treatments are worth discussing: Ronald Weber's discussion of Tarkington in *The Midwestern Ascendancy in American Writing* (1992) and Thomas Mallon's reconsideration of Tarkington in *The Atlantic* (2004).

Weber uses Tarkington principally to illustrate his case that many of the popular writers associated with the midwestern regionalist movement, especially in its earlier years, left no works of "unquestioned quality." The central achievements of the midwestern "ascendancy," for Weber, include *The Hoosier School-Master, Main-Travelled Roads, Sister Carrie, Chicago Poems, Spoon River Anthology, O Pioneers!, My Ántonia, Main Street, Giants in the Earth, The Grandmothers,* and *Winesburg, Ohio*. Tarkington's *Alice Adams* and *The Magnificent Ambersons* are conspicuously excluded from his list.

Weber's critique of Tarkington, and the low level of importance he assigns him, faithfully represents the view of Tarkington held by most partisans of Dreiserian naturalism and literary modernism, as well as the lack of sympathy with which they approach Tarkington and the sort of society for which he wished to speak.[21] Weber implies, for example, that Tarkington shared with other Indiana writers—James Whitcomb Riley, Gene Stratton-Porter, Meredith Nicholson, et al.—a devotion to the "uncritical celebration" of the Midwest. Like them, Tarkington was a romanticizer with a "quality of easy and uncritical sentiment."[22] Indiana writers like him were guilty of the "impulse to gild life by looking at the more smiling aspects of the region or, as was more often the case, looking beyond it altogether."[23] Riley and Tarkington remain worthy of our attention, concedes Weber, only for "their usefulness in illustrating the removed vision at the heart of even the best ... Indiana writing of the period than for lasting literary qualities."[24]

To support his claims with respect to Tarkington, Weber focuses on *The Gentleman from Indiana*. That book, with "its roots firmly in the conventions of the sentimental novel of a local-color variety," is out of touch "with the actualities of rural life."[25] Weber acknowledges that Tarkington himself thought the novel inferior to his later work, so he produces a reading of Tarkington's 1902 article "The Middle West" to confirm that "Tarkington's sense of urban life ... was as narrowly restricted as his sense of the country."[26] "The Middle West"'s defense of midwestern gentility versus its supposedly superior eastern counterparts shows how ignorant Tarkington was of the grittier realities of the region, realities with which his set rarely came into contact. Sherwood Anderson, by contrast, resisted and rebelled against "the kind of comfortable front-porch, country-club, middle-class Midwestern life that Tarkington had hailed in the pages of *Harper's Monthly*."[27]

In short, while Tarkington and his fellow Indiana authors produced literature that was "wistful," "folksy," and "homey,"[28] writers like Anderson and Dreiser manifested the spirit of opposition that marks the superior artist. They courageously challenged conventional views and experience, whereas the Indiana writers believed in "an imagined world of serene images and untroubled lives"[29] and indulged in the "tradition of literary escapism."[30] Not until Dreiser did a Hoosier author really practice literary realism, claims Weber. Unlike Tarkington and other Indiana writers, Dreiser rejected the tradition of "neighborly, warm-hearted, backward-looking fiction" that was "based on the shared experience of comfortable life in a genteel and secluded American heartland basking in the afterglow of the garden myth."[31]

Like Dreiser and Anderson, Sinclair Lewis's work also helped to usher in the age of midwestern realism. When *Main Street* was published, writes Weber, the reading public's interest was still "fixed on the traditional and sentimental depictions of village life emanating from the popular Indiana writers, Riley and Tarkington," but all that would now be swept away.[32] Tarkington may have been Lewis's "only competition" in the depiction of the American businessman, but as Lewis himself knew, Tarkington romanticized the businessman and portrayed the industrial world in a deeply unrealistic way.

Such is Weber's brief against Tarkington. A few of its features are worth noting. In this important study of midwestern literature, Weber provides no account whatsoever of the major works of Tarkington's realist period. You would never know from Weber that Tarkington grappled directly and at length with the changes in American life wrought by the rise of industry and the flight to the city, since Weber does not deal at all with the *Growth* trilogy (consisting of *The Turmoil*, *The Magnificent Ambersons*, and *The Midlander*), *Alice Adams*, or any other post-1913 work. That is rather remarkable.

At least with respect to this later period—by far the most important—of Tarkington's career, Weber's charges simply don't stick. *Alice Adams*, for instance, can hardly be accused of being "wistful." None of Tarkington's major realist works deals with "village life," much less its sentimental depiction. All of them situate their action within the context of industrialization, urbanization, and other dynamic late-nineteenth- and early twentieth-century social forces, and so can hardly be classified as escapist. And all portray American businessmen as socially and historically ambiguous figures whose evaluation is a complex matter. Only those who prefer their industrial titans drawn in caricature can credibly accuse Tarkington of romanticizing them in these books.

What *is* true is that Tarkington did not share the spirit of cultural opposition that animated Dreiser, Anderson, and others. If greatness is more or less a function of thoroughgoing rebellion against the characteristic views of one's place and time, as Weber argues, then Tarkington does not pass the test. As Jon Lauck has shown, for a century now many celebrated writers and critics have chosen to depict the Midwest "as a repressive and sterile backwater filled with small-town snoops, redneck farmers, and zealous theocrats"—a place against which all courageous and humane writers felt they must rebel.[33] Tarkington demurred. He found in the Midwest and its people goods to be defended, even celebrated. And when, rather early in his career, that sort of conviction became noticeably unpopular, he not only persisted in holding it but used his literature more directly to present his views. This shift came, sometimes, to the detriment of his art, but it is unfair to leave the impression that he was unconcerned with the great issues of the day.

For his part, Thomas Mallon brutalized Tarkington in a 2004 *Atlantic* retrospective. Mallon praises *Alice Adams* as perhaps one of the top fifty American novels of all time. He finds *The Magnificent Ambersons* "fine." And he hails *In the Arena* (1905)—a collection of early short stories inspired by Tarkington's term in the Indiana House of Representatives—for its "vivid characters" and for showing that Tarkington could have become a "memorable novel-writing politician." Yet he nevertheless concludes that Tarkington was a compromised and ultimately failed "full-time Author."[34]

Tarkington's work is so "wildly uneven," writes Mallon, as to suggest "a blood-sugar problem, or some seasonal affective disorder." *Ambersons* and *Alice Adams* are "suffocated" by the "vast body of his mediocre work." Tarkington wrote "in the throes of nostalgia" and was afflicted by a "fatal eagerness to please—the impulse that time and again, between his best productions, would cause Tarkington to lose his nerve and play to the cheap seats."

Tarkington's cowardice was complemented by distasteful social views. He displayed "a sort of regretful nativism" when it came to immigration, and on race "one can locate him somewhere between the normal, automatic bigotries of his era and a positively oafish delight in the way things were. Paul Fussell, in an otherwise level-headed defense of *Penrod* against PC expurgation, sees in that novel only 'affectionate condescension toward Negroes.'" But Fussell was too kind, writes Mallon, who accuses Tarkington of treating the *Penrod* books' black characters Herman and Verman like characters in a minstrel sideshow.

Tarkington was progressive in being "an emerald-Green decrier of internal combustion," but even here Mallon does not credit Tarkington for his foresight. For on the one hand, Tarkington's emphasis on the baleful effects of the automobile ultimately became "abrasive." And on the other, while he "would speak his piece on the subject," Tarkington "was finally more intent on offering his readers a pleasant Sunday drive—along with the sociological reassurance that they weren't really the Babbitts and boobs that Sinclair Lewis and H.L. Mencken kept taking them for."

One gets the sense that with Mallon, Tarkington can hardly win. Mallon concedes that in the *Plutocrat*, Earl Tinker, the millionaire who was Tarkington's "philanthropic, shrewd, and tolerant" answer to Babbitt, is allowed to take his "victorious leave" standing in an automobile. Mallon further allows that Tarkington made the "impressive" artistic decision to make the most sympathetic and winning character in *Ambersons*, Eugene Morgan, the new automobile man, whereas the awful snob Georgie Minafer speaks for "the author's own wistful values." A lesser critic might conclude that Tarkington's attitude toward the automobile, and the new socioeconomic order it represented, was more ambivalent and complex than what he had just been charged with—perhaps not even "wistful."

But Mallon soldiers on. Not only did Tarkington have nothing of import to say about the Depression, but Mallon speculates that Tarkington *welcomed* it, since it "was undoing only a smoky prosperity he hadn't liked to begin with." Tarkington, who was routinely mocked and upbraided by left-leaning critics for overvaluing business—Tarkington the Republican and praiser of Rotarians—was apparently simultaneously fatuously pro-growth and damnably anti-growth. It was quite a trick.

Even more remarkably, Mallon finds the popular *Penrod* a "tame ... production" whose lead protagonist, "remains a nice young woman's idea of a boy," a judgment one must at least note is wildly at odds with others'. Penrod's "charmlessness" vitiates the entire effort, writes Mallon. *Seventeen* is "even worse." William Baxter is "inspid" and his love interest Lola Pratt "spoiled and nauseating" (which of course she is intended to be). The best moments in the book, says Mallon in another fine instance of backhanded praise, reveal Tarkington "writing above himself." Usually, the narrator evinces a "constant superiority, however fond, toward his subjects." One of the characters, Mr. Parcher, "longs to be reading Plutarch—and twenty pages into *Seventeen*, so do we."

---

While many more instances might be mentioned, this sketch of Tarkington criticism more or less exhausts the catalogue of charges lodged against Tarkington from the height of his fame until the present day. Many of these charges consist of critiques of the Midwest itself—of its characteristic culture, points of view, and personality types. Tarkington and his Midwest, we are told, were nostalgic, sentimental, reactionary, old-fashioned, repressive, racist, xenophobic, insipidly pro-business, hopelessly bourgeois, and blandly ignorant of real life, or life as it was lived below the middle class and beyond the bounds of Middle America.

Tarkington heard it all, and by the latter half of the 1920s he was directly responding. In this regard, several texts are of primary interest: the aforementioned *Plutocrat*, a novel; *Looking Forward and Others*, a collection of essays, most of them dialogic in form; and the (mostly) autobiographical *The World Does Move*. Further insight into Tarkington's mind during this period can be gleaned from a small biographical pamphlet put out by his publisher and the letters collected in *On Plays, Playwrights, and Playgoers*.[35]

Three areas of disagreement become clear from the literary reply Tarkington began to make in the 1920s. First, he thought his critics' portrayal of Midwesterners as essentially stupid provincials ridiculously self-congratulatory. He thought he spied as much provincialism among the sophisticated as he did among the supposed rubes of his home region. Second, he believed the enthusiasm of the typical midwestern bourgeois for prosperity and growth—and the region's individualism—not characteristics to be wholly scorned but rather to be qualifiedly appreciated and harnessed for the common good. And third, he believed the naturalist/modernist anthropology to be inadequate, precisely from a realist point of view.

What about, though, Tarkington's racial and ethnic views? Were they as bad as Mallon claims? Much depends on how charitable one is inclined to be. It is not obvious, from Tarkington's published work at least, that he was especially retrograde, though neither was he a champion of racial equality. To be concerned about the effects of mass immigration, as Tarkington seems to have been, looks fairly silly now, but at the time it was a mainstream position. And Tarkington not only puts these concerns into the mouths of others; he also allows other characters to interrogate them. Such a technique suggests both ambivalence and a decent amount of humility.

As for race, we have already seen that Paul Fussell rose to Tarkington's defense. Most recently, so has Colin Fleming, who regards Herman and Verman as "beyond clever." The brothers are "little adults who act as a kind of two-man Greek chorus with more savvy than Penrod and his mates combined. They are also auteurs of trouble, sagacious, and rightly proud imps who back down from no one."[36] Jonathan Yardley's judgment is a balanced one. Although Tarkington "portrays black characters in antiquated and occasionally offensive ways ... a good deal of evidence indicates that Tarkington is more respectful and sympathetic to his black characters than first impressions suggest." Yardley notes that "Penrod and Sam play with their black friends Herman and Verman pretty much as equals, and Tarkington invests them with a certain dignity. When Verman is insulted by Georgie Bassett with a racial slur, Sam quickly and emphatically comes to his defense, making plain that Verman 'won't let anybody' call him that."[37]

Then there is the incident reported by Tarkington's friend George Ade, the humorist. Tarkington was strolling down the street with a bouquet of flowers for a friend when he saw a black woman carrying a load of laundry on the other side of the road. Impulsively, he crossed over, paid her "lavish compliments," and "removed the covering of the bouquet and presented it to her. We had to walk all the way back with him while he bought another bouquet but Tark was smiling and happy. He had defeated the conventions, brought a burst of sunshine into the life of a lowly worker and given a certain dark female something to talk about for days to come."[38]

Finally, one ought to keep in mind that in 1920s Indianapolis, when the Ku Klux Klan controlled the local Democratic Party and counted roughly one-third of the city's native-born white men as members, to be publicly a progressive Republican who treated African Americans with a reasonable degree of sympathy was to side clearly *against* the out-and-out racists, even if it didn't quite qualify as moral heroism.[39]

Tarkington might have said that to be so quick to believe Midwesterners racists typified the provincial attitude of coastal elites toward his region, an attitude never more manifest than when they accused Midwesterners of provincialism. For example, he and his fellow playwright Harry Leon Wilson were astonished when New York drama critics thought that their midwestern character Daniel Vorhees Pike, in *The Man from Home*, spoke for *them* when he said he "wouldn't trade our State Insane Asylum for the worst ruined ruin in Europe." They hadn't realized just how invested the critics were in portraying hinterland playwrights as philistines.[40]

Tarkington had been introduced to east-coast regional snobbery when he went off to college. "I'd first begun to feel the hurt, rather puzzledly, when from Princeton I visited Eastern classmates and their families, and observed that my Hoosier origin was ignored with conscious tact by these kindhearted people. It was as if I had a physical defect.... Friendly girls spoke teasingly of the Middle West; gentle elderly ladies said forgivingly that they didn't think of me as Hoosier born and bred; I was more like one of them."[41] Tarkington would always chafe at this kind of thing. It was precisely what he didn't like about Lewis's *Main Street* (even though he claimed not to have read it). He believed that it presented a caricature of midwestern types that played precisely to the prejudices of eastern elites. To one correspondent, he wrote that the attitude of *Main Street* was similar to that of the knowing New Yorkers who had recently showed up at a Kennebunkport baseball game and made fun of the team the whole time, leaving early once "they'd made the crowd aware of their wise guy superiority."[42]

Tarkington thought that Lewis and like-minded writers missed the fundamental point: "The *Essentials* in human beings seem to me the same in city and in village, and I'd make a guess that provincialism is the defect in a man that prevents him from seeing that this is true."[43] To him, the rebels against the midwestern village were just exchanging one kind of provincialism for another—and one that made them less self-aware of the limits of their vision. As Madame Momoro, an elegant French woman who serves as the voice of broad-mindedness and historically aware wisdom in the *Plutocrat*, explains to Laurence Ogle, a self-consciously modernist east-coast playwright, true "sophistication is always provincial." "Cosmopolitanism is a little knowledge about many places and kinds of people," but "sophistication is a great deal of knowledge about a very few places and a very few people, usually about one place and one kind of people."[44] Even Wendell Berry has never made the localist case more concisely.

Nothing demonstrated to Tarkington the provincial closed-mindedness of modern intellectuals more than the ideologies and doctrines that were becoming popular in the 1920s. Nihilism and determinism, in particular, struck the deeply humanist Tarkington as fantastically wrongheaded. The title essay in *Looking Forward and Others* consists of a dialogue between Tarkington and an elderly doctor, who observes that to increasing numbers of people, man's "life seems to him but a moment of consciousness between two eternities of black nothing," largely because the advance of science had led to increased agnosticism.[45] But to the doctor, the conclusion that life was meaningless was the result of a startling incuriosity about death. The dialogue presented by Tarkington is impressive, the doctor making points still being made today against philosophical materialism and laying out a case that the nihilists and materialists are too smug, too lacking in proper skepticism, to subject their trendy views to rigorous examination. Nearly a century later, the dialogue holds up. If nothing else Tarkington showed that the "conventional" belief in a human soul and universe suffused with meaning was an intellectually defensible position.

In another essay in *Looking Forward*, a business tycoon recovering from a life-threatening illness is moved to think about the big questions, including the question of determinism. In dialogue with his doctor (this time the medical man representing progressive rather than traditional thought), he proceeds to work out his reasons for not believing "himself a mere Jumping Jack—an automaton produced by evolution."[46] The patient doesn't deny that heredity and environment are responsible for the actions most people take most of the time, but he concludes "that a man can be superior to his natural responses," and that "the truly wise man is one who can look down with serenity upon the mastered demons in his own soul."[47] There is a psychoanalytic dimension to the patient's theorizing. But instead of believing humans to be principally driven by sexual urges or death wishes, he concludes that they are driven unconsciously by the "urge to happiness." Freedom lies in understanding this urge and its effects, in being able to "look down upon" ourselves "from the heights of understanding, and observe [our] own 'reactions' and refuse to be bound by the demons among them."[48] Tarkington adumbrates here a limited sort of freedom, a freedom achievable to those who can release themselves from the cares and demands of everyday existence—and the new conventional wisdom.

Materialism and determinism are intrinsic to Marxist socialism, of course, which was one reason Tarkington could not accept it. About socialism, especially in its Soviet manifestation, Tarkington can hardly be said to have been less perspicacious than those legions of younger writers who expressed admiration for the USSR. Then, too, Tarkington believed that the human egoism—the voracious self, the insistent *I*—that was so thematically central to his fiction could not be eradicated, as he thought socialists believed. His statesmanlike solution to the problem of self-interest and the inequality it inevitably generated was to harness it for the common good.

Inequality was part of the structure of this imperfect world, Tarkington believed, and in any case, communism ultimately offered no real solution, as even under communism people would remain unsatisfied with what they had. Acquisitiveness would remain. A communist regime would therefore reproduce inequality just as surely as any other, and no more justly.[49] The "socialist remedy for human selfishness" he therefore found laughably inadequate. "Abolish private ownership; put 5,000 Gov't Clerks in place of 8 or 10 capitalist-appointed superintendents. Pay the bill in taxes. Commissars get the limousines instead of the capitalists. Destroy our freedom, incentive and other things—with no charge in return except a backward one."[50] He further prophesied that the centralized administration of all enterprise could end in nothing but economic disaster.

Yet, with his typical fair-mindedness, Tarkington profoundly admired his fellow Hoosier Eugene Debs, the great Socialist Party and union leader. He once found himself sitting in the same train car as Debs, and the two men spoke for hours—Debs having no idea who Tarkington was. "It seemed to me that I'd never encountered a sounder or more steady-minded, fair, and profoundly intelligent patriotic American citizen," Tarkington later recalled.[51]

Tarkington, in fact, had ambivalent feelings toward big business and the tycoons who did so much to change American life during the end of the nineteenth century and beginning of the twentieth. His mature views could fairly be described as quasi-Hegelian; he had faith in a sort of providential progress that advanced by stages in zigzag fashion, in which the industrialist played his fate-appointed part.[52]

Certainly no literary figure was ever more aesthetically oriented than Tarkington. Beauty, to him, was life. He deplored the terrible ugliness that accompanied the industrial-capitalist dispensation: the hideous smoke, grime, dirt, noise, and architecture. He was troubled, too, by the fissures in the old social order and changes in manners and mores brought about by the rapid growth that was industrial capitalism's fruit—so troubled, in fact, that earlier in his career Tarkington was thought to harbor left-leaning, anti-American beliefs because of his critique of the ideology of growth and the mania for what he called "bigness."[53]

But he was just as irritated by portraits of businessmen that presented them as cartoon villains, or that ignored the extent to which society—including artists and writers—benefited from their efforts. To ignore this fact simply seemed dishonest to Tarkington. As he aged, he found himself offering a defense of business and those civic-minded men and women who promoted its interests, including the intellectual class's despised "Rotarians."[54] Tarkington knew a number of prominent financiers and industrialists personally, and he generally seems to have enjoyed their company as much as, if not more than, that of other writers. Not only did he get material from them—the *Plutocrat*'s Earl Tinker is based on his friend Howard Fisher—but he found that often their vices, such as hyper-patriotism, could be channeled toward more virtuous ends, such as civic investment. Tarkington thought that capitalism's pioneers were inevitable types playing inevitable historical roles. They were like Roman emperors, persons of stupendous energy and possessing even more stupendous egos. However uncouth they were, and however ugly, at first, their works, they ironically laid the necessary material foundation on which the arts, high culture, philanthropic institutions, and social advancement rested.[55]

It is not clear how many of his critics ever considered these rebuttals. Certainly we never hear about them. But forget the establishment. Outside the literary guild Tarkington has always had many fans, not a few of them prominent. His fellow Indianapolis native Kurt Vonnegut was one. Late in life he credited Tarkington's example for the success he had achieved as a writer. "When I was a kid, I wanted to be like him. We never met. I wouldn't have known what to say. I would have been gaga with hero worship."[56] Roger Ebert and Jonathan Yardley greatly admired the

*Penrod* books, Yardley writing that Tarkington's "piercingly observant" eye makes them "nothing less than primers on boyness."[57] Roy Blount Jr. has said he was influenced by Tarkington's work. The novelist John P. Marquand praised Tarkington's "deep knowledge of human beings," which was consistently relayed with a "high level of technical achievement."[58] The Marx Brothers, with their wives, even once dropped in on Tarkington in Indianapolis, and Tarkington and Groucho were correspondents.[59]

All of these figures found in Tarkington a man capable of illuminating the human condition with wisdom, common sense, and humor. One suspects that most of the members of this varied group, if not all of them, appreciated the counterpoint he offered to the village-protest, these-people-are-idiots, life-here-sucks thrust of much midwestern literature after Dreiser—the *best* midwestern literature as defined by the establishment. Tarkington's works were surely imperfect, his range of vision also limited. But as a writer and social historian, he has perennial value in providing us with the other side of the story.

## Notes

1. Asa Don Dickinson, *Booth Tarkington: A Biographical and Bibliographical Sketch* (Garden City, NY: Doubleday, Doran & Co., 1928), 11. Dickinson interviewed Tarkington for what was essentially a public-relations pamphlet put out by Doubleday, Tarkington's publisher. It has no value as literary criticism, but it is quite useful for the Tarkington quotations and biographical information it contains, and for the sense it gives of the literary and public perception of Tarkington at the time.
2. Dickinson, *Booth Tarkington*, 10–11.
3. The quotation comes from a Hutner interview with the publisher of his book, *What America Read: Taste, Class, and the Novel, 1920–1960* (Chapel Hill, NC: University of North Carolina Press, 2009). See www.uncpress.unc.edu/browse/page/600.
4. James Woodress, *Booth Tarkington: Gentleman from Indiana* (Philadelphia: J.B. Lippincott Co., 1955), 287.
5. The biographical information in this and later paragraphs comes primarily from Woodress, *Booth Tarkington*; Booth Tarkington, *America Moved: Booth Tarkington's Memoirs of Time and Place, 1869–1928* (Eugene, OR: Wipf and Stock, 2015); Keith J. Fennimore, *Booth Tarkington* (New York: Twayne Publishers, 1974); and Dickinson, *Booth Tarkington*. Booth's paternal Tarkington ancestors had migrated to Indiana by way of North Carolina. His mother, Elizabeth Booth's, family had arrived by way of Connecticut and tended to claim a socially superior ancestry.

6. Tarkington, *America Moved*, 110. For a very fine recent article on Riley and his immense popularity, see John E. Miller, "The Funeral of Beloved Hoosier Poet, James Whitcomb Riley," *Studies in Midwestern History*, 2, no. 6 (July 2016), 70–78.
7. Woodress, *Booth Tarkington*, 7.
8. Fennimore, *Booth Tarkington*, 48.
9. From February 2016 to February 2017, the museum mounted an exhibition titled "A Gentleman Collector from Indiana: Portraits from the Collection of Booth Tarkington" in honor of the seventieth anniversary of Tarkington's death.
10. Both the Lewis and the Glasgow letters are quoted in Woodress, *Booth Tarkington*, 249.
11. Woodress, *Booth Tarkington*, 336.
12. In Commager's article on Arthur Meier Schlesinger Sr.'s *The Rise of the City* and in Atherton's *Main Street on the Middle Border*, respectively. The quotation is from Fennimore, *Booth Tarkington*, 18.
13. Welles always claimed that Eugene Morgan, the book/film's automobile-manufacturing entrepreneur, was based on his father, Richard, a businessman who successfully transitioned from making bicycle headlamps to car headlights. This is plausible, as Dick Welles was good friends with Tarkington pals George Ade and John McCutcheon. Tarkington's letters, never published and scattered across various archives (principally at Princeton University, the University of Virginia, Colby College, and the Indiana Historical Society), might be able to corroborate the claim. See Patrick McGilligan, *Young Orson: The Years of Luck and Genius on the Path to Citizen Kane* (New York: Harper, 2015).
14. Carl Van Doren, "Contemporary American Novelists: Booth Tarkington," *The Nation*, February 9, 1921, 233–35.
15. Cited in Ronald Weber, *The Midwestern Ascendancy in American Writing* (Bloomington, IN: Indiana University Press, 1992), 54.
16. Claude Bowers is the original source of this quotation from Dreiser. See W.A. Swanberg, *Dreiser* (New York: Charles Scribner's Sons, 1965), 296.
17. Andrew Jewell and Janis Stout, eds., *The Selected Letters of Willa Cather* (New York: Alfred A. Knopf, 2013), 308.
18. Cited in Weber, *The Midwestern Ascendancy*, 55.
19. F.O. Matthiessen, *Theodore Dreiser* (New York: William Sloane Associates, 1951), 65.
20. Mark Schorer, *Sinclair Lewis: An American Life* (New York: McGraw-Hill, 1961), 283.
21. Naturalists of the Dreiser or Zola school generally attempted to take a detached, skeptical, and therefore, from their point of view, more clinical and "scientific" view of humans and their behavior. Their version of literary realism is significantly more pessimistic and less open to transcendence than was the earlier, alternative realism of Howells and Tarkington.

22. Weber, *The Midwestern Ascendancy*, 16.
23. Ibid., 50.
24. Ibid., 51–52.
25. Ibid., 53.
26. Ibid., 54.
27. Ibid., 107.
28. Ibid., 55.
29. Ibid., 16.
30. Ibid., 51.
31. Ibid., 55.
32. Ibid., 162.
33. Jon K. Lauck, "The Myth of the Midwestern 'Revolt from the Village,'" *MidAmerica* XL (2013), 39–85. This thoroughly researched article is seminal in reshaping our understanding of how this interpretation of the Midwest arose and spread, and of how the numerous midwestern writers who rejected this interpretation have been scrubbed from most scholars' historical consciousness.
34. Thomas Mallon, "Hoosiers: The Lost World of Booth Tarkington," *The Atlantic*, May 2004. "Author" is capitalized in the original. All subsequent Mallon quotations are from this article.
35. In later novels, too, including *Mary's Neck* and *The Heritage of Hatcher Ide*, Tarkington satirizes or responds to the critics of midwestern conventionality.
36. Colin Fleming, "From Pen to Penrod: An Appreciation of Booth Tarkington," *Weekly Standard*, May 2, 2016.
37. Jonathan Yardley, "Attaboy! Booth Tarkington's Rascals," *Washington Post*, August 7, 2004.
38. *Letters of George Ade*, ed. Terence Tobin (West Lafayette, IN: Purdue University Press, 1973), 169.
39. The statistic on Klan membership comes from *The Encyclopedia of Indianapolis* (Bloomington, IN: Indiana University Press, 1994), 879. I don't wish to portray Tarkington as angelic on racial and ethnic matters. There are a number of scenes, remarks, stereotypes, and word choices throughout his oeuvre that provoke cringing today. But rarely if ever does any kind of animus seem to be present.
40. Booth Tarkington, *On Plays, Playwrights, and Playgoers: Selections from the Letters of Booth Tarkington to George C. Tyler and John Peter Toohey, 1918–1925*, ed. Alan S. Downer (Princeton, NJ: Princeton University Library, 1959), 18.
41. Tarkington, *America Moved*, 106.
42. Tarkington, *On Plays, Playwrights, and Playgoers*, 42.
43. Ibid.
44. Booth Tarkington, *The Plutocrat: A Novel* (Garden City, NY: Doubleday, Page & Co., 1927), 272–73.

45. Booth Tarkington, *Looking Forward and Others* (Garden City, NY: Doubleday, Page & Co., 1926), 3.
46. Tarkington, *Looking Forward*, 73.
47. Ibid., 76.
48. Ibid., 77.
49. Tarkington, *On Plays, Playwrights, and Playgoers*, 39.
50. Ibid., 27.
51. Woodress, *Booth Tarkington*, 111.
52. See especially *The Plutocrat, Looking Forward and Others*, and *The World Does Move* (Garden City, NY: Doubleday, Doran & Co., 1928).
53. Dickinson, *Booth Tarkington*, 21–22.
54. See Tarkington's "Rotarian and Sophisticate," *World's Work*, January 1929, 42–44.
55. *The Plutocrat* is the key novel here.
56. Kurt Vonnegut, *Armageddon in Retrospect* (New York: G.P. Putnam's Sons, 2008), 27.
57. For Ebert quotations related to Penrod, see http://dramatic-insights.org/tarkington/index.php/2010/roger-ebert-penrod-fan/. The Yardley quotation is from "Attaboy! Booth Tarkington's Rascals."
58. J.P. Marquand, "Tarkington and Social Significance," *Saturday Review*, March 1, 1941, 7.
59. *The Groucho Letters: Letters from and to Groucho Marx* (New York: Simon and Schuster, 1967), 295–97.

Harl A. Dalstrom | "Let us write like inspired artists and sell like shrewd Yankees"

Bess Streeter Aldrich's Early Twentieth-Century Middle West

From the 1920s to the 1940s, Bess Streeter Aldrich (1881–1954) of Elmwood, Nebraska, won fame as a short-story author and novelist. Her most famous work, *A Lantern in Her Hand* (1928), is an historical novel, as are *Spring Came on Forever* (1935), *Song of Years* (1939), and *The Lieutenant's Lady* (1942). All emphasized nineteenth-century frontier experiences in settings from northeastern Iowa to eastern Nebraska to Montana Territory, and all reflect Aldrich's commitment to accuracy and realism coupled with genuine affection for the rural Midwest. *Lantern* and *Spring* provide generally positive images of rural life and especially midwestern small towns in the early twentieth century as do *The Rim of the Prairie* (1925), *A White Bird Flying* (1931), and two books of stories previously published in magazines, *Mother Mason* (1924) and *The Cutters* (1926). A gifted observer with a strong talent for description, Aldrich portrayed material and social changes that broadened human horizons and intensified the interdependence of rural, small-town, and urban life. Her narratives show that this change created tensions between old and new values, especially the role of women as wives and mothers. Frontier settlement brought ethnic diversity to the Midwest, and Aldrich ably illustrates the stresses and accommodations accompanying this cultural dynamic in rural Nebraska. In contrast to writers who emphasized the shortcomings of midwestern life, she gave her readers a warm but honest depiction of her region.

Bessie ("Bess") Genevra, the eighth and last child of James and Mary Anderson Streeter, was born in Cedar Falls, Iowa, soon after her family moved to town after years of farming nearby. Bess's parents had experienced life in frontier Iowa in the 1850s, and she was reared amid stories of pioneering. Indeed, lore from both sides of her family, along with her innate abilities, did much to shape her future. After graduating in 1901 from Iowa State Normal School in Cedar Falls, Bess taught in elementary schools and in 1907 earned a Primary Training Certificate from her alma mater. That year, she married attorney Charles Sweetzer Aldrich and relocated to Tipton, Iowa, her husband's home town.

In 1909, Bess and Charles ("Cap") moved to Elmwood, Nebraska, a community of some 585 people in western Cass County, east of Lincoln. There, Charles and Bess's brother-in-law had purchased the American Exchange Bank, and Cap established a career as bank cashier and as an attorney. In May 1925, Cap's death made Mrs. Aldrich's writing essential to supporting herself and their four children. She lived in Elmwood until 1946, when she moved to Lincoln, residing near her daughter Mary and family.[1]

Despite her loss of Cap, Aldrich's writing reflects a positive view of life from her Iowa childhood through her many years in Nebraska. Her cheerful mother, Mary, was a particular inspiration for this outlook. Aldrich, a Methodist of Scottish-Presbyterian background, was traditional in her values and her narratives reflect this traditionalism. Topics such as spousal abuse, infidelity, alcoholism, or other aspects of dysfunctional family life were not part of her experience and are absent from her narratives. Still, as she said, her type of writing was not "Pollyanna stuff" and she emphasized that "the decent things of life" are as realistic as the darker elements.[2] Biographer Carol Miles Petersen, Annie Russell Marble (an early commentator on her work), and *Omaha World-Herald* book critic Victor P. Hass have rightly described her as a "Romantic Realist."[3]

Because Aldrich typically set her works in the central United States, she often used the term "middle-west" or "Midwest," a fairly new concept in the 1920s when she wrote her first novels. By then, "Middle West" had come to mean the dozen states from Ohio to the Dakotas, Kansas, and Nebraska.[4] In Mrs. Aldrich's novels, her northeastern Iowa family background and early life and the rolling land of eastern Nebraska where she later lived are basic to her regional identity. In *White Bird*, one of her characters describes the Middle West as extending to the "ten thousand lakes of Minnesota," the "Bad Lands of Dakota," and "the sandhills of northern Nebraska."[5] In *Mother Mason* she used "Mid-West" to symbolize a quintessential American lifestyle.[6]

Mrs. Aldrich's fiction often portrays the interaction of three or four generations of characters, from old-timers surviving from the frontier era to young folks of the 1920s and 1930s. The heart of the settlement period from 1870 to 1890 remains the most dynamic generation of growth in Nebraska's history as national and international demographic, economic, and technological realities acted within the new state's highly variable physical environment, yielding breath-taking change. Aldrich's historical novels set primarily in eastern Nebraska— *Lantern* and *Spring*—ably show the growth dynamics of her adopted state from frontier times to the early twentieth century. Her writing is faithful to what historian Frederick C. Luebke described as the interaction of "Time, Place, and Culture" in the settlement process, an interaction which had a lasting impact upon Nebraska's character.[7]

A prominent theme in Mrs. Aldrich's treatment of the twentieth century is an intense commitment to defending the Midwest, set forth most forcefully in her first novel, *The Rim of the Prairie*. In her preface, Aldrich, speaking of fictitious Maple City, Nebraska, *Rim*'s primary setting, said:

> Small and midwestern is Maple City, which in the eyes of many modernists is synonymous for all that is hideous and cramping. A handful of people, they say we are, knotted together like roots in the darkness. Blind souls, they call us—struggling spirits who can never find deliverance from sordid surroundings. Poor thinkers! Not to know that from tangled roots shimmering growth may spring to the light in beautiful winged release.

Here, in the context of *Rim*'s 1925 publication, Aldrich assumes that her readers will recognize the "many modernists" as those contemporary writers and literary critics who portrayed small towns—especially those of the Midwest—as havens of cultural and social stagnation. From this perspective, America's great cities were the home of open-mindedness and modern values, a notion easily perverted into jocular ridicule of small and seemingly remote places.

Reflecting upon slights against their region, two of *Rim*'s characters, banker O.J. Rineland and Nancy Moore, a young woman central to *Rim*'s romantic plot, speak defensively and eloquently in

Ad for *Rim of the Prairie*. *Sunday World-Herald* (Omaha). Nov. 15, 1925. p. 8E [p. 48 online].

support of the culture, values, and achievements of midwestern people and the natural beauty of their land. Nancy thereby inspires Warner Field, a young author beset by writer's block and debt, to recover his creativity and produce a manuscript telling "the simple story of the land that is neither east nor west," which a New York publisher soon buys. This is remarkable because Warner, an eastern-educated Omaha native, had previously authored material critical of the Midwest.[8] Aldrich also vigorously defended the cultural life of the small midwestern town in "Meadows Entertains a Celebrity," published in *American Magazine* in August 1923, and reprinted in *The Cutters*.[9]

Aldrich was working against a growing literary trend. Sinclair Lewis's 1920 novel, *Main Street*, with its negative portrayal of life in fictional Gopher Prairie, Minnesota, seemingly opened the door to attacks on small towns. Although Lewis did not limit his critique to midwestern communities, Carl Van Doren, reviewing *Main Street*, said that Lewis possessed "so enormous an acquaintance with the foibles and folklore of the Middle West that he has literally set a new standard for novels dealing with the section."[10] In "The Revolt from the Village," published in *The Nation* in October 1921, Van Doren, a professor at Columbia University, named other recent authors in addition to Lewis who had helped solidify the idea that thoughtful people were rejecting the complacency, mediocrity, and smugness that they associated with midwestern towns. This interpretation gained credibility, despite the fact that Lewis and other writers who had seemingly revolted from their home communities subsequently revealed more balanced perspectives.[11]

Aldrich steadily resisted these literary currents. Carol Petersen notes that in December 1925, Mrs. Aldrich responded sharply to a New York book reviewer who, evaluating her *Mother Mason*, made a snide comment about Nebraska's people.[12] But much earlier, before *Main Street*, Aldrich defended the quality of small-town life. In April 1920, some six months before *Main Street*'s release, *American Magazine* published her story, "Tillie Cuts Loose," which questioned whether a person could live in a place like "Springtown" and have a lively, growing intellect. The key figure in the narrative, "Mother Mason," concluded from personal experience that indeed one could live in a small town and be familiar with the broader world. Because the plot in "Tillie Cuts Loose" did not have a pejorative regional implication, Aldrich, speaking through Mother Mason in defending small-town living, was seemingly responding to the influence of a local critic. Still, the fact that this story predated *Main Street* and the "Revolt from the Village" theme suggests Mrs. Aldrich's sensitivity to an emerging direction in American thought. In 1925, when *Rim* was released, the linkage of small-town parochialism with the Midwest again caused her to reject what she saw as the denigration of her state and region.[13]

Aldrich's defense of the Midwest is based on her own positive experience and exposure to the wider world. Most towns and farms in the heart of the Midwest were reasonably accessible by rail to an urban center, the rail system generally offering public transportation far superior to that of the early twenty-first century. One could readily ride a Missouri Pacific train between Elmwood and Lincoln; hence, it makes sense that Mrs. Aldrich begins *Mother Mason* with Mrs. Henry Mason catching the morning train from "Springtown," Nebraska, to "Capitol City" for a few days of shopping, rest, and recreation. The Mason children attend university in Capitol City; two daughters marry prominent educators from there, and we have a glimpse of "Father" (Henry) reading the *Journal*.[14] In *Spring*, a banker's wife in a Nebraska town takes her daughter to Omaha to purchase a wardrobe suitable for university activities.[15] Aldrich also mentions medical emergencies in rural Nebraska in which a *"trained* nurse" came from Omaha. Indeed, nurses' training programs in Omaha and elsewhere offered attractive career opportunities for young women from town and countryside.[16]

Aldrich's Nebraskans are hardly "trapped" on the farm. In *Lantern,* Aldrich tells the story of pioneering in eastern Nebraska through the eyes of Abbie Deal, who settled in the Stove Creek (Elmwood) area in 1868 where she lived until her death circa 1927. Like the author, Abbie had grown up in the Cedar Falls, Iowa, area, and her Nebraska home, "Cedartown," resembles Aldrich's Elmwood. Although Abbie Deal, her deceased husband, Will, and their neighbors had molded their frontier locale into prosperous farms and a community to serve this countryside, none of the Deal children became farmers and only one remained in Cedartown. Three built careers in Chicago, Omaha, and Lincoln, and one was a Lincoln housewife and artist.[17] The dispersion of all but one of the Deal children to cities foretold the future of the Midwest. Her defense of small towns notwithstanding, Mrs. Aldrich well expressed the lure of a nearby city to a young person when Mother Mason's daughter Marcia, who was completing her university studies, proclaimed her teaching plans: "'I don't want to go to any little two-by-four burg. Capitol City for *me!*'"[18] Indeed, in Aldrich's writings, second and later generation characters are often college-educated, which reflects the lives of Bess and Cap Aldrich and their children. In *Lantern*, before Abbie Deal's son John settled down as a Cedartown attorney, his fictional story paralleled Cap's actual career. However, in the closing pages of *White Bird* and *Spring* we see young university-educated couples in the 1930s, descended from pioneers, making their futures in farming, showing the relevance of higher education to agriculture.

Mrs. Aldrich routinely treated the material changes that came to the Midwest in the early twentieth century. She noted the introduction in the 1890s of winter wheat and alfalfa, and these crops—which Abbie Deal planted—would profoundly shape Nebraska's agriculture. In *Lantern*, Abbie lived to hear her daughter Isabelle sing on the radio from Chicago and to see her children and grandchildren come in automobiles to visit.[19]

Because her husband and brother-in-law were Elmwood bankers and she believed that authors should write about familiar subjects, bankers and banking are prominent in Bess Streeter Aldrich's works and are not cast in a negative light, as would become common in literature in coming years. Indeed, after Cap's death, she was elected to the board of directors of the American Exchange Bank.[20] Speaking of "The country banker" in *Mother Mason*, Aldrich said, "He is the financial pastor of his flock.... He carries a burden of confidences that is far from being merely financial, a burden of greater proportions than the minister's." In *Rim,* she remarked that "It is a favorite indoor sport of fiction writers to picture him [the banker] as a Shylock, whetting his knife behind the grated window. The country-banker is a high-type man, calm, level-headed, just. Where one goes wrong, a hundred stay right."[21] Reflecting her knowledge of banking in Elmwood, Mrs. Aldrich in *Rim* gives her readers a good sense of why the beginning of March was a critical time in the rural Midwest. March 1 was the common date for farm tenancy agreements, and her depiction of the atmosphere and challenges of this hectic day with its sometimes complex real estate transactions illustrates the interdependence of town and countryside.[22]

In *Lantern,* Aldrich's description of Abbie Deal's son, Mack, who had left the farm to make a career as an Omaha banker, captures the business atmosphere of urban America in the 1920s. As she said, "He wore horn-rimmed glasses, went in for golf and Rotary and the Commercial Club."[23] Indeed, the actual Commercial Club of Omaha, renamed the Omaha Chamber of Commerce in 1918, promoted regional development and in *Rim* we are told that banker Rineland of Maple City "held an out-of-town-membership." This illustrates the business network intrinsic to the Midwest as a region.[24]

By the 1920s, however, Nebraska banking was in crisis. By law, state-chartered banks were required to contribute to building a bank guaranty fund, which would presumably protect their depositors. Yet there were too many small banks and when the agricultural boom of the World War I era ended, a massive collapse of the state-chartered banks brought severe consequences.[25] In *White Bird,* Mrs. Aldrich, speaking through Abbie Deal's sons, John, a lawyer and state legislator, and Mack, the banker, provides a well-balanced treatment of this controversial topic. For Aldrich, this became a real-life crisis, because in 1933 the future of the American Exchange Bank of which she was an officer and owner was in danger. Mindful of the suffering that its failure would bring to her community, she quietly committed all of her financial resources needed to save the bank.[26] The problem was not limited to Nebraska, and other states in the region experienced similar disasters.[27]

In *The Cutters,* the depressed economy after World War I impaired attorney Ed Cutter's income, forcing hard decisions in the family's spending.[28] Economic depression and climatic challenges in the

Midwest are basic to Aldrich's January 1938 *Cosmopolitan* magazine story, "The Drum Goes Dead," subsequently republished in other formats. The setting is a Christmas Eve during the 1930s Depression in "Bellfield," a town much like Elmwood. Banker Richard Lanning, depressed by the hard times, wants to avoid his customary function of playing Santa to the children at Bellfield's Christmas Eve program. In addition to the economic debacle, drought had killed many trees while grasshoppers and wheat rust beset the land. The past summer brought blazing heat and desiccating wind, ruining much corn, and occasionally making that crop toxic to livestock. Newspaper and Cooperative Extension Service (county agent) reports confirm the accuracy of Aldrich's portrayal of local conditions and suggest a time frame of 1934 to 1937. But Richard Lanning could not escape his duty as Santa, and as the evening unfolded he saw that Christmas was still a wondrous time for youngsters, and that the world was far from uniformly bleak and depressing. Indeed, "Drum" reminds us that no historical period is thoroughly described by our general images of it.[29]

From her childhood, Bess Streeter Aldrich lived amidst people of recent European background. In *White Bird*, she illustrates ethnic distribution within rural Nebraska, concluding "All were highly efficient farming people. But everywhere came the Germans, equally efficient and thrifty."[30] With the exception of the older American stock, Germans were by far the largest ethnic group in Cass County.[31] Aldrich's most significant treatment of ethnicity is in *Spring Came on Forever*. A group of Germans who had lived in a colony in Illinois came to Nebraska in 1866 where they maintained their inter-family associations and German-Lutheran congregation. By the early twentieth century, however, their cultural bonds were eroding. The public school, routine association with Anglo-Americans, intermarriage, and the passing of the older generation all advanced this acculturation. The old white frame Lutheran Church was replaced with a red brick edifice, but as Mrs. Aldrich said:

> More than these material changes, the services were part English,—there had been almost a rumpus over it, and again over whether to have a short sermon in German and another in English immediately following, or the German every other Sunday ...

This passage aptly describes the tension that accompanied ethnic group adjustment in the early twentieth century Midwest.³² Aldrich did not suggest that Nebraska's ethnic identities were obliterated, but she showed that by the 1930s the acculturation of early immigrants was well advanced. In *Miss Bishop* (1933), set in a midwestern college town, Aldrich portrayed the negative impact of World War I upon the study of the German language and literature and upon a professor who taught these subjects. Likewise, in *Spring* she described the embittered human relations that World War I brought to rural Nebraska, a situation reflected in real-life Elmwood.³³

Aldrich's works also address the rise of a new set of cultural values that challenged old mores in the Middle West and the nation. Aldrich's misgivings about modern values are unmistakably clear in *Spring Came on Forever,* in which she writes that the World War I era was marked by "a wild aftermath of economic and moral breakdown that swept into every village and farm."³⁴ Myrtie Holmsdorfer (who got her married name Anglicized to Holms), for example, becomes a club woman who does not have time for household work or child-rearing. Myrtie's selfishness and superficial values, including a disdain for farm life, compels her husband to move to town and make big financial mistakes.³⁵ In *Lantern,* Abbie Deal, who had sacrificed her artistic yearnings for home and family, cannot understand the decision of daughter Isabelle and her husband to forego having children. They wish to pursue musical careers and conclude that they could not make enough money to support a family. Abbie also regrets that women were spending so much time with activities outside their homes when they might be building solid relationships with their children. Aldrich reiterates this point in *Lantern*'s sequel, *White Bird*.³⁶

In *Rim, White Bird,* and the last part of *Spring,* Mrs. Aldrich presents even bolder challenges to traditional ideas of love and marriage. Young Nebraska women—Nancy Moore in *Rim* and Laura Deal, Abbie's granddaughter, in *White Bird*—are college graduates and each becomes strongly attracted to a fine young suitor. However, Nancy and Laura have material or urban career interests that lead them to make seemingly firm, but emotionally deficient marital decisions rejecting traditional romance. In *Spring,* Hazel Meier breaks her engagement to a university classmate when he tells her that he will be a farmer rather than practice law.³⁷

In each work, Aldrich brilliantly uses the Midwest's capricious weather in the denouement. The *Rim* chapter "April Sixth" describes a windy, sultry Sunday, and in the next chapter, a tornado strikes, producing a romantic ending. (Indeed, on Sunday, April 6, 1919, a destructive tornado hit near Elmwood.)[38] In *White Bird*, a severe summer storm combines tragedy and romance, and in *Spring* the great flood in the Republican River valley in southwestern Nebraska in 1935 does likewise. In all three books, the imminent prospect or reality of death brought the triumph of values underlying romantic realism.[39]

The relationship of people to the land is fundamental, and it is hard to imagine a farmer having a deeper bond to his soil than does *Rim*'s "Uncle Jud" Moore, who lives near Maple City. Uncle Jud and his wife, "Aunt Biny," confronting the realities of old age, sell their farm to a neighbor. The neighbor then tells Jud that he plans to remove the orchard and other trees so as to increase crop land. These comments devastate Jud, an environmentalist generations before the term came into vogue. He also worries about the fate of some virgin prairie that he had retained and that school children visit on field trips. A terror seizes him, augmented by the reality that he simply does not want to retire. Hence, he works out a settlement with the buyer to cancel the land sale, and he and Aunt Biny go to the home of banker Rineland to see if his old friend and financial advisor approves the arrangement. There, Uncle Jud stands and makes a heartfelt declaration of the environmental cause. As Carol Petersen notes, this desire to preserve a tract of virgin prairie reflected Aldrich's childhood awareness of remnants of prairie having been kept near her Cedar Falls home.[40]

If Aldrich was, on balance, a defender of the midwestern rural order in her fiction and a skeptic of modern values, she was also willing to lay bare the difficulties of life in the Midwest. In "Meadows Entertains a Celebrity" in *The Cutters*, she lamented that rivalry between churches hindered the planning of a community event.[41] There are worthy characters in *Rim*'s Maple City, but the town has poverty, snobbery, and a young woman whose life began as a foundling child born out of wedlock to two prominent families.[42]

Aldrich captured the household grind and monotony facing women. As Nell Cutter exclaims to husband Ed, "I have spells when I just want to fly—get off somewhere away from everybody in this town.

'Think of it! To wash on Monday and iron on Tuesday and clean on Wednesday—and *always* the youngsters and three meals!'" In *Mother Mason*, Aldrich takes her readers to the home of Mother's daughter-in-law, who, expecting her second child, finds everything going wrong. She is overwhelmed with house-cleaning, ironing, and kitchen tasks and oppressed by the beastly heat of a midwestern summer decades before home air-conditioning, and finds her husband less than fully understanding.[43]

Aldrich's writings will casually introduce today's readers to routine details of life in bygone days. In the early twentieth century, boarding houses were an important feature of town and city living. Bess Streeter and Charles Aldrich met at a boarding house in Marshalltown, Iowa, and a novelist could hardly find a better setting for exploring personalities and grass-roots dramas. So in *Rim* we soon meet some of the book's characters in the dining room of a boarding house, once the home of one of Maple City's eminent families.[44]

Maple City was probably among the many midwestern towns served by now long-gone railroad branch lines. Aldrich's fine image of travelers standing on the station platform amid the milk cans and chicken crates waiting for a train carries us back to the early twentieth century.[45] We are also reminded that after World War I high schools still had "normal-training" programs for elementary teachers, that electricity in its early home use was relatively expensive, and that smallpox remained a menace.[46] The use of rural party lines was common (as was eavesdropping).[47] We find vestiges of rural life in towns—families might keep chickens or buy butter from a farm woman, or residents on the edge of town might have a cow and pasture.[48]

Aldrich was an exponent of what we call "traditional family values," but her life illustrates the evolution of the status of women in the Midwest and nation. In "How I Mixed Stories with Doughnuts" in *The American Magazine* in February 1921, her remark that "I believe sincerely in equal suffrage, but I have never turned my hand over to help obtain it," suggested that her priorities were home and writing. That she took pride in her craft is shown in the 1920 Census, which gives her occupation as "authoress (national magazines)." In *Miss Bishop* we learn that at "Midwestern College" a woman faculty member who married was required to resign. But times were changing: Ella Bishop, who taught at Midwestern for over half a century, admired the directness and ambition of her students in the 1930s, including the women, compared to the reticence of her classmates of 1880.[49] In *Mother Mason* and *The Cutters*, the women protagonists are college graduates and although their community activities are gender-delineated, we may see their leadership roles preparing the way for their granddaughters to make wider-ranging use of their ambitions and talents. Above all, Mrs. Aldrich had the values, ability, motivation, and discipline to be highly successful as a modern professional woman while being an outstanding parent.[50]

All these features of Aldrich's work demonstrate her commitment to place and regional writing. In 1909, the kind reception she and her family received in Elmwood bespoke an enduring community goodness that, with her innate optimism, explains her decision to emphasize "the better features of the small town and its people."[51] Gifted in expressing sensory perceptions of her midwestern landscape, Aldrich found her surroundings laden with dramatic potential, and through her writings she demonstrated that ordinary people everywhere have meaningful lives.[52]

To tell the stories of her rural Midwesterners and to become a well-known writer, however, Aldrich had to be a keen marketer. In *White Bird*, Abbie Deal's daughter-in-law and granddaughter make a vacation acquaintanceship with a prominent author—surely a surrogate for Aldrich—who discusses the marketing side of writing, which Aldrich understood well.[53] Selling books and stories was her mission. In 1925, shortly before Cap's death, Aldrich told the Writers' Guild of Nebraska, "Let us write like inspired artists and sell like shrewd Yankees."[54] And sell she did. In 1931, *White Bird*'s national sales placed third after Pearl Buck's *The Good Earth* and Willa Cather's *Shadows on the Rock*. Aldrich's continued publication and the 1941 release of the motion picture, *Cheers for Miss Bishop*, based upon her novel, *Miss Bishop*, ensured her additional financial success.[55] In 1971, book critic Victor Hass said that "writing, as was her lot, in the all-but-overpowering shadow of the great Willa Cather, Mrs. Aldrich went her tranquil way to fashion a literary legacy of which any state could be proud." Hass observed that "Mrs. Aldrich was a very nearly perfect example of the regional novelist who … interpreted and illuminated a particular area for those who inhabit it," likening her to Sarah Orne Jewett, Ruth Suckow, Ellen Glasgow, and Edith Wharton.[56] In 1973, nineteen years after her death, Aldrich joined her fellow Nebraskan Willa Cather in the Nebraska Hall of Fame, where she holds a well-deserved place, for her contributions not only to Nebraska, but to midwestern literature in general.

## Notes

1. Amelia Mabel Meier, "Bess Streeter Aldrich: Her life and Works" (Kearney, Nebraska: Master of Science in Education thesis, Kearney State College, 1968), 6–16, 55, 94; Carol Miles Petersen, *Bess Streeter Aldrich: The Dreams Are Real* (Lincoln: University of Nebraska Press, 1995), 1–24, 194, 196–97, 199, 229–30; Petersen (ed.), *Bess Streeter Aldrich: The Collected Short Works 1920–1954* (Lincoln: University of Nebraska Press, 1999), 135 (headnote); *Elmwood Leader-Echo*, May 8, 1925 (hereafter cited as *EL-E.*) Items in *EL-E*, Feb. 23, Apr. 27, June 15, July 13, 1917, Apr. 4, 1919, March 27, Apr. 3, 1925, illustrate Charles Aldrich's business and professional career in Elmwood. U.S. Bureau of the Census, Thirteenth Census of the United States, Volume III, *Population 1910*, Nebraska: 25, shows the Elmwood village population as 635, but the MS census, T624_840, shows fifty Greek railroad workers, who were probably transients.
2. Petersen, *Aldrich*, 12, 63–65; Aldrich, "Why I Live in a Small Town," in Petersen (ed.), *Collected Short Works 1920–1954*, 221 (quotes). For her mother's influence, see Aldrich, "Nebraska History in Novels" [typed MS, half sheets], 7, Box 10, Bess Streeter Aldrich Papers, MS3263, Nebraska State Historical Society, Lincoln (hereafter cited as Aldrich Papers, NSHS).
3. Petersen, *Aldrich*, XVII; Meier, "Aldrich," 55–58; Annie Russell Marble, "A Daughter of Pioneers: Bess Streeter Aldrich and Her Works" [New York: D. Appleton and Company], *Boston Transcript* reprint, 9, copy in Bess Streeter Aldrich info file, *Omaha World-Herald* morgue, Douglas County Historical Society, Omaha (hereafter cited as *WH* morgue, DCHS); "VPH" [Victor P. Hass], "Bess Streeter Aldrich," *Sunday World-Herald Magazine*, Aug. 15, 1954, p. 28 (hereafter cited as *SWHM* + date).
4. James R. Shortridge, "The Emergence of 'Middle West' as an American Regional Label," *Annals of the Association of American Geographers* 74 (June 1984): 211–13.
5. Aldrich, *A White Bird Flying* (Lincoln: University of Nebraska Press, Bison reprint, 1988), 113.
6. Aldrich, *Mother Mason* (Lincoln: University of Nebraska Press, Bison reprint, 1987), 45, 69–70.
7. For an outstanding interpretation of the Cornhusker State, see Frederick C. Luebke, "Time, Place, and Culture in Nebraska History," in James H. Madison (ed.), *Heartland: Comparative Histories of the Midwestern States* (Bloomington: Indiana University Press, 1988), 226–45, reprinted in *Nebraska History* 69 (Winter 1988): 150–68.

8. Aldrich, *The Rim of the Prairie* (Lincoln: University of Nebraska Press, Bison reprint, 1966), preface (quote), 59–60, 76–78, 84–88, 213 (second quote), 219, 243, 351–52. See 251–52, illustrating a supercilious urban commentary on small-town life.
9. Petersen, *Aldrich*, 71, 227; Aldrich, *The Cutters*, 179–81, 183–84. See also Aldrich, *White Bird*, 88–90.
10. Sinclair Lewis, *Main Street* (New York: Harcourt, Brace & World, 1920, copyright 1948), preface; Carl Van Doren, in *New York Evening Post*, Nov. 20, 1920, cited in *Book Review Digest: Reviews of 1920 Books* (New York: The H.W. Wilson Company, 1921), 324.
11. Jon K. Lauck, "The Myth of the Midwestern 'Revolt from the Village,'" *Mid-America* XL: 39–42; 54–63.
12. Petersen, *Aldrich*, 68. A review of *The Cutters*, *The Saturday Review of Literature*, Sept. 4, 1926, 91, is an exercise in nastiness.
13. Aldrich, "Tillie Cuts Loose," *American Magazine* (April 1920): 50–52; 272, 274, 276, 279); reissued with modified introduction in Aldrich, *Mother Mason* (Lincoln: University of Nebraska Press, Bison reprint, 1987), 74–97.
14. Aldrich, *Mother Mason*, 8–16, 47, 120, 145, 148, 228, 247–50. On Elmwood's rail service, see *EL-E*, Nov. 16, 1906, May 9, 1935. The *Nebraska State Journal* was a forerunner of today's *Lincoln Star-Journal*.
15. Aldrich, *Spring*, 258.
16. Ibid., 202–203, 218–20; Aldrich, *White Bird*, 128–29; Aldrich, "The Day of Retaliation," in Petersen (ed.), *Collected Short Works 1920–1954*, 194–95 (quote); Harl A. Dalstrom, "*Garlic and Old Horse-Blankets*: Medical Services and Omaha's Trade Area in the Early Twentieth Century," paper presented at Northern Great Plains History Conference, Fargo, ND, Sept. 29, 2012.
17. Aldrich, *A Lantern in Her Hand* (New York: Signet-Vista, 1983), 51–61, relates the Deal family's move to Nebraska. On the Deal children, see 118–19, 158–59, 163–65, 167, 171, 182, 187, 193–94, 203–204.
18. Aldrich, *Mother Mason*, 121 (quote), 126.
19. Aldrich, *Lantern*, 157, 179–80, 222–24, 232; James C. Olson, *History of Nebraska*, second edition (Lincoln: University of Nebraska Press, 1966), 198, 251–52.
20. *EL-E*, May 22, 1925. For her belief that authors should stick to topics with which they are familiar, see *White Bird*, 63.
21. Aldrich, *Mother Mason*, 2, 22 (quotes); Aldrich, *Rim*, 155. See also Aldrich, "The Drum Goes Dead," in *Journey into Christmas and Other Stories* (Lincoln: University of Nebraska Press, Bison Book reprint, 1985), 56, on the role of the cashier in a small-town bank.
22. Aldrich, *Rim*, 292–93; *EL-E*, Feb. 27, 1925 (advertisement, American Exchange Bank). A bleak view of March 1 is found in Deborah Fink, *Agrarian Women: Wives and Mothers in Rural Nebraska, 1880–1940* (Chapel Hill: University of North Carolina Press, 1992), 53.

23. Aldrich, *Lantern*, 194.
24. Aldrich, *Rim*, 60; Louise Gilmore Donahue, *Pathways to Prosperity: A History of the Greater Omaha Chamber of Commerce* (Omaha: Greater Omaha Chamber of Commerce, 1993), 10.
25. Aldrich, *Spring*, 261–63; Aldrich, *Miss Bishop*, 302–304.
26. Aldrich, *White Bird*, 56–57; Memo by Landale, Dec. 8, 1950, Aldrich info file, WH morgue, DCHS; Petersen, *Aldrich*, 118–20. For the state banking crisis, see Earl C. Hald, "State Bank Failures in Nebraska Since 1920" (Lincoln: University of Nebraska, M.A. thesis, 1932), and Dalstrom, "Kenneth S. Wherry" (Lincoln: University of Nebraska, PhD dissertation, 1965), Vol. I, 23–43.
27. For example, see Herbert S. Schell, *History of South Dakota* (Lincoln: University of Nebraska Press, 1961), 265, 277–78.
28. Aldrich, *The Cutters*, 206–208.
29. Aldrich, "The Drum Goes Dead," in *Journey into Christmas*, 46–74; Dalstrom, "Fiction and Fact: Bess Streeter Aldrich's *The Drum Goes Dead* and the Hard Times of the 1930s," *Great Plains Quarterly* 34 (Fall 2014): 293–315. A prototype of "The Drum Goes Dead" is Aldrich's "The Cashier—and Christmas," *McClintock's Magazine* 2 (Dec. 1922): 3–4, set amidst the hard times following World War I, Box 14, Aldrich Papers, NSHS. See Petersen (ed.), *Collected Short Works 1920–1954*, XIII, for comments on Aldrich's articles in *McClintock's Magazine* (Minneapolis), a banking equipment firm publication.
30. Aldrich, "I Remember," in *Journey into Christmas*, 234, 244; Aldrich, *White Bird*, 34 (quote).
31. Bureau of the Census, Volume III, *Population 1910*, Nebraska: 52. See "Old Poke," *EL-E*, Sept. 28, 1900.
32. Aldrich, *Spring*, 1, 71, 75–76, 175, 178, 187–88 (including quote), 198. See especially Carol K. Coburn, "Ethnicity, Religion, and Gender: The Women of Block, Kansas, 1868–1940," *Great Plains Quarterly* 8 (Fall 1988), 232, note 36. Two works essential to an understanding of this topic are Luebke, *Immigrants and Politics: The Germans of Nebraska, 1880–1900* (Lincoln: University of Nebraska Press, 1969), and Jon Gjerde, *The Minds of the West: Ethnocultural Evolution in the Rural Middle West, 1830–1917* (Chapel Hill: University of North Carolina Press, 1997).
33. Aldrich, *Miss Bishop* (Lincoln: University of Nebraska Press, Bison reprint, 1986), 256–58; Aldrich, *Spring*, 214–16; Recollections of Rosemary John, in Cindy Steinhoff Drake (comp.), *Elmwood: The Life of a Community, 1886–1986* (Elmwood Centennial Committee, 1986), 79.
34. Aldrich, *Spring*, 217. See also Willa Cather, "Nebraska: The End of the First Cycle," *The Nation*, 117 (Sept. 5, 1923): 238.
35. Aldrich, *Spring*, 203–204, 208, 210, 228–32, 237–41, 263–68.

36. Aldrich, *Lantern*, 168–69, 180; Aldrich, *White Bird*, 122–32. For a provocative treatment of Aldrich's character, Abbie Deal, see Fink, *Agrarian Women*, 182–85.
37. Aldrich, *Rim*, 169–72, 202, 262–63, 266–69, 315–16, 330–35; Aldrich, *White Bird*, 80, 87, 108–12, 174–78, 187–89, 197; Aldrich, *Spring*, 259–60, 269, 274–81.
38. Aldrich, *Rim*, 320–22, 329–35, 340; see Donald J. Gonzales (ed.), *Elmwood: A Village Portrait: Commemoration of Nebraska's Centennial, 1867–1967* (Elmwood: Elmwood Centennial Committee, 1967), 12; Drake (comp.), *Elmwood*, 76. For the real tornado, see *EL-E*, Apr. 11, 1919.
39. Aldrich, *White Bird*, 200–205; Aldrich, *Spring*, 282–97; 300–310, 319; *EL-E*, June 13, 1935. See also "The Family Takes a Vacation," in Aldrich, *The Cutters*, 82–106. On Aldrich and storms, see Hass, "Aldrich," *SWHM*, Aug. 15, 1954, p. 28; Abigail Ann Martin, *Bess Streeter Aldrich* (Boise: Boise State University Western Writers Series Number 104, 1992), 29; Foreman, "Fiction of Aldrich," 172–76.
40. Aldrich, *Rim*, 216–17, 222, 274–78, 283–87; Petersen, *Aldrich*, 12.
41. Aldrich, *The Cutters*, 184–85.
42. Aldrich, *Rim*, 114–17, 160, 176–80, 222, 228, 283, 342–44, 348–49. Mrs. Aldrich's story, "Star Across the Tracks," in *Journey into Christmas*, 18–45, illustrates social and economic disparities in "River City."
43. Aldrich, *The Cutters*, 82–83; Aldrich, *Mother Mason*, 171–202. See also Petersen, *Aldrich*, 41–43.
44. Aldrich, *Rim*, 9–16, 152–53, 182, 209–211, 214, 222–23, 350; Petersen, *Aldrich*, 17.
45. Aldrich, *Rim*, 219.
46. Ibid., 52, 150, 207.
47. Ibid., 21. See Gonzales (ed.), *Elmwood*, 78.
48. Aldrich, *Rim*, 121, 283, 338; Aldrich, *Mother Mason*, 118, 174; Aldrich, *The Cutters*, 83.
49. Aldrich, in Petersen (ed.), *Collected Short Works 1920–1954*, 35 (quote); 1920 U.S. Census, Cass County, Nebraska, T625_1982; Aldrich, *Miss Bishop*, 229, 283–84. See Fink, *Agrarian Women*, 118–19, 178–80.
50. On life in the Aldrich family, see comments of Mary Aldrich Beechner, Robert and Charles Aldrich, in Harold Cowan, "A Kind and Gentle Writer," *SWHM*, July 8, 1973, p. 6.
51. Aldrich, "Why I Live in a Small Town," in Petersen (ed.), *Collected Short Works 1920–1954*, 221.
52. Martin, *Aldrich*, 28, 33, 39, 41.
53. Aldrich, *White Bird*, 60–63.
54. Margaret H. Doorly, *SWHM*, Apr. 5, 1925, p. 7.
55. Petersen, *Aldrich*, 112, 179–82, 194.
56. Hass, "Leaves from a Bookman's Notebook," *SWHM*, Apr. 18, 1971, p. 30.

Cherie Dargan | The Realistic Regionalism of Iowa's Ruth Suckow

Ruth Suckow (1892–1960) was an itinerant writer and realistic regionalist whose description of the people, small towns, and farms of Iowa was based on her keen observation of life in the early 1900s. Suckow's portrayal of the lives of ordinary "folks" enables modern readers to empathize with her characters, many of whom were Midwesterners. Her poetic descriptions of the Iowa farmland evoke the artistic realism of Grant Wood paintings and place her squarely in the midwestern regionalist milieu of the interwar years. Suckow was recognized during her lifetime as a gifted writer and she was widely anthologized from the 1920s through the 1950s.[1] Suckow's nearly fifty short stories include "Midwestern Primitive," "A Rural Community," and "A Start in Life." The latter focused on a young teen's first day as a hired girl and became Suckow's most widely-anthologized story. Her nine novels include *Country People* (1924) and the best-selling *The Folks* (1934). Suckow's prose was so descriptive that Allan Nevins called her "a painter of Iowa" in his review of *The Bonney Family* (1928) and he called her short stories "among the most authentic and veracious of all records of middle western life."[2] Even *Smart Set* editor H.L. Mencken said Suckow was "unquestionably the most remarkable woman ... writing stories in the republic."[3]

Suckow biographer Leedice Kissane observed that although Ruth Suckow was correctly classified as a literary realist and a regionalist, "she was something more. That 'something more' has never been adequately assessed."[4] That "something more," I argue, includes Suckow's remarkable story-telling abilities, her realistic portrayal of characters—especially women—and her contribution to the regionalism debate. These are the qualities that make Suckow an outstanding midwestern writer and a key figure in the early twentieth-century Midwestern Moment in American literary history and a voice that deserves to be heard again.

Suckow grew up in Iowa but also lived in New York, New Mexico, Colorado, and California, so she offers a particularly "mobile" view of midwestern regionalism.[5] The daughter of a Congregational minister, Suckow and her family lived in eight Iowa towns as her father moved from one church to the next, and this pattern of moving around continued throughout her life. Suckow attended college in Grinnell before enrolling in the Curry School of Expression in Boston in 1916. She then went to the University of Denver, earning both her bachelor's and master's degrees. She worked as a waitress in Yellowstone Park, and drew on all of these experiences to create her characters, such as Marjorie, the heroine of *Odyssey of a Nice Girl* (1925), who studies at a School of Expression in Boston. *New Hope* (1942) is set in Suckow's birthplace of Hawarden, Iowa, while other stories unfold in a small college town like Grinnell, Iowa. Despite these literary allusions to her own life, Suckow resisted the idea that her fiction was merely autobiographical, although her many links to the Midwest, and Iowa especially, shine through.[6]

Suckow's stories focused on daily life in midwestern towns and farming communities, or on Midwesterners traveling elsewhere. Her extended German-American family also provided her with material, as Clarence Andrews has noted.[7] While Suckow never lived on a farm, she frequently visited her grandparents' farm in Hancock County, Iowa.[8] She also had opportunities to closely observe the Iowa countryside and rural and small-town people when Rev. Suckow took her along on visits to his parishioners (her father became an important influence because her mother was ill during much of her childhood). As a result, her writing, especially *New Hope*, is filled with a love for the land, as well as specific details about the daily lives of the people living there.[9]

Suckow's connections to the Iowa countryside were also deepened by her apiary interests. While attending the university in Denver, Suckow studied bee-keeping as a way to support herself as a writer once she returned to Iowa. She joined her father, who was now pastoring in Earlville, and from 1920 to 1926 she divided each year between keeping bees in Earlville and writing stories in New York City. She kept eighty hives, selling her honey to farmers' markets in Dubuque, and "was known ever afterward as the beekeeping author."[10] This added to her reputation as a practical midwestern writer.

Suckow's pursuit of a literary career was also aided by her marriage to Ferner Nuhn. In 1929, at age thirty-seven, Suckow married Nuhn after a brief correspondence and courtship. A fellow Iowan, he was an artist, writer, and critic, and eleven years younger. They were together for over thirty years and shared a passion for writing, travel, and cats.[11] An observer described them: "Nuhn found an artist who could translate the Midwest, and in Nuhn, Suckow found a critic who could understand the translation."[12] Above all, they supported each other's work. After getting married in California, they spent time in several writers' colonies, including Yaddo in New York. They lived in New Mexico and Washington, DC, and passed a summer with Robert Frost in his Vermont home. They always returned to Iowa, however, where they twice lived in Cedar Falls until health problems forced them to move to Arizona and then California. Suckow died there in 1960: she was still writing, and left behind an unfinished novel.

Suckow's literary legacy remains an impressive corpus of work deeply influenced by the Midwest and steeped in the traditions of realism and regionalism. Suckow is often called a realist because of her focus on portraying characters as real people, living the ordinary lives of common folks. Her vivid descriptions of the countryside made readers visualize Grant Wood's paintings of Iowa farm fields. The *Christian Science Monitor* compared Wood's 1936 painting *Spring Turning* to Suckow's first novel, *Country People* (1924): "The farmer with his team of horses which accent the foreground of the painting might have been her fictional Iowa farmer, August Kaetterhenry, out early on a spring morning to plow his lush field."[13] The writer and painter shared "an eye for the minutiae of everyday life as well as a deep love for the beauty of the Iowa farm land."[14]

American literary realism gained traction in the 1860s and became associated with Mark Twain, Kate Chopin, and Henry James. Of that group, both Twain and Chopin were born in the Midwest. Literary realism became linked with regional writing because authors captured their "local color" in setting and dialogue. Other components included a focus on the middle class, characters making complicated ethical choices, describing events that seemed possible, using the local slang and language, objectivity, and writing in a detailed, realistic way, according to Evan Luzi.[15] Suckow's writing embodies all of those elements in her portrayal of her characters, especially women. Frank Mott, who helped edit the Iowa-based literary journal *The Midland*, said Suckow was "advantageously placed" to observe the realities of life in a small midwestern town, given her proximity to the parsonage.[16]

Ruth Suckow. Publicity photo (1931).

Suckow consistently "shunned the critics' term of regionalist as a misinterpretation of her intent" because she valued the common and universal.[17] She was reluctant to be labeled a regionalist, even though her writing fits the category. She was not merely a regionalist, however. As Kissane pointed out, Suckow's books "are not period pieces or local-color oddities. Though they reflect their region and their era, they have universality" and thus great merit.[18] Suckow explained her perspective about regionalism in her Introduction to the book *The Carry-Over*: "The writer has always believed that the matter of locality has been overemphasized in estimations of her fiction, and re-reading, she is happy to say, has confirmed that belief."[19] Indeed, her fiction explored themes including farm couples retiring and moving into town, sacrificial daughters caring for aging parents, women striving for independence, and small-town pastors struggling to lead their congregations. Although many of her stories are set in the Midwest, they explore universal conflicts.

Suckow explained her distinctive realistic regionalism in several essays. In the essay "The Folk Idea in American Life" (1930), she argued that to capture the life of the "folks" was to grasp the authentic American life. American identity rests on the principle of folk life, she insisted, and the folk spirit is the common element that could unite the nation: "If our artists do not include themselves ... they are giving away their own heritage to the philistines."[20] In her 1926 essay "Iowa," she addressed her region more directly. She insisted that Iowa was forming its own culture, one "innocently ingenuous, fresh and sincere, unpretentious ... strengthened by the simplicity and severity of its hard working farmer people." These people, she wrote, are "the folk element and the very soil and bedrock." If Iowa had a culture, it would be founded on that bedrock, where the state's varying nationalities met.[21]

While Suckow was reluctant to be labeled a "regional" writer, she recognized a midwestern canon, starting with Mark Twain's *Huckleberry Finn*, which "comes first, both as literature and sociology. It is the epic— delicate, sly, meandering, and grand—of the Mississippi, the great central life-stream of this region."[22] Other selections included: Willa Cather's *My Ántonia*, Sinclair Lewis's *Main Street*, Hamlin Garland's *Main-traveled Roads*, Theodore Dreiser's *Sister Carrie*, Harriet Connor Brown's *Grandmother Brown's Hundred Years*, Glenway Wescott's *The Grandmothers*, and Sherwood Anderson's *Winesburg, Ohio*. To that list she added the poetry of Vachel Lindsay and Carl Sandburg and Edgar Lee Masters's *The Spoon River Anthology*.[23] Still, while Suckow embraced her midwestern roots and a midwestern literary canon, she did not want to be pigeonholed as "only" a midwestern writer.

## Midwestern Literature and Regionalism

Suckow's concerns about regionalism limiting her audience were part of a growing debate in the first decades of the 1900s. During that era, John Albert Macy, author of *The Spirit of American Literature* (1913), argued that no one had explained what was uniquely American about American literature.[24] Macy called on novelists, in particular, to write about their regions: "the whole country is crying out for those who will record it, satirize it, chant it. As literary material, it is virgin land, ancient as life and fresh as a wilderness."[25] John T. Frederick, Suckow's first editor, read Macy's book and went on to found *The Midland*, which H.L. Mencken called the most influential literary periodical ever set up in America. *The Midland* ran from 1915 until 1933. For eighteen years Frederick published poetry, short stories, reviews, and essays written by midwestern writers like Ruth Suckow, James Hearst, Paul Engle, and others.[26] A book profiling the magazine, *The Midland: A Venture in Literary Regionalism*, explained Frederick's guiding philosophy for the literary magazine: "it's better here, at home."[27] Frederick believed that there was dignity in rural and small-town life, wisdom in the older generation, and a "Thoreauvian rapture" to be discovered in the region's outdoors.[28] Decades after the last issue rolled off the presses, Frederick "read one of those *Midland* stories by Ruth Suckow to an Iowa University class of eighty graduate students. When he finished, they applauded."[29]

Frederick became Suckow's mentor when he published one of her early poems in 1918, three stories in 1921, and another story in 1922. He saw a "vital sense of place" in her writing."[30] Suckow also served as his editorial assistant during the winter of 1921–1922.[31] Frederick described Suckow as "not hostile towards the Middle West, not a resentful critic. Miss Suckow loves the Middle West."[32] Of Suckow's female characters, he wrote: "Suckow's women are not magazine cover heroines. They are human beings of terrible veracity."[33] In the early 1920s, Frederick introduced Suckow to H.L. Mencken, editor of *The Smart Set* and *The American Mercury*, who went on to publish twenty-one of her short stories.[34] Mencken became an important mentor to Suckow: she called him "Uncle Henry" and said that he taught her to read things out loud because "you don't know what you've written until you've heard it ... it's like reading lyrics without music."[35]

### From Iowa Girl to Recognized National Writer

While *The Midland* was a regional publication, both of the magazines that Mencken edited were published in New York, moving Suckow into the national spotlight. Suckow's work was soon appearing in *Good Housekeeping, Scribner's, Harper's Magazine,* and *The Century*. Her novel *The Folks* (1934) was a Literary Guild selection for October 1934. In addition, five of her novels and one volume of short stories were published outside of the United States, another indication of her success.[36]

Many critics praised Suckow during her lifetime. In the 1930s, George Jean Nathan felt that Suckow was "the most important short story writer that America has produced in the last decade."[37] Carl van Doren said Suckow "came nearer than any other writer has done to representing the whole of American life on farms and in small towns."[38] Kissane compared Suckow to Sarah Orne Jewett in Maine and Eudora

Ruth Suckow on farm.

Welty in Mississippi: "Readers ... come to know Iowa as she knows it—the feel of its atmosphere, the lay of the landscape, and the intellectual climate and prevailing spirit of its people."[39]

Most critics agree that Suckow's best work was done with her short stories because they allowed her to focus on a single situation, character, and mood.[40] An example of a Suckow story that did well was "Just Him and Her," which appeared in the anthology *Contemporary Trends: American Literature Since 1914* (1933), under the section entitled "The Renewed Interest in Regional Life," along with selections by Willa Cather and Eugene O'Neill, signaling Suckow's place as a regional writer of significance.[41]

In all, sixteen of Suckow's short stories appeared in fifty anthologies from 1924 through 1954, but few appeared after that, in keeping with the broader diminishment of regionalist energies after World War II.[42] Most of Suckow's books were out of print by the 1960s until *Country People* and *Iowa Interiors* were reprinted in 1977. Then *A Ruth Suckow Omnibus* was published in 1988, followed by a new edition of *The Folks* in 1992, giving a new generation of readers the opportunity to discover Suckow. A resurgence of interest in Suckow's work occurred during the 1970s through the 1990s, with the reprinting of four books and several critical biographies. Scholars began looking at Suckow differently: one article called her "Iowa's First Feminist Author."[43]

## Suckow's Short Stories and Regionalism

Three short stories in particular showcase Suckow's regional realism. The first story, "Midwestern Primitive" (1928), explores the concept of what is "primitive" in midwestern culture. As it opens, a woman named Bert has prepared a meal and set the table, using ideas from her women's magazines. She wants to establish her home as the Hillside Inn: Bert is expecting her first paid guests and wants to please them. Her visitors are coming from quite a distance; she wants to make a good impression and worries about her mother, who is out digging in the garden. The guests arrive and Bert apologizes for not having an indoor bathroom but says they can freshen up in a bedroom with a wash bowl. Finally, they sit down and she serves them, trying to remember all of the little tips from her national magazines. Bert overhears little snatches of conversation and worries that her dinner is going too quickly.

Her mother comes in, wearing her old dress, and offers the guests dandelion wine and a tour of her garden. The group goes out and praises her flowers: one man says it is like going back thirty years. The old woman picks flowers for her guests, they drink from the old pump, and then the guests go back inside and look at old photo albums and listen to her mother's stories. While Bert is cleaning up in the kitchen, she feels frustrated. But they praise her meal, pay her more than she asked, sign her guest book, and leave—after getting more flowers from her mother. As they drive away, Bert doesn't understand why the guests seemed to like her mother so much more than her: "she didn't yet see what their idea was."[44]

Bert planned her table setting and menu based on the standards presented in the magazine articles; however, this group wanted a "real" meal, or authentic country cooking. This is why they were so pleased with her mother's dandelion wine: it was memorable because it was something she made and valued. They enjoyed the garden tour and looking at the photos with Bert's mother because she was just being herself—genuine and fresh. Suckow shows us the contrast of the mother and her daughter: both want to make their guests feel welcome, but they reveal their different values. Like many, Bert doesn't value the genuine culture of her small midwestern town, while Suckow uses Bert's mother to examine the word "primitive."

A second story, "Auntie Bissel," appeared in 1935. An unnamed narrator tells us about her trip to California, where she looks up Auntie

Bissel. Auntie Bissel had been married to the station agent at the railroad depot back in Woodside, Iowa. Everyone called him Uncle Harvey. The couple lost a child named Gracie, so their small town became their family. Children came to their home because Auntie Bissel baked biscuits and cakes, curled their hair, tied sashes on them, and called them her girlies; Uncle Harvey always had candy. However, Uncle Harvey died years ago and Auntie Bissel moved to California and the narrator had not seen her since.[45]

A woman, Alice, answers the door and welcomes her into a lovely Spanish-style home. Auntie Bissell comes in and surprises the narrator with her bobbed hair and makeup, and they chat. They smell a cake and go to the kitchen. Auntie Bissell baked it for the birthday of a neighbor girl, an aspiring child actress. Auntie Bissell explains that she came to California to help her brother, who later remarried. She then met an older man, whose wife had died, and she cared for him; when he died, he provided for her in his will. Later, she met Alice, who had cared for her mother until her death: Alice moved in and became a surrogate daughter to Auntie Bissell—perhaps her lost Gracie.

The children arrive to claim the cake and Auntie Bissell shows them off, but Suckow's narrator responds to the overly commercialized California culture. She sees the birthday girl "as the most obnoxious infant on the earth" while recognizing that "all was glowing in the happy light of Auntie Bissel's pure naiveté."[46] The narrator recognizes that Alice and Auntie Bissel, in "coming to the land of eternal sunshine, both had reached the last stand of their tribe and race. They had come into its final flowering, whether real or unreal none could say."[47] Again, Suckow asks us to decide what is real and unreal and what might become of the old Midwest that she knew so well.

They take the narrator to visit a mausoleum, making the narrator feel that they were entering the happy ending of the great American fairy tale.[48] The mausoleum was the ultimate sanctuary, "wrought in marble and gold." Auntie Bissel talks about having Gracie and Uncle Harvey transferred to this resting place, which makes the narrator think of the contrast between the simple cemetery back in Iowa and this place—where Auntie Bissel and Alice wish to be buried.

Afterward, they go back to Auntie Bissel's house for lunch. The narrator lingers in the garden to admire the city lights and the ocean, and senses the mix of brand new and prehistoric old. She hears the women talking: Auntie Bissel's voice seems more authentic than Alice's, more naïve too, and fabulous. Auntie Bissell has arrived at her promised land and is living in her own happy ending. Even so, the narrator senses a threat of violence in the hills from possible fire and flood. The story ends with the narrator's epiphany that she, too, could have her dream. However, "when destruction came to this glittering mirage-land, when some Samson shook the pillars on some final day, she would have 'passed on' and her contented ashes be resting in a marble post office shrine inscribed in indestructible bronze ... 'Auntie Bissel.'"[49]

Many people see California as a promised land: a place of sunshine, beaches, the movies, and a place to reinvent yourself, as Auntie Bissel has done, though only in part. However, the narrator thinks the state offers a happy ending at the price of a lost midwestern culture. The reference to Samson shaking the pillars is from the Old Testament and may be a metaphor for judgment day. The marble post office box refers to the gaudy mausoleum where Auntie Bissel wants her ashes to be placed. Although Auntie Bissel worked hard all of her life and deserves her happiness, the narrator finds it ironic that she has so readily adopted California styles, while maintaining her old midwestern caring ways. Indeed, Suckow suggests that Auntie Bissel has retained her midwestern values and seems more authentic than Alice. Thus, her story probes the complexities of transplanted midwestern culture. Although Suckow ended her days in California, she did not believe in fairy tale happy endings, and her fiction is marked by more realistic and, at times, even ambiguous, ironic, and challenging endings. As Kissane points out, Suckow was a very honest writer.[50]

A final story, "A Rural Community," has long been a reader favorite. As the story begins, Ralph arrives on the morning train to Walnut, Iowa, and asks for directions to Luke Hockaday's house. He has been away for fifteen years, and in his absence, his adopted parents moved to town, retiring from the farm where he was raised. Ralph walks through town and sees things have changed in the old town. "Changes—even here!—you couldn't escape them." Later, however, he realizes the streets had scarcely changed at all. It was almost the same![51]

Ralph is a journalist and has flown all over the civilized world, where "change was the only thing he saw."[52] He approaches his parents' house on the outskirts of town, and sees his father; Ralph greets the old man and his father recognizes him and calls to his mother from inside the house. They go into the house to visit and Ralph thinks they should still be living in the little farmhouse. Ralph had been an orphan when he came to live with them—they were the only parents he has known. He left the farm at sixteen to go to college and then he went into newspaper work. He came back just once, for a wedding for Jack, one of his brothers. However, he always sent a letter on Christmas Day with a check to his adopted parents.

Ralph is now a successful man who travels a lot and thinks of himself as not needing a home, but he had an urge to see the old couple before he went off on his next assignment. His mother goes to make lunch and he offers to help but she turns him down. So he looks at the family photo album—full of several generations of pictures of couples and babies, and his mother's treasures.

They say a blessing and eat lunch: fried chicken, mashed potatoes, and lots of relishes and sides. He learns that all of the children and grandchildren come for lunch every Sunday. After the meal, Ralph calls his brother Jack, a farmer, on the telephone and they agree to visit that evening after milking. Ralph tries to explain to his mother why he cannot stay longer. He says, "I can't settle yet, mother … too many places to go. Too much to do."[53] However, his parents ask when he's going to settle down. His father mentions his old high school girlfriend and he is shocked, because he is seeing his life from a different point of view. His mother brings out a scrapbook with many of his articles, which surprises him. "Ain't you one of my boys? Sure you are." Ralph sits back, smiles, and doesn't trust himself to speak as he feels "a kind of resurrection of his boyhood self." "You was always a fine talker," she said fondly. "better'n any of the boys. He was, wasn't he, pa?"[54]

His father goes off to take a nap, while Ralph accompanies his mother to the nearby cemetery and watches her tend to the graves of friends and family. He jokes that "this wouldn't be such a bad place to sleep in, some day." She replied, "so ye can, my dear, but I hope it won't be for a long while yet. You're one of us, sure you are."[55]

They have supper and then his siblings arrive with their families. They sit down and begin to visit. Ralph sits back, listening to them talk, and feels a sense of satisfaction. It pleases him to think of how deeply rooted they are in the rich Iowa soil of their farms. By 9:30, the old couple is tired and his siblings become solemn and formal as they say goodbye; Ralph watches them leave. His train leaves at 11:30 and Ralph doesn't want his parents to go with him to the train depot, so his father shakes hands and says, "Ralph, the Lord keep ye." His mother has tears in her eyes: "Have a good safe journey." He walks to the train station: the agent is the only one there. Ralph gets his ticket and waits. He gets onboard and settles down, but:

> he was aware that since he had stepped off the train in the morning, the current of his thoughts had changed. He felt steadied, deeply satisfied. He looked toward the dark pastures beyond the row of dusky willow trees. They widened slowly into the open country which lay silent, significant, motionless, immense, under the stars, with its sense of something abiding.[56]

    This story showcases the elements that mark Suckow's fiction as both regional and universal: the detailed description of the small town and surrounding farm fields evokes the country scenes in Grant Wood's paintings; the depiction of Ralph's mother caring for family and friends' tombstones connects with many Midwesterners as a familiar ritual; dialogue with his extended family reflects the time period and farm community; and the description of the food at the meal he shares with his parents makes one's mouth water with a familiar menu. Suckow uses the arrival and departure of a train to frame the story, and allows her readers insight into Ralph's state of mind. The reflective, quiet story conveys deep emotion. Ralph, also an itinerant writer, reconnects with his family, and the small town, and leaves feeling more connected to both: his mother tells him that he's one of their children several times, and finally, it connects with him and seems real.

    In spite of the fact that "A Rural Community" was written in 1922, my community college literature students were able to relate to Suckow's characters and setting and the theme of returning home, finding it both changed and changeless. They feel there is something magical in the story's concluding paragraph. I've read it to my students numerous times, at a presentation to librarians at the Iowa Library Association, and on Iowa Public Radio, with similar responses. As I read it out loud,

I'm filled with wonder at the power of language to convey emotion, and my listeners seem to relate with Ralph's experience and feel some of the same deep emotions—something "significant" and "abiding" as they reflect on their midwestern legacy. Suckow retains her regionalist powers even after nearly a century since her work was first published.

The short story "A Rural Community" alone justifies Ruth Suckow's designation as a prominent writer in midwestern literary canon. Like Ralph, Suckow traveled the world as an itinerant writer—yet she came home to Iowa and her midwestern roots. In fresh scenes and language, Suckow captured what is both sustaining and abiding in midwestern life as well as the challenges that confront life in the region. Because of stories such as "A Rural Community" Suckow should be considered a combination of a regional writer, a realist, and a Midwesterner. She also transcended those labels, however, and found many new readers after her death, as scholars of the 1980s proclaimed her Iowa's first feminist writer. She was recognized by her peers, critics, and editors alike for her realistic storytelling skills and her ability to capture the realities of life for people who lived on the Iowa farms and in the small towns of the early 1900s. Her work is worthy of being remembered and preserved for future generations of readers, especially those who want to understand an era of midwestern regionalist enthusiasm that has long faded from memory.

## Notes

1. Margaret Stewart Omrcanin, Appendix II: "A Chronology of Writings of Ruth Suckow: 4. Anthologized Stories," in *Ruth Suckow: A Critical Study of Her Fiction* (Philadelphia, Pennsylvania: Dorrance & Company, 1972), 208–11.
2. Allan Nevins, "A Painter of Iowa: Review of the Bonney Family," *The Saturday Review of Literature*, March 10, 1928, accessed February 14, 2016, https://www.unz.org/Pub/SaturdayRev-1928mar10-00666.
3. Tom Longden, "Famous Iowans. Ruth Suckow: Writer, 1892–1960, Hawarden," *Des Moines Register*, April 5, 1992, accessed February 6, 2016, http://data.desmoinesregister.com/famous-iowans/ruth-suckow.
4. Leedice McAnelly Kissane, preface to *Ruth Suckow, Twayne's United States Authors Series* (New York: Twayne, 1969).
5. Kissane, 11–12.
6. Rebecca Christian, "Just Suppose: The Story of Iowa Novelist Ruth Suckow, A One-Woman Show in Two Acts," Commissioned by the Ruth

Suckow Memorial Association for the Centennial of Ruth Suckow's birth (1992), 15.
7. Clarence Andrews, "Ruth Suckow: Introduction," in *A Ruth Suckow Omnibus* (Iowa City, Iowa: University of Iowa Press, 1988), ix.
8. Rebecca Christian, "She Wrote of Iowa—and Life," *The Iowan,* September 30, 1992, 61.
9. Patricia Ellen Martin Daly, "Foreword" to *New Hope,* A Bur Oak Book (Iowa City, Iowa: University of Iowa Press, 1998), xv.
10. Christian, "She Wrote of Iowa and Life," 60.
11. Daly, "Foreword," xvi.
12. Christian, "She Wrote of Iowa and Life," 61.
13. "Evolving a Beauty Born of the Earth." *Christian Science Monitor,* June 18, 1981, accessed February 10, 2016, http://www.csmonitor.com/1981/0618/061813.html.
14. Ibid.
15. Evan Luzi, "On American Realism and Mark Twain's 'The Man Who Corrupted Hadleyberg,'" The Blackandblue.com, March 17, 2008, accessed February 8, 2016, http://www.theblackandblue.com/2008/03/17/on-american-realism-and-mark-twains-the-man-who-corrupted-hadleyberg/.
16. Andrews, Introduction to *Omnibus,* ix.
17. Omrcanin, Preface.
18. Kissane, 2.
19. Ruth Suckow, "Comments and Addenda," *The Carry-Over* (Farrar & Rinehart, 1924), vii.
20. Ruth Suckow, "The Folk Idea in American Life," *Scribner's,* September 1930, 245–55.
21. Ruth Suckow, "Iowa," *The American Mercury* , September 1926, 39–45.
22. Ruth Suckow, "Middle Western Literature," *The English Journal* XXI, no. 3 (March 1932), 176.
23. Ibid.
24. John Albert Macy, *The Spirit of American Literature,* (New York: Doubleday, Page & Company, 1913), 8.
25. Ibid., 16.
26. Clarence Andrews, "Chapter 7—Ruth Suckow: The poetry of place," in *A Literary History of Iowa* (Iowa City, Iowa: University of Iowa Press, 1972), 81–82.
27. Brooke Workman, "Review of *The Midland: A Venture in Literary Regionalism*" by Dr. Milton Reigelman, *The Annals of Iowa,* The State Historical Society of Iowa, 43, no. 6 (Fall 1976), 477.
28. Ibid.
29. Ibid., 478.
30. John T. Frederick. "Ruth Suckow and the Middle Western Literary Movement." *The English Journal* XX, no. 1 (January 1931), 1.
31. Omrcanin, 6.

32. Frederick, 5.
33. Ibid., 7.
34. Andrews, *A Literary History of Iowa*, 82.
35. Christian, *Just Suppose*, 8.
36. Omrcanin, 6.
37. Daly, xiii.
38. Omrcanin, 10.
39. Kissane, 15–16.
40. Omrcanin, 182–83.
41. John Herbert Nelson, ed., *Contemporary Trends: American Literature since 1914*. (The Macmillan Company, 1933). University of Texas for PDF of Table of Contents.
42. Omrcanin, 208–11.
43. Mary Jane Sweet, "Ruth Suckow: Iowa's First Feminist Author," *Cedar Falls Record*, June 15, 1982.
44. Ruth Suckow, "Midwestern Primitive," in *A Ruth Suckow Omnibus* (Iowa City, Iowa: University of Iowa Press, 1988), 270.
45. Ruth Suckow, "Auntie Bissel," *Scribner's*, August 1935, 84.
46. Ibid., 88.
47. Ibid., 90.
48. Ibid., 90.
49. Ibid., 92.
50. Kissane, 18.
51. Ruth Suckow, "A Rural Community," *The Midland*, July 1922, 1. PDF available at http://www.ruthsuckow.org/home/ruth-suckow-s-short-stories.
52. Ibid., 2.
53. Ibid., 10.
54. Ibid., 12–13.
55. Ibid., 15.
56. Ibid., 19–20.

Zachary Michael Jack | The Curious Case of Jay G. Sigmund

The Midwest's Most Rooted Regionalist?

> He guesses not, that as I plod along
> My heart's a seedbed for a crop of song!
> —Jay G. Sigmund, "A Plowman Sings"

To speculate on the curious case of writer Jay G. Sigmund, the Midwest's Most Rooted Regionalist, is to be reminded of this regrettable truth: History is often a merciless, unaccountable, and wholly unrepentant bastard. To wit: sadly few contemporary midwest literary scholars know Jay Sigmund's name; fewer still know that Ilya Tolstoy hailed the Bard of the Wapsipinicon River as "an American Chekhov and Maupassant," a man who published over 1200 poems, 125 short stories, and over 25 plays[1] all while mentoring Iowa regionalist writers and painters—Paul Engle, Marvin Cone, and Grant Wood among them—until their legacy far eclipsed his own. At the time of his passing in 1937, at the age of fifty-one, Sigmund had authored at least six volumes of poetry and four books of short fiction, an output made doubly impressive by the demands of his day job as an insurance executive in Cedar Rapids, Iowa.[2]

To my mind, the real mystery is not Sigmund's (like Shakespeare's) preternaturally late start (Sigmund didn't begin writing seriously until age thirty-six and died at fifty-one), nor his swift, dark-horse, come-from-behind ascent. Nor for me is the principal enigma his productivity—how a full-time insurance executive could be so prolific in so many genres. No, the most interesting, and most relevant, question for the modern-day neo-regionalist is this: How could a writer of Sigmund's talent and influence be so rudely, roundly forgotten?

The fashion in the past has been to tie Jay Sigmund to Grant Wood, the latter having sufficiently long coattails for a forgotten regionalist scribe to ride. The method invoked here is similar to the way we apologetic neo-regionalists, when meeting cosmopolitan scholars or strangers at an airport, locate ourselves in reference to the nearest big city in our universe—oh, I'm about an hour northeast of Iowa City, we might say, saving our interlocutor their geographic ignorance, or three hours east of Des Moines. Thus scholars of the recent past have located Sigmund in relation to, and proximity of, the far busier metropolis of Grant Wood.

In his small monograph written in partial fulfillment for a Masters in English in the graduate college of the University of Iowa in 1985, Edward Ferreter wrote a short thesis under the title "Grant Wood Meets Jay G. Sigmund: From Word to Image: From Image to Word." Ferreter's project is to illuminate and articulate the lesser-known Sigmund by attempting to point out the synergies, confluences, and shared sympathies of the two regionalist maestros. The budding scholar does an admirable job of synthesizing the well-established facts of that convergence: that the backyard and streets of Sigmund's home in Waubeek, where Wood would occasionally summer, were used as models for two of his paintings;[3] that Sigmund's car accident on the way to the Stone City Art Colony in the early 1930s served as the direct inspiration for Wood's brooding, vertigo-inducing canvas *Death on Ridge Road*. But the circumstantial similarities do not end there. Both men lived and worked in Cedar Rapids for much of their lives; both were born on eastern Iowa farms in the Wapsipinicon River watershed; both attended the Stone City Art Colony as experts in their crafts, bon vivants, luminaries, and masters of ceremonies. While Sigmund for a time belonged to the pungent salon Grant Wood presided over with much pomp in Cedar Rapids—the Garlic Club—it was Sigmund, Ferreter argues, who first insisted Grant Wood quit living the life of the expatriate poseur in Europe and return to capture the indigenous folkways of his midwestern homeland. Both Sigmund and Wood died too young, in their early fifties, completing the uncanny similarity between the two in the eyes of the few critics who have considered such things.

In doctrine and ideology Sigmund and Wood were so close as to be virtually indistinguishable. In fact, they discussed the idea of co-writing an *esprit de corps* in the 1930s; this aborted manifesto, no doubt, ultimately turned into Wood's only "book," a short credo entitled *Revolt Against the City*, believed by some to have been ghost-written by writer-publisher Frank Luther Mott. In it Wood devotes nearly a page to a discussion of Sigmund, Sigmund's home of Waubeek, and the "heirloom" people who inhabit that place.[4] "My friend and fellow-townsman Jay Sigmund," he writes, "devotes his leisure hours to the writing of verse celebrating the kind of human beings I have been discussing. He is as much at home in Waubeek—perhaps more so—as in the office of his insurance company."[5] Wood's discussion of Sigmund, while laudatory, suggests an uncertainty regarding in which camp he ought rightly to put his good friend, the hybrid insurance man-poet. Wood opines, "I have been interested to find in the little town of Waubeek, near my home, farmer-descendants of the folk of New England fishing villages. Waubeek has not changed or grown much since it was originally settled, because it was missed by the railroads and by the paved highways. The people of this community have kept as family heirlooms some of the old whaling harpoons, anchors, and so on which connect them with the struggle which their ancestors waged with the sea."[6]

Is Sigmund, a man who came from the land even if he was not then working it, likewise an example, in Wood's mind, of one of those picturesque heirloom residents of Waubeek ripe for artistic rendering and exploitation? Or is he one of the class, like Wood, charged with capturing, documenting, packaging, and preserving their local color for the rest of a thoroughly urbanizing Mississippi Valley region fast losing its agrarian roots? Perhaps Wood himself felt a certain ambivalence toward Sigmund, whose verse he highly valued and quoted at length, but who at times he presented as emblematic of the "farmer material" needing "interpretation" by the natural aristocracy of college-educated artists, writers, thinkers, and intellectuals to which Wood, despite occasional protests to the contrary, firmly belonged.

Sigmund, however, offers an altogether different model than Wood, and here is where the two-for-one treatment of Wood and Sigmund offered by some critics diverges. While Wood had moved to one of Iowa's largest and most diverse cities—Cedar Rapids—by the age of ten—well in time for his formative years, Sigmund remained in and around Waubeek until he was nineteen and ready to enter the workforce, a few years later, as a junior insurance agent eventually to work his way into a vice presidency at the Cedar Rapids Life Insurance Company. While Wood left the United States for Europe to apprentice and generally learn at the feet of the masters, Sigmund, Ferreter tells us, "never got beyond Chicago."[7] Of Sigmund's deep roots, Paul Engle wrote, "He saw nothing so evil in Iowa life that he had to run away from it to New York or Paris. He wanted not an ivory tower but the water tower of his own village."[8] Yet both Engle and Wood went on to teach at the University of Iowa and hold advanced degrees (Engle was a Rhodes scholar), earned or honorary, while Sigmund carried on in the tradition of the self-styled auto-didact then generally dying out in American arts and letters.

Why then is Sigmund not better remembered in the company of iconic writers of the midwestern experience to which he was so often compared—writers like Theodore Dreiser, Sherwood Anderson, Sinclair Lewis, and Edgar Lee Masters? After all, critical reception of Sigmund's work, while not as voluminous as that of Wood's, was equally as positive. Writing in 1929, Carl Sandburg praised the literary revolution begun by Sigmund and his fellow Iowa regionalists in his weekly column "From the Notebook of Carl Sandburg" in the *Chicago Daily News*.[9] Sandburg was one of Sigmund's many champions. H.L. Mencken, Sherwood Anderson, and Ilya Tolstoy, among others, corresponded with him. California poet Robinson Jeffers lauded Sigmund's "fine powers of imagination and imaginative sympathy, as well as musical verse."[10] Sigmund earned a *New York Times* review for just his second full-length book of poetry, 1923's *Pinions*, of which the *Times* reviewer opined, "To say that they [the poems] are somewhat in the vein of Edgar Lee Masters is not to suggest imitation, for they are fresh and original both in content and in rendering."[11]

When, building on the success of his poetry, Sigmund turned to fiction in the late 1920s, his efforts likewise garnered positive notice. Editors tapped his short fiction not only for the prestigious Best Short Stories series, but also for numerous anthologies, including *The American Caravan*, where his work appeared beside Ernest Hemingway's and Gertrude Stein's. In 1930 alone, Boston editor Edward J. O'Brien listed six Sigmund shorts as among the best short stories of that year.[12] By 1937, the year of his premature passing, the *Chicago Tribune* described him as an "established author" then winning "increasing regard by thoughtful critics."[13]

In his *All's Well* literary magazine, Newberry Award–winning author Charles Finger lionized his friend's courage in writing plain-spoken material for which, "as all the world knows, there is no market ... in the magazines of today when the cry is all for unconvincing romanticism, success and sex tales, and stories of impossible adventure—but that matters no more to Sigmund than it mattered to Millet that no dealer wanted his pictures."[14] For others, Sigmund's unflinching realism had itself become an imitation. "Mr. Sigmund deals in tragic materials," a 1931 *New York Times* review of Sigmund's book *The Ridge Road* read, "but it takes a [Sherwood] Anderson to bring out the essentials of tragedy among the dwellers in a Winesburg—or a Wapsipinicon Valley."[15] Finger argues that Sigmund's greatness is missed by the present generation, yet certain to be redeemed in the sweet by-and-by: "The fact is that Jay G. Sigmund ... seems to have an eye on readers of the future."[16]

Yet by the early 2000s, when I set out to provide Jay Sigmund his posthumous due, I found that Charles Finger's prophesy had utterly failed to come to pass. Among prominent writer-scholars, only New York's Bill Kauffman seemed conversant with the Sigmund legacy, writing, in "his best Wallace Stevens fashion, Sigmund combined his insurance with his poetry. He also wrote badly undervalued short stories ... animated by his affection for the people of his home region."[17] As I pitched possible anthologies to well-regarded university presses throughout the Midwest, nary an acquisition editor had, at the time, even heard of Sigmund, much less felt his work worthy of a selected edition prepared in the spirit of literary stewardship with which Engle had first compiled a posthumous Sigmund collection in 1939. One unusually thoughtful acquiring editor to whom I broached the idea kindly referred my query to an "expert" on such things. But when the home-state expert commissioned to weigh in likewise failed to recognize the Bard of the Wapsipinicon River, a renaissance was, for a time, dead in the water, at least in Sigmund's home state and mine.

The Bard's wholesale neglect made a sad kind of sense to me. After all, two generations had passed since the definitive book of its ilk, *A Literary History of Iowa*, penned by Michigan Technological University professor Clarence Andrews. Andrews's book was a thorough and in many ways seminal treatment of its subject, and while it names Sigmund in passing as one of a few Iowa poets to earn distinction writing about rural life, the treatment he receives is notably slight relative to his contemporaries.[18] Sigmund and his work, for example, earn approximately ten unique mentions in the book's comprehensive index, while the references to Sigmund's contemporary Ruth Suckow require a full column. Critics who don't know better often put Sigmund and Suckow in the same silo—both were known for rooting down close to home and earning their literary fame by writing about the "home folks." But while Ruth Suckow's titles remain in print by the dozens, and on offer by reputable presses, Jay Sigmund's work was, prior to the publication of the 2008 anthology *The Plowman Sings,* the stuff of used book stores and interlibrary loan consortia. Indeed, so careless had librarians and literary critics grown with Sigmund's legacy that by the early 2000s, when I set about acquiring his lesser known tomes, I received via interlibrary loan a signed original from a state university library in Illinois inscribed in the author's own hand: "For Ralph H. Kastner, with the author's compliments, Jay G. Sigmund, November 2nd, 1927." Kastner, I learned, was an up-and-coming Chicago lawyer around 1927, a Sigmund reader among many who had been born in Iowa and migrated to the Windy City. Some dutiful academic librarian had penciled the word "signed" at the top of Kastner's personally inscribed volume, but continued to ship it out merrily to the few interested parties in urgent need of Sigmund's short story collection *Wapsipinicon Tales,* even as its pages had grown so brittle as to break in the hands. Any other signed original by a regionalist writer of Sigmund's import would surely have long ago been squirreled away and sequestered in special collections, or else sold at auction to an established antiquarian. Certainly, a signed Suckow original would not be so thoughtlessly and blithely circulated.

    Here again, however, the usual differences in educational attainment, geodemographics, and mobility perhaps explain the variously experienced legacies of analogous Iowa regionalists, as well as attitudes and endowments in the home community entrusted with shaping and shepherding the historical reputations of their native daughters and sons in the hereafter. Ruth Suckow, for example, as Tom Lutz rightly points out, was a preacher's daughter who moved around widely and well as a child,[19] unlike Sigmund, who liked to point out that his formal schooling had occurred in country schools with names like Buzzard's Folly[20] and Rabbit Grove.[21] Indeed, while the Bard of the Wapsipinicon had no formal education beyond the tenth grade, Suckow attended an elite liberal arts college, Grinnell, before moving, like

Hamlin Garland, to Boston in her early twenties. Not to be outdone, she relocated from Boston to Denver, returning to Iowa in her late twenties just as regionalism hit its vogue in the journals to which she sold her work, including John T. Fredericks's iconic *The Midland*. Throughout her nomadic life, Suckow, portrayed as the quintessential small-town writer and beekeeper, was, in fact, as happily itinerant as most of the other regionalists, living in cosmopolitan Cedar Falls (a university town), Santa Fe, Tucson, Greenwich Village, Vermont, Chicago, and Claremont, California, among other destination cities. Home to the University of Northern Iowa, the city of Cedar Falls claimed Suckow as its own in 1966, forming a Ruth Suckow Memorial Society that recently celebrated its 50th successful year.[22] The organization's webpages abound with historical photos, chronologies, timelines, and connections that testify to a legacy well-preserved, despite the fact that Suckow lived in Cedar Falls off and on for just seven years, sporadically from 1931 to 1932 and for the better part of 1935 to 1940.

Meanwhile, Sigmund turned down an executive position in Omaha to stay home with his wife, Louise, and their three children. Unlike Wood and Suckow, who cultivated their artistic talents early, Sigmund came to his craft at the relatively ripe old age of thirty-six, a point of pride but also a serious handicap in an era when artists and writers of social if not financial capital benefited from the head starts offered by the educations and connections their class entitlements afforded them. Suckow, for example, had graduated from the Curry School of Self Expression in Boston—the equivalent of a fine arts college—by her early twenties.

All of this is to say, or begin to say, that the regionalists whose reputations have survived and thrived far in excess of the dark horse Sigmund's largely followed the pattern now well-established by out-migrating cosmopolites and brain-drainers even when they do hail from relatively disadvantaged rural and small-town environments. The pattern, applicable to nearly every known regionalist of history's so-called Midwestern Moment, is as follows: first, leave home to secure a college education, a credential, even if one maintains a healthy distaste and distrust of exactly the class of liberally educated patrons and benefactors whose favor one hopes eventually to cultivate; second, secure one's literary or artistic reputation by becoming an ambivalent critic of the home place. If one comes from a place like Waubeek, Iowa, as Sigmund did, simply positive treatments of the home folks in the pages of the nation's elite periodicals would not make muster in 1930 any more than they might now. Citified readers in the Jazz Age and shortly thereafter, most of whom had long since left their own midwestern Wobegons to pursue their fortunes in the great "funeral procession of the nation cityward,"[23] wanted at least a ceremonial nod to the goodness of the bucolic nests they had left, to be sure, but ultimately sought out the ilk of writers who had, like them, transcended that homey, homely environment in word as well as in deed. Hence the assured literary reputation of the out-migrating, itinerant regionalists such as Dreiser and Lewis. Hence Sandburg. Hence Anderson. Hence fellow Iowans Aldrich, Garland, Glaspell, Quick, and Suckow. Here, as elsewhere, Sigmund broke the mold by insisting on staying home, even shaming others, including Engle and Wood, for their leave-takings. It was all well and good for critics in cosmopolitan cities like New York and Iowa City to praise Sigmund's work for its downhome genuineness, its sincerity, its utter lack of guile or artifice, but their interest in such places as Sigmund called home remained purely literary. In fact, in many ways, regionalism could be read as a thumb in the eye of the class of readers and critics populating the cities, a point Wood himself makes in his essay "A Definition of Regionalism," wherein he describes the movement as "a revolt against the cultural dominion of the city ... and the tendency of metropolitan cliques to lay more emphasis on artificial precepts than on more vital human experience."[24]

Certainly, part and parcel of the glee with which the upwardly mobile literati inhabiting American cities embraced writers and artists like Wood and Suckow was the Victorian-like thrill implicit in "discovery"—coming upon some raw, rusticated writer the way one came upon a quaint roadside curio shop or wayside inn to be talked up excitedly with one's more sophisticated friends: "You simply wouldn't believe the hole-in-the-wall place I found on my way home. To think such places still exist!" No doubt, among out-migrating writer-critic Sigmund supporters such as Sherwood Anderson, Carl Sandburg, Charles Finger, and H.L. Mencken there was true glee in finding an insurance man (of all things!), in Cedar Rapids, Iowa (of all places!) writing top-drawer literature full of local color. Even as cosmopolitan as Suckow was by comparison to Sigmund, she too carried the sex appeal of the rustic for regionalist sympathizers gone off to the city, chief among them Mencken. Writing Sinclair Lewis, Mencken fairly gushed that he had "lately unearthed a girl in Iowa who seems to me to be superb. She follows after Dreiser and Anderson, but she is also a genuine original."[25] Suckow, Mencken claimed, could "write like the devil" and was "unquestionably the most remarkable woman ... writing stories in the Republic." Truth be told, the "genuine original" Mencken "unearthed" was a sophisticated woman and literary technician who by 1929 had earned a BA and an MA while matriculating, piecemeal, at educational institutions across the country, a worldly author who had begun a cosmopolitan life that would take her and her partner across the country and to political appointments and government work in Washington, DC

The hesitation among the literati regarding Sigmund, it seemed, was not just that he refused to come to them in the monied, cultured East, but that he was actually stubbornly, unrepentantly happy where he lived, writing portrayals of home that, while sometimes dark, lacked the satiric nudge-nudge, wink-wink inside joke of Anderson's *Winesburg, Ohio*, for example, or Wood's canvases *American Gothic* and *The Appraisal*. Works like these carried with them a critical subtext easily decoded by those "in the know"—the farm wife in *American Gothic* could be read by them as the Gothic in *American Gothic*, repressed and imprisoned—while Sigmund's work seemed resistant to sending even the most coded and subtextual messages of outright criticism or class condescension.

In their book *Writing Out of Place* Judith Fetterley and Marjorie Pryse parse the difference between local color and regionalist texts that "look with" the region versus texts that "look at" the region. If a text looks *with* its subjects—in other words when the author legitimately looks on and laughs with the people written about—the location about which the author writes is "marked rather than transcended."[26] Conversely, when a text, like Wood's or Anderson's or Dreiser's, looks *at* its subject, geography and location play second fiddle to the artist's need for transcendence and universality. While their distinction may be a bit too tidy, it could be argued that Sigmund looked *with*, while many of his better-known, far more cosmopolitan contemporaries looked *at*, consistent with the worldviews of their more metropolitan, liberally educated buyers and benefactors. Similarly, the sorts of presses with whom Sigmund published most of his books—including, for example, Cedar Rapids's homegrown Torch Press and Cornell College's chapbook series—published "with" a local and regional readership in mind, rather than "at" a national demographic. Sadly, where historical legacy is concerned, "lookers with" lose to "lookers at" by more than a nose.

What then does the curious case of Jay G. Sigmund have to teach a latter-day, neo-regionalist vested in both a reexamination of that long-ago Midwestern Moment of regionalist centrality and preeminence? It tells us in part that the "amateurs," whether painters, historians, or writers, who stubbornly stay home inevitably damage their legacies relative to their more credentialed, better circulated ("networked" in contemporary parlance) peers. It teaches us that the so-called rustic or primitivist beholden for his or her literary or artistic legacy to the fickle opinion-makers and aesthetes in the nearest ivory tower cosmopolis is likely to be vulnerable in the end; history proves the shapers of literary fashion to be capricious at best and duplicitous at worst. So long as the genuine, or the simple, or the sincere (words used to pay backhanded compliments to the conspicuous lack of artifice in Jay Sigmund's work) in literature are *de rigueur,* the stock in trade of the "rustic" regionalist remains high. But when these same attributes fall out of literary vogue he or she will be cast aside for the next big thing, in much the same way that the reputations of early Iowa local color writers—scribes such as Hamlin Garland, Alice French, Ellis Parker Butler, and even Herbert Quick—had begun to be downgraded by the 1930s in favor of a less folksy, more academically circumspect regionalist aesthetic. Finally, Sigmund's example reminds us that someone must stay home to keep the home fires burning; someone must open the door to the prodigal come home to make his or her art; someone must be the steady enough Sigmund in temperament, income, and vocation to offer a meal and room to the itinerant genius who blows in with the wind. Sigmund played this paternal role for creatives as varied as Grant Wood and Paul Engle, but, like any father, he watched as his "sons"—those whom he had counseled, debated, cheered, vexed, and sometimes censored—easily surpassed him in reputation by choosing a life unlike his own. In his introduction to Sigmund's chapbook *Burroak and Sumac,* Cornell College Professor Clyde Tull took care to lower expectations regarding his talented yet overlooked friend, writing, "While his [Sigmund's] work has never been marked by the qualities that lead to sudden or spectacular fame, it has won increasing regard from thoughtful critics."[27]

Sigmund's protégé and spiritual inheritor, Engle, wrote this definition of regionalism based on the literary harvest his good friend had every reason to hope for: "This is the way it must be if great art of any kind is to be produced here. That is the word—produce, what a countryside grows naturally,"[28] and the produce must be distributed for the "nourishment" of the writer's people in their "little area of the earth." Yet the neo-regionalist writers and artists living in the hinterlands beyond their states' major cities know that if their cause is taken up, or their "produce" in the form of books or paintings bought, it will mostly be by the highly mobile elites, be they conservative or progressive, whose likes and dislikes shape public opinion and literary taste. Our home folks cannot ensure our literary reputation in the wider world, much as they would like, though they can vouch for our character. This then is the Faustian bargain for the true regionalist, then as now: real and lifelong rural roots or national reputation, recognizing that it is nearly impossible to have both for an artist, like Sigmund, unwilling or unable to frequently travel. Sigmund emphatically chose roots and bled to death of an accidental gunshot wound in the remote woods and wilds alongside his native river—the one whose praises he helped sing in countless poems. He was too far from the village to be heard as he cried for help.

I am grateful that, since I first set out to raise Jay Sigmund's historical reputation from the dead, the cognoscenti in our shared home state have begun to pay him proper respects. Linn County, Iowa, where Sigmund lived and worked for the entirety of his adult life, belatedly honored its native son with a seven-acre park. In the intervening years a Sigmund film documentary has been produced; reassessments of the Bard of the Wapsipinicon have appeared in journals like *Modern Age*, where scholars, building on and echoing my enthusiasm for Sigmund, have suggested that in the long run critical esteem for Sigmund's work will surpass that of his mentee, Engle.[29] Even the biographical dictionary published by the home state university press finally conceded the importance of the insurance man-poet, granting him a brief but well-deserved entry.

Lately, a whole new generation of ardent pro-localism cosmopolites have rediscovered Sigmund, leveraging his worthwhile example not only in county parks but in cultural scavenger hunts and digital exhibits of the kind mounted by the Silos and Smokestacks Natural Heritage Area in eastern Iowa, where a trip to Sigmund's memorial park is listed as an excursion fit for a well-intentioned urbanite or suburbanite determined to secure the feel-goods associated with historical-literary tourism. The same website that hopes to attract young, curious viewers in offering video links advertising titillations-cum-cultural-literacies like "Watch baby pigs being born!"[30] likewise offers, however belatedly, a breadcrumb trail leading back to the Midwest's most forgotten regionalist.

## Notes

1. Ed Ferreter, "Jay Sigmund and Grant Wood," *Books at Iowa* 42 (1985), 26.
2. Thomas K. Dean, "Sigmund, Jay G.," *The Biographical Dictionary of Iowa* (Iowa City, IA: University of Iowa Press, 2009), accessed July 2, 2016, http://uipress.lib.uiowa.edu/bdi/DetailsPage.aspx?id=346.
3. Edward Pierce Ferreter, "Grant Wood Meets Jay G. Sigmund: From Word to Image: From Image to Word" (MA thesis, University of Iowa, 1985), 14.
4. Grant Wood, *Revolt Against the City* (Iowa City, IA: Clio Press, 1935), 34.
5. Ibid., 35.
6. Ibid., 34–35.
7. Ferreter, "Grant Wood Meets Jay G. Sigmund," 7.
8. Paul Engle, ed., "The Poet and the Man," in *Jay G. Sigmund: Select Poetry and Prose* (Muscatine, IA: The Prairie Press, 1939), viii.
9. "From the Notebook of Carl Sandburg," *Chicago Daily News*, 1929; in Papers of Jay Sigmund, Special Collections Department, University of Iowa, box 1, "Newspaper Clippings."
10. Robinson Jeffers, letter to Jay Sigmund, June 22, 1926, Box 1. Papers of Jay Sigmund (MsC 697), Special Collections Department, University of Iowa Libraries, Iowa City, IA.
11. "Poetic Brushstrokes: *Pinions*: By Jay G. Sigmund," Review of *Pinions* by Jay G. Sigmund, *New York Times*, February 24, 1924, BR 21.
12. Zachary Michael Jack, *The Plowman Sings: The Essential Poetry, Prose, and Drama of America's Forgotten Regionalist, Jay G. Sigmund* (Lanham, MD: University Press of America, 2008), 2.
13. John Evans, "Iowa College Out with New Chapbooks," *Chicago Daily Tribune*, April 25, 1937, E2.
14. Charles Finger qtd. in Jack, *The Plowman Sings*, 13.
15. Unsigned review of *The Ridge Road*, by Jay G. Sigmund, "Of the Soil," *New York Times*, Feb. 1, 1931, 9.

16. Charles J. Finger, "A Kind of Introduction," in *Wapsipinicon Tales*, by Jay G. Sigmund (Cedar Rapids, IA: The Torch Press, 1927), 12.
17. Bill Kauffman, *Look Homeward, America: In Search of Reactionary Radicals and Front Porch Anarchists* (Wilmington, DE: ISI Books, 2006), 63.
18. Clarence A. Andrews, *A Literary History of Iowa* (Iowa City, IA: University of Iowa Press, 1972), 148.
19. Tom Lutz, *Cosmopolitan Vistas: American Regionalism and Literary Value* (Ithaca, NY: Cornell University Press, 2004), 147.
20. Engle, "The Poet and the Man," vi.
21. Jay G. Sigmund, letter to C.G. Stookey, November 14, 1933, accessed January 16, 2017, http:// www.campsilos.org/excursions/hc/one/s1d.htm.
22. Ruth Suckow Memorial Association Website, accessed July 3, 2016, http:// www.ruthsuckow.org.
23. Martha Foote Crow, *The American Country Girl* (New York, NY: Frederick A. Stokes, 1915), 85.
24. Grant Wood, "A Definition of Regionalism," *Books at Iowa* (November, 1965), 3.
25. H.L. Mencken, qtd. in Tom Lutz, *Cosmopolitan Vistas*, 146.
26. Judith Fetterley and Marjorie Pryse, *Writing Out of Place: Regionalism, Women, and American Literary Culture* (Urbana and Chicago, IL: University of Illinois Press, 2003), 36.
27. Clyde Tull, ed., foreword to *Burroak and Sumac*, by Jay Sigmund (Mount Vernon, IA: Cornell College, 1935).
28. Engle, "The Poet and the Man," viii.
29. Allan C. Carlson, "Bard of the Wapsipinicon: An Assessment of Jay G. Sigmund," *Modern Age* vol. 55, no. 4 (Fall, 2013), 44.
30. Silos and Smokestacks National Heritage Area, "From Native Prairie to Present, Our Agricultural Heritage," accessed January 16, 2017, http:// www.campsilos.org.

Michael J. Pfeifer | A Symphonic Midwest

The Minneapolis Symphony Orchestra and Regionalist Identity, 1903–1922

The development of symphonic music in the early twentieth-century United States was shaped by strong regionalist and transnational currents. Boston and New York had long dominated the American classical musical scene, which was largely (although hardly exclusively) populated by musicians born or trained in German-speaking lands, even as midwestern urban centers such as Chicago, Cincinnati, Minneapolis, and St. Louis had long supported orchestral cultures. By the late nineteenth and early twentieth centuries, symphonic music was financially supported as a matter of local prestige by business classes seeking to demonstrate that their metropolis possessed "culture."[1] The case of the Minneapolis Symphony Orchestra nicely reveals the intersection of early twentieth-century symphonic culture with a regionalist midwestern identity. The performance of orchestral music in Minneapolis dated to the city's founding in the mid-nineteenth century as ad hoc ensembles often led by or involving German-born musicians staged concert series. However, in 1903, a Munich-born organist, Emil Oberhoffer, organized a symphonic orchestra that presented a full series of subscription concerts. Over the next decade the orchestra grew in size and recruited many musicians from abroad, most significantly from German-speaking lands, but also from elsewhere in Europe and the United States.[2] Meanwhile the president of the orchestral association, E.L. Carpenter, relentlessly recruited support and subscriptions from Minneapolis's leading businessmen, sometimes at the behest of their wives (whose husbands sometimes professed boredom and disinterest with attending the symphony).[3] By the mid-1910s, the orchestra toured extensively around the Midwest as well as further afield and presented concerts in New York's Carnegie Hall and in Boston's Symphony Hall; Minneapolis residents took significant pride that their orchestra was now ranked among the nation's top three or four despite its location far from the East Coast.[4] Until 1914, the Minneapolis Symphony rose while in competition with the ambitious efforts of the St. Paul Symphony, backed by St. Paul business boosters, who wished to deny Minneapolis the privilege of having the Twin Cities' only major orchestra; the St. Paul Symphony collapsed amid the uncertain economic environment brought about by the onset of World War I.[5]

In many respects, then, the first decades of the Minneapolis Symphony, which conductor Emil Oberhoffer led until 1922, chart the development of a midwestern regionalist symphonic orchestra culture, linked to a larger transnational context of German musicians crossing the Atlantic, in the early twentieth century. This chapter will analyze the regionalist and transnational dimensions of the early history of the Minneapolis Symphony using a variety of primary and secondary sources such as reminiscences of musicians and orchestra board members, concert programs, newspapers, and histories of the orchestra.

The history of orchestral music performance in Minneapolis, a flour-milling metropolis on the upper Mississippi River commanding an extensive agricultural and extractive (iron mining and timber) hinterland,[6] drew substantially on the contributions of musicians who had been born or trained in the German-speaking lands of Prussia and Austria. Hamburg-born Ludwig Harmsen arrived in Minneapolis in 1868 and organized the Orchestral Union in the 1870s, pairing Schubert and Schumann with lighter fare, even as some critiqued "Professor" Harmsen's ostentatious conducting style.[7] Franz Danz, a violist and cornetist from Darmstadt via New York City arrived in the late 1870s, began organizing band and orchestra concerts, and within a few years lured his son Franz Jr., who had been serving as concertmaster in the Theodore Thomas Orchestra in New York, to Minneapolis. Franz Danz Jr. took over conducting duties for the Danz Orchestra and initiated a long-running series of orchestral concerts in 1884, juxtaposing serious music by composers such as Wagner with light classics, initially in Turner Hall, a beer hall popular with German Americans. In 1886 the Danz Orchestra moved its concerts to Harmonia Hall, where alcohol and smoking were forbidden and Danz in the new venue effectively maneuvered around Sabbatarian sensibilities by styling his Sunday afternoon performances as "sacred concerts," thus broadening the orchestra's appeal from German immigrants to Yankee Protestant Minneapolis and its mercantile elite.[8]

German musicians played a pivotal role again after the turn of the century as Minneapolis's symphonic life deepened with the founding of the Minneapolis Symphony Orchestra in 1903. The orchestra's first concert on November 3 opened with the Prelude to Act I of Wagner's opera *Die Meistersinger;* musicians included personnel from the Danz Orchestra, conducted by Emil Oberhoffer. Oberhoffer, born into a musical family in Munich in 1867, had studied with the prominent organist and composer Josef Rheinberger before leaving in 1885 for New York City, where he served as a church organist and associated with Anton Seidl, a Leipzig-trained assistant to Richard Wagner who led crucial performances of Wagner's operas in New York in the mid-1880s that helped to popularize the music of the quintessential mid- to late-nineteenth-century German composer in the United States.[9] Venturing west to Minnesota as a musician in the orchestra of a Gilbert and Sullivan troupe, Oberhoffer took a job with Danz's orchestra and then as an organist at churches around the Twin Cities. By the late 1890s, Oberhoffer competed with a soprano from the Rhineland, Anna E. Schoen-René, as transplanted German cultural entrepreneurs seeking to raise the musical culture of the Twin Cities to elevated Teutonic standards. Schoen-René, who would later lead the voice department at the Julliard School in New York, led an abortive effort to create a Northwestern Symphony Orchestra to serve the Twin Cities and the region. Oberhoffer for his part led increasingly ambitious efforts to put on oratorios and operas with the Danz Orchestra, culminating with performances of Saint-Saëns's opera *Samson and Delilah,* which Oberhoffer conducted in late 1902.[10] Embarking on the founding of a full-fledged symphony orchestra in 1903, the Bavarian Oberhoffer enlisted the financial backing of "fifty-four guarantors, representing much of Minneapolis industry and wealth," including a young lumberman and frustrated opera singer from Clinton, Iowa, Elbert L. Carpenter, who would become the orchestra's long-time financial manager.[11] Traveling to Europe in the months before the Minneapolis Symphony embarked on its inaugural season, Oberhoffer filled out the orchestra's ranks by hiring European musicians and purchased scores for the orchestra's library, including several works by Richard Strauss, the leading German composer of the era.[12]

Over the next two decades the Minneapolis Symphony developed a regional and national reputation as Oberhoffer hired additional

European and European-trained musicians, the quality of the orchestra's playing improved markedly, and the orchestra toured extensively in the United States and Canada, particularly in the midwestern and plains states and prairie provinces, but also around the West and in the Northeast, including concerts in New York and Boston, the leading American cities for classical music. The *Musical Courier*, a New York–based classical musical trade journal, evincing the geographical imprecision that sometimes still hampered those who sought to characterize the Upper Midwest, in 1913 lauded the Minneapolis orchestra as "the new orchestral voice of the Northwest." A *Musical Courier* writer evoked the role of timber in the Upper Midwest's economy as he described a visit to the orchestra's Minneapolis concert hall, the Auditorium at Eleventh Street and Nicollet Avenue. "Like a whiff of the invigorating ozone from such a forest of pine is the vim with which the Minneapolis symphonic players make attack in response to the decisive beats of the director [Oberhoffer]."[13] John K. Sherman, a mid-twentieth-century Twin Cities newspaper music critic and historian of the Minneapolis Symphony, noted that Oberhoffer grew into the persona of Minneapolis maestro, taking on the role of "a kind of civic symbol of musical culture" that embodied a Teutonic "high seriousness and spirit of consecration" as a dedicated practitioner of the sacred art of serious music.[14] Yet Sherman notes that Oberhoffer had studied not only in Munich but also in Luxembourg and Paris and he was hardly a German chauvinist in his programming, even as German and Austrian composers were well-represented in the orchestra's programs. With time, through "dexterous spoon-feeding" and adventurous programming that included serious evening programs and mixed programs that included lighter fare on Sunday afternoons, Oberhoffer built up sizable audiences in Minneapolis and St. Paul for not only Beethoven and Brahms but also for Tchaikovsky, Dvořák, Franck, and, eventually, Sibelius. Sherman writes that Richard Strauss visited the Twin Cities twice during the Oberhoffer years, on one visit "expounding on the absurdity" of both Minneapolis and St. Paul trying to maintain their own separate symphony orchestras (St. Paul's orchestra, conducted by the Austrian composer and conductor Gustav Mahler's student Walter Henry Rothwell, lasted only eight years, until funding dried up amid the start of the war in 1914). The Minneapolis Symphony gave the American premiere of Strauss's Festival Prelude in October 1913.[15] As the

Minneapolis orchestra rose in stature in the 1910s, its members shared a common German cultural background; while thirteen nationalities were represented among the personnel, most of the musicians were either from German-speaking lands or had been German-trained.[16]

Oberhoffer and his Minneapolis Symphony musicians were typical among symphonic musicians in the United States in the early twentieth century in their German identity. Since the mid-nineteenth century, symphonic music and orchestral performance in the United States had developed in a distinctly Germanic mode as Prussia, Great Britain, and France laid competing claims for cultural supremacy among inferiority-complex-laden American elites convinced, along with many European intellectuals, that the United States lacked a meaningful high culture. As historian Jessica Gienow-Hecht convincingly demonstrates, musicians from German-speaking lands, who had inculcated the emergent nineteenth-century notion of the German Empire as a "kulturnation" (that is, a nation based upon a cultural canon) successfully established the dominance of German composers in the classical canon even as a "symphony craze" took root among urban U.S. business elites who funded the establishment of symphony orchestras in the late nineteenth and early twentieth centuries. German musicians such as Oberhoffer, aided by the advent of the ocean-going steamer and the comparatively rapid transatlantic voyages it afforded, had significant advantages over American musicians. German musicians could claim, in the Romantic tradition, to be authentic interpreters of the German composers (Beethoven, Schubert, Brahms, Wagner) who were now seen as central to the classical canon. While according to Victorian notions, American male musicians risked being perceived as inappropriately effeminate, German male musicians, who were often idolized in the American press, were seen by contrast as "emotionally gifted." Gender played a role as well in the reception of symphonic music not only among urban elites but among a wider American audience that took to symphonic music in the years before and after the turn of the century. While business class men sometimes complained of being dragged to boring symphony concerts by their wives who were seeking to culturally elevate them, many American men could identify with the "power of the orchestra" and "the sex of the performers" (male), while for their part American women thrilled to "the emotional impact of music."[17]

By the fin de siècle period, German music and musicians dominated the symphony hall. Between 1890 and 1915, more than sixty percent of the works performed by major American orchestras were the compositions of German and Austrian composers, while by contrast Russian and French composers contributed merely twelve percent each to the repertoire of American orchestras, and native-born American composers only four percent.[18] Conductors from German-speaking lands, including Emil Oberhoffer, led all major American orchestras during this period, and musicians with a German pedigree filled the ranks of their ensembles, even as the American Federation of Musicians sought to unionize orchestras and to establish strict residency requirements for union membership. For example, Karl Muck, the Darmstadt-born conductor of the Boston Symphony who had served as music director of the Berlin State Opera, hired many Germans to play under his baton in Boston; by 1917, five years into Muck's second stint as music director in Boston, the orchestras included twenty-two Germans, eight Austrians, two Italians, and two French musicians.[19] In short, as Gienow-Hecht persuasively argues, German music and musicians achieved a "monopoly on the public display of 'emotion'" in fin de siècle America as German serious music came to be perceived as a refuge from capitalism and modernization and indeed as a language of emotion for many Americans.[20] Yet the German domination of the symphony hall had also long provoked concern of a nationalistic Prussian strategy of cultural imperialism that betrayed the universalistic ideals of high art, weakened home-grown American art, and risked compromising American ideals of democracy and patriotism. Long-standing tensions in the American reception of German serious music and musicians would erupt during the anti-German backlash after the American entry into World War I in April 1917.[21]

In its early decades the Minneapolis Symphony toured extensively around the Midwest and the Plains states, performing and traveling in often challenging conditions and bringing symphonic music sometimes for the first time to far-flung corners of the region and often eliciting an enthusiastic reception from locals. In 1916 the orchestra's tour manager, Iowa-born Wendell Heighton, tallied seventy-nine communities that had experienced their first symphonic concert at the behest of the Minneapolis Symphony.[22] Playing a mixture of light classical and more serious fare and accompanying local choral societies and operatic soloists that traveled with the orchestra, the Minneapolis Symphony filled an important gap in the dissemination of classical music in an era before the advent of radio and when few other orchestras were touring widely. The traveling and performing situations could be difficult; for example, the orchestra was delayed in February 1912 by Wisconsin snowdrifts and in May 1913 by flooding in Indiana. Venues could also be demanding, ranging from the Corn Palace in Mitchell, South Dakota, to a curling rink in Duluth, to scorching or leaky tents. Often extraneous noise competed for the audience's attention, such as "a piercing whistle" that interrupted the opening of the Prelude to Act I of Wagner's *Tristan und Isolde* as the orchestra sought to perform it in Aberdeen, South Dakota, in Spring 1914, or the wild animals, traveling with a circus troupe, that disrupted a performance on the fairgrounds in Fort Dodge, Iowa.[23] Wherever they traveled throughout the Midwest and Plains, the Minneapolis Symphony often received an appreciative response. A newspaper in Devils Lake, North Dakota, captured the ebullient reaction in that community in its headline rendered in capitals: "ONE OF THE GREATEST ORCHESTRAS IN THE UNITED STATES PLAYING IN SMALLEST CITY IT EVER APPEARED IN CERTAINLY HAD THE MOST APPRECIATIVE AUDIENCE IT EVER PLAYED TO." A subheading, though, captured more layers of complexity in the audience's response in Devils Lake: "PROGRAM WAS ALMOST TOO HEAVY FOR MAJOR PORTION OF AUDIENCE."[24] Prominent locals sometimes reveled in the orchestra's visit; one musician recalled, for example, that on tour in Fargo in 1908, Maestro Oberhoffer and the orchestra repaired post-concert to a local brewery, where they celebrated their performance by raising steins with, among others, the governors of North Dakota and South Dakota.[25]

Seeking to raise its national profile, the Minneapolis Symphony ventured east to play in New York in 1911, returning to the informal capital of the American classical world in 1913, 1914, and 1916, and traveling several of these years as well to Philadelphia and Boston, also centers of the eastern musical establishment. The ambitious visits of the upstart orchestra from the Upper Midwest provoked conversation over the quality of the Minneapolis orchestra's music-making compared to that of more well-established American orchestras and speculation as to whether audiences in the eastern metropoles would actually benefit from hearing a midwestern orchestra. Minneapolis music critic Caryl

Storrs argued that Emil Oberhoffer and his Minneapolis Symphony were reversing the eastern hegemony that had long characterized the country's classical musical scene. "For 50 years the tide of American music had been flowing from east to west, and now a serious musical organization from the banks of the distant Mississippi river, where but yesterday the buffalo roamed unmolested and the only music was the song of birds and the pine tree symphony played by the wind, was to start the first wave of the new tide from west to east."[26] The critics in the New York papers, however, had decidedly ambivalent reactions to the Minneapolis orchestra's 1911 performance, which included works of Richard Strauss, Brahms, and Mozart. The *New York Tribune* expressed the mixed view of the hinterland interlopers, asserting somewhat condescendingly that the midwestern orchestra "played as well as could be expected but that the manner of the conductor was extremely distasteful 'to the veteran concertgoers of New York.'"[27]

The Minneapolis Symphony's next New York visit in 1913 provoked similar irritation in the New York musical press, with music critics assaying little need for a concert by a provincial western orchestra when New York was already overwhelmed with symphony concerts. "Why does the orchestra of the Northwest go out of its beaten path to challenge comparison with the Boston Symphony, the Chicago Symphony, the New York Philharmonic and the New York Symphony? It is mistaken ambition and no one is deluded as to the means for employing audiences [that is by handing out free tickets]." The *Musical Leader* held that the Minneapolis orchestra was simply not good enough to be venturing east to perform in the citadel of American orchestral life and that its music-making held little interest for sophisticated New Yorkers. "The young Lochinvar-from-the-West argument is all right if his steed is the best, but should he bring only a fresh young untrained colt, then he had better go back to the place whence he came." Yet the *Musical Observer* found this all rather "patronizing," arguing that the visiting Midwesterners merited better treatment. "When an admirable organization like this Minneapolis orchestra visits us, when undeniable proof is given of the liberality, enthusiasm and artistic spirit of a comparatively small western community, with no other view than the gaining of a foothold or an appreciative word, our critics reward them with a few remarks that the woodwind section might have been better, that the brass at times was somewhat noisy, that the strings at times played well or they didn't, and that the conductor, Mr. Oberhoffer, was a man of some talent."[28] Subsequent New York visits in 1914 and 1916 elicited a similarly mixed response of incredulity and praise from the New York critics for the enterprising midwestern orchestra, with the *New York Sun* for example acidly remarking, "the Minneapolis orchestra once more enters the domains of the effete east to shed sweetness and light in those places where orchestral music is yet in its infancy."[29]

In sum, from its founding in 1903 to its rise to regional and national prominence by the 1910s, the Minneapolis Symphony embodied the interaction of regionalist and transnational trends in the making of an American symphonic orchestra culture in the early twentieth century. Employing many German-born and -trained musicians and funded by a Yankee urban mercantile elite, the Minneapolis orchestra carried symphonic music to communities throughout the Midwest and earned the grudging, if patronizing, admiration of New York classical music critics who had doubted a worthwhile orchestra could come from the Upper Midwest. The Minneapolis Symphony's rapid rise to prominence, aided by its extensive touring, roused envy and admiration in other major midwestern cities. The *Musical Courier*, which would later report that Detroit was hoping to revive its orchestra along similar lines after its symphony had fallen defunct, stressed the significance of Minneapolis's achievement. "That a western city the size of the Minneapolis should develop and maintain an orchestra that is ranked by leading musicians and critics as one of the four leading orchestras in the country is a fact that emphasizes the marvelous development of music in America in recent years."[30] In February 1913, in the wake of a recent visit to St. Louis by the Minneapolis orchestra, which it praised for being "backed by hardheaded [sic] business men on hard-headed [sic] grounds," the *St. Louis Times* lamented that its own St. Louis Symphony lacked a similarly august profile and urged that the St. Louis orchestra should tour nearby "southern and western states" to "advertis[e] ... this city in a wholly helpful way."[31] Comparing St. Louis unfavorably with Minneapolis and other U.S. cities, such as Boston, New York, Philadelphia, and Cincinnati, that possessed prestigious symphony orchestras, a columnist in the *St. Louis Times* styled as "an observer" similarly despaired, "Our own atmosphere seems to consist mostly of smoke, commercialism, and old families ... Let it be our ambition to be a center of things other than beer, shoes, and hardware—say, art, for instance, and beautiful parks and handsome public buildings and music, especially music."[32] The columnist lauded the Minneapolis Symphony as an example of an orchestra that elevated its city's status throughout the Midwest and the country at large and hoped that the St. Louis Symphony might do the same. "Minneapolis has the double glory of a great State University and an orchestra whose achievements have put Minneapolis distinctly on the map. The Minneapolis orchestra has the business men of the city solidly behind it in ungrudging and generous support, and it advertises the city from New York to Denver, and from Duluth to Galveston, as being itself the flower of the city's achievements. Let's get into the game ourselves, and make the waster places—musically—of the West and Southwest glad because of the regular coming of our orchestra, for even the former high-grass towns in our territory are hungering and thirsting for the good things in art and music and look to St. Louis to supply them with their heart's desires. If we can't have championship baseball teams, let's have something more enduring and far-reaching as an advertisement of our city as a center and dispenser of sweetness and light."[33] For the St. Louis editorialists, the Minneapolis Symphony offered an exemplary model for how a symphony orchestra could marry commerce and art, project high culture into the midwestern hinterland, and raise the regional and national status of a midwestern metropolis.

## Notes

1. For these developments see Joseph Horowitz, *Wagner Nights: An American History* (Berkeley: University of California Press, 1994); Lawrence W. Levine, *Highbrow/Lowbrow: The Emergence of Cultural Hierarchy in America* (Boston: Harvard University Press, 1990); Jessica C.E. Gienow-Hecht, "Trumpeting Down the Walls of Jericho: The Politics of Art, Music, and Emotion in German-American Relations, 1870–1920," *Journal of Social History*, Vol. 36, no. 3 (Spring 2003), 585–613. Jessica C.E. Gienow-Hecht, *Sound Diplomacy: Music and Emotions in Transatlantic Relations, 1850–1920* (Chicago: University of Chicago Press, 2009) offers a valuable history of the rise of American symphony orchestras in the context of German-American relations. Gienow-Hecht, *Sound Diplomacy*, p. 120, argues that German Americans, who were typically not in the circle of the urban elites at this time and whose "political heritage strongly opposed private donations," may have constituted a portion of the audience for symphonic concerts but were not important financial supporters of the symphony,

even in heavily Germanic midwestern cities such as St. Louis. For scholarly debate over how diverse and democratic the audience for symphony music actually was in the late nineteenth and early twentieth centuries, see Joseph Horowitz, "Music and the Gilded Age: Social Control and Sacralization Revisited," *The Journal of the Gilded Age and The Progressive Era*, Vol. 3, no. 3 (July 2004), 227–45. Horowitz, p. 231, contends that the key institutions of American classical music in the Gilded Age were not "fundamentally patronizing and anti-democratic." Horowitz, p. 243, holds that composers and performers, "not monied elites," were the primary drivers of sacralization, which "essentially documents aesthetic, not sociological change." By contrast Alan Trachtenberg and Lawrence Levine writing in the 1980s held that Gilded Age high culture, including the opera house and the concert hall, involved elites imposing feminized social control on the masses and thus, in Levine's signal interpretation, establishing a powerful dichotomy of sacralized high culture versus vulgar low culture that would eventually exclude the working classes from institutions of high art. Alan Trachtenberg, Ch. 5, *The Incorporation of America: Culture and Society in the Gilded Age* (New York: Hill and Wang, 1982), 140–81; Levine, *Highbrow/ Lowbrow*. For an important study of the rise of popular musical cultures in the Midwest, see James P. Leary, *Polkabilly: How the Goose Island Ramblers Redefined American Folk Music* (New York: Oxford University Press, 2006).
2. John W. Sherman, *Music and Maestros: The Story of the Minneapolis Symphony Orchestra* (Minneapolis: University of Minnesota Press, 1952). For the history of the Detroit Symphony, see Laurie Lanzen Harris and Paul Ganson, *The Detroit Symphony Orchestra: Grace, Grit, and Glory* (Detroit: Wayne University Press, 2016).
3. "Eva Blanchard Letter and Notes, re: Oberhoffer," John Sherman Research Notes, PA 12, Ser. 14, Minnesota Orchestra Archives, Manuscript Division, University of Minnesota-Minneapolis.
4. "Wendell Heighton, Orchestra Manager, 1909–1912, 18 p Reminiscence," John Sherman Research Notes, PA 12, Ser. 14, Minnesota Orchestra Archives, Manuscript Division, University of Minnesota-Minneapolis.
5. Sherman, *Music and Maestros*, 131–32.
6. For an economic and social profile of early twentieth-century Minneapolis, see Elizabeth Faue, *Community of Suffering and Struggle: Women, Men, and the Labor Movement in Minneapolis, 1915–1945* (Chapel Hill: University of North Carolina Press, 1991) 23.
7. Sherman, *Music and Maestros*, 11–14.
8. Ibid., 16–28.
9. Ibid., 38–39; Horowitz, *Wagner Nights*, 81–104.
10. Sherman, *Music and Maestros*, 39–48.
11. Ibid., 49–52, quotation from p. 52. Interview with Mrs. E.L. Carpenter, July 15, 1946, John Sherman Research Notes, PA 12, Ser. 14, Minnesota Orchestra Archives, Manuscript Division, University of Minnesota-Minneapolis.

112    A Symphonic Midwest

12. Sherman, *Music and Maestros*, 52–53, quotation from p. 53.
13. "Minneapolis in Music," *Musical Courier*, December 17, 1913, 26, in Wendell Heighton Scrapbook: Clippings from *Musical Courier*, PA 12, Ser. 9, Minnesota Orchestra Archives, Manuscript Division, University of Minnesota-Minneapolis.
14. Sherman, *Music and Maestros*, 71–73, quotations from p. 71 and p. 73.
15. Ibid., 131–32; *The Bellman* (Minneapolis, 1913), Vol. 15, 506.
16. Sherman, *Music and Maestros*, 74–75, 100, quotation from p. 74.
17. Philip Hart, *Orpheus in the New World* (New York: W.W. Norton, 1973), 59; Gienow-Hecht, "Trumpeting Down the Walls of Jericho," 586–92, quotations from p. 592.
18. Hart, *Orpheus in the New World*, 59, 404–26.
19. Gienow-Hecht, "Trumpeting Down the Walls of Jericho," 592–93; 599, 602–603.
20. Ibid., quotation from p. 600.
21. Ibid., 600–604. For the anti-German backlash and the experiences of German musicians in the United States during World War I, see Edmund A. Bowles, "Karl Muck and His Compatriots: German Conductors in America during World War I (and How They Coped)," *American Music*, Vol. 25, no. 4 (Winter 2007), 405–40.
22. *Musical Courier*, March 2, 1916, Wendell Heighton Scrapbook: Clippings from *Musical Courier*, PA 12, Ser. 9, Minnesota Orchestra Archives, Manuscript Division, University of Minnesota-Minneapolis.
23. "Minneapolis Orchestra on Tour," Wendell Heighton Scrapbook, PA 12, Ser. 9, Minnesota Orchestra Archives, Manuscript Division, University of Minnesota-Minneapolis; Sherman, *Music and Maestros*, 92–98, quotation from Sherman, p. 97.
24. Quoted in Ibid., 107.
25. "Talk with Karl Scheurer, November 3, 1946," John Sherman Research Notes, PA 12, Ser. 14, Minnesota Orchestra Archives, Manuscript Division, University of Minnesota-Minneapolis.
26. Quoted in Sherman, *Music and Maestros*, 108–109.
27. Ibid., 109–10, quotation from p. 110.
28. Quoted in Ibid., 110–11.
29. Quoted in Ibid., 112–13.
30. *Musical Courier*, February 9, 1911; "Minneapolis Protests," *Musical Courier*, October 24, 1914, Wendell Heighton Scrapbook: Clippings from *Musical Courier*, PA 12, Ser. 9, Minnesota Orchestra Archives, Manuscript Division, University of Minnesota-Minneapolis.
31. "Music and Business," *St. Louis Times*, February 14, 1913, in Wendell Heighton Scrapbook: article re: M.S.O. from "an observer," PA 12, Ser. 9, Minnesota Orchestra Archives, Manuscript Division, University of Minnesota-Minneapolis.
32. Ibid.
33. Ibid.

Paul Emory Putz

The Homer of Middle-Western America

Walt Mason's Syndicated Midwestern Poetry

Readers of Sinclair Lewis can be forgiven if they do not remember T. Cholmondeley "Chum" Frink. A minor figure inhabiting Lewis's fictional mid-sized midwestern city of Zenith, Frink appears in both *Babbitt* and *Arrowsmith*. Like many characters in Lewis's novels, Frink represents an American type: the cheery syndicated newspaper columnist. Lewis's notes indicate that he created Chum Frink as a composite of popular real-life writers like Eddie Guest, Walt Mason, Frank Crane, and Bruce Barton.[1] Thanks to syndication, essays and poems offering practical advice from these columnists reached a daily readership in the millions. Eschewing "highbrow" literary culture, they wrote in a simple style that supposedly appealed to the "common man"— in essence, white, English-speaking, middle-class Americans.[2] So, too, as Lewis biographer Richard Lingeman explains, the real-life Chum Frinks were "bard[s] of business" preaching "salesmanship, optimism, and pepism."[3] Most of them also had links to the Midwest. Crane and Barton grew up in Illinois, while Mason and Guest were born in Canada and England, respectively, before finding newspaper homes in Kansas and Michigan. But while most had midwestern connections, Walt Mason, more than the others, claimed a distinctly midwestern voice.

Precious few scholars take the syndicated writers behind Lewis's Frink character as serious subjects of study. Joan Shelley Rubin and Joseph Harrington are two important exceptions, the latter of whom has taken a particular interest in Mason.[4] For Harrington, Mason exemplifies the popular, nonmodernist poetry that reached a wide readership in the early twentieth century, only to be ignored by literary scholars ever since.[5] Harrington, however, is not as much interested in Mason as a voice from the Midwest as in exploring the questions of what counts as poetry, and why, and how those answers have changed over time. Yet, for scholars of the Midwest, Mason's writing should be of particular interest. He possessed a style and image shaped by and linked with the region, particularly between 1909 and 1920. During those years Mason lived in Emporia, Kansas, working for William Allen White's *Emporia Gazette* while reaching a national audience through his humorous syndicated poems.

To be sure, Mason's work is likely too conservative, celebratory, and sentimental for contemporary tastes.[6] But it has value precisely because it does not fit within the canonized "revolt from the village" tradition, which prizes writers who offered penetrating explorations of the hypocrisy and banality of life in the Midwest. A complete picture of the midwestern literary landscape of the early twentieth century must extend beyond the village revolt writers, bringing popular and middlebrow voices alongside those deemed suitable for modernist standards.[7] By examining Mason's writings, his popularity, and his surprisingly supportive critical reception in the 1910s, we can broaden our understanding of midwestern writing in the early twentieth century, and better understand the cultural power of the small-town Midwest in an age of mass consumption.

Born in Ontario, Canada, Mason was an adopted son of the Midwest.[8] He immigrated to the United States around 1880, working for a time as a common laborer in New York. Unsatisfied with that work, he headed west and tried his hand as a jack-of-all-trades in the newspaper business. In 1885, E.W. Howe, editor of the *Atchison* (Kansas) *Globe*, gave him one of his early jobs. Mason's arrival came soon after the publication of Howe's first novel, *The Story of a Country Town* (1884). A gloomy and melodramatic tale, it earned Howe a place among the early group of writers who painted the midwestern town with the brush of realism.[9] What impact Howe's literary style had on Mason is difficult to say, but the two became lifelong friends. Howe would later declare with pride that Mason created rhymes "more easily than any other living man."[10]

By 1887 Mason had departed from Atchison, becoming something of a nomad in the industry. For the next twenty years he worked for numerous newspapers, particularly in Nebraska. In the 1890s he served for a time on the staff of the *Lincoln Journal* with Willa Cather. But thanks in part to his drinking habit, he never managed to stay in one place for long.[11] Still, editors in Kansas and Nebraska continued to respect his journalistic abilities. In 1907 one such editor—William Allen

White of the *Emporia Gazette*—heard that Mason was looking for work and offered him a job. The forty-five-year-old Mason moved once more.

Mason could hardly have tied his fortunes to a better patron than White. A decade earlier White had earned a national reputation thanks to his 1896 anti-Populist editorial "What's the Matter with Kansas?" In the ensuing years White's political views shifted towards progressivism. Even so, the 1896 editorial opened the door to a national audience, and White did not let the opportunity slip. By the early 1900s White had become a go-to national spokesman for the small-town Midwest.[12] White did not confine his writing to journalism; he also had literary ambitions. *The Real Issue* (1896) and *In Our Town* (1906), collections of short stories about small-town life in Kansas, earned White a reputation as a pioneering midwestern realist.[13] With White's political commentary and literary output, the town of Emporia and the *Emporia Gazette* earned a regional and national importance that belied its 3000-person subscriber base.[14]

While the *Emporia Gazette* was uniquely positioned to give Mason's rhymes a wide and influential audience and to connect his poetry in the minds of readers with the small-town Midwest, the layout of the newspaper also helped to facilitate Mason's rise to prominence. At the top of its front page, the *Gazette* routinely carried a local news story set apart by a starred border. During a slow news day on a Saturday in late October, 1907, Mason was asked to provide filler for the box. Due to space constraints, Mason's poem—which encouraged readers to attend church—appeared in prose form, reading in part: "Let us all proceed tomorrow humbly to the house of prayer. The prediction from Chicago says the weather will be fair."[15] The poem resonated with readers, and Mason began regularly contributing short "prose poems" to fill the *Emporia Gazette*'s starred front-page box. By December 1907 Mason's unsigned poems had earned plaudits from fellow journalists in Kansas. The Kansas City *Journal* went so far as to compare Mason favorably to Walt Whitman. The *Journal* admitted that Whitman would be seen as superior by cultural elites. But "the average man, not gifted of the gods with the sixth sense of literary self-hypnosis and who is too honest to be hypocritical" preferred Mason.[16]

The *Journal* would not be the last to make such claims about Mason. Over the next year his poems grew increasingly popular as newspapers throughout Kansas copied and printed them. On Memorial Day in 1908 Mason penned what would become his most well-known poem, "Little

Green Tents."[17] And by October 1908 Mason began signing his poems, bringing more notoriety. The *Emporia Gazette* dutifully reported the praise their poet received. In November 1908 they reprinted a declaration from a Salina, Kansas, man: "I don't know Walt Mason from Adam but those poems which the *Union* reprints from his pen every day are humdingers. I clip every one of them out and paste them in my scrapbook."[18]

Mason's celebrity quickly grew beyond the bounds of Kansas, and by November national magazines *Collier's* and *Puck* had featured his work. But Mason's big break came when William Allen White recommended Mason's poems to George Matthew Adams, who had recently formed a newspaper syndicate. Adams took up White's suggestion and in 1909 began distributing Mason's poems to newspapers across the country. By 1919 Mason's poems reached an estimated 12 million readers through the pages of 200 daily newspapers.[19] Along with their newspaper run, Mason's best work was collected and published in volumes such as *Uncle Walt* (1910), *Business Prose-Poems* (1911), *Rippling Rhymes* (1913), *Horse Sense* (1915), *Walt Mason: His Book* (1916), and *Terse Verse* (1917).

The role of syndication in bringing Mason fame—and its connection with standardization and mass culture—seems at first glance to undercut any specific midwestern identity. Yet, as Charles Johanningsmeier has shown, newspaper syndication involved a complex process of negotiation. Adams and other independent syndicators operated more or less as middle men. They identified and located talented or famous writers, bought their work outright, and then attempted to sell it to as many newspapers in non-overlapping circulation areas as possible. In this scenario, local editors, rather than syndicators, held the position of power.[20]

Newspaper syndication was not new in the early twentieth century. Many famous fiction writers syndicated their work during the late nineteenth century, as did some poets, including Eleanor Wheeler Wilcox.[21] But the idea of having short poems written daily by a single author specifically for newspapers within a national syndication network did not truly take off until Adams brought Walt Mason to the public in 1909.[22] The feasibility of Adams's operation owed much to technological improvements in communication and transportation, improvements that ultimately extended the influence and reach of urban centers and severely curbed the self-sufficiency of small towns.[23] Yet, for Mason at least, these developments also had the effect of bringing his small-town voice to a national audience.

Far from a top-down imposition of culture, then, Mason's ascendance occurred because local newspaper editors believed that his writing would meet the demands of their readers. That Walt Mason proved so popular across the nation speaks to his ability to resonate with a wide audience. That he did this while maintaining a voice tied distinctly to the small-town Midwest speaks to the cultural power of that ideal during the early twentieth century.

Deemed by cultural observers as "the Kansas poet," Mason's identity in the 1910s—like that of William Allen White—was inseparable from his home base of Emporia. White in particular helped to cement this connection. In numerous columns and advertisements over the 1910s White reiterated Emporia's pride in Mason. "Here is a town he has made famous all over the world," White proclaimed in 1912. "It is a fearful 'case'—that between the town and Walt Mason—and long may it wave."[24] Emporia's role in Mason's rise to fame had special prominence for Prohibition supporters. Mason credited the small-town environment of Emporia—a "dry" town—with helping him beat his dependency on alcohol.[25] In a 1918 article for the general interest monthly *American Magazine*, White made a similar claim. He noted that Mason had struggled for his entire adult life with alcohol. But in Emporia Mason faced no temptations to drink. He could focus on his work and, as White put it, benefit from an entire town that "stood by and cheered him."[26] In White's telling, Mason's success exemplified the supposed virtues of small-town living.

Although Mason represented small-town midwestern values, for many observers at the time those values were not provincial. Rather, they were the essential American values. In the 1910s, many believed that the Middle West stood as the most American thing about America.[27] Thus Mason could earn praise for "quaintness" of style while simultaneously being lauded as a representative of the "common" man; he was heralded as the "high priest of horse sense," and the "poet laureate of American democracy."[28] Or, as White put it in 1918, "Walt Mason is the Homer of modern America, and particularly of Middle-Western America, the America of the country town."[29]

Even beyond the fact that Mason lived in Emporia, White had good reason to claim that Mason represented the country town. Mason's writings constantly evoked the small town world of such places as "Pumpkinville" and "Pruneville."[30] So, too, Mason often defended the opportunities that small-town life provided. But Mason did not drench his depictions in nostalgia. His small town was very much a part of the modern world, with automobiles roaming its streets, theaters playing the latest movies, and mail-order catalogues encroaching on the business of local shopkeepers.[31]

Mason's poetic treatment of baseball—one of his favorite subjects—is especially revealing of his basic philosophy. Although baseball's popularity encompassed city and small town, in "The Great Game," we can see the way that Mason privileged small-town life and community:

> The pitcher is pitching, the batsman is itching to punish the ball in the old-fashioned way; the umpire is umping, the fielders are humping—we're playing baseball in our village today! Two thousand mad creatures are perched on the bleachers, the grand stand is full and the fences the same, the old and the youthful, the false and the truthful, the plain and the lovely are watching the game.[32]

Another baseball poem, "Play Ball," highlights Mason's preference for practical action, or what Lewis Atherton called the "cult of the immediately useful and practical."[33] Mason describes a baseball scene in which players stand around arguing. Such talk is fruitless, Mason writes. Eventually one has to "get down to Old Brass Tacks and play ball."[34] This poem also reflects Mason's scorn for the "loafer." Mason consistently made such characters the target of his humor, preaching the old-time gospel of hard work as the cure for all ills.[35]

Mason's "just play ball" philosophy could render invisible the realities of class- and race-based hierarchies built into midwestern and American life. For example, in 1922 Mason eulogized famed baseball player and manager "Cap" Anson, urging readers to "keep his watchword, 'Play the game.'" Such a watchword was especially ironic, given that Anson helped lead the charge in the 1880s for racial segregation in professional baseball.³⁶ Just as Mason praised Anson's work ethic without recognizing Anson's support for a system that barred blacks from opportunities to work, many living in the small-town Midwest did not reflect on how their own communities were shaped by white supremacy.³⁷ In Mason's world and that of his readers, hard work, not pleas to address what white residents regarded as special grievances, offered the best approach to life's difficulties.

If work provided one answer to life's problems, another could be found through the consumption of popular culture. Mason praised baseball for offering respite from the chaos of the modern world. Take, for example, his poem "The Greatest Thing":

> ... The orator shrieks and clamors, and kicks up a lot of dust, and larrups and whacks and hammers the weary old sinful Trust; the congressman chirps and chatters, pursuing his dream of fame; but there's only one thing that matters, and that is the baseball game.³⁸

Mason's appreciation for baseball as a means of escape dovetailed with his antipathy towards highbrow culture. In a few poems Mason writes of putting on airs around "the cultured crowd." In their company he praises Thomas Hardy, Henry James, and other respected authors. But when the cultured crowd leaves, Mason sets aside the acclaimed authors and reaches instead for the latest detective novel, "however poor in diction, however punk in plot."³⁹

One final baseball poem worth examining is "The Umpire." Here, Mason urges an angry and raucous crowd to treat the baseball umpire with kindness, who, after all, is "doing the best he can."⁴⁰ "The Umpire" highlights Mason's knack for tweaking overzealous reformers.⁴¹ Mason's mindset and his politics were conservative—White described him as a "standpatter from Standpatville"—but he was usually not an activist conservative participating in a culture war.⁴² Although Mason supported Prohibition, he lampooned religious reformers who sought to build on Prohibition's success with anti-cigarette laws and blue laws prohibiting Sunday activities. And when evolution became a topic of debate in the mid-1920s, Mason (a Unitarian) expressed disinterest in the debate.⁴³ Faced with society's problems, more often than not Mason's response was to "sit and smoke and let things slide."⁴⁴ This conservative escapist style stood in contrast with that of midwestern progressives like William Allen White and William Jennings Bryan. Yet, even if Mason was no reformer, he articulated and represented the same small-town values that Bryan and White sought to preserve or promote through various reform efforts.[45]

Those small-town values, what historians Andrew R.L. Cayton and Peter S. Onuf have called the "ideology of the nineteenth-century middle class," formed much of the basis of Mason's moral world.[46] For Mason, the old virtues of honesty, industry, sobriety, good credit, and cheerfulness stood as one's best options for dealing with the complexities of modern life.[47] This understanding of life, built upon a nineteenth-century world of farmers and producers in "island communities," faced a credibility problem in the face of the increasingly industrialized and urbanized society of the early twentieth century.[48] Indeed, the disparity between the middle-class myths of the nineteenth century and the reality of life in the twentieth century provided much of the impetus for artistic expressions of disillusionment that emanated from the Midwest at the time. Yet, as Cayton and Onuf have noted, this dissonance did not eliminate the power of the old ideology; it could lead some to double-down, to "adher[e] to certain values without being sure of what they meant."[49] Through his syndicated newspaper poems Mason provided a way in which the nineteenth-century virtues of the small town could be experienced and given new meaning in the modern world.

The advertisements for Mason's poems are an especially useful way to understand this phenomenon. A 1909 promotional pamphlet created by George Matthew Adams, for example, explained that Mason's poems "may be taken as a tonic at almost any hour of the day," providing an "American atmosphere" in homes and hearts that could help "cure the blues" and "cleanse the head."[50] The medicinal suggestions are telling: faced with the ills of modern life, Mason's poems, containing a dose of the old-time virtues, offered readers temporary relief. Such a suggestion fit the long-time view, reformulated for an age of mass consumption, that poetry's value could be found primarily in terms of its practical effects on the reader.

By writing poems about small-town life and current events from his perch in Emporia, all filtered through a nineteenth-century middle-class moral lens, Mason provided a distinctive midwestern voice. At the same time, by meeting the desires of ordinary newspaper readers and by engaging so directly in the commercial world, Mason became perhaps the wealthiest poet of his day.[51] Although open entanglement with commercial culture was often viewed as a mark against a writer's artistic integrity and ability, in the 1910s some of America's leading literary critics—including William Dean Howells—did not seem to mind. Twice in 1912 Howells boosted the poetry of "that Kansas man" in his "Editor's Easy Chair" column for *Harper's Monthly*. Howells praised Mason's verse with its "baseball parlance, with the street corner and corner store of a small town, with that absolute village freedom of tongue which is dearer to you the farther you get from the small town in time and space." He also lauded Mason's "realistic study of country-town character and event."[52]

William Marion Reedy, editor of *Reedy's Mirror*, also lent his support to Mason. "[H]is work is not trivial, properly estimated," Reedy wrote. "It is important and it is none the less so for being irrefragably American in its strongly love-diluted cynicism."[53] Reedy's estimation of Mason is especially revealing because of Reedy's close connection with the more "legitimate" midwestern poets of the 1910s.[54] In 1914, for example, Reedy championed Edgar Lee Masters's work, printing the poems that became *Spoon River Anthology*.[55] Reedy also boosted pioneering midwestern realist Theodore Dreiser, author of *Sister Carrie* (1900)—as did Mason. In a 1913 letter to Dreiser, Mason praised his books for their "profound knowledge of human nature." Dreiser returned the warm feelings, remarking that Mason "has entertained me on many a dreary railway journey."[56]

That Howells, Reedy, and Dreiser, all proponents of literary realism, counted themselves as supportive readers of Mason has mystified later commentators. One of Howells's biographers felt compelled to apologize for his subject's "deplorable weakness" for Mason.[57] Yet, as Joan Shelley Rubin and Joseph Harrington have shown, the early twentieth century was a particularly fluid time for artistic tastes. One could be a realist and also enjoy optimistic light verse.[58] At the same time, there was a subtle realism in Mason's poetry that his critics often missed. Mason preached a general message of optimism but he did not ignore the harsh reality of life.

Perhaps the best way to illustrate this is to compare Mason with James Whitcomb Riley, a poet to whom he was often compared.[59] Riley, an Indiana poet, gained fame in the late nineteenth century for his dialect verse, earning wide popularity until his death in 1916.[60] Written in the vernacular of rural Indiana dwellers, Riley's poetry emphasized cheer and wholesomeness, sentimentalism and nostalgia.[61] Mason and Riley expressed mutual admiration for each other, and Mason was clearly influenced by the Hoosier poet.[62] But Mason's style, while in the tradition of Riley's popular verse, reflected a more modern sensibility. To be sure, Mason trafficked in sentimentalism, writing poems about the pleasures of traditional domestic life and the glory of the United States. But unlike Riley he did not often yearn for the idyllic village life of his youth. He lampooned old-timers who "rant and scold" about changes in modern society.[63] And, as we've seen above, Mason embraced modern consumer culture, peppering his poems with references to automobiles, movies, and dime novels. Riley represented the small-town Midwest of the nineteenth century; Mason exemplified its transition into the modern consumer-driven twentieth century.

But even if Mason was more up-to-date than Riley, he, too, fell out of favor at the same time that Riley's poetry was becoming passé among the literary elites. Modernist poetic forms, prizing more experimentation in style, increasingly gained traction in the 1910s. Thus, when H.L. Mencken linked Mason with Riley in 1919, it was not intended as a compliment. Mencken contrasted the "new poetry" of Vachel Linsday, Carl Sandburg, Amy Lowell, Edgar Lee Masters, and Ezra Pound with the popular poetry of Riley, Ella Wheeler Wilcox, and Mason. In Mencken's view the popular poetry was not really poetry at all; it found an audience only because it articulated the "simple, rubber-stamp ideas" of the unthinking masses.[64]

Mencken's dismissal of Mason's poetry was not entirely new. The blatant commercialization and light touch of Mason's verse had long rendered him suspect in the eyes of some critics. For example, a 1915 *Literary Digest* article on Mason noted that some viewed his work as "poetic chewingum." Throughout the 1910s Mason was sensitive to such criticism, defending his work by emphasizing what Joseph Harrington describes as the "practical function" of poetry.[65] Readers, Mason explained in 1914, wanted "clean and wholesome" poetry with "a jingle in it" that "treats the things and conditions they are familiar with." While literary-minded Americans might dismiss it, Mason argued that his poetry "is doing more good than all the highbrow stuff on the shelves."[66]

Of course, as the support from Howells and Reedy attests, Mason's base of support in the 1910s was not confined to a popular audience. But by the end of World War I it was increasingly difficult to find leading literary critics like Howells or Reedy—both of whom died in 1920—who treated Mason's work as legitimate poetry. Instead, critics followed Mencken's path in dismissing it entirely. In 1922 Harriet Monroe, editor of *Poetry,* described Mason's writing as "placid rhyming journalese."[67] In 1924 English professor Bruce Weirick expressed similar views, writing that Mason's "humdrum doggerel written as prose reveals daily to several million readers the shrewd but unpoetic Kansan."[68] These were the critical assessments informing the punchline when Sinclair Lewis had a character in *Arrowsmith* (1925) praise Chum Frink for "rank[ing] with Eddie Guest and Walt Mason as the greatest, as they certainly are the most popular, of all our poets."

By the 1920s, then, it was clear that Mason's poetry, like the image of the Midwest itself, had become associated in literary circles with banality and conformity. For his part, Mason struck back at critics of his poetry and of the Midwest. In a syndicated poem, for example, Mason blasted Lewis's *Main Street* as "twaddle for the twaddling mob."[69] Unlike William Allen White, Mason was unable to appreciate the ambivalence within Lewis's novels, viewing them as a wholesale attack on small-town life.[70]

But if Mason did not understand Lewis, so Lewis did not seem to understand Mason. Take, for example, a 1922 article written by Mason for *Hearst's International.* In the article Mason criticized *Main Street*–style books that would "have us believe that all country towns are alike." To counteract such notions Mason emphasized the uniqueness of Kansas's small towns. But even as Mason criticized Lewis, in his analysis Mason echoed the very critiques that Lewis made in *Main Street* and would make again in *Babbitt* (1922). Small towns, Mason lamented, were falling prey to the "live wires" of the "Chamber of Commerce" crowd. These groups clamored for growth and standardization; they were "the blighting influence which kill off originality in country towns, and strive to make ... so many Gopher Prairies."[71] Mason's criticism of "live wires," along with the gently cynical notes of his poetry, reveals the problem with classifying him as a bard of boosterism and pep, as Lewis did in the character of Chum Frink.

Despite the critics' barbs, Mason continued to churn out his daily poems to a wide newspaper readership until the eve of World War II. Although he moved to California for health reasons in 1920, his connection with the Midwest remained strong. After his death in

1939, the *New York Times* remembered him for his "farm philosophy of the Western prairies," while his old employer, the *Nebraska State Journal*, described him as "of the middlewest, reared and developed in the Missouri valley country."[72] As for the *Emporia Gazette*, they honored Mason's memory by running tributes to Mason on their editorial page for an entire month after his death.

It was fitting for Emporia's residents to claim Mason as their own, even though Mason spent the last twenty years of his life in California. It was in Emporia that Mason fully developed his distinctive style, and it was in Emporia that he penned his best-loved poems.[73] Although syndicated poets like Eddie Guest eclipsed Mason's star by the mid-1920s, in the 1910s no other poet reached as wide an audience as Mason. Fusing elements of literary realism with celebratory and sentimental popular poetic styles, Mason took the middle-class ideology of the nineteenth-century Midwest and repackaged it into new cultural forms fit for an age of mass consumption. The fact that he so firmly represented the small-town Midwest while standing preeminent among the popular poets of the 1910s speaks to the primacy of the Midwest not only in the early twentieth-century development of "legitimate" American literature, but also within the realm of popular culture. Mason may have been an easy target for Sinclair Lewis's satire, but scholars who seek to get a full sense of the midwestern literary landscape and its place within American culture in the early twentieth century should take a closer look at Mason and his fellow real-life Chum Frinks.[74]

## Notes

1. James M. Hutchisson, *The Rise of Sinclair Lewis, 1920–1930* (University Park, PA: Pennsylvania State University Press, 1996), 51–53.
2. Hutchisson, *The Rise of Sinclair Lewis*, 51.
3. Richard R. Lingeman, *Sinclair Lewis: Rebel from Main Street* (St. Paul, MN: Borealis Books, 2002), 176.
4. Joan Shelley Rubin discusses Eddie Guest in *Songs of Ourselves: The Uses of Poetry in America* (Cambridge, MA: Harvard University Press, 2007), 66–74. The best source on Bruce Barton is Richard M. Fried's *The Man Everybody Knew: Bruce Barton and the Making of Modern America* (Chicago: Ivan R. Dee, 2005). On Frank Crane, see Paul Emory Putz, "From the Pulpit to the Press: Frank Crane's Omaha, 1892–1896." *Nebraska History* 96.3 (Fall 2015): 136–53. Harrington discusses Mason in *Poetry and the Public: The Social Form of Modern U.S. Poetics* (Middletown, CT: Wesleyan University Press, 2002). Harrington has also written the best single biographical source

on Mason. See "Walt Mason," *American National Biography Online* (Oxford University Press) http://www.anb.org/articles/16/16-01067.html.
5. Harrington, *Poetry and the Public*, 21–55. Two other books that recover nonmodernist poetry are Cary Nelson's *Repression and Recovery: Modern American Poetry and the Politics of Cultural Recovery* (Madison: University of Wisconsin Press, 1989) and Lisa Szefel's *The Gospel of Beauty in the Progressive Era: Reforming American Verse and Values* (New York: Palgrave Macmillan, 2011). Both focus on poetry written by ethnic and racial minorities and by politically progressive poets, categories into which the white, male, and stand-pat Republican Mason does not fit.
6. See, for example, Ronald Weber's dismissal of Indiana writers like James Whitcomb Riley in *The Midwestern Ascendency in American Writing* (Bloomington: Indiana University Press, 1992), 15–16, 59–53.
7. On the need to extend beyond the one-sided "revolt" interpretation of midwestern literature, see Jon K. Lauck, "The Myth of the Midwestern 'Revolt from the Village,'" *MidAmerica* XL (2013): 39–85.
8. Unless otherwise noted, biographical details are drawn from the files on Walt Mason located within the William Allen White Collection, Kansas Collection, RH MS 929, Kenneth Spencer Research Library, University of Kansas Libraries, and from Harrington's entry for Walt Mason in *American National Biography Online*.
9. Weber, *The Midwestern Ascendency in American Writing*, 11; Anthony Channell Hilfer, *The Revolt from the Village, 1915–1930* (Chapel Hill: University of North Carolina Press, 1969), 37–39.
10. E.W. Howe, *Plain People* (New York: Dodd, Mead & Company, 1929), 233–34.
11. Patricia C. Gaster, "Pen Pictures and Prose Poems: Walt Mason in Nebraska," *Nebraska History* 96.4 (Winter 2015): 180–87.
12. Sally Foreman Griffith, *Home Town News: William Allen White and the Emporia Gazette* (New York: Oxford University Press, 1989), 50.
13. Griffith, *Home Town News*, 29, 140, 151; John DeWitt McKee, *William Allen White: Maverick on Main Street* (Westport, CN: Greenwood Press, 1975), 43. White's biographers view him as a predecessor to the more critical writing on small-town midwestern life by Edgar Lee Masters, Sherwood Anderson, and Sinclair Lewis.
14. Griffith, *Home Town News*, 77.
15. "Fair Weather Sunday," *Emporia Gazette*, October 26, 1907, 1.
16. *Emporia Gazette*, December 2, 1907, 2.
17. "Little Green Tents," *Emporia Gazette*, May 30, 1908, 1.
18. *Emporia Gazette*, November 9, 1908, 5. On the practice of clipping poetry, see Mike Chasar's *Everyday Reading: Poetry and Popular Culture in Modern America* (Columbia University Press, 2012), 52.
19. Mason, "Are You a Misfit?" *American Magazine* (April 1919), 27.
20. Charles Johanningsmeier, *Fiction and the American Literary Marketplace: The Role of Newspaper Syndicates, 1860–1900* (Cambridge: Cambridge

University Press, 1997), 48–88, 180–82. Although focused on fiction, Johanningsmeier's book is the best historical account of the development of newspaper syndication.
21. Elmso Scott Watson, *A History of Newspaper Syndicates in the United States, 1865–1935* (Chicago: 1936), 55.
22. Ibid., 58–59.
23. Richard O. Davies, *Main Street Blues: The Decline of Small-Town America* (Columbus, OH: Ohio State University Press, 1998), 80–88.
24. *Emporia Weekly Gazette*, May 30, 1912, 1.
25. Mason, "A Town with a Lid," *Collier's*, June 27, 1914, 16.
26. William Allen White, "What Happened to Walt Mason," *American Magazine* (September 1918): 19.
27. James R. Shortridge, *The Middle West: Its Meaning in American Culture* (Lawrence: University Press of Kansas, 1989), 33–34.
28. *Emporia Gazette*, April 17, 1912, 2. These descriptions of Mason can be found in the front matter to his various books: *Uncle Walt* (Chicago: George Matthew Adams, 1910); *Business Prose-Poems* (Chicago: George Matthew Adams, 1911); *Rippling Rhymes* (Chicago: A.C. McClurg & Co, 1913); *Horse Sense in Verses Tense* (Chicago: A.C. McClurg & Co., 1915); *His Book* (New York: Barse & Hopkins, 1916); and *Terse Verse* (Chicago: A.C. McClurg & Co., 1917).
29. White, "What Happened to Walt Mason," 19.
30. Mason, "Confidential," *Emporia Gazette*, December 5, 1912, 1; "Justitia," *Judge*, October 17, 1914; "Too Many Churches," *Emporia Gazette*, November 23, 1915, 1; "Wider Fields," in *Terse Verse*, 24; "The Home Town," *Emporia Gazette*, October 2, 1925, 4.
31. See, for example, Mason, "Your Own Town," in *His Book*, 53; "Town and Country," in *Terse Verse*, 36; "Hollywood," *Emporia Gazette*, April 10, 1922, 2; "Mail Order Clothes," in *Uncle Walt*, 169; "The Danger Car" in *Terse Verse*, 22; "Back to the Farm," in *Business Prose-Poems*, 135.
32. Mason, "The Great Game," in *Horse Sense*, 17–18.
33. Lewis Atherton, *Main Street on the Middle Border* (Bloomington: Indiana University Press, 1954), 111–21. On midwestern utilitarianism see also William Barillas, *The Midwestern Pastoral: Place and Landscape in the Literature of the American Heartland* (Athens, OH: Ohio University Press, 2006), 33–37.
34. Mason, "Play Ball," in *Rippling Rhymes*, 38.
35. On the prevalence of this gospel of hard work elsewhere in the Midwest, see Jon K. Lauck, *Prairie Republic: The Political Culture of Dakota Territory, 1879–1889* (Norman: University of Oklahoma Press, 2010), 39–40.
36. Mason, "Pop Anson," *Emporia Gazette*, May 22, 1922, 2. On Anson's support for segregation, see Steven A. Riess, *Touching Base: Professional Baseball and American Culture in the Progressive Era* (Urbana: University of Illinois Press, 1999), 195.

37. On the use of racist violence in the nineteenth century to ensure that Kansas's small towns stayed dominated by whites, see Brent M.S. Campney, *This Is Not Dixie: Racist Violence in Kansas, 1861–1927* (Urbana: University of Illinois Press, 2015), 141–42.
38. Mason, "The Greatest Thing," in *Rippling Rhymes*, 61–62.
39. Mason, "Literature," in *Horse Sense in Verses Tense*, 142; "Theory and Practice," in *Rippling Rhymes*, 96–97. On "highbrow" and "lowbrow," see Lawrence W. Levine, *Highbrow/Lowbrow: The Emergence of Cultural Hierarchy in America* (Cambridge, MA: Harvard University Press, 1988).
40. Mason, "The Umpire," in *Rippling Rhymes*, 63–65.
41. Mason, "Some Protests," in *Rippling Rhymes*, 69–70.
42. *Emporia Gazette*, October 7, 1912, 2.
43. Mason, "The Great Issue," *Des Moines Register*, July 6, 1923, 7; William E. Connelly, *A Standard History of Kansas and Kansans* Vol. III (Chicago: Lewis Publishing Company, 1919), 1368.
44. Mason, "Waste of Effort," *Judge*, June 12, 1920, 9.
45. Griffith, *Home Town News*, 142–46.
46. Andrew R.L. Cayton and Peter S. Onuf, *The Midwest and the Nation: Rethinking the History of an American Region* (Bloomington: Indiana University Press, 1990), 122.
47. See, for example, Mason, "The Old Virtues," in *His Book*, 49.
48. Cayton and Onuf, *The Midwest and the Nation*, 116–19. The well-worn "island communities" is taken from Robert Wiebe's *The Search for Order, 1877–1920* (New York: Hill & Wang, 1967).
49. Cayton and Onuf, *The Midwest and the Nation*, 117.
50. Pamphlet located in Box 2, Folder 26, William Allen White Collection, Kansas Collection, RH MS 929, Kenneth Spencer Research Library, University of Kansas Libraries.
51. "A Kansas Poet's Income," *Literary Digest*, February 14, 1914, 339–43; "News Notes," *Poetry: A Magazine of Verse* (August 1939), 292.
52. William Dean Howells: "Editor's Easy Chair," *Harper's Monthly Magazine* (June 1912): 148–51; "Editor's Easy Chair," *Harpers Monthly Magazine* (July 1912): 310–13.
53. William Marion Reedy, "Overture," in *Terse Verse*.
54. The three "canonized" midwestern poets from the 1910s are Edgar Lee Masters, Vachel Lindsay, and Carl Sandburg. See, for example, Alan Shucard, Fred Moramarco, and William Sullivan, *Modern American Poetry, 1865–1950* (Boston: Twayne Publishers, 1989), 50–54
55. Herbert K. Russell, *Edgar Lee Masters: A Biography* (Urbana: University of Illinois Press, 2001), 67–76; Weber, *The Midwestern Ascendency in American Writing*, 99.
56. Walt Mason to Theodore Dreiser, 11 February 1913, Box 72, Folder 4006, Theodore Dreiser Papers, Department of Special Collections, the

University of Pennsylvania. Dreiser's comment is printed in the preface to *Rippling Rhymes*.
57. Edwin H. Cady, *The Realist at War: The Mature Years of William Dean Howells, 1885–1920* (Syracuse: Syracuse University Press, 1956), 239. See also Edward Wagenknecht, *William Dean Howells: The Friendly Eye* (New York: Oxford University Press, 1969), 27.
58. Rubin, *Songs of Ourselves*, 74; Harrington, *Poetry and the Public*, 144.
59. Irving S. Cobb, William Dean Howells, and William Allen White all compared Mason to Riley. See, for example, *Emporia Weekly Gazette*, May 30, 1912, 1; William Dean Howells, "Editor's Easy Chair," *Harper's Monthly Magazine* (February 1917): 442–45.
60. John E. Miller, "The Funeral of Beloved Hoosier Poet, James Whitcomb Riley," *Studies in Midwestern History* 2.6 (July 2016): 70–78.
61. Szefel, *The Gospel of Beauty in the Progressive Era*, 63–66; Elizabeth J. Van Allen, *James Whitcomb Riley: A Life* (Bloomington: Indiana University Press, 1999).
62. Mason, "The Poet Balks," in *Uncle Walt*, 134; "Riley's Birthday," *Emporia Gazette*, October 7, 1915. In the preface to *Rippling Rhymes*, Riley describes Mason's poetry as "facetious, capricious [and] delicious."
63. Mason, "The World of Knockers," *Judge*, July 8, 1922, 12. See also "Farm Life," in *Terse Verse*, 135; "Good Old Days," in *Horse Sense*, 182–83.
64. H.L. Mencken, *Prejudices: First Series* (New York: Alfred A. Knopf, 1919), 92–96.
65. Harrington, *Poetry and the Public*, 31–34.
66. "A Kansas Poet's Income," 339–43.
67. "Newspaper Verse," *Poetry: A Magazine of Verse*, March 1922, 327.
68. Bruce Weirick, *From Whitman to Sandburg in American Poetry* (New York: Macmillan, 1924), 55.
69. Mason, "Main Street," *Emporia Gazette*, June 15, 1921, 2.
70. William Allen White to Sinclair Lewis, 23 November 1920, in Walter Johnson, ed., *Selected Letters of William Allen White, 1899–1943* (New York: Henry Holt and Company, 1947), 210–12.
71. Mason, "If I Owned Hay Center," *Hearst's International*, January 1922, 51–52.
72. "Walt Mason," *Emporia Gazette*, July 5, 1939, 4; "More or Less Personal," *Nebraska State Journal*, June 23, 1939, 12.
73. These poems are listed in "Walt Mason Dies in California," *Emporia Gazette*, June 22, 1939, 1. All the anthologies of Mason's poems were published during Mason's Emporia years from 1909 to 1920.
74. Along with the individuals Lewis cited as inspiration for Chum Frink—Mason, Bruce Barton, Frank Crane, and Eddie Guest—other early twentieth-century syndicated newspaper writers from the Midwest who deserve further study include George Ade and George Matthew Adams. Jay "Ding" Darling, a nationally syndicated cartoonist based in Des Moines, would be a worthy subject of study as well.

John E. Hallwas | Village Realism but
No Revolt

Frazier Hunt's
*Sycamore Bend*

The most famous literary works about small-town life in the Midwest are Edgar Lee Masters's celebrated *Spoon River Anthology* (1915, 1916), Sherwood Anderson's acclaimed *Winesburg, Ohio* (1919), and Sinclair Lewis's phenomenal bestseller *Main Street* (1920). All three depict problematic local individuals, who are often alienated, commonly frustrated, and frequently damaged (or made insensitive to others) by their town's provinciality, conventional values, and repressive social environment. These works epitomized the so-called "revolt from the village" among midwestern writers of the early twentieth century. Of course, that development in literary realism countered the previous idealization of the American small town.

Commentary on the supposed "revolt" and on small-town life as depicted by those writers has been fairly extensive. The most thorough discussion of these and similar literary works—by midwestern writers and others—is Anthony Channel Hilfer's *The Revolt from the Village 1915–1930* (1969). He correctly views those realistic depictions of small towns as having greater complexity and psychological insight than such earlier idealizations as Booth Tarkington's *The Gentleman from Indiana* (1900) and Zona Gale's *Friendship Village* (1908).[1]

Another significant discussion is John T. Flanagan's article "Literary Protest in the Midwest" (1949).[2] For example, he briefly summarizes the negative portrayal of small communities during the revolt: "By the early 1920s, when what Carl Van Doren called [in 1921] the revolt from the village was in full swing, the Midwest small town had been recorded as an ugly, gossip-ridden, materialistic, hypocritical, prurient, stolid community."[3] Recently, historian Jon Lauck has written an article, "The Myth of the Midwestern 'Revolt from the Village'" (2013), that appeals for a more balanced understanding of the small-town views of leading writers like Masters, Anderson, and Lewis, and also argues that "the 'village revolt' interpretation is simplistic and flawed, and its institutionalization within the annals of history clouds our vision of the midwestern past."[4]

If readers only know the small-town Midwest from certain famous works by Masters, Anderson, and Lewis, as well as some notable fiction by Hamlin Garland, E.W. Howe, and Mark Twain, their view may be distorted indeed. However, none of the above-mentioned commentators refers to a novel that appeared during the "revolt from the village" era (1915–1930) and directly challenged the negative portrayals of small-town midwestern life that were receiving so much attention. Frazier Hunt's forgotten *Sycamore Bend: Population 1300* (1925), although not a great literary achievement, effectively portrays some troubled small-town individuals who live in a socially responsive and personally meaningful cultural environment, and it centers on a newspaperman whose experience epitomizes the conflict—rampant in our own time—between the struggle for self-realization and the need for belonging in a community. The realistic novel has a distinctive style, too, which blends a developing plot with local reporting.

Hunt (1885–1967) was born in Rock Island, Illinois, to parents who had met and married in nearby Aledo.[5] Because his mother died soon after he was born, he and his brother were raised by an aunt and uncle, first in rural Missouri for five years and then in North Manchester, Indiana, where Hunt graduated from high school in 1903. He spent a year at a military academy before attending the University of Illinois (1904–1908), and afterward he worked for two years in Chicago as an advertising writer for a newspaper, and then lived for most of three years in Mexico. Of direct importance for his later novel, Hunt then became the editor of the *Alexis Argus* (1912–1916), which his father bought for him. That small town in western Illinois was on the border of Mercer and Warren counties, near Aledo, where the widowed aunt who had raised him then resided. As he later said in his autobiography, *One American and His Attempt at Education* (1938), his years as a small-town newspaperman were "the last of the horse-and-buggy days," before changes came along that started "the long and slow process of killing off small towns."[6]

Of course, that period was also marked by the first noted work in "the revolt from the village" movement, Masters's *Spoon River Anthology*, which appeared in 1915 and then was issued in a more complete version (identical to all later editions) in 1916. That stunning volume of poetic monologues was inspired by the poet's experience at Lewistown, in Fulton County—which borders on Warren County, to the northwest, where Alexis is located. Hunt, who was already writing and submitting short stories for publication, was surely aware of that much-discussed poetic depiction of midwestern small-town life set in the nearby Spoon River country.

Hunt got along well in Alexis, but his own ambitions and the advice of friends eventually prompted him to sell the *Argus* and move with his wife and pre-school son to New York City. There he worked as a reporter for the *New York Sun*. Hunt eventually became a famous American journalist, a foreign correspondent who traveled the world, reported on various issues and conflicts, and interviewed people like Ghandi, Hitler, Lenin, and Pancho Villa. He wrote fourteen nonfictional books, including biographies of Billy the Kid, George Armstrong Custer, and General Douglas MacArthur.[7]

But early in his career as a foreign correspondent, during the 1920s, while living for five years in London, Hunt became the close friend of Sinclair Lewis. Despite their friendship, Hunt nevertheless viewed Lewis as self-centered and often intolerant of others.[8] Of course, they had in common their midwestern small-town boyhoods, but those experiences were different. As Hunt later said in his autobiography, "When Lewis started to write *Main Street*, the fictional town he saw and hated was the real town [Sauk Center, Minnesota] of his own unhappy youth"—and such a boyhood "had been the exact opposite of my own full and satisfying one."[9] That was surely an important reason why Hunt wrote *Sycamore Bend* (his only novel)—to shed some positive, and more accurate, light on small-town life in the Midwest. Published by Harcourt Brace, the novel appeared in September 1925, and it directly reflected not his boyhood in North Manchester but his years as a country editor in Alexis.

Set in 1922, the novel centers on a small-town newspaper editor named Will Hadley, who owns the *Sycamore Bend Sentinel*. Although doing well, and a leader in his small-town world, he yearns to escape to a big city, like Chicago or New York, where he might better realize his talent "and end up a real writing man."[10] As he says to a local youth who asks him for career advice, the "little towns are only for second-raters—the left-overs—the people who didn't have enough ambition to move out of their tracks" (4). Although he is a lifelong resident, Will wants to leave town before his approaching fortieth birthday, but his wife, Madge, calls that plan "foolishness" (23). Afraid that he might fail in the big city and be economically ruined, she also can't imagine leaving Sycamore Bend:

> "We're happy here, Will. This is where we belong. We've lived all our lives here. We're part of the town. We've a car and a home here, and friends and family. What more could you want?"
> 
> Will bit his lip. "I want my own chance," he whispered. (22)

The novel's central issue is conveyed in their conflict—between the deep need for self-realization and the equally powerful need to remain in a familiar place, filled with personal connections, and have a sense of belonging.

Will is soon attracted to Jean Simpson, the lovely wife of a local store owner, who also feels frustrated by small-town life. Appreciative of his writing, she encourages him to follow his heart and leave Sycamore Bend. The reader soon realizes that Will is inwardly conflicted, too, for he cares about, and relates to, local residents, yet feels trapped, as he tells the sympathetic new woman in his life:

> "There's plenty of nice people here—and kindness and gentleness and affection. Everybody in the town is sort of like a relative to me. And I'd do almost anything for any of them. But they've got me shut in a cage—and I want to get out. I want to try my wings." (99)

Will has developed a two-sided perception of Sycamore Bend, and as he heads into middle age the negative aspects of his situation are coming to the forefront. While he chronicles the doings of the townspeople for his next issue, he is so caught up with recording it all that he does not reflect on the larger concern of what those matters reveal about life itself or the nature of people. The narrator comments on what is being overlooked: "Will dreamed of some great life in the outside world, yet here in his little corn-belt village there came unknowingly into his hands all the wonder of life—all the mystery of life—all the beauty and cruelty" (72).

The extra-marital love relationship slowly deepens, as Will's marriage to Madge becomes more troubled over the leaving-or-staying debate, and he associates Jean with his hopes for self-fulfillment in the city and considers running away with her. Although they express their love, Will cannot go through with their planned escape. Partly to avoid hurting his family with an affair, and partly to insist on fulfilling his dream, Will eventually sells his newspaper and takes his wife and son to New York. His lover ultimately maintains a decent set of values, too, and while she asserts that he has been "the very best thing" in her life, she also wants to avoid doing something that's "wrong—and cheap" (258).

Will is initially excited about being in New York, viewing Madge and himself as "pioneers" creating a new life, "emigrants from America to New York"—reversing the traditional, much-celebrated American experience of going west to find "a home for ourselves" (261). The new challenge pulls them back together. But he struggles to find a job and he ends up having to work a nighttime newspaper copy-desk shift— from 7:00 p.m. to 2:30 a.m. After well over two years in that impersonal environment, with no sign of some larger success, he develops a negative view of New York: "He saw it for what it really was—a cruel, muddling beehive of millions of tired, discouraged human beings, pulled in from all the corners of the world by the lure and promise of success and adventure; a trap ... a squirrel cage with an endless, purposeless turning wheel" (283). As that experience-based view indicates, *Sycamore Bend* proclaims that individuals can feel trapped in cities, too—which midwestern writers such as James T. Farrell, Richard Wright, and Willard Motley would soon reveal in their famous, Chicago-based naturalistic novels.

Will realizes that "I belong back there [in Sycamore Bend]," as he says to a friend (284). But ironically, Madge has meanwhile adjusted well to the city—and has "found a newer, broader life here"—so she doesn't want to leave (286). In that way, Hunt avoids a simplistic condemnation of the impersonal city, in contrast to socially connected small-town life. The novel clearly asserts that some people can indeed find a meaningful place for themselves in a big city—but not everyone. Feeling appropriately placed is a result of interaction between someone's complex selfhood and his or her cultural-social environment. Because Will is so desperate to return home to Sycamore Bend, however, Madge agrees to leave New York. Once they are settled in their old home town, Will manages to buy back his weekly newspaper. The novel closes as he is welcomed back by old friends and joins them in playing horseshoes, a game which he realizes is "slow and friendly and intimate, like the town itself" (67).

Dramatizing the New York misadventure in the life of newspaperman Will Hadley is only one focus of the novel. The other is Hunt's depiction of small-town people and their struggles. Most of the novel reflects the very personal world of Sycamore Bend, where—unlike the situation in city culture—townspeople are very aware of each other's stories. Among the many individuals that Will knows about, for example, is Link Peters, a disadvantaged, inwardly troubled, overly talkative man that everyone tolerates and some people have tried to help:

> Link, slender, cadaverous, eternally talking and never saying anything worth listening to, was satellite ... and general assistant and hanger-on to the horse doctor. When he was three years old, Link's mother had died of consumption, and the boy had been brought up after a fashion by his father. The two had lived together in a shanty by the river, grubbing out an existence by trapping, gardening, and wood-chopping, with a little horse-trading thrown in on the side. When his father died some fifteen years ago, Link, then seventeen, had wandered into the Bend and allied himself with the Kemple Livery Stable. Ten years later, when the Fords [i.e., cars] had driven Dick Kemple out of business and forced him to sell the old stable to Doc Butterbaugh, Link, like a pre-war slave, was sold with the plantation. He continued sleeping in the tiny back room of the stuffy, horsy, livery-stable office that Doc now used as the headquarters for his veterinary practice. Unappointed, he became Doc's office manager, car washer, stable boy, and social and business secretary. (10–11)

Link has been impacted by forces beyond his control, and with psychological problems that prevent him from having a normal life, he seems like a character in *Winesburg, Ohio*.

Another troubled small-town figure is Nell Morrison, whose mother died when she was fourteen, and who had to end her schooling in order to keep house for "her father and a lazy lout of an older brother" (78). Poor and lonely, she is seduced by a local jeweler, becomes pregnant, and is then abandoned by him. After she faces disgrace and the baby dies at birth, she commits suicide. Will writes a sympathetic obituary, saying, "She had found life cruel and difficult, and she had chosen her own way of solving it," which he even suggests might be viewed as "a brave and beautiful way" (88–89). In fact, Will realizes, from her case and others, that lives are shaped by unchosen forces—"with something called Luck, or Fate, or Destiny blindly and thoughtlessly pulling strings that have made men dance all their lives to wrong tunes and with wrong partners" (75).

Yet another struggling individual, of the many who are reported about in the novel, is old Mrs. Lindberg, a Swedish immigrant whose lazy, difficult husband finally dies, after she spent years struggling to support them both:

> For almost ten years the little Swede woman had earned the family living from the sale of her early vegetables and tomato and cabbage plants and chickens. She had labored day and night, trying her best to keep her self-respect and full independence. His bad health and failing mind had doubled her tasks. (182)

The entire town is sensitive to her long struggle, so people pitch in to help with the funeral—including Will, who agrees to serve as one of the pallbearers. People also join the procession to the local cemetery, whether they knew her personally or not, and even the stores close down during the funeral event, to show their sympathetic regard for her.

As Will persists in dreaming of escape from Sycamore Bend, to achieve self-realization as a writer in the city, he nevertheless continues his work as a chronicler of the town's "long voyage across time," with all sorts of local commentaries (71). And the narrator reflects on the significance of his role, as "the [Alexis] country paper, with its fifteen hundred circulation, [remained] a dear and priceless record of humanity to its readers" (72). As that suggests, there is a connection between the two components of the novel—the frustration and yearning for fulfillment of

Will Hadley and the nature of the small community in which he already functions. He is, after all, the chronicler of, the chief sympathizer with, and the spokesman for the community, who helps to hold it together. But he fails to see the significance of that role, especially for his own self-fulfillment, until after his disappointing struggle in New York.

As this commentary reveals, *Sycamore Bend* is hardly a shallow idealization of small-town culture, filled as it is with flawed and struggling people, as well as a central character who is unsatisfied—and unaware, for most of the story, that his true literary purpose, and social impact, involves seeing into those local lives. Nor is it a "revolt from the village" novel that portrays midwestern small-town culture as an often-insensitive place, filled with shallow, selfish people. Coming just five years after *Main Street*, Hunt's realistic novel finds a middle ground.

The main reason for its effective fidelity to real life in a midwestern village, and avoidance of a negative depiction, is that *Sycamore Bend* is based directly on the author's well-informed and largely positive experience as a small-town newspaperman, which nevertheless ended forever when he sold out and moved to New York to continue his writing career. Hunt himself is clearly the basis for Will Hadley. In fact, during his Alexis days, he was in his late thirties and was married and had one son—just like his main character.

Moreover, the author's autobiography also reveals many connections between his own experience and Will Hadley's. Although he was not a native of Alexis, Hunt's mother's family was from Mercer County, so he was quickly "accepted ... as one of them," and he developed many friends.[11] While in Alexis, he wrote a column on local life called "Main Street Waftings," which inspired the "Alley Waftings" column that Will writes.[12] Also, some of the episodes involving colorful townspeople in *Sycamore Bend,* such as an old colonel who accidentally sets off all the Fourth of July fireworks at once, and a woman who complains about Will's article on her drunk husband, and another local lady who wants her travel letters from the Holy Land published, and the poor, hard-working Swedish woman (mentioned above) whose difficult husband dies, are all based on real people and events from Hunt's days as a newspaperman in Alexis.[13] Some friends that Will often interacts with in Sycamore Bend are based on friends that Hunt had in Alexis as well—including Doc Butterbaugh, who was derived from Doc Windbigler, "an immense, dog-loving, trapshooting, roaring village sport," and Baldy Hobson, the printshop foreman, who eventually advises Will to leave town, and who was based on Hunt's typesetter and shop foreman, named Baldy as well.[14]

No wonder the 1925 editor of the *Alexis Argus*, who had succeeded Hunt, said in a page-one review of the novel, "All [locals] who read the book will see that he might as well have named it *Alexis*, and that some of his characters bear a striking resemblance to certain flesh and blood Alexians."[15] Unfortunately, the 1912–1916 issues of the *Alexis Argus* do not survive, for there were surely various other townspeople and activities in Hunt's local writings that later inspired components of *Sycamore Bend*.

After referring, in his autobiography, to a couple dozen people he knew well back in Alexis, Hunt also attempts to explain why his novel has a different, less critical view of the midwestern small town than writings by others: "These [townspeople] and more were to give my Alexis days a flavor and meaning that many observers of small-town life have completely missed," for so many of those other writers "discover only what they are looking for—failure, bitterness, inadequacy, repression—all of which are largely their own."[16] In other words, since Masters, Anderson, Lewis, and other writers had a difficult time, in some respects, during their early years in the small towns where they lived, they would naturally project their own issues (conflicts, resentments, lack of appreciation) onto the villagers they created from that experience. While that is perhaps an oversimplification—for talented writers sense psychological problems in people that others miss—there is a relationship between the quality of any writer's social interaction and his or her depiction of that same cultural environment in whatever kind of writing. And Hunt's social experiences were deep, positive, and meaningful.

Related to this point, Hunt also refers to the significance of his role, and Will Hadley's fictional role, as a small-town newspaper editor:

> Only a doctor and a preacher fit as closely and enduringly into the pattern of small-town life as does a country editor. His little weekly can mean a great deal to his community. It can reflect its true mood and be an articulate part of its being.[17]

Because Hunt was so committed to what we might call the spiritual impact of a small-town newspaper on its readership, he devotes much of his novel to Will Hadley's work, which derives from meaningful social awareness, for the townspeople are there for him to comprehend, appreciate, and depict through his articles and his "Alley Waftings." And because Will's work had been Hunt's work back in Alexis, *Sycamore Bend* is a kind of fictionalized memoir—except that his main character returns to the village.

The author's dual focus—on both a journalist-writer's struggle for self-realization, in a story that takes him into a temporary love affair and then on to New York, and a country editor's role, as the sensitive reflector of his small community—was a new approach. It combined a developing plot with reportorial writing from Hunt's experience. And that resulted in mixed reviews. An anonymous reviewer in the *New York Times Book Review*, for example, asserted that "*Sycamore Bend* stands out as a thoroughly homely and agreeable little tale," with "a theme of strong, elemental appeal," and he even praised all the community detail, which "suits rather than detracts" from the novel.[18] The reviewer saw the purpose for all the small-town reportorial material, which doesn't advance the plot but illuminates the world of Will Hadley and eventually helps us realize why he wants to return to Sycamore Bend. Ultimately, the frustrated newspaperman realizes what the experience of his small-town past, in a commonplace but thoroughly known world, means to him. In contrast, the reviewer for *The New Republic*, while recognizing that "Mr. Hunt has willfully reversed the usual formula ... to lift from the small town the curse laid upon it by so many of its former children, so happily exiled," finds the depiction of small-town people that Will Hadley interacts with to be ineffective:

> Mr. Hunt has something that he is burning to say: that the small town is, after all, full of all kinds of people, all different, worth knowing, worth telling about. Unfortunately, his zeal outruns his pen, and his people, buried under their creator's too manifest good-will, are ... not particularly alive or interesting.[19]

As this reveals, the strong nonfictional aspect of *Sycamore Bend* bothered some reviewers. Hunt was, after all, trying to be truthful about his own experience, but mentioning troubled or colorful townspeople, whose issues aren't being fully dramatized or resolved, yet who surround the main character, was not in sync with the fictional purpose of drawing readers deeply into complex lives. But one reviewer, H. Walker, who did praise that very aspect of the book in the *International Book Review*, asserted that "the real hero of the thing, the real center of interest, is not the man but the country newspaper itself," and "Mr. Hunt manages to make that a curiously living entity in well-nigh unique fashion."[20] As this comment suggests, Walker saw it as essentially a reflection of small-town life, through a perceptive and sympathetic, if anxiety-ridden, country editor. Had Hunt simply written a memoir of his years in Alexis, the expectations of some other reviewers, and their responses, would have been different—and more in agreement with Walker's appreciation for the expression of small-town culture as related to, and viewed through, a weekly newspaper.

In any case, for those of us who now look back at the Midwestern Moment, when small-town life in the region was receiving broad and penetrating literary attention for the first time, Frazier Hunt's long-overlooked novel deserves thoughtful attention. If nothing else, the conflict between striving for individual self-realization and belonging in a deeply placed community is more evident in the twenty-first century than it was a hundred years ago, when the "revolt from the village" was getting into high gear with the frustrated figures Masters presented in *Spoon River Anthology*, and when Frazier Hunt in the same Illinois area was realizing meaningful social connection and inner growth through a role that would soon inspire *Sycamore Bend*. It is interesting, in fact, that Masters portrays a country editor in the *Anthology* as perhaps the worst person in Spoon River, for Editor Whedon admits from the grave that he would not only often "pervert truth" for his own purposes but would "use great feelings and passions of the human family / For base designs, for cunning ends."[21] It is tempting to reflect that Hunt's novel may have been partly motivated by his desire to counter that extremely negative portrait of the very role that he then filled in an adjoining county.

Aside from the issue of literary quality, in which the famous poetry volume is admittedly superior, we might also acknowledge from our twenty-first century cultural perspective that it was to be expected that Masters's small-town world of outspoken, conflict-ridden, isolated, and largely dissatisfied individuals would become the most widely read (and performed) American poetry volume of the past century, while Hunt's fictional village of appreciative and socially connected, if often struggling, townsfolk would be forgotten.²² Masters anticipated the coming decline of American community, which has been discussed in our time by many scholars.²³ And Hunt has been largely forgotten as well. After all, he was once a nationally known figure, who made a kind of ultimate departure from the Midwest to live in famous cities and report from many countries, and who wrote fifteen books, some of which were widely and positively reviewed, but when the *Dictionary of Midwestern Literature* appeared in 2001, he was not even mentioned.

## Notes

1. Anthony Channel Hilfer, "The Revolt: What It Was About," *The Revolt from the Village 1915–1930* (Chapel Hill: University of North Carolina Press, 1969), 3–34. The rest of his book expands on his opening commentary, focusing largely on midwestern writers but also dealing with such other significant figures as H.L. Mencken and Thomas Wolfe.
2. John T. Flanagan, "Literary Protest in the Midwest," *Southwest Review*, vol. 34, no. 2 (Spring 1949), 148–57.
3. Flanagan, 155.
4. Jon K. Lauck, "The Myth of the Midwestern 'Revolt from the Village,'" *MidAmerica XL* (2013), 39–85. Lauck's discussion is extensively annotated.
5. The most extensive source of biographical information on Hunt, and his relationship to Alexis, is his autobiography, *One American and His Attempt at Education* (New York: Simon and Shuster, 1938), but the following shorter items are helpful as well: Hunt, "My Little Old Home Town," *Cosmopolitan*, June 1924, pp. 51–52; Walter Trohan, "Frazier Hunt, Ex-*Tribune* Writer, Buried" (obituary), *Chicago Tribune*, December 28, 1967, p. A24; Earle Bennett, "Once Country Editor Frazier Hunt Made the World His Beat," *Aledo Times Record*, July 29, 1970, sec. 3, p. 3; John E. Hallwas, "Frazier Hunt: Newspaperman and Novelist," in *Western Illinois Heritage* (Macomb: Illinois Heritage Press, 1983), 185–87; and "Frazier Hunt" in Wikipedia.
6. *One American and His Attempt at Education*, 80.
7. For a list of his book titles, see the website www.nmanchesterhistory.org/biographies-frazier-hunt.html.
8. *One American and His Attempt at Education*, 253.
9. Ibid., 253–54.
10. *Sycamore Bend*, 4.
11. *One American and His Attempt at Education*, 74.
12. Ibid., 75.
13. Ibid., 75–80.

14. Ibid., 74, 71.
15. "New Book by Noted Alexian Received Here," *Alexis Argus,* September 19, 1925, p. 1.
16. *One American and His Attempt at Education,* 75.
17. Ibid.
18. "A Country Editor," *New York Times Book Review,* September 6, 1925, p. 8.
19. "Americans All," *The New Republic,* September 16, 1925, p. 105.
20. H. Walker, "Sycamore Bend," *International Book Review,* November 1925, p. 829.
21. "Editor Whedon," *Spoon River Anthology: An Annotated Edition,* ed. John E. Hallwas (Urbana: University of Illinois Press, 1992), 213. See my extensive note on the background to the poem (399–400), which reveals that Masters had personal reasons for the negative portrait and that the man who inspired the poem, William T. Davidson, actually had a good reputation. For a discussion of this poem and several other works about country editors (but which also fails to mention *Sycamore Bend*), see Gerald K. Wells, "The Small Town Editor: Guardian of Respectability," in *Order and Image in the American Small Town,* ed. Michael W. Fazio and Peggy Whitman Prenshaw (Jackson: University Press of Mississippi, 1981), 150–60.
22. For discussion of the relationship of *Spoon River Anthology* to Masters's early life and to the people of Lewistown and Petersburg, see Hallwas, *Spoon River Anthology: An Annotated Edition,* 1–71, 363–435.
23. The scholarship on community decline in America is extensive. The two most widely known, and acclaimed, general studies are by Robert N. Bellah, et al., *Habits of the Heart: Individualism and Commitment in American Life* (Berkeley: University of California Press, 1985), and Robert D. Putnam, *Bowling Alone: The Collapse and Revival of American Community* (New York: Simon and Schuster, 2000). The best view focused on small-town life is by Robert Wuthrow, *Small-Town America: Finding Community, Shaping the Future* (Princeton, N.J.: Princeton University Press, 2013). It has an extensive bibliography.

John E. Miller | South Dakota Artist Harvey Dunn
 | 
 | Expressing Midwestern Regional Values and Identity on Canvas

Among the artists the Midwest has produced, many were better known but few are more indicative of what the region represents than Harvey Dunn of South Dakota. While he was recognized during his heyday from around 1910 through the 1920s and 1930s as one of the United States' foremost magazine illustrators, he also deserves to be recognized along with Thomas Hart Benton, Grant Wood, and John Steuart Curry as one of the major regionalist American scene painters of the Depression decade. That he did not achieve this sort of acclaim resulted from his keeping his prairie paintings, inspired by the South Dakota landscape where he had matured, locked away in his studio in Tenafly, New Jersey, across the river from New York City, until shortly before he died in 1952.

Dunn was born on March 8, 1884, on a homestead three miles south and one mile east of the little town of Manchester in southeastern Dakota Territory.[1] The village, which had sprung up just four years earlier along a line of the Chicago and Northwestern Railroad, grew to no more than a hundred or so residents (unincorporated, the town was not listed in the census) by the time the young man left home in 1901 to pursue further education. As a youth, he loved to draw. After obtaining advanced training in art during stints at the nearby Land Grant institution—South Dakota Agricultural College—in Brookings, the Art Institute of Chicago, and the studio of famed illustrator Howard Pyle in Wilmington, Delaware, the budding artist was able to quickly ascend the professional ladder. Demand for his illustrations grew impressively between 1906 and World War I. But it would be the prairie paintings he turned out during the 1920s, 1930s, and 1940s that constitute his distinctive legacy as a regional artist. Dunn's work richly evoked the kinds of lives he and his fellow midwestern agriculturalists had experienced along the Middle Border separating the Great Plains from the Midwest during the time that he was growing up. His life and career constitute an important entryway into turn-of-the-century midwestern culture.

Dunn's inquisitiveness, enthusiasm, creativity, energy, work ethic, and powerful ambition revealed themselves early in life. He liked people and he enjoyed observing them, interacting with them, and painting them. Endowed with a deep, rich voice, around 6 feet, 2 inches tall, muscular, and handsome, he attracted people's attention at first meeting. They especially noticed his large hands and expressive eyes. Action-oriented and full of life, he remained remarkably modest, down-to-earth, and self-controlled. No beret-topped, dreamy, unworldly artistic bohemian was he.

While attending the nearby one-room Esmond Township country school in Kingsbury County for nine years, he grew up to be an active and curious boy and a better-than-average student. His classmates remembered especially the pictures sketched endlessly on the blackboard, requiring the teacher to hide the chalk box to prevent him from using it all up. By age fourteen, he had grown up into a stout young lad, capable of doing a man's work on the farm, but yearning already to make his escape and pursue his dream of making art. His practical-minded, Scotch-Irish father, Thomas Dunn, an immigrant from Canada, harbored little interest in or patience with his artistic yearnings. But Harvey's mother, Bersha, a former schoolteacher, was a sensitive and poetic soul, harboring some artistic inclinations of her own. Recognizing the boy's latent talent and passion for drawing, she sometimes joined him in the evenings making art, and she encouraged him to pursue his dream.

Beyond his family circle and neighborhood friends, the youth was most influenced as a teenager by the beautiful but daunting landscape that surrounded him, reaching out seemingly endlessly in all directions. Straddling the border separating the Midwest from the Great Plains, the verdant land yielded bumper crops in a good season, but could be fickle when environmental conditions deteriorated. Rainfall, never profuse in the region, remained unusually abundant during the early 1880s, but fell off later in the decade. By the early 1890s, drought prevailed. Through all of this, young Harvey developed a fierce attachment to the land and to the environment of the Redstone Valley and Redstone Creek that ran through his family's farm and then in a southerly and westerly direction until it ran into the James River.

Dunn remained a resident of the Midwest from birth to age seventeen. His experiences on the South Dakota prairie and the memories and impressions he retained exerted a profound influence on him in later life. The town of Manchester lay about fifteen miles east of the ninety-eighth meridian, often identified as the point where the West begins. Somewhere between it and the one-hundredth meridian—the line zigzagging and varying considerably in position from year to year, depending upon rainfall levels and environmental conditions—the Midwest gradually gives way to the Great Plains. Rainfall declines, tall-grass prairie undergoes a transition into short-grass, and soil types shift at the transition zone separating the two regions. Culture also undergoes a significant change, reflected in behavioral practices and belief patterns.[2] Harvey Dunn's heart remained east of this divide—he was a quintessential Midwesterner and remained one throughout his life. The art that he produced marked him as a midwestern type, something that he took deep pride in.

Dunn's friend and early publicist, Aubrey Sherwood, editor of the *De Smet News*, observed that he "loved the land and its people—the South Dakota prairies and its pioneers."[3] Dunn's countless hours spent as a youth walking behind a plow, planting and harvesting, caring for animals, and performing all of the chores a farm requires did not sour him on the occupation of farming. Rather, it cemented his attachment to the landscape. All his life, he expressed his love for the land. He was in perfect agreement with the author Joyce Carol Oates's notion that the landscape itself takes on the cast of a character. "So I never write without a sense of where it is, and I wouldn't want to," she writes. "It wouldn't be much fun for me. Really, I think the people are expressions of the landscape. Of the atmosphere of a special place."[4] Just as landscape continues to inspire Oates's writing, it animated Dunn's painting.

Like the author Hamlin Garland, who also spent time in South Dakota as a young man, Dunn was proud to be a "Son of the Middle Border." As an artist, he was determined to capture its essence on canvas, and especially its best qualities. While Garland's brand of literary realism often took a critical turn and he could be acerbic in describing the faults and deficiencies of life in the region, Dunn's artistic depictions of the subject were almost always positive and admiring. Both artists in their own separate ways limned and celebrated local color and regional distinctiveness. In *Crumbling Idols* Garland asserted that "it is the most natural thing in the world for a man to love his native land and his native, intimate surroundings." When young artists started thinking about the people they grew up with and the connections that bound them together, Garland wrote, they were likely to conclude that "the near-at-hand things are the dearest and sweetest after all."[5]

Like Garland and other writers and artists who placed the Midwest at the center of their work, Harvey Dunn was driven by a variety of impulses. Chief among them, as already noted, were a strong attraction to the land and to the environment as well as a liking for and sense of kinship with the people who dwelled there. Every writer and artist must negotiate the treacherous tensions mediating criticism and nostalgia, realism and idealism, the mundane and the dreamlike. Relevant to this, Dunn urged his art students, "Paint a little less of the facts, and a little more of the *spirit*. Look a little at the model and a *lot* inside."[6]

During the early 1920s, entering into the fifth decade of his life, he began returning annually to South Dakota to revisit old haunts, renew acquaintances, and execute sketches of people and the land, which he then took back with him to New Jersey to use in manufacturing his growing cache of prairie paintings. As he approached his old home place in South Dakota, he would sometimes start to sing, once pausing to exclaim, "This is *my* country. Now I'm living again!"[7] By the early 1920s, his mind began more and more to wander back to his South Dakota heritage. "For all his commercial success, Harvey Dunn was most at home when his brushes were depicting the rigors and the romance of homesteading," wrote his biographer. "He readily admitted his preference for painting the Dakota scenes above all others." When asked why he remained so loyal to the land of his birth long after he had moved away, Dunn frequently alluded to a verse from the Bible, Matthew 6:21: "For where your treasure is, there will your heart be also."[8]

Several individuals I talked to remember meeting Dunn or sitting on his lap when they were young children and testify to his kindness and lack of pretense.[9] He felt at ease and at home among the types of people he had grown up with in Kingsbury County, and as time went by the urge to return to his boyhood haunts and to reminisce about the time of his youth became more and more important to him. His art students recalled that while he could be a demanding critic, he was also honest, helpful, considerate, enthusiastic, and inspirational. One of them quoted Dunn in a letter he had written to South Dakota Art Museum director Joseph Stuart: "The native sweetness of people clutches at my very heart."[10] The love affair was mutual. Nessa Forman, art editor for the *Philadelphia Bulletin*, quoted another writer who said of him, "Nobody likes Harvey Dunn's pictures—except the people." Forman went on to observe, "They like them because they feel they can understand them, and they can understand them because Dunn understood the people. He neither glamorized nor romanticized homestead life. Neither did he place undue emphasis on the seamy side." Rather, in her opinion, "He captured the realism of a frugal, heroic, lonely existence, and he did it simply, without symbolism or artistic allegory."[11] Dunn, a philosophical sort, posited a sort of mystical union existing between him as an artist and the audience for his work.[12]

In attempting to tell a story of a people, of their hopes and heartbreaks, dreams and disappointments, Dunn liked to say, "It's the *invisible* something in a picture which makes it a good one. The feeling you have when you think of those mysterious people."[13] Dunn was one of those "mysterious" people himself, and although he stands as a certain "type" of Midwesterner, it would be a stretch to argue that he was a "typical" or "standard" type. To the degree that one associates midwesternness with qualities that were often attributed to him, Dunn was indeed *a* recognizable type of Midwesterner. Dean Cornwell, one of his best-known students and one who was closest to him, observed that Dunn was "bluff, hearty, powerful, intensely honest with others and with himself—quite a show-off—and would use his great physical strength in parlor tricks. He dramatized everything he did—a poet—as Dunn himself put it, he was 'a sentimental old fool,' never ashamed of being sentimental—he would cry at the drop of a hat—yet he would go out of his way to blast a phony."[14] Another of Dunn's students, Grant Reynard, called him "a whale of a man, a veritable pioneer hulk of a man with a head reminding you of a cross between an Indian chief and a Viking." Mesmerized by his charisma, Reynard added, "He overpowered you before he spoke and absorbed the attention of every gathering without saying a word."[15] Yet, these same individuals, along with others, also testified that Dunn could be gentle, soft-spoken, meditative, philosophical, and tender. He was a man of many contradictions, but he also displayed some distinct tendencies. Many of his most characteristic attitudes and practices derived from factors connecting him to his native region.

Echoing themes first developed in detail by the historian Frederick Jackson Turner, many writers and artists emphasized the democratic nature of the culture and polity of the Midwest. Indiana author Meredith Nicholson, for example, extolled the region's democratic tendencies in his classic 1919 volume, *The Valley of Democracy*. The three great midwestern regionalist painters of the 1930s—Benton, Wood, and Curry—all took democratic approaches to their art, and Harvey Dunn fit easily into their mold. It would be hard to argue that the Midwest had or has a monopoly on democratic ideas and practices, but to the degree that the region embraces democracy and opposition to elitism, Dunn stood out as a prominent exemplar of those tendencies.[16]

Beyond that, the South Dakotan was significantly shaped by several important midwestern institutions, all of which left strong impressions on his habits and thinking. In the first place, he was a product of the homestead frontier, facilitated by the passage of the Homestead Act of 1862. Enacted by Congress after the Confederate states withdrew from the Union at the beginning of the Civil War, the law possessed especially close ties to the Midwest, which played a significant role first in its passage and then in implementing it and taking advantage of it. The newly minted Republican party, whose birthplace was in the old Northwest and which was closely identified with the Midwest, had spearheaded the drive for free homesteads, while the South, fearing rapid population expansion into new lands in the North, had stood adamantly opposed to the idea while it remained in the Union. New Englanders, meanwhile, remained lukewarm on the subject or firmly opposed to it, fearing further drains on their population base. The explosion of the Homestead frontier during the late 1860s and 1870s centered primarily in the Midwest in the eastern portions of Kansas, Nebraska, and the Dakotas.[17]

Eastern Dakota Territory lay at the center of the Homestead boom of the early 1880s, during the time that the Dunn family arrived and Harvey was born.[18] South Dakota achieved statehood in 1889 and became one of the most agriculturally oriented states in the Union. Thomas and Bersha Dunn, like other settlers, ventured out onto the Dakota prairies in order to wrest a living from the land. Their son Harvey grew into a strong, broad-shouldered young man, tilling and harvesting the prairie sod. Later as an artist he would achieve his greatest renown for painting remembered and imagined scenes revolving around the settlement of the land and life on the agricultural frontier.

The Midwest was also closely associated with a second major American institution—the one-room country school. Although common throughout the nation and not exclusive to the region, it was a quintessentially midwestern type of cultural phenomenon. Dunn's Kingsbury County and others like it sometimes contained as many as 80 to 100 one-room schools scattered across the landscape. Settlers on the post–Civil War frontier were quick to establish common school districts, erect classroom buildings, hire teachers, and enroll their children. Faith in education as a tool of social leveling, economic progress, and cultural improvement was strong, although most rural residents retained fairly realistic expectations about what actually could be accomplished.[19] Whatever else young Harvey Dunn acquired from the young, meagerly trained women who were hired to teach him, he remained motivated by a strong spark of ambition and evidenced a driving desire to learn and a willingness to work. As a result, by the time he arrived at the agricultural college in Brookings, he was fully prepared to take advantage of whatever the art instructors there were able to teach him.

Land Grant colleges were also closely associated with the Midwest, which provided the most enthusiastic base of support for the passage of the 1862 law that created them. Although it was a Republican representative from Vermont—Justin Morrill—whose name was attached to the enabling act and some Midwesterners remained skeptical of or actively opposed to the idea, once the new schools started in operation, midwestern residents stood out among their strongest and most enthusiastic proponents. South Dakota Agricultural College (later named South Dakota State College and then South Dakota State University) and its sister schools in Minnesota, Nebraska, Iowa, Wisconsin, and elsewhere became pacesetters in America's higher educational system. They injected a huge dose of democracy into it and greatly widened opportunities and expectations for farm youth like Harvey Dunn.[20]

During the single year that Dunn spent at S.D.A.C. in Brookings, approximately fifty miles east of Manchester along the railroad line, he came under the excellent tutelage of a young, recently arrived art instructor named Ada B. Caldwell, trained at a number of places, including the Art Institute of Chicago and the Teachers' College of Columbia University. At the time, S.D.A.C. boasted fewer than 250 collegiate students and only about three dozen faculty members. Dunn later wrote admiringly that Caldwell had "opened new vistas for me. For the first time I had found a serious, loving, and intelligent interest in what I was vaguely searching for."[21]

Only seventeen at the time and having completed only one year of school beyond eighth grade, he enrolled in the "Aggie School" at S.D.A.C.—a prep school that provided the equivalent of a high school education, being open only during the winter months when boys could be spared from farm work. That did not prevent him from catching the attention of Miss Caldwell, who quickly ascertained that she had an unusual talent on her hands. Working with him for a couple of semesters, she suggested that he pursue further training in Chicago, and he enthusiastically followed her advice. It was a rather unusual and ambitious plan of action for a raw farm kid from the South Dakota prairie still in his teens.

The aspiring artist—only a year off the farmstead and still only eighteen—moved on to Chicago in 1902. With a population of 1.7 million, it was already the second-largest city in the United States, full of bustle and excitement. Dunn was a long way from home now and in a completely foreign environment—scary and alluring at the same time, but somewhat familiar all the same. Like the hub of a wheel, with spokes reaching out into all corners of the region, Chicago operated as the metaphorical "capital" of the Midwest. The Chicago and Northwestern railroad that transported Dunn to the city also hauled South Dakota grain and livestock to the city's grain terminals and stockyards and carried manufactured goods from Montgomery Ward and Sears and Roebuck warehouses back to eager homesteaders and town dwellers in the region. The "Windy City" was its heartbeat—an economic powerhouse and a cultural mecca for writers, artists, and intellectuals from Carl Sandburg, Sherwood Anderson, and Harriet Monroe to Clarence Darrow, Jane Addams, and John Dewey.[22]

A young man like Dunn, just arrived from the hinterlands, hardly possessed the time or the intellectual background to absorb all of the lessons that he might have learned from these impressive intellects and from the surrounding circumstances, but he shared in the excitement of the place, soaked up the atmosphere, and tested his mettle in the cauldron of activity going on all around him. Dunn's biographer notes that "during the two years from 1902 to 1904 the transition from farm boy to man-of-the-world began to take place."[23] Rejecting "friendly" advice proffered him by a group of older students who suggested that his rural background and lack of culture precluded him from advancing in the world of art, and also judging the instruction advanced by some of his teachers to be less than helpful, he relied heavily upon his own instincts and upon his fierce determination to hone his skills and advance in his studies. From the beginning, Dunn charted his own path, and memories of his origins on a South Dakota farmstead were never far from his thoughts.

During his second year in Chicago, he attended a lecture by the renowned illustrator Howard Pyle and asked how he might apply for the art school he conducted in Wilmington, Delaware. Pyle, impressed by examples that Dunn sent him of his work, welcomed him into his classes. For the next two years, the former South Dakota farm boy absorbed the accomplished master's approach and philosophy more than any particular techniques that the great man might have taught him. When it came time to set out on his own, Dunn rose quickly in the world of magazine illustration, obtaining numerous commissions from popular magazines, ranging from *Scribner's* and *Harper's* to *Century* and *Outing*. Over the next several years, his illustrations became a staple in popular magazines, especially in the *Saturday Evening Post*.[24] Dunn took a practical, business-like approach to his work, cranking out in rapid succession color paintings that were immediately transformed into black-and-white illustrations, which were in great demand by the mass-circulation magazines that were immensely popular during the early decades of the twentieth century. In this, his timing was impeccable, for he entered the illustration market just at the confluence of rising magazine circulations, a shift in illustration techniques from line drawings to illustrative paintings, and a major transformation in American reading habits.[25]

Dunn's career can be conveniently divided into three parts. The first decade and a half witnessed his rise to the top of the magazine- and book-illustration markets, as he produced in profusion images of knights and maidens, pirates, sailors, soldiers, swashbucklers, gunmen, domestic scenes, sportsmen, seascapes, railroads, workers, builders, business moguls, animals, and anything else that might provide dramatic visuals for readers of the short stories and books that were so popular at the time. Some of his subjects were pioneers and homesteaders, but they constituted only a small part of his repertoire. Then, during a brief period that lasted less than a year during the latter part of World War I, he was commissioned by the United States government as one of eight official artists of the Allied Expeditionary Force. Although his finished output was less than that of most of his fellow artists, Dunn's work was widely recognized as the most impressive and the most popular with the general public. Having entered the project with great enthusiasm and an intense desire to capture the war as it actually was being waged, Dunn was profoundly influenced by the experience and was determined to transform the scores of sketches he had made on the foreign battlefronts into powerful paintings once he returned home. However, the program's directors foreclosed that possibility by ordering the artists to turn in all of their materials immediately upon returning home. Greatly disappointed, Dunn was left with a compelling impulse to achieve something of significance—something that went beyond the routine type of magazine work he had been doing before the war. Now he wanted to accomplish something great.[26]

That unfinished business decisively influenced his shift of direction during the third stage of his career, which continued from the early 1920s until his death in October 1952. In the meantime, he turned forty in 1924, and the transition into middle age helped bend his thoughts increasingly back to the days of his youth on the Dakota prairies. He later expressed his feelings in an oft-quoted statement, "I find that I prefer painting pictures of early South Dakota life to any other kind, which would seem to point to the fact that my search of other horizons has led me back to my first."[27] During a modernizing era when American society and culture were undergoing profound stress and change, Dunn entered into a nostalgic mood, reverting back to his childhood on the homestead frontier.

Magazines, meanwhile, were switching over to using photographs instead of artistic renditions of scenes, and Dunn was becoming

Harvey Dunn in his studio in Tenafly, New Jersey. Courtesy South Dakota Art Museum, Brookings, South Dakota.

somewhat bored with the whole process. His illustration productivity declined significantly during the 1920s and 1930s, pretty much dropping off altogether by the early 1940s. Facilitating this shift of emphasis was the affluence he had acquired from his successful career, supplemented by the wealth brought to his marriage in March 1908 to the socialite Johanne Louise ("Tulla") Krebs, daughter of a wealthy Wilmington businessman. In 1914, the couple had moved from Wilmington to Leonia, New Jersey, across the Hudson River from New York City, bringing Dunn closer to the offices of the major magazines for which he did most of his illustration work. Five years later, they moved to a large estate in Tenafly, several miles further north.

During the early 1920s, the South Dakotan began journeying back home on sketching trips to visit his sister, Carrie Reiland, who was living on the old family farm, and former friends and acquaintances in and around Manchester. An added appeal of these excursions was that he could get away from the stilted and artificial atmosphere that prevailed among his family and friends on the East Coast. He could loosen up and revert to boyhood habits for a time, wearing old boots and clothes, laughing and joshing with the home folks, and recalling old stories that drew them together. He liked midwestern folks' straightforward, practical, unpretentious, and down-to-earth behavior.

Continuing during the 1930s and 1940s, driving out almost every year, he would bring along sketch pads and fill them with drawings of landscapes, billowing clouds, trees, streams, houses, farm buildings, animals, and people, returning with them to Tenafly, where he would utilize them to dredge up memories of his boyhood years in South Dakota. As time went by, he replaced his former high-horsepower, expensive automobile with a more practical woody station wagon that he would slip an old mattress in so that he could pull over to the side of the road and get some sleep along the way when he got tired. The paintings that emerged out of the sketchbooks recreated the conditions that had existed back around the turn of the century as he remembered them. The people may have still looked much the same, but their clothing had changed, as had their houses, artifacts, and surroundings. Dunn's prairie paintings contained very little in the way of vehicles, farm machinery, railroads, or other modern technologies and conveniences. He was picturing the past, after all, not the present.[28] The titles of some of his paintings, starting with his most famous work, the iconic *The Prairie Is My Garden*, indicate the general scope of his interests: *In Search of the Land of Milk and Honey, Going West, Buffalo Bones Plowed Under, Pioneer Woman, A Driver of Oxen, Something for Supper, Homesteader's Wife, Abandoned Farm, Woman at the Pump, After School*, and *Old Settlers*.

The images he produced were largely complimentary of the region, featuring strong men and women—ordinary and unpretentious, but formidable, staunch, determined, and hard-working. Mostly, they were depicted as individuals, striding across the prairie, gun in hand perhaps, or sowing, reaping, stacking hay, fixing fence, planting gardens, tending chickens, pumping water, and riding horses or in wagons. Seldom were people pictured in groups of more than two or three, but there *were* grain threshers, children walking home after school, travelers in wagons or other conveyances, and mothers with children picking flowers. In one dramatic rendition, a funeral party was enclosed within a fenced-in cemetery out on the open countryside. But larger groupings like this were uncommon. Almost all of Dunn's prairie painting subjects were rural. Seldom did towns appear in this work. I believe that was because he felt that picturing them would have required him to invent objects and clothing, storefronts, consumer goods, vehicles, signs, machinery, games, activities, and other accoutrements of the time.

A strong whiff of nostalgia pervades these pictures. Like the outputs of many other American artists, Dunn's body of work displays a complex mix of realism and romanticism. Working as a realistic artist at

Harvey Dunn, *The Prairie Is My Garden*. Courtesy South Dakota Art Museum, Brookings, South Dakota.

a time when abstraction was on the ascendant, Dunn was also a fabulist in that his paintings conjured up an ideal world—a place made up of dreams as much as reality. Never one to deny the presence of hardships, challenges, and dangers in an unpitying environment, Dunn also sought to capture the triumph of human beings over nature and the value of the work that they did with such great diligence. "How they sing of love and light and praise of this country he knows so well," observed his student Grant Reynard about those pictures. "He has captured in a superb impressionism the light and feel and lift and inspiration of this land ... [His paintings] shall continue to sing a great hymn of South Dakota and his America in color and light and joy across the years."[29]

Although Dunn's oeuvre consisted largely of portrayals of individuals, couples, or small groups, implicit in his work was a strong intimation of community. The labor of farm men and women, their trading of work with each other, and the building of cooperative institutions on the land and in the towns that were connected to the countryside also provided a foundation for community development, which complemented the rival sense of individualism that was required for survival in a challenging environment. Paradoxically, the expression of individualism and the uniqueness of the eastern South Dakota prairie countryside that were portrayed in Dunn's paintings coexisted with more universal meanings that were implied in them. "Certainly his pictures lack subtlety," wrote Edgar M. Howell of the Smithsonian Institution, "And all have something of the universality that he preached from the depths of his physical size and strength, 'all the farmers of America rolled into one.' So many of them seem to be Dunn himself, directly transposed into his subjects and their surroundings, 'byproducts' of his life as he told his students to let their pictures be of theirs."[30]

By a stroke of good fortune, Dunn's collection of close to four dozen prairie paintings wound up back in South Dakota at the same school where he had begun his artistic career—South Dakota State College in Brookings. While visiting his artist friend in Tenafly in May 1950, *De Smet News* editor Aubrey Sherwood, who for a number of years had been a one-man publicity machine for Dunn's work,[31] was invited to look at the artist's prairie paintings, which were scattered about in his studio. When Sherwood offhandedly mentioned that he was certain that many South Dakotans would love to view these works, the artist, who was increasingly feeling his mortality (he would be dead of cancer within two years), immediately offered to ship a group of them out to De Smet if a practical place could be found in which to display them. That summer, while forty-two of them were on exhibition at the Masonic lodge in De Smet for fourteen weeks, Dunn accepted an offer from S.D.S.C. president Fred Leinbach to provide a home for them in Brookings, donating them to the college for nothing.[32] They later became the foundational collection for the building of a South Dakota Art Museum on the institution's campus.

Thus Dunn's magnificent work, which had been completed in virtual secrecy—overlapping with the work being done during the 1930s by Benton, Wood, and Curry—could finally be viewed in comparison with the work that these three more prominent regionalists had produced. Until putting his prairie paintings on display in De Smet in 1950, this project had been his own personal testament to his background growing up on the Dakota prairie. He was affluent enough to not need the money that might have come from their sale; he seemed to have a deep, almost spiritual, relationship with the work; and, for whatever reason that he kept hidden in his heart, Dunn had no interest in putting them up for public viewing. Despite the similarity of theme and treatment, Dunn's output, while widely appreciated and valued by art connoisseurs and art historians, never managed to acquire the recognition and acclaim of that of his counterparts. Nevertheless, it deserves to be recognized for what it is—an excellent example of the values, industry, character, and spirit of the Midwest around the turn of the twentieth century, the place that inspired and nurtured one of the country's foremost illustrators of his time.

### Notes

1. Harvey Dunn left behind few letters and almost nothing in the way of diaries or memoirs. The standard biography is Robert F. Karolevitz, *Where Your Heart Is: The Story of Harvey Dunn, Artist* (Aberdeen, S. Dak.: North Plains Press, 1970). Biographical information, a detailed listing of and discussion of Dunn's paintings and illustrations, and several of Dunn's letters are contained in William Henry Holaday III, "Harvey Dunn: Pioneer Painter of the Middle Border" (PhD dissertation, The Ohio State University, 1970). Unless otherwise noted, most of the biographical information in this chapter comes from the above sources. A lavish collection of Dunn's artworks is reproduced in full color in Walt Reed, *Harvey Dunn: Illustrator and Painter of the Pioneer West* (Santa Cruz, Cal.: Flesk Publications, 2010).

In addition, there are a number of informative articles on Dunn, including, for instance, Edgar M. Howell, "Harvey Dunn: The Searching Artist Who Came Home to His First Horizon," *Montana: The Magazine of Western History* 16 (Winter 1966): 41–55 and Mari Sandoz, "Dakota Country," *American Heritage* 12 (June 1961): 42–53. I also consulted materials on Dunn in the South Dakota Art Museum Archives and in the Hilton M. Briggs Library Archives, South Dakota State University, both in Brookings.

2. A classic meditation on the transition to the Great Plains is Walter Prescott Webb, *The Great Plains* (Boston: Ginn, 1931); See also James D. McLaird, "From Bib Overalls to Cowboy Boots: East River/West River Differences in South Dakota, *South Dakota History* 19 (Winter 1989): 454–91; and John Milton, *South Dakota: A Bicentennial History* (New York: W.W. Norton, 1977), chap. 7.
3. Aubrey Sherwood, "Harvey Dunn," *South Dakota Conservation Digest* 35 (July/August 1968), 12. Sherwood was a self-appointed, one-man publicity bureau promoting the careers of both Dunn and children's author Laura Ingalls Wilder during the period before they achieved their greatest fame. See Dale Blegen, "Aubrey Sherwood of the *De Smet News*" (Master's thesis, South Dakota State University, 1979).
4. Joyce Carol Oates, quoted in Julie Keller, "First: The Land," *Chicago Tribune Magazine*, October 29, 2006, p. 20.
5. Hamlin Garland, *Crumbling Idols: Twelve Essays on Art and Literature* (1894, reprint Gainesville, Fla.: Scholars' Facsimiles & Reprints, 1952), 64–65.
6. Harvey Dunn, *An Evening in the Classroom* (Tenafly, N.J.: Mario Cooper, 1934), reprinted in Reed, *Harvey Dunn*, 245.
7. Arvella Lewallen (family friend), quoted in Karolevitz, *Where Your Heart Is*, 99.
8. Karolevitz, *Where Your Heart Is*, 101. On pioneer landscapes generally, see David Lowenthal, "The Pioneer Landscape: An American Dream," *Great Plains Quarterly* 2 (Winter 1982): 5–19; John Milton, "Plains Landscapes and Changing Visions," ibid., 55–63.
9. This discussion of Dunn's personal characteristics is based on interviews the author did in 1989 and 2016 with a number of people who knew him.
10. Charles J. Andres to Joseph Stuart, May 6, 1991, South Dakota Art Museum Archives, Brookings, South Dakota.
11. Nessa Forman, "H.T. Dunn: Prairie King," *Philadelphia Bulletin*, September 15, 1974.
12. See especially his musings captured in *An Evening in the Classroom*.
13. Dunn, *An Evening in the Classroom*, 251.
14. Notes from interview with Dean Cornwell, by Ed Howell, November 30, 1959, in South Dakota Art Museum Archives.
15. Grant Reynard, Notes for a talk on Harvey Dunn to be delivered at Brookings, South Dakota, on July 24, 1952, in South Dakota Art Museum Archives.

16. Frederick Jackson Turner, "Middle Western Pioneer Democracy," in Turner, *The Frontier in American History* (New York: Henry Holt and Co., 1920), 335–59; Meredith Nicholson, *The Valley of Democracy* (New York: Charles Scribner's Sons, 1919); John E. Miller, "Midwestern Regionalism During the 1930s: A Democratic Art with Continuing Appeal," *Mid-America: An Historical Review* 83 (Summer 2001): 71–93.
17. Everett Dick, *The Lure of the Land: A Social History of the Public Lands from the Articles of Confederation to the New Deal* (Lincoln: University of Nebraska Press, 1970), 135–36, 140–42; Heather Cox Richardson, *The Greatest Nation on Earth: Republican Economic Policies During the Civil War* (Cambridge, Mass.: Harvard University Press, 1997), 140–49; Eric Foner, *Free Soil, Free Labor, Free Man: The Ideology of the Republican Party before the Civil War* (New York: Oxford University Press, 1970), 27–29, 175.
18. On the society and political culture of Dakota Territory during the 1880s, see Jon K. Lauck, *Prairie Republic: The Political Culture of Dakota Territory, 1879–1889* (Norman: University of Oklahoma Press, 2010).
19. Wayne E. Fuller, *The Old Country School: The Story of Rural Education in the Middle West* (Chicago: University of Chicago Press, 1982); Paul Theobald, *Call School: Rural Education in the Midwest to 1918* (Carbondale: Southern Illinois University Press, 1995); Andrew Gulliford, *America's Country Schools* (Washington, DC: Preservation Press, 1984).
20. Earle D. Ross, *Democracy's College: The Land-Grant Movement in the Formative Stage* (Ames: Iowa State College Press, 1942); R.D. Christy and L. Williamson, eds., *A Century of Service: Land Grant Colleges and Their Universities, 1890–1990* (New Brunswick, N.J.: Transaction Publishers, 1992); Roger L. Geiger and Nathan M. Sorber, *The Land-Grant Colleges and the Reshaping of American Higher Education* (New Brunswick, N.J.: Transaction Publishers, 2013)
21. Harvey Dunn to H. Dean Stallings, August 29, 1941, in Holaday, "Harvey Dunn: Pioneer Painter of the Middle Border," 289.
22. William Cronon, *Nature's Metropolis: Chicago and the Great West* (New York: W.W. Norton, 1991); Dale Kramer, *Chicago Renaissance: The Literary Life in the Midwest, 1900–1930* (New York: Appleton-Century, 1966); Carl S. Smith, *Chicago and the American Literary Imagination, 1880–1920* (Chicago: University of Chicago Press, 1984).
23. Karolevitz, *Where Your Heart Is*, 23.
24. Ibid., 35–37.
25. Over time, he also worked for other publications, including *Country Gentleman, Ladies' Home Journal, McCall's, Cosmopolitan, American Legion Monthly, American Magazine, Redbook,* and *Hearst's International*. An extensive listing of Dunn's illustrations and paintings is contained in Reed, *Harvey Dunn*, 286–91.
26. Karolevitz, *Where Your Heart Is*, 49–67. See also Alfred Emile Cornebise, *Art from the Trenches: America's Uniformed Artists in World War I* (College

Station: Texas A & M University Press, 1991) and Peter Krass, *Portrait of War: The U.S. Army's First Combat Artists and the Doughboys' Experience in WW I* (New York: Wiley, 2006).
27. Dunn to H. Dean Stallings, August 29, 1941, in Holaday, "Harvey Dunn: Pioneer Painter of the Middle Border," 290.
28. See reproductions of Dunn's illustrations and paintings contained in Reed, *Harvey Dunn*.
29. Grant Reynard, Notes for a talk on Harvey Dunn to be delivered at Brookings, South Dakota on July 24, 1952, South Dakota Art Museum Archives, Brookings, South Dakota.
30. Howell, "Harvey Dunn: The Searching Artist Who Came Home to His First Horizon," 53, 55.
31. Blegen, "Aubrey Sherwood of the *De Smet News*," 36–43.
32. Aubrey H. Sherwood, *Harvey Dunn: Master Mason* (South Dakota Lodge of Masonic Research, 1964), 56–59.

Kimberly K. Porter

The Most Talked-About Personality in the Middle West

Henry Field's Struggle to Maintain the Midwestern Ideal on Iowa Radio

Early in 1925, Secretary of Agriculture William Jardine enthused that "radio's greatest contribution to civilization may lie in its influence upon the life and actions of the farm population.... It is to become a vital necessity for their economic, spiritual, and intellectual life ... by delivering the farmer and his family from the sense of isolation, by coping with class and sectional differences, by keeping boys and girls on the farm, and by making possible a system of agricultural education through the radio-extension courses of the agricultural colleges."[1]

Other modernizers of the *Country Life* ilk perceived that radio would break down the barriers that bad roads, expensive and unreliable telephone installations and gas-consuming automobiles had only begun to eliminate. A professor from the University of Minnesota argued that the greatest benefit rural Americans could gain from their radios was in the bringing of urban culture to the countryside, rather than requiring farm families to travel to cities to imbibe the latest urban trends. Elsewhere the *Rural New Yorker* correspondent I.W. Dickerson observed that radio "connects you with the whole world and breaks down the invisible but real barriers that separate the country from the city."[2] That radio *might* be used to bring rural life to urban listeners was not hazarded. Midwestern rural radio stations did not seek to replicate the offerings of urban stations; those could readily be tuned in if desired. Rather, rural radio offered midwestern listeners the opportunity to celebrate their culture via an agrarian idealism, traditional music, and Christian spirituals. In doing so, rural stations aided in the maintenance and even expansion of the regionalist energies of the early twentieth-century Midwestern Moment.

Henry Field and his multitude of KFNF listeners—he estimated that each evening nearly two million individuals tuned in—clearly did not see matters in the same form as their Secretary of Agriculture, their agricultural extension agents, or the purveyors of agricultural opinion as voiced by farm publications. While some rural folks *did* pine for worldly excitement, the greater portion seemed quite willing to seek out Henry and his fiddlers on the dial, to listen to "hillbilly" music, harmonicas, old gospel tunes, and untrained voices of amateur performers. Moreover, they seemed quite content to listen to Field expound at length on the values of rural life and what dreadful fate awaited a nation divorced from its agricultural heritage.[3]

In the perceived struggles underway in post–World War I America, Field took the local approach, proclaiming that he was simply a "Missouri jake" reliant upon straightforward, plain English devoid of "highfalutin'" words and phrases. Others could debate, and often decry, the mixed verb tenses, the malapropisms, the perpetually truncated gerunds, and the derision reserved for long-haired men, short-haired women, and the overly educated. Field himself stood firm at the center of a debate questioning the maintenance of distinctive midwestern mores, populist pronunciations, and downhome dialect.

Born and bred an Iowan, Henry Field, the first child of Solomon and Celestia "Lettie" Eastman Field, made his appearance in early December 1871. His birth was followed in relatively quick succession by those of Stephen, Helen, Martha, Jessie, Solomon, Jr., Leanna, and Susan. Before the babies came, both Solomon and Lettie taught in the one-room schools of Page County. Indeed, Solomon is given credit for teaching the first school ever in the county and his wife receives similar billing for teaching the first school within the confines of the new village of Shenandoah, in the far southwestern corner of the state.[4]

Finding teaching not entirely to his liking, Solomon dabbled in a number of arenas, but seemed most content to farm, to raise truck garden, and to occasionally serve in elected office. Indeed, Solomon, Sr., served two terms as a Republican in the Iowa House of Representatives, taking young Henry to Des Moines with him to serve as a personal page during one session.[5] During hours off from his labors as an errand boy for his father, Henry served a sort of apprenticeship with Livingston Seeds in the capital city.[6] For filling, labeling, and pasting envelopes, he received $3.50 per week. Of this, $3.00 per week was returned to the firm for room and board.

For Field, filling seed envelopes fulfilled a long-term ambition, that of being a seeds man. Although Field's memory can occasionally be considered vague and rather heroic, he noted in his 1911 seed catalog that he became aware of his true calling at a quite young age. As he recalled, "I think it all started from the reading of the James Vick catalog, when I was a boy five years old. James Vick was really the father of the mail-order seed business, and I can remember just how that catalog looked to me. It was my dearest possession, and I can remember having my mother read it out loud to me. After studying that catalog, I wanted to be a seedsman, and I insisted that my mother write to Mr. Vick to that effect." Vick, in his kindness, replied to young Field encouragingly, including a color picture of a gladiolus, the first he had ever seen.[7]

Despite attending Shenandoah's Western Normal School, Field did not pursue one of the learned professions, nor did he actually graduate from the college. When it burned in December 1891, he chose not to return to its resurrected form the next autumn. Impatient to start his career and provide for the woman he intended to marry, Field tried his hand at teaching for three terms, surveying for the county, and truck gardening, before returning to his first love, the seed and nursery business.[8]

As his business grew from his kitchen table to several buildings in the community of Shenandoah, Field's family also grew. Having lost his first wife after but six years of marriage, and when their son was only five, Henry remarried a scant year later, eventually siring a dozen children total: Frank, Faith, Hope, Phillip, Josephine, Jessie, Charity, Ruth, Georgia, John Henry, Celestia, and a stillborn son. Upon the death of his second wife, he married again. This time, however, he married a member of his seedhouse crew, a divorced woman, one of a category of humanity he both earlier and later cast considerable aspersions upon.[9]

As his business developed, so did Field's conservative nature. While he had benefited from three years' study at Western Normal School, and several of his sisters had attended there and elsewhere, Henry took to deriding college education, declaring that it had taken him at least ten years to overcome his "book learnin'," forget his "high falutin'" ways, and return to a useful way of living.[10] When his children came of age, Field discouraged their attendance at institutions of higher learning, going so far as to refuse to support any of his children's education beyond the high school level.[11]

Within a decade after he began to publish seed catalogs in 1899, Field was using his semiannual catalogs as a platform for his social and political ideas, albeit phrased with caution to avoid offending potential customers. He took care to emphasize his growing family, the independence he attempted to foster within them, his refusal simply to provide jobs for his children, his fiscal conservatism, his belief in "old-fashioned" ways, and the vital importance to the nation of its agricultural past. With regard to the agricultural past, Field was clear that rural life was good for the mind, the soul, the body, and the nation. In one catalog, he noted: "we all need a garden. Whether it's for profit or pleasure—to help out our living or as a hobby for our leisure—a poor man's necessity or a rich man's hobby—or anywhere in between—we all need a garden, and get a world of help in every way from it. Physical, mental and moral. The best cure for most of our troubles is to get back to earth and plant a garden."[12]

In *Seed Sense*, his small-scale, occasional magazine—sent to all customers and anyone else upon request—he often waxed poetic on the profound moral, physical, and financial benefits of gardening. Accompanied by a photograph of his long-suffering third wife, Bertha, and literally hundreds of jars of canned goods, Henry observed that a "little hard work, patience, and perseverance is all it takes. Good seed goes without saying. You'll be blessed with plenty; you'll be healthy and happy. Of course you might not get rich off a small farm, but you will have plenty to eat, plenty to wear, a comfortable home, happy children, and who could be richer than that?"[13]

Always enjoying a new toy or two—he was particularly fond of cameras, cars, and business machines—he and his younger children enjoyed many evenings of "listening in" on a crystal set, a very simple radio receiver. Believing that his customers would find an inexpensive radio worthy of purchase, Field announced his intention to start selling the Gilbert receiver as soon as it became readily available. As for radio's role within the seed house, Field had not yet made a determination, awaiting opportunities to see how it impacted business and sales at other early adopters.[14]

Field, his daughter Lettie, and son John Henry "listening in" on a crystal set, ca. 1923.

WOAW, associated with the fraternal and insurance organization Woodmen of the World, provided Field an opportunity to test the new gadget as a sales tool late in 1923. Traveling the 60 or so miles to Omaha, Nebraska, on wretched roads, Field and his seed house gang took to the airwaves at 9:00 p.m. His employees offered up old standards, such as "When the Roll Is Called up Yonder," "Softly and Tenderly," "Shall We Gather at the River," and "I Love to Tell the Story." In a leaflet included in that autumn's seed catalog, Henry touted the experience as providing an "evening of old fashioned music," bringing "back the memories of the simple tuneful music of other days, and to have an entire evening of good music, free from either Jazz or Grand Opera, but to our notion better than either."[15]

Having received over 5000 letters and telegrams "from every state in the Union, all parts of Canada, Cuba and even from ships at sea," begging for more of the gospel hymns, Field promised a return engagement on WOAW in both January and February of 1924. He was willing to take requests for his seed house gang, but would not honor calls for "Jazz, Grand Opera, or the banana song."[16]

A springtime leaflet in the 1924 catalog offered comments on the second and third appearances of Field and his fellows on WOAW. Once again gospel standards predominated: "He Leadeth Me," "Will Jesus Find Us Watching," "Throw Out the Life Line," and "Pass Me Not Gentle Savior." With his second appearance, however, Field also threw a bit of the "fiddle" into the mix with performances of "Buffalo Girls," "Darling Nellie Gray," and assorted instrumentals, including "Turkey in the Straw."[17]

With over 6000 telegrams and letters in hand commending Field for his efforts at providing quality music, he promised his listeners and readers continuing music via WOAW. Unfortunately for Field, a conflict arose with station manager Orson Stiles. In a letter to Senator Morris Sheppard of Nebraska, W.A. Fraser, sovereign commander of the Omaha branch of the Woodmen of the World, complained that while Field's performances had been well-received, he failed to heed the rules placed before him by the Woodmen: no direct advertising of his firm or its products. After the first two Field presentations, Stiles demanded that the seedsman stay away from the microphone entirely rather than have the opportunity to push his products.[18] Frustrated and seeing considerable opportunity to make sales, Field declared Stiles's "statements to the effect that direct or undisguised indirect publicity was prohibited were all 'bunk'" and forthwith determined to start his own broadcasting firm in Shenandoah, free from the oversight of the Woodmen.[19]

Within a matter of weeks, Field had secured the licensing agreements and cobbled together the broadcasting equipment to free himself from the perceived strictures of flawed interpretations of the Department of Commerce's statements regarding direct advertising and undisguised indirect publicity. Harley Bartles, a long-term Field employee, traveled to Ft. Dodge, Iowa, to purchase a used transmitter from a defunct radio station. Other employees crawled atop Henry Field Seeds's main office building to erect two windmill towers from which to string the transmission lines. And while Field touted the forthcoming station as a benefit "to be used for the general good of Shenandoah and Southwest Iowa," few could fail to recognize that the station came "under the personal direction of Henry Field." Moreover, Field concluded that if listeners felt so inclined to give him their seed orders he would be "well satisfied."[20] Clearly, Field had every intention of offering products for sale via his newest gadget.

Secretary of Commerce Herbert Hoover had made his opinion known regarding the use of radio for product promotion at the Department of Commerce's Conference on Radio Telephony in 1922. According to Hoover, the thought of radio being used for advertising, allowing quality news, entertainment, education, and "vital commercial purposes" to be "drowned in advertising chatter" was simply unthinkable. Moreover, that quality programing could "interlard discussion as to the approaching remnant sale" was inconceivable to the Secretary.[21] Indeed, the final report of the conference, not acted upon by Congress, urged that "direct advertising in radio broadcasting service be absolutely prohibited and that indirect advertising be limited to a statement of the call letters of the station and the name of the concern responsible for the matter broadcasted, subject to such regulations as the Secretary of Commerce may impose."[22]

Despite the lack of limiting legislation, many in authority decried the presence of advertising on the radio, seeing it as an intrusion upon the listener that she could not avoid, as she could do with an advertisement in print. As RCA President James Harboard complained in 1923, "Even Sundays are not sacred to these people, and the most touching and affecting church services are often interrupted by the raucous voice of some wide-mouthed barker serving an advertising agency."[23]

Hoover offered similar sentiments at the onset of the Third National Radio Conference, declaring, "I believe that the quickest way to kill broadcasting would be to use it for direct advertising. The reader of the newspaper has an option whether he will read an ad or not, but if a speech by the President is to be used as the meat in a sandwich of two patent medicine advertisements, there will be no radio left."[24] Exactly how radio would pay for itself remained a question to which Hoover and many others could not foresee an answer. However, by the fall of 1924, Henry Field had the clear answer: full-force direct advertising. As he later noted in an issue of *Radio Digest*, "what real harm is there in naming the price of a thing that is for sale? The selling is the story and the price is the climax. It's the answer to the inevitable question in the mid of the listener, 'Well, how much is it?'"[25]

And despite the presence of more and more direct advertising, which most Americans seemed to prefer to a tax on their receivers, some held firm against the use of advertising as the bread of a meaty sandwich. Loudly leading the pack against direct advertising, and specifically targeting Field, was the British-born Francis St. Austell, self-proclaimed president of the Iowa Radio Listeners' League of Des Moines. In the *Radio Broadcast Advertiser*, St. Austell raged against his subjugation to

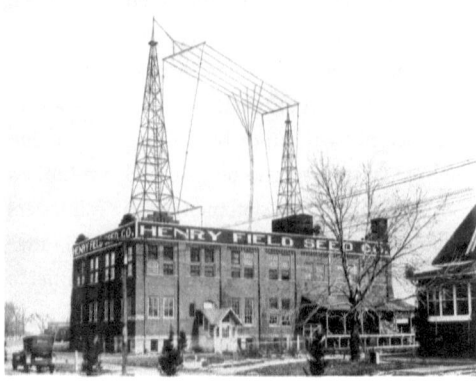

KFNF transmitting antenna system atop the Field Seed building, Shenandoah, Iowa, ca. 1925.

Field's advertisements for tires, Chinese bowls, pencils, fountain pens, peaches, coffee, overcoats, corn, and canned paint. Decrying Field's popularity, St. Austell suggested that a man with such considerable influence should be treated carefully. Indeed, "Henry Field arouses a feeling among his followers that is akin to worship. He is becoming a cult.... The magnetic personality of Henry Field makes him stand alone, a national figure, a creation of radio, a leader of hundreds of thousands, almost a prophet, a Moses of the common people."[26]

But the "Moses of the common people" did not readily take to criticism from the likes of St. Austell, the Woodmen of the World, the *Des Moines Register*'s radio critic Gordon Lathrop, or pretty much anyone else when it came to running his seedhouse or to spreading his message of agrarian superiority, the benefits of gardening, or his own line of merchandise. At least at the outset, Field, the savvy businessman, did not argue specifically for direct advertising as his motivation for starting his own station.

Rather, he noted during the first night of broadcasting on KFNF's makeshift towers, that while experimenting with his children and their newest gadget, he heard little more than "those raggy, jazzy tunes, and I wondered if people didn't really get tired of that sort of music." After a few letters to radio stations asking for a greater variety of music, Field determined to set out on his own, despite the naysayers of his firm and family who declared that it would be too expensive and too time-consuming to begin a radio station.[27] And when he took to the air in February, 1924, his first regular broadcast commenced with the station's policy: "This is to be a station where old-fashioned music is to predominate. I believe there are enough of us in the world old-fashioned enough to enjoy old-fashioned tunes and the old-fashioned hymns. We are going to give you music you heard around the old family organ before jazz was thought of."[28]

An examination of early programming records proves the validity of Field's declaration. Little programming could be considered jazz, or for that matter modern. In the autumn of 1924, KFNF broadcast a series of concerts, performed without cost to the studio, by local churches, student groups, farm organizations, neighborhood associations, and the like.[29] The Cornfield Canaries proved particularly popular, as did accordion contests, old fiddlers' reviews, whistlers, and harmonica concerts. On a daily basis, LuEtta, a seed house secretary, sang "sacred songs," "gospel tunes," and "old-fashioned favorites."[30]

Field clearly understood his audience, as did those who reflected on his life. At the time of the broadcaster's death in 1949, W.D. Archie of *The Shenandoah Evening Sentinel* explained that Field's purposeful

> success hinged largely on his understanding of the people he loved. Thus when he started in radio, as a great pioneer, his station attained great success. He knew what his people wanted to hear and no one could sway him from what he knew to be right. Thus there was the morning prayer service, the Sunday school lessons, gospel singing, talks on trees, flowers and vegetables, old fashioned fiddling, the barn dance, and a comfortable, chatting style in his own programs. It was a personalized radio station and a personalized business all built around his amazing understanding of his people and a love for the soil.[31]

Eulogizing aside, it quickly became apparent that individuals either loved or hated Henry. There did not seem to be much, if any, middle ground. As the *New York Times* observed, one could be neutral with regard to the McNary-Haugen bill, the tariff, the naval build up, and "whether Coolidge means it or not," but one could not find neutral ground with regard to KFNF. A "radio addict," according to the *Times*, "can hardly escape having a positive opinion as to whether KFNF is a desirable station which should be at the head of the radio commission's preferred list or a bad station which should be banished to the radio limbo."[32] And in recalling the early days of radio in 1974, Iowa author Carl Hamilton could state with clarity that his father "Didn't like 'Old Henry' at all!"[33] Others were a bit more charitable, noting that KFNF was "the most loved and the most hated broadcasting station in the country."[34] One either appreciated Henry Field, his music, and his direct advertising, or not.

In his "appreciation" of radio station KFNF, F.E. Way, MD, of Wahoo, Nebraska, waxed far beyond what one might expect of a physician regarding the Shenandoah broadcaster. In a dozen, colloquial verses, dialectically styled "Missouri English," the doctor trilled:

> Yes, we all tune in and lissen
> When Henry's on the air;
> Not a word we will be missin'
> For there's not a thing to spare.
> We don't care what he talks about,
> Plantin' peas or mendin' fence;
> It's allus interestin'
> And full of common sense.
>
> And I love the old time music—
> How it makes my muscles twitch;
> When Wilbur tunes that violin
> My feet just fairly itch.
> And Bill, with his harmonica—
> Say! Ain't that music swell?
> Just fairly lifts me off my feet
> With it's [sic] entrancin' spell.
>
> ...
>
> But when old Henry starts to read
> The telegrams. Oh! Gee!
> They only prove there's others
> Who like it just like me.

> They bring 'em up in baskets
> And dump 'em on his lap.
> He just can't read the half of 'em
> 'Cause there's other things on tap.
>
> So we never lack variety,
> And we never lack for spice;
> There's somethin' doin' all the time
> And that's what makes it nice.
> But best of all is Henry,
> With his friendly common ways;
> We all have learned to love him,
> And joy to sing his praise.
>
> A friendly voice from a friendly town,
> Just let them call us "Rubes";
> I love old Henry at the Mike,
> Here's blessings on his tubes.
> K F N F, Kant Find No Fault,
> And would not if I could;
> I hear him every morn and night,
> And all I hear is good.
>
> ...
>
> A hundred thousand folks like me,
> Stand up to say, "God Speed.
> The message from K F N F
> O'er mountain, vale and mead."
> A hundred thousand humble ones,
> Who lissen in each day,
> Remember Henry and his Mike
> When they bow down to pray.[35]

Dr. Way did not stand alone in his affection, support, or talent when it came to station KFNF and its owner. Rather, he might be considered among the better educated of those who felt sufficiently inspired to take pen in hand to celebrate Field and his endeavors.

To commemorate the second anniversary of KFNF in early 1926, the nearby *Essex Independent* proclaimed:

> A funny sort of geezer, is Henry,
> An entertainment, teaser, our Henry,
> Old fashioned as the deuce,
> But he never wastes the juice,
> For they have a lot of use, for Henry.
> Though these many years he's toiled, has Henry,
> Just for two years has he coiled, queer Henry,
> Round the universe his fame
> Do the ether waves proclaim,
> Everybody knows the name of Henry.
> May he ever make us glad, kind Henry,
> When these radio days are o'er
> And we reach the other shore,
> Hope to meet him at the door, our Henry.[36]

Not to be outdone in the celebration of KFNF's second anniversary and its prairie broadcaster, Will M. Maupin in his *Omaha World-Herald* "Sunny Side Up" column also devoted a few too many lines of poetry to "Henry Field":

> Ain't one of them highbrow men, our Henry
>     He's jus' made o' common stuff, like you and me
> Talks our language, an' he gits his big joys
>     Out'n common things o' life we all kin see.
> Likes th' ol' time tunes an' songs, does Henry;
>     Don't go much on jazz an' way-up operays.
> Druther call t' mind old home ties an' friendships,
>     Old-fashioned tunes that brightened other days.
>
> Religion? Got workin' kind, has Henry,
>     Don't put it off along with Sunday clothes.
> Lives it ev'ry day, an' by example provin'
>     It helps a feller on where'er he goes.
> Allus git good tunin' in on Henry,
>     'Cause he's just brimmin' fun o' sense an' cheer;

Talkin' o' flowers an' seeds an' trees an' roses—
    Makes a feller young our Henry's voice t' hear.

Highbrows pretend they never tune in Henry,
    But they don't count along with common herds.
Millyuns o' us an' highbrows ain't so plenty.
'At Henry needs t' worry 'bout them birds,
Explainin' why he clings to things old-fashioned,
    He knows them things was allus good an' clean,
Just like th' shrubs an' seeds 'at he is sellin',
    With words o' hope an' cheer strung in between.

Mother an' me we string along with Henry;
    Tunin' in on KFNF ev'ry night:
An' sometimes too tune in on mornin' worship,
    'Cause mother says it starts th' new day right.
Highbrows may sneer an' say harsh things o' Henry.
    But O, th' good influence he does wield
Among us common folks, an' so I'm allus wishin'
    Long life an' more o' power t' Henry Field.[37]

As suggested by Maupin, not all folks found Henry Field to be as entertaining as he. Rather, Field came in for considerable criticism by early radio enthusiasts for his colloquial language, his "old-fashioned" ways, his potentially new-found religion, and his willingness to push the products of his seed house via "direct advertising."[38]

But as Maupin suggested, "[I]t is doubtful if a broadcasting station in the country has more devoted listeners. Henry Field is a character. He knows his clientele and is one of them. He talks to farmers and citizens of the small towns in their own language. He figures it out that what he likes will be the things that men and women like him will like— and goodness knows there are a lot of them, millions and millions. Do they love Henry?" For Maupin and hundreds of thousands of listeners, the answer was a resounding "Yes." After all, he "talks our language."[39]

Moreover, he understood their prejudices with regard to entertainment. In the first *Seed Sense* published after the commencement of his radio broadcasting, Field put forth his general rules for KFNF, "believ[ing] so far as possible that the following classes of entertainment should be barred, and will use every effort to keep them off the programs of this station: Jazz, Elocution, Child Prodigies, Heavy or Long Speeches, Heavy Classic Music and Over use of Dedications." Field also "reserved the right to pull the plug on any speaker who talks too long or gets mean or tiresome."[40]

That he talked their language did not comfort all of those who could tune in KFNF. In a letter to the editor of the *Des Moines Register*, Albert Haldeman condemned the station for its informal nature, as well as for its legion of "mispronounced words, incorrect English and billingsgate." Of the recent Christmas-day broadcast Haldeman fairly fumed that the program seemed like little more than a Field family reunion with untrained singers, unrehearsed chatter, and lessons in how not to broadcast. Indeed, he asked, "How can we expect our children to speak good English after listening to this nonsense from radio?"[41]

For the *Des Moines Register*'s radio critic Gordon Lathrop, Henry's habit of using poor grammar to relate to his customers could scarcely be considered admirable. His use of "ain't got," "we was," "have went," and the like when talking directly over the air to his "folks" did not necessarily reflect a lack of education, but rather a shrewd tool which made him "the most talked-about personality in the Middle West." Given his college education and ability to speak perfect English in common conversation, Lathrop could only consider Field to be "grossly unethical in his invidious comparison of his own prices with those of the small town merchants, throwing on them the suspicion of gouging their customers; he is aggressive, arrogant."[42] Nonetheless, he was effective. Lathrop noted, "I have heard him wax eloquent on the excellencies of a certain brand of pig meal. One wanted to buy a bucket of it for breakfast food for his family. He can make women tear their hair in impatience to get the pen and ink to order dress goods."[43]

In an essay published in the Grinnell College [Iowa] *Tanager* in September 1927, Thornell Barnes, the son of a Shenandoah banker, let loose his opinion of the proprietor of KFNF. In an essay titled "Culture Waves from KFNF," Barnes took Field and his admirers to task for a multitude of sins, as only a young collegian fresh from his home town can do to its most prosperous citizen. Not only did Henry appear in public without a collar and tie, but he also showed the world his suspenders and bare forearms as he generally rolled the sleeves of any shirt. Moreover,

Henry displayed considerable willingness to drop his "g"s, appreciate the "sweet, untrained voice" of his prize singer LuEtta, and push his own merchandise unmercifully upon his listeners. That Field seemingly appreciated "musical saws," "cracked fiddles," harmonicas, and accordion playing did not elevate him in the eyes of Barnes, who also broadly hinted that Henry's deep and abiding Christian faith had first manifested itself at the same time he discovered the power of broadcasting to line his pockets.[44]

According to historian Clifford J. Doerksen, Field's "farmer station" shared a common difficulty, whether or not it was recognized as such, with other rural-based stations. With federal limitations on the use of phonograph music to fill the air-time hours, rural stations needed to rely upon local talent, preferably cheap and readily available. For Field this came in the form of his own seed house employees, a fact he readily shared with his listeners. "Unlike the city stations, which strove to distance themselves from the taint of amateurism, KFNF proudly advertised the fact that its most popular female vocalist, LuEtta Minnick Armstrong, was the office assistant to company treasurer Fred Tunnicliff, who was familiar to listeners as the announcer of KFNF Sunday devotional services."[45] As needed, and by request, LuEtta could be called to the microphone at a moment's notice. Later, Field would broadcast LuEtta's wedding ceremony to a fellow seed house employee, to great fanfare and mixed acclaim.[46]

As Field put it in an office memo, "Are We 'Small Town'?":

> In our entertaining we must stick mainly to our own old time type of music and talks. They all try to copy it but most of them cannot get the spirit of it. Our successes in the past have been with our fiddling and gospel hymns and old time ballads. With music of the type of the Smith-Beldings, and LuEtta, and the girls chorus and the quartettes and trios when they sing old time songs and negro [sic] spirituals, and Edith when she sings the familiar old time ballads and spirituals. We can beat the world with these.
>
> When we get into the modern music we are competing with professionals, trying to beat them at their own game. And that's always a hard proposition.[47]

Field's techniques of popular, old-fashioned music, harmonica and fiddler contests, common sense English, and the like proved exceptionally popular, particularly when the available choices on the tuner were limited, and few broadcasters managed to stay on their assigned frequencies. Moreover, many radio stations could not find sufficient talent to fill their allotted hours, often leaving Field quite alone in the ether of any given night.

To celebrate the second anniversary of his first broadcast, Field determined to go all out. Newspapers around the nation, including the *New York Times*, reported on the events of the week. Breaking the rules of his station's licensing agreement, Field broadcast for 30 hours straight. With fiddling contests, harmonica contests, female, male, and mixed quartets, eight separate orchestras, devotionals, gospel groups, handy gardening advice, barn dance music, encouragement to visit the station and the test gardens, as well as an assortment of speakers touting both Field and Shenandoah, the hours passed. Field, urging that any individual who could hear the sound of his voice should send a postcard, was inundated with telegrams, postcards, long-distance calls, and letters. All told, office personnel tallied some 226,000 responses to the call for recognition. For those who kept track of such things, this was a new record in response to a radio broadcast. The number of telegrams arriving overwhelmed the local Western Union office, making an accurate count impossible. An estimated 500,000 letters also arrived to celebrate Henry's conquest of the air.[48]

And while some could proclaim their disdain for "just plain Henry," the impact of KFNF could not be ignored. Despite the nation's turning toward an urban aspect, Field could generate fame and fleeting fortune for himself by promulgating a form of agrarian localism. While other radio stations might fail or suffer along with music of "highbrow" origins, Field told the nation that his rural station could hold its own with the very best of the urban purveyors of radio. Moreover, his listeners could acquire the accoutrements of a quality life, even if not an urban one, simply by ordering the merchandise he so shamelessly pushed: garden seed; china dishware; wall paper; purebred hogs; clothing for men, women and children; fresh fruit; harness; tires; canaries; goldfish; wedding rings; nostrums against horse and mule ailments; and much more.

As some listeners dreamed of traveling abroad or perhaps to Chicago, New York, or San Francisco, Field encouraged his listeners to grab hold of their own vacation dreams and visit Shenandoah, Iowa. A day trip, perhaps expanded to a week, would permit the rural folks a true vacation. When in Shenandoah, they could take in a radio broadcast, tour Field's manicured Sleepy Hollow gardens, look at the latest productions from the test gardens, watch the pole sitter attempt a world record, meet with the folks they regularly heard on the radio, stay at one of the cabins Field erected for summertime traffic, buy their gasoline from his station, and dine at his café. For the children, there were free rides on the miniature train and the Ferris wheel, a chance to observe trained bears and monkeys, and the captive mountain lion sent by Field's brother Solomon from California.[49]

Visitors to Shenandoah were encouraged to tour the city with the provision of a free map, directing them to sites important to the Henry Field Seed Company, as well as to those of his occasional competitors: the Earl May Seed & Nursery Co. and its KMA radio studios, Mt. Arbor Nursery, Nishnabotna Nurseries, and Ratekin's Seed House. Depending on the time of year, they might celebrate the jubilee with free watermelon slices, pancakes, sausage, and coffee. Or, they might take in the show of oddly shaped fruits and vegetables, oversized swine, prize bulls, and towering draft horses. Along with a souvenir or two to take home—Field offered free pamphlets, but charged for dishware and silver-plated spoons touting KFNF, as well as for postcards illustrating everything from his station and gardens to prize pigs, to multiple versions of his children.[50]

Moreover, when a day or two could be spared from the farm, KFNF listeners did not hasten to Omaha, Chicago, Des Moines, Kansas City, Lincoln, or Sioux City. Rather, they sought their cultural experiences in Shenandoah, absorbing what could only be described as centralized rural culture. It was what Henry provided, and what Field as a businessman knew he could sell. As observed by Lathrop, Field "play[ed] small town and farmer prejudices against cities and city folk."[51]

In the "KFNF Listeners' Guide" for each of the years 1925, 1926, 1927, 1928, and 1929, the daily schedule, Sundays excepted, included several 15-minute blocks per day devoted to "promotion." The men and women responsible for the various lines of goods and services offered by Field were profiled in the guide, just as were Henry's children, company officers, vocalists, and musicians. Field had no qualms about direct advertising in support of his station and his ideas; he also could argue with the best of his critics that farm families actually *wanted* to hear details regarding the products they might be purchasing, such as price, testimonials, colors, qualities, and available styles.⁵²

Lathrop found much to be concerned about with regard to Field and KFNF. He squarely divined that Field wanted to play both ends of the street, both rural and urban, both modern and fundamentalist. In Field, Lathrop found "a stroke of genius on Henry's part now to make of his station the model, the sanctuary of the old-fashioned, the humble, the fundamentally religious, while at the same time to erect upon that sort of a foundation the most modernly prosecuted mail order business in the country. Thus does fundamentalism rail against the modern, yet declare a dividend on it."⁵³

Still, when it seemed that KFNF might be forced to reduce its coverage area and operating hours, Field's fans found their pens and pencils and wrote letters to the Federal Radio Commission. William M. Jones of Clay Center, Kansas, offered that he wrote "spechel there to bege of you to let the Radio station K.N.N.F. [sic] the Henry Feld's station alone as it is the best one on the eair for us in the middle west here do not cut the power down but let them alone as they are fin. They are a great blessing to us all here."⁵⁴ Mrs. E.J. Ernst of Johnson, Nebraska, offered that KFNF was the only "real farmer's station."⁵⁵

The quality of Field's programming gathered the attention of many who feared the loss of his voice to a lower broadcasting power. "KFNF has quite a lot of relishious songs and talks too that I like so well and that is to the good. So much of the Jass sure is tiresome,"⁵⁶ wrote one Nebraska woman, while another urged the Federal Radio Commission, "We find Mr. Field a man of great service, and ever ready to serve in time of need. His station inspires many hundred listeners. One never tires of his station, for he does not have the sickening jazz."⁵⁷

Perhaps the most inspiring letter in support of Field maintaining his wavelength came from fellow Iowan D.J. Cowden, "dealer in telephones and accessories." After praising Field's station for its accomplishments—good music, excellent agricultural talks, timely weather and market reports, Sunday services for shut-ins—Cowden offered his opinion, favorably, on what KFNF did *not* offer. "Lastly, let the dance halls and leg shows hold open all night if they want to and play their Jazz and sing their smutty songs, and have their TRAINED?????? singers tremule nonsense like a Coyote ad-lib-itum, but you stay just where you are. You are doing the country more good than all the Jazz houses in the world." To ensure that both Field and the FRC got the message clearly, the quoted passage was written in red ink.[58]

While the opponents of Field and his form of broadcasting also took the time to write members of the Federal Radio Commission, Secretary of Commerce Hoover, assorted congressmen, and governors, the vast majority of the letters in KFNF's National Archives files supported his efforts. Some authors even went so far as to suggest that Henry Field had their interests at heart far more than did the recipients of their letters, and that perhaps he should consider a run for public office in order that the voice of the farmer might again be heard in the affairs of government.[59]

That this fear had occurred to some of his airwave adversaries had also become clear. As Gordon Lathrop saw it, "[Henry] could take 3,000,000 letters from admirers of his radio station and himself to Washington and could say to the timorous politicians there: 'Do you dare refuse 3,000,000 farmers and small towns people their right to hear me on the air and buy my goods?' Politicians don't dare. Henry, smilingly being himself, has put the fear of God or its equivalent, defeat at the hands of the opposition, into the hearts of Middle West politicians. He is a sort of Moses of the common people, so called."[60]

M.E. Stanley, in "Henry Field—A New God in the Middlewest," wondered why the man he referred to as a "messiah" with "the showman instincts necessary in one who would lead the multitudes, a sure touch for the spectacular" had not yet chosen to enter the arena of politics. As Stanley perceived the situation, Field's following was larger than that of William Jennings Bryan, and should he wish the "nomination" it most assuredly would be his.[61]

Politics, however, could wait. For the next decades, Field used KFNF, garden catalogues, and *Seed Sense,* as well as his immense popularity with the nation's farm population, to support his rural ideal: hard work, simple language, self-reliance, ties to the land, Republicanism, and common sense. High falutin' highbrows had no place in Field's Middle West.

## Notes

1. "A College Course by Radio," *Literary Digest* 84 (March 14, 1925): 23–24.
2. See, among others, *Wallaces' Farmer* (January 9, 1925): 42; *Progressive Farmer* (June 13, 1925): 680; *Literary Digest* 100 (February 23, 1929): 24; *Rural New Yorker* (September 20, 1924): 1207–1208.
3. Field was not alone in his labors; rural radio stations of the 1920s and 1930s remain an area for academic consideration. Given the ease of erecting a radio transmitter and the lack of federal regulations (or at least of their enforcement), dozens of stations made their appearance in the Midwest in the industry's early years. Besides Field's KFNF of Shenandoah, Earl May Seeds, his cross-town competitor, broadcast a somewhat more elevated programming on KMA, "The Corn Belt Station in the Heart of the Nation." Joining the list of seedsmen on the air were A.A. Berry Seed Company, Clarinda, Iowa, on KSO, "Keep Serving Others," and D.B. Gurney of the Gurney Seed and Nursery Company, Yankton, South Dakota, on WNAX. The stations' need for live performers offered such fledgling artists as Lawrence Welk and his Hotsy Totsy Boys, the Blackwood Brothers Gospel Quartet, and the Everly Brothers a starting point. Elsewhere in the Midwest, the Omaha Grain Exchange operated WAAW; *Drover's Journal*, a farm publication, broadcast from Chicago on WAAF; Norman Baker blasted his opinions on all matters from KTNT, Muscatine, Iowa; WTAX of Streator, Illinois, offered up the wisdom of the Williams Hardware Company; Council Bluffs's Mona Motor Oil Company operated KOIL; and the United States Playing Card Company served up music and news from WSAI, Mason, Ohio. Not all stations, of course, had connections with businesses hoping to cash in on direct advertising to potential customers. Assorted colleges and universities around the Midwest offered educational fare and the opportunity to listen to student musical offerings and athletic contests. Churches also took to the airwaves in the 1920s and 1930s. Methodists, Baptists, Lutherans, Catholics, Congregationalists, the Reorganized Church of Jesus Christ of Latter Day Saints, Presbyterians, Seventh Day Adventists, Evangelicals, Universalists, and the "People's Pulpit" all held radio licenses and could be tuned in at midwestern homes on a clear night. For a listing of radio stations and their owners in the mid-1920s, see *The U.S. Radio Dial*, June 30, 1927 and June 30, 1930, as well as the Department of Commerce, "United States Radio Stations as of June 30, 1925."
4. Frances Hope Field Pawek, *The Story of Henry Field* (privately printed, 1994), 3–6.
5. Solomon Field served two terms in the Iowa House of Representatives, 1887–1888 and 1889–1890. He did not stand for re-election following his second term of office.
6. Pawek, *Story of Henry Field*, 27. Livingston Seed Company is one of the oldest seed firms in the United States, having begun in Ohio under the direction of Alexander Livingston, the man considered to have popularized

the tomato for broad scale consumption in the United States. Fearing an economic downturn in Ohio, Livingston determined to move his firm to Des Moines, Iowa, only to later return his business to Cincinnati. See A.W. Livingston, *Livingston and the Tomato* (Columbus, OH: A.W. Livingston's Sons, 1893; repr., Columbus, OH: Ohio State University Press, 1998).

7. *The Henry Field Seed Catalog*, (Shenandoah, IA: 1911), 2. James Vick (1818–1882) ran a seed firm from Rochester, New York, in the latter portion of the nineteenth century. Having started life as a printer under Horace Greeley, he later edited *The North Star*, an abolitionist paper founded by Frederick Douglass, and the *Rural New Yorker*, the latter leading him into the seed business. See Claribel R. Barnett, "Vick, James," *Dictionary of American Biography*, 19 (New York, NY: 1936); Elliot Fitch, "James Vick," *Encyclopedia of Biography* (New York, NY: 1916), Donald B. Marti, "Vick, James," *American National Biography*. 22 (New York, NY: Oxford University Press, 1999); "James Vick," Victory Horticultural Library, accessed January 16, 2017, http://www.saveseeds.org/biography/vick_bio.html; "Vick, James," Smithsonian Libraries, accessed January 16, 2017, http://www.sil.si.edu/silpublications/seeds/vickjames.html.
8. Pawek, passim.
9. Ibid. Marriages: Annie Hawxby, November 24, 1892 to April 29, 1899; Edna Lois Thompson, May 8, 1900 to April 3, 1925; Bertha McMullen Mitchell, April 10, 1929 to Field's death in 1949.
10. Wayne Gard, "Henry Field of Iowa," *Plain Talk* (May, 1929): 607–12; M.E. Stanley, "Henry Field—A New God in the MiddleWest," *Haldeman-Julius Monthly* (1928): 29–40.
11. John Henry Field, interview with the author, Denver, CO, July 7, 2008. Field also chose not to employ any of his children in the nursery business until late in his life.
12. *Seed Sense* (Spring, 1936): 16.
13. *Seed Sense* (March 1, 1941): 1.
14. *Seed Sense* (May 1, 1922): 1.
15. Leaflet, Autumn, 1923, Henry Field Seeds Catalog, in possession of Margery Strom, Shenandoah, IA, niece of Field. WOAW would later change its call letters to WOW.
16. Ibid.
17. Leaflet, Spring 1924, Henry Field Seeds Catalog, in possession of Margery Strom, Shenandoah, IA, niece of Field.
18. W.A. Fraser, letter to Morris Sheppard, November 10, 1924, National Archives, Records of the Federal Communications Commission, Radio Division, Correspondence Relating to Applications for Broadcasting Station Licenses, 1928–1932, Record Group 173, Box 410 (hereinafter FCC Records).
19. Ibid.
20. *Seed Sense*, March, 1924, 2.

21. "Minutes of Open Meetings of Department of Commerce Conference on Radio Telephony," Washington, DC, February 27–28, 1922, Herbert Hoover Presidential Library, West Branch, IA, Commerce Papers (hereafter Commerce Papers), Box 496, "Radio-Conferences-National-First."
22. "Report of the Department of Commerce Conference on Radio Telephony," Commerce Papers, Box 496.
23. "Broadway Brought to the Farm; Lonely Days Ended by Radio," *New York Times*, February 4, 1923, VIII10.
24. Herbert Hoover, "Address before the Third National Radio Conference," October 7, 1924, Commerce Papers, Box 491, "Radio Advertising, 1924–1927."
25. "Listeners Like Henry Field," *Radio Digest* (October, 1929): 50.
26. Francis St. Austell, "Direct Selling by Radio: Is It a Menace to the Retail Business Structure?" *Radio Broadcast Advertiser* (May 1928): 59.
27. William H. Graham, "KFNF: Just for Old Fashioned Folks," *Radio in the Home* (September, 1924): 17.
28. Ibid.
29. *Shenandoah Daily World*, September 30, 1924, 5.
30. See assorted newspaper issues of 1924–1927 and KFNF brochures, in possession of the author.
31. W.D. Archie, "Along the Banks of the Nishna," *The Shenandoah Evening Sentinel*, October 20, 1949, 2.
32. "Henry Field's Radio Corn Belt Feature," *New York Times*, August 28, 1927, E7.
33. Carl Hamilton, *In No Time at All* (Ames, IA: Iowa State University, 1974), 111.
34. Gard, "Henry Field of Iowa," 29–30.
35. F.E. Way, M.D., "K.F.N.F.: An Appreciation," copy in scrapbook of Margery Strom, Shenandoah, IA, niece of Field (spelling and grammar as in original).
36. *Essex Independent*, "To KFNF," undated, copy in scrapbook of Margery Strom, Shenandoah, IA, niece of Field.
37. Will L. Maupin, "Henry Field," *Omaha World-Herald*, ca. 1926, copy in scrapbook of Margery Strom, Shenandoah, IA, niece of Field (spelling as in original).
38. Ibid.
39. Ibid.
40. *Seed Sense* (March, 1924): 2.
41. Albert Haldeman, "Radio English," *Des Moines Register*, January 4, 1928, 4.
42. Gordon Lathrop, "Henry Field of KFNF is the Commission's Greatest Problem," *New York Sun* Radio Section, October 22, 1927, unpaginated.
43. Ibid.
44. Thornell Barnes, "Culture Waves from KFNF," *Tanager* [Grinnell Iowa], September, 1927, 7–10.

45. Clifford J. Doerksen, *American Babel: Rogue Radio Broadcasters of the Jazz Age* (Philadelphia, PA: University of Pennsylvania Press, 2005), 79.
46. Barnes, "Culture Waves from KFNF."
47. Henry Field, "Are We 'Small Town?,'" State Historical Society of Iowa, Henry Field Collection, Ms. 134, Box 1, Folder 1.
48. "KFNF Makes Record: Gets 225,899 Telegrams," *New York Times*, March 21, 1926, XX21.
49. Assorted KFNF studio brochures, 1924–1930; Pawek, passim.
50. Pawek, passim; *Shenandoah Sentinel*, 1924–1927.
51. Lathrop, "Henry Field of KFNF"; Gard, "Henry Field of Iowa," 29–40.
52. "Listeners Like Henry Field," *Radio Digest* (October, 1929): 50.
53. Lathrop, "Henry Field of KFNF."
54. William M. Jones, Clay Center, KS, letter, May 12, 1927, FCC Records (spelling as in original).
55. Mrs. E.J. Ernst, Johnson, NE, letter, December 19, 1927, FCC Records.
56. Mrs. Eugene Webb, St. Edward, NE, letter to Secretary of Commerce Herbert Hoover, March 25, 1925, FCC Records.
57. Mrs. Charles H. Schultze, Brainerd, NE, letter, October 26, 1925, FCC Records.
58. D.J. Cowden, Adair, IA, letter December 15, 1925, FCC Records (capitalization and punctuation as in original).
59. See Mr. and Mrs. M.L. Dale, Pleasanton, IA, letter, May 12, 1927, FCC Records; Earl Tessman, Ross, IA, letter, January 9, 1926, FCC Records; Mrs. W.S. Courtright, Howard, KS, letter, January 20, 1926, FCC Records; Mr. and Mrs. John Letholt, Braymer, MO, letter, July 15, 1926, FCC Records.
60. Lathrop, "Henry Field of KFNF."
61. Stanley, "Henry Field," 64–70. Stanley did not make clear which nomination would be Field's for the asking.

Allan C. Carlson | "Flee to the Fields"
Midwestern Catholicism
and the Last Agrarian
Crusade, 1920–1941

The presidential campaign of William Jennings Bryan in 1896 revealed the extent of the new American rural crisis. Low commodity prices, rising debt, and a wave of farm foreclosures underscored the weak economic foundations of the remnant agrarian Republic. It also stimulated a "higher agrarianism," a primarily intellectual campaign to defend and promote family-scale farming and a distinctive rural life.[1] The initial thrust came from Progressives in the Northeast such as Liberty Hyde Bailey. While born in Michigan, Bailey assumed the Chair of Practical and Experimental Horticulture at New York's Cornell University in 1888. A pioneer in turning universities toward "extension work" with farmers, he founded the journals *Country Life in America* (1901) and the *Cornell Countryman* (1903) as outlets for his more philosophical efforts. Farming, he argued, produced strong families and an abundance of children, which supplied cities "with fresh blood, clean bodies, and clear brains that can endure the strain of modern urban life."[2] Moreover, contact with the earth made a person "original" in thought and "independent of group control," turning the farmer into "the fundamental fact in democracy."[3] Impressed by Bailey's 1907 speech on "The State and the Farmer," President Theodore Roosevelt appointed him to Chair a National Commission on Country Life. Joined by his friend Kenyon Butterfield, President of the Massachusetts Agriculture College, Bailey crafted a report in early 1909 that urged "the gradual rebuilding of a new agriculture and a new rural life."[4] Bailey also launched the American Country Life Association to promote this work. To the degree that religion was involved, the dominant form was liberal Protestant.[5]

This Country Life movement, though, would fall into decline during the late 1920s. Replacing it on the national stage was a distinctly Roman Catholic agrarianism. This came as a surprise, for the Catholic

Church in America at this time was overwhelmingly urban in composition and focus. All the same, a band of primarily midwestern writers and activists built a school of thought and a movement that gained national attention during the 1930s. Under the banner of "Flee to the Fields,"[6] and with a sometimes strange cast of allies, these midwestern, Catholic Agrarians mounted the last serious crusade to save and renew small-scale, family-centered agriculture on the American landscape.

Such rural activism represented a break with other currents within Catholicism. In 1899, Pope Leo XIII had condemned "Americanism," the attempt to reconcile Roman Catholicism with American-styled liberal democracy and religious pluralism. Eight years later, Pope Pius X issued an encyclical denouncing "Modernism." Meanwhile, the American Church itself was largely a self-contained cosmos, dominated by recent immigrants in ethnic parishes. This intense, inward-looking faith featured Marian parades, personal confessions, meatless Fridays, Latin masses, parochial schools, and otherworldliness. The dominant moods were alienation from the dominant culture and defensiveness.[7]

The founder of modern Catholic agrarianism was Edwin Vincent O'Hara. Born 1881 in Fillmore County, Minnesota, O'Hara enjoyed a childhood on a fairly prosperous 320-acre family farm. He attended the local public school, with most of his classmates being of Norwegian Lutheran descent. With his local priest's consent, O'Hara also took part in the month-long summer Bible schools held at the Lutheran church, a model he would later adopt for Catholic Agrarian ends.[8] In 1898, he began full-time study at The College of St. Thomas in St. Paul. Founded thirteen years earlier, St. Thomas was the project of Bishop John Ireland. He was "an unabashed flag-waving American," who emphasized the harmony between Catholic truths and American ideals. Considered dangerous by most of his German-American colleagues, Ireland embraced "reason, education, liberty, and amelioration of the masses." As a progressive on matters of economics, Ireland frequently referenced Pope Leo XIII's 1891 social encyclical, *Rerum Novarum*. By 1900, O'Hara had resolved to enter the priesthood and Ireland's exuberant Americanism transmitted to him "not only the character of Holy Orders but an entire approach to church and society."[9]

Another key figure in O'Hara's intellectual growth was John A. Ryan. Also born on a Minnesota farm and ordained by Ireland, Ryan had been dispatched for graduate training at the Catholic University of America. Here he wrote his dissertation on "A Living Wage," destined to become one of the most important volumes on economic justice of the early twentieth century. When Ryan returned to St. Thomas as a young professor of moral theology, O'Hara took courses from him over four semesters. They left a lasting mark on the student.[10] Following ordination in 1905, O'Hara became a parish priest in the Diocese of Portland, Oregon. During World War I, he served in France as a Chaplain with the U.S. Army. This sojourn in Europe also allowed him to grow more familiar with new currents in continental social thought. His focus on rural issues came after his return to the United States in December 1918. During a meeting with officials of the Catholic Educational Association, he found that they shared a concern with him over the poor state of rural Catholic churches. He agreed to study the problem and prepare a thorough report. O'Hara presented the paper, entitled "The Rural Problem in Its Bearing on Catholic Education," at the organization's 1920 meeting in New York.[11]

O'Hara's rural philosophy and program grew out of this report. They were, in their foundation, primarily inward-looking and pastoral. O'Hara noted that with new restrictions on immigration looming, the Catholic Church could no longer look to that source for growth. Rather, the future source of population would be on farms, where average family size was still three children per home, compared to 1.6 in the cities. "The primary product of the farm," he reported, "is not wheat or potatoes or cattle, it is people." In a line routinely repeated, O'Hara called the farm "the natural habitat of the family." Why was this so? Country life embraced "home ideals and attitudes," avoided "social competition" in consumption, favored more and earlier marriages, cemented the functional partnership of husband and wife, and received children as economic assets. In short, "on the farm alone ... the economic forces work for the unity of the home."[12]

Alas, only eighteen percent of American Roman Catholics resided on farms, compared to nearly fifty percent of Protestants. Meanwhile, ninety percent of Church resources—parish buildings and schools—were in cities. Given urban sterility and institutional rural neglect, the Church faced a dismal demographic future. This was ironic, O'Hara maintained, for "the Catholic Church is the strongest and most cohesive social force known to history" and there were compelling examples of a vital Catholic agrarianism to be found in Belgium, Germany, Italy, and Spain. He concluded that "the future will be with the Church that ministers to the rural population." Knowing the realities of farming, he was skeptical about back-to-the-land campaigns that planted unprepared city people in rural locales. Rather, the goal must be "stay-on-the-land," counselling young, rural, Catholic men and women to remain in farming. The church should train more priests for service in rural parishes and upgrade their status. It should build more rural schools. And it should launch projects to make farm living more socially, culturally, and religiously attractive.[13]

As O'Hara moved to implement these plans, he found willing partners, all centered in the Midwest. The oldest and largest of these was the Central Verein. Founded in 1855 as a loose union of German Catholic fraternal mutual aid societies, the organization's initial locus was in northeastern cities. The group's center-of-gravity and purpose shifted in 1908, however, through creation of the Central Bureau, with the mission to promote social justice. Established in St. Louis, this office soon reflected the "Christian-corporative social philosophy" of its first director, the energetic, Chicago-born, German-language journalist Frederick Kenkel. By 1920, the group had also turned to rural issues, driven by the strong Iowa, Minnesota, and Missouri chapters, which contained large contingents of German Catholic farmers. As one frustrated Eastern member complained as early as 1911: "What consideration can we expect from the men living on both sides of the Mississippi for our needs now? They have the Central-Verein mostly in the West."[14]

Also lending enthusiastic support were Alphonse and Joseph Matt, editors of *Das Wanderer*. Based in St. Paul, this periodical began in 1867 as a journal of religious instruction for German Catholic immigrants in the Midwest. Following the issuance of *Rerum Novarum*, it became a critic of finance capitalism and industrialism and a staunch advocate for Catholic social justice.[15] In addition, the monastic orders of the Midwest rallied to the rural cause. Prominent were the Benedictine monks of St. John's Abbey in Collegeville, Minnesota, which would become a national center for rural life education. Meanwhile, the midwestern Jesuits chose St. Mary's College in Kansas as the place for their rural pursuits.[16]

The most prominent of the early Jesuit ruralists was Joseph Husslein. Born in German-American Milwaukee in 1873, he spent most of his career at St. Louis University, where he founded the School of Social Work. Denouncing "liberalism and rationalism" alongside "the selfish spirit of rationalistic capitalism," Husslein yearned for a restoration of medieval social principles. He praised the old guilds for providing a ceiling to personal wealth and building a family-centered economic order. He defended the hierarchy of male over female and maternal austerity as "right order." He distrusted democracy. And he favored a countryside of contented peasants. His books were antiquarian, "decorous and full of strange lore," and drawn primarily from nineteenth-century German and Austrian Jesuit scholarship.[17]

For his part looking forward, O'Hara resolved to create Catholic rural organizations that would be functionally independent of the Church's hierarchy.[18] In 1920, the social justice activities of the American Catholic bishops were coordinated by the Social Action Department of the National Catholic Welfare Conference, based in Washington, DC. Its director was his former professor at St. Thomas College, John A. Ryan, while its episcopal chair was Bishop Peter Muldoon of Rockford, Illinois. O'Hara convinced them to create a Rural Life Bureau as part of the Department, "to study the rural Catholic problem, to suggest remedies and to enlist the active cooperation of all forces necessary to apply these remedies." O'Hara became its part-time Director.[19] Still serving as a rural pastor in Oregon, he also launched in 1922 a publication at his own expense: *St. Isidore's Plow*. Named for a patron saint of farmers, the monthly carried a familiar theme: "the Church which ministers to rural congregations is assured of the future in the city as well as in the country."[20]

The next year, O'Hara convened the "First National Catholic Rural Life Conference" in St. Louis. Held in conjunction with the Annual Meeting of the American Country Life Association, local arrangements were made by Frederick Kenkel and his Central Bureau. Seventy-one registrants and over a hundred observers attended the Catholic sessions. The participants approved a resolution to create a permanent National Catholic Rural Life Conference (NCRLC) that would promote "the spiritual, social and economic welfare of the rural population." Elected to its board were rural priests from Michigan, Missouri, Illinois, Wisconsin,

Ohio, Maryland, and Oregon. The director of the already existing Rural Life Bureau—Father O'Hara—would also serve as executive secretary of the Conference.[21] Concentrating on pastoral matters, O'Hara resolved to counter the deplorable catechetical education that most rural children received. Parish schools were relatively few and the Catholic population often scattered. O'Hara's response was to draw on his experience as a boy in Lutheran Vacation Bible Schools. He designed a curriculum for and promoted Religious Vacation Schools, to enroll all Catholic children in a parish, ages 6 to 14, to attend daily morning sessions for four summer weeks. By 1930, over 1000 of these schools were in operation.[22]

In all these matters, O'Hara kept his focus on the Catholic "population" problem. Through his ties with the Country Life Association he did experiment with a novel, practical, and "American" ecumenism. However, there were limits to or flaws in his approach. Notably, he and other Catholic ruralists remained fixated on Europe. O'Hara's own references to "Catholic Rural Action" usually turned to European experiences.[23] The German accent of the Central Verein often seemed too heavy.[24] And the romantic medievalism, "corporatist nostalgia," and "arcane vocabulary" of figures such as Joseph Husslein came across as strange and certainly not "American."[25] The turmoil of interwar Europe also produced a confusing message. The example of Iowa priest Luigi Ligutti is telling. Joining the Catholic rural cause in the mid-1920s, celebrated for launching a fairly successful subsistence homestead community in Granger, Iowa, during the 1930s, and taking the helm of the NCRLC in 1940/41, he remained mired in the politics of his native Italy. Throughout the interwar years, he regularly defended in the Iowa press the fascist government of Benito Mussolini. Indeed, as late as 1939, he was still publicly justifying the Italian conquest of Ethiopia.[26]

In 1930, O'Hara gained appointment as Bishop of Great Falls, Montana. These new responsibilities required resignation from his posts at the Rural Life Bureau and the NCRLC. The change also coincided with the worsening of the Great Depression. As economic paralysis spread, faith in the American gospel of prosperity and confidence in the capitalist system waned. In addition, the early 1930s witnessed a reversal of the long-time city-ward trend in migration; the greater number was now returning to the country. Many of these migrants were "determined to be self-sufficient and independent of the marketplace."[27] The time was ripe for creative, even radical thinking about the place of farming within American culture and agriculture.[28]

Moreover, a curious gap in American agrarian thought and activism had emerged. By the early 1930s, the American Country Life Association was in clear numerical decline; so were the rural life offices of the larger Protestant denominations.[29] A new group of Catholic ruralists found themselves standing, partly by default, as the nation's leading religious agrarians. Their focus quickly shifted from Catholicism's "population" problem to a campaign to save and energize the whole of American agriculture. Conscious of their midwestern roots, they deemed the pattern of the 160-acre farm still dominant in the Upper Mississippi Valley to be the modern version of the Jeffersonian ideal. In contrast to the convoluted land holdings of the South and the industrial farms in California's Central Valley, the Midwest's model was available for nationwide replication.[30]

Encouraging this shift were broader developments within Catholicism itself. To begin with, a Catholic "literary revival" was already under way, involving a rediscovery and a re-tuning of Thomistic neo-scholasticism, the medieval theology of Thomas Aquinas repackaged for the twentieth century. John Henry Newman was "the prophet and inspiration for the initial stages" of this revival; another English convert, G.K. Chesterton, fed the flame. The latter's genius here came in taking the whole argument against Christianity and turning it on its head: Christian Orthodoxy liberates; materialism and rationalism restrain. Orthodoxy brings true progress; unbelief brings stagnation. Other European authors drawn in included Emmanuel Mournier, Étienne Gilson, Jacques Maritain, and Christopher Dawson. Long on the defensive, Catholic thinkers and apologists now boldly entered American debates over culture and social politics, supremely confident that their creed "represented immutability and cohesion" and "resolute authority" amidst cultural despair and intellectual confusion.[31]

Further energy came from Pope Pius XI's 1931 encyclical, *Quadragesimo Anno*. Issued on the fortieth anniversary of *Rerum Novarum*, Pius's commentary on economics, morality, and social justice was far bolder and more specific than Leo XIII's had been. It provided a framework for a Catholic "third way" economics that was entirely compatible with basic agrarian ideas.[32] A third factor was an

G.K. Chesterton's only visit to the Midwest came in autumn, 1930, when he served as a Visiting Professor at the University of Notre Dame in Indiana. At the end of his tenure, he received an honorary Doctor of Laws degree from University President Charles O'Donnell, CSC [pictured here, courtesy of the Notre Dame Archives]. The Englishman's duties also included attendance at the dedication of Notre Dame's new football stadium. In honor of the occasion he wrote a poem, "The Arena," comparing American footballers to the gladiators of ancient Rome.

emerging contest over informal control of the Church in America, part of a shift in Catholic influence from the predominantly Irish East to the predominantly German Midwest. As Michael Dolan explains, this was also "evidenced in George Cardinal Mundelein's plans to make Chicago the Catholic capital of the United States."[33]

These developments gave a new spirit to the Catholic Agrarian cause. As John LaFarge, associate editor of the Jesuit publication *America*, told the 1936 conference of the NCRLC: "American culture can be saved, and Catholicism can save it, and will save it, if we get a chance." Why? Because the Catholic Church "preserves what is individual, unique, local, regional, special, historic, in our American culture, because it essentially tends to organic forms."[34] As they charged into America's culture wars, Catholic Agrarians also found new allies. Prominent among these were the Southern Agrarians, loosely tied to Vanderbilt University, who issued the volume *I'll Take My Stand* in 1930. Theirs was a clarion cry of resistance to both the "New South" creed (what Robert Dorman has called "a kind of Dixie Babbitry") and "the powerful acid of the great Progressive Principle."[35] Catholic ruralists adapted most of the arguments made by the Southerners into their own framework, including the Vanderbilt group's interpretation of the Civil War (where "success to Northern arms was in reality success for the cause of industrialism").[36]

The second and more important alliance came through contact with the distributists of Great Britain. Ties first emerged in the 1920s. An early issue of *St. Isidore's Plow*, for example, featured an essay by Hilaire

Belloc on "The Mowing of a Field."[37] And in 1926, the "Distributist priest" Vincent McNabb dispatched a remarkable "Open Letter" set in old gothic type to the NCRLC's 1926 conference, where he supported local food ("things should be produced where they can be most economically consumed") and celebrated the husbandman "whose craft demands and provides the home and the homestead" that were "alone efficient to safeguard family life."[38]

The deeper influence, though, came from their colleague, G.K. Chesterton. Simply put, Chesterton rescued Catholic ruralists from the medievalism of Husslein, delivering instead a rhetoric of liberty and democracy, laced with a remarkable, almost childlike gaiety and optimism.[39] Chesterton admired the Middle Ages for providing an economic order grounded in widely distributed property, but he never became a "Medievalist."[40] Indeed, following Belloc here, Chesterton—the great apologist for Christian orthodoxy—actually celebrated the French Revolution for its opposition to aristocracy, its defense of the common man, and its commitment to human freedom and democracy. This support for the Revolution even extended to a defense of the anti-Catholic "Civil Constitution of the Clergy," promulgated in 1790.[41]

Chesterton stood, in the words of his American disciple Herbert Agar, for "life on the human scale, life organized so that the plain man can understand it, enjoy it, love it…. It follows that he was one of the truest democrats of modern history."[42] Chesterton praised Thomas Jefferson and the Jacobins Robespierre and Danton as "men of the forum and the marketplace, ruling among the people under an open sky."[43] Meanwhile, the Englishman's love of liberty approached philosophical anarchism.

Chesterton also delivered to Catholic Agrarians in America a fairly clear economic program. It began with a strident denunciation of capitalism as enemy of the family, which attracted American attention. As Chesterton wrote: "It is not the Bolshevik, but the Boss, the publicity man, the salesman and the commercial advertiser who have, like a rush and riot of barbarians, thrown down and trampled underfoot the ancient Roman statue of Verecundia."[44] In another context, Chesterton declared: "Our purpose is revolution. We do not want to tinker with the capitalist system, we want to destroy it." His distributist alternative required a broad redistribution of productive land, homes, and shops from the "plutocrats" to common men and their families, a "revolution" to be achieved through differential taxation. As the original name for Chesterton's Distributist League nicely summarized, it was "The League for the Preservation of Liberty by the Restoration of Property."[45]

Here was a language and a political platform that seemed to reconcile Christianity and conservative family values with liberty, democracy, and social justice, that brought Aquinas and Jefferson under the same philosophical tent, that linked the radical to the reactionary, and that implicitly blessed the relatively egalitarian midwestern pattern of the 160-acre family farm. As Paul K. Conkin quipped, "Was Jefferson back on earth, or was it St. Thomas speaking?"[46] This was a heady brew.

In 1928, the American journalist Herbert Agar moved to England, where he took a junior editorial post at *G.K.'s Weekly*, Chesterton's journal. Agar subsequently became an exuberant "translator" of distributism into an American idiom. In his Pulitzer Prize–winning book, *The People's Choice*, and in a long essay on "The Task for Conservatism," Agar basically rewrote American history through a distributist lens.[47] His 1936 volume, *Land of the Free*, advanced his development of an American agrarianism built on distributist principles, including a return to self-sufficient family farms based on the midwestern 160-acre model and policies "to eliminate the purely commercial farmer by means of differential taxation."[48] Agar joined with the Vanderbilt agrarian Allen Tate to co-edit still another volume, *Who Owns America?: A New Declaration of Independence*, which also appeared in 1936. In addition, Agar was the driving force behind the launch in 1937 of a new monthly journal, *Free America*, bankrolled by the wealthy Catholic convert Chauncey Stillman. Claiming to be equally opposed to finance capitalism, communism, and fascism, the journal sought to unify "The Southern Agrarians and their allied Distributist Groups ..., the Consumer Cooperative Movement, the Catholic Rural Life Conference," and other agrarian causes.[49]

Importantly, all of the new, post-O'Hara Catholic Agrarian leaders were products of the Midwest. The almost complete domination of the organization after 1940 by Luigi Ligutti has tended to obscure the work and contributions of these men. Unlike the "activist" Ligutti, they were persons committed to ideas and to the articulation of a distinctly Catholic rural philosophy with a national appeal and influence. They included: Aloisius Muench, born in Milwaukee, who became the Bishop of Fargo and oversaw the drafting of the NCRLC's 1939 *Manifesto on*

*Rural Life;* Edgar Schmiedeler, a Kansas-born Benedictine priest, who earned a PhD in rural sociology from Kansas State University and replaced O'Hara as director of the Rural Life Bureau and executive secretary of the NCRLC; Joseph A. Campbell, a priest from Ames, Iowa, who became president of the NCRLC in 1934, convinced that "our first concern must be economic rather than spiritual"; and Vincent J. Ryan, one of "the Fargo Trio" who drafted the *Manifesto* in 1939 and who soon thereafter became the Bishop of Bismarck, North Dakota.[50]

Three others, though, stand out. James Byrnes, born in Minnesota, became a priest overseeing the parochial schools of the Diocese of St. Paul. Following a power struggle of sorts, he replaced Schmiedeler at the NCRLC in 1934, becoming the organization's first independent executive secretary. "[S]trongly conscious of their rural and Midwestern roots," he and Fr. Campbell successfully moved the NCRLC office from Washington, DC, to St. Paul. Of equal importance, he also resolved to raise the intellectual tone and output of the organization. Starting in 1935, he produced for several years a compilation of the best papers from the NCRLC's annual conferences, under the title *Catholic Rural Life Objectives.* And in 1938, he founded a new periodical, *The Catholic Rural Life Bulletin.* Despite its title, this was a journal of ideas and policy prescriptions, not a newsletter. It drew generously on secular agrarian theory. In format, typeface, and graphics, it closely resembled *Free America.*[51]

Born 1890 to a German Catholic family in St. Paul, George Michel spent his summers and winter vacations working on his grandparents' farm in Scott County, Minnesota. At age twenty, he joined the Benedictine Order at St. John's Abbey, taking the new name Virgil. Ordained in 1916, he earned a doctorate from the Catholic University of America. Subsequent study in Europe opened his mind to distributist ideas in Britain and to the need for liturgical renewal. Emphasizing the Mystical Body of Christ, Virgil Michel sought a more "natural" celebration of the Mass and active participation by the laity, goals tied to his budding agrarianism. For example, he argued that the Eucharist in the Catholic Mass took place as a community, so pointing as well toward a political economy built around producer cooperatives. His nine books on social questions included *Ownership, Critique of Capitalism,* and *Ideas of Reconstruction.*[52]

The third key figure was John C. Rawe. Born in Omaha and raised on a farm, "he had a feel for the soil and small towns." Entering the Jesuit order, he studied and taught at St. Louis University, St. Mary's College, and Creighton University. Agrarianism came naturally to him, absent the "gothic Catholicism" and continental Jesuit musings. As one biographer has noted, he was wholly American: "He glorified the American yeomanry, and the times he yearned to restore were Jeffersonian."[53] In 1940, Rawe co-authored with Luigi Ligutti *Rural Roads to Security: America's Third Struggle for Freedom*. One historian has called it the "Summa" of Catholic agrarianism; two others "the most explicit and most radical presentation" of the NCRLC's rural philosophy.[54] The more ideologically charged portions of the book were clearly the work of Rawe.

The first purpose of the Catholic Agrarian cause was deeply conservative: the protection and promotion of the procreative family. To this end, the Agrarians favored the usual Catholic social principles: relatively early and indissoluble marriage; distinct gender roles within marriage, with mothers focused on the nurture of children and the care of homes; a strict condemnation of birth limitation, except through abstinence; and a consequent high fertility. They were notable on such matters only by the extra emphasis that they gave to large families as a deliberate goal, the legacy of Edwin O'Hara.

On all matters economic, though, their platform was radical, indeed. To begin with, the Catholic Agrarians saw their campaign as part of a global "Green Rising," what G.K. Chesterton hopefully labelled a "vast victory" for European peasants and American family farmers and "a vast defeat both for the communists and the capitalists," "a huge historical hinge and turning point like the conversion of Constantine or the French Revolution."[55] In *Rural Roads to Security*, Luigi Ligutti and John C. Rawe labelled the American version of this Green Rising the "third struggle for liberty," the first being against the British King in the Revolution and the second against slavery in the Civil War. The third campaign was against "the Liberalistic system" of economics fostered in Europe, which paved the way for imposition of a materialist philosophy.[56] Speaking at the 1935 NCRLC meeting, journalist Michael Williams called for "a moral revolution, a revolution of spiritual force," a "Green Revolution" in America that would "restore the original bases of American life which the first American Revolution laid down ... but which the Industrial Revolution [partly] overthrew."⁵⁷

Midwestern Catholic ruralists also embraced a strident anti-urbanism. In a fictional "airplane survey" of America, John Rawe began in the Northeast where families led "congested" lives in "brick caves and canyons of steel and stone," where "belching factories" reduced "millions of men, women and children" to dependence "upon the low wage incomes from subdivided, dehumanized, unskilled, monotonous jobs," where home production had been abandoned, where women—"mothers too"—engaged in industrial work to the detriment of home life, and where the 200 giant corporations that largely owned America resided. In cities, James Byrnes added, "the sanctities of marriage are treated with pagan indifference." Edgar Schmiedeler reported "that the present American city is doomed ... to destroy human beings." *The Catholic Rural Life Bulletin*, under the banner of "Flee to the Fields," described American cities as "the graveyards of our civilization." As Virgil Michel summarized: "Eden was a farm. Sodom was a city."⁵⁸

Capitalism received an equally strong denunciation. The Conference's *Manifesto on Rural Life* held that industrial capitalism "works against the family and in favor of divorce, desertion, temporary unions, [and] companionate marriage." Rawe denounced the joint-stock corporate charter as "a legal-social structure of privilege and concentration completely alien to the fundamental democratic provisions in our laws." The movement of industrial capitalism onto the land, he argued elsewhere, "will reduce a nation of free citizens to slaves, bring death to living things, [and] barrenness to its soils." He described the Middle West as "a peaceful country, where we peacefully destroy our land with tractors" driven by a landless rural proletariat for the benefit of "banker owners and absentee investors." Byrnes found the status of "our so-called common people" under capitalism to differ "but slightly from that of slavery."⁵⁹

A "Property State," Catholic Agrarians held, was the just alternative. The cardinal prescriptive principles of their rural theory were: the wide diffusion of productive property; ownership of the land by those who till it; and promotion of the family-scale farm, with the 160-acre midwestern model clearly in mind. Rawe insisted that widely divided farmland among a free yeomanry was an implicit part of the

American Constitution. He praised a 1932 Kansas Supreme Court decision that had abolished as a "public menace" a 64,000-acre corporate farm, and urged a wave of such judgments. Justifying this sweeping agenda, Michel argued (citing Thomas Aquinas): that "[a]ll the things of earth apart from men are there to serve the needs and the comforts … of all men, of all mankind"; that "all men have the strict right by natural law to as much of these goods as they need for attaining the purposes of their creation by God"; and that "superfluous" property beyond the needs of a man and his dependents fell under "the wider social aspect of all things human," subject to redistribution.[60]

In this regard, Catholic writers openly acknowledged the need to use government power for agrarian ends. The 1939 *Manifesto* held that state action "is not only warranted but even necessary to check the trend toward tenancy and make it possible for farmers to become owners again." It favored a rural "homestead exemption" from property taxes, a "progressive land tax" to discourage speculation and break up large commercial farms, and a tax on "the unearned increment of land values." Casting a broader policy net, Rawe called for laws that "would restrict advertising campaigns," prevent the formation of agricultural joint stock companies, and abolish the bank ownership of land.[61]

Catholic ruralists also called for a mandatory "Parity" in prices. The *Manifesto* reasoned that if "[t]hirty-five to forty million farm people of the nation receive an unfair price for agricultural products, their purchasing power is reduced." Adapting the old Catholic economic concept of "just price" to American conditions and new policy language, the document declared "the maintenance of a parity in prices between agriculture and industry" to be of "great importance."[62]

Echoing both Aristotle and Jefferson, these agrarians urged as well a return to self-sufficiency on farms and in homes. According to Byrnes, the "true agrarian is a person of simple tastes and habits." He "wants a balanced life for all," Rawe added, "lived out in a definite social tradition, a life in which religion, arts, good manners, conversation, hospitality, sympathy, family life, and all other social exchanges can reveal and develop sensibility in human affairs in an equitable economy founded on the right relations of man to nature." This "homestead basis of life" required, according to John LaFarge, that "the majority of citizens grow some of their own vegetables; that women again learn the arts of home production; that the home workshop come into its own." Rawe concurred, suggesting that study of the classics in schools give way in part to the training of both boys and girls in "self-sufficiency" and a "way of life" form of agriculture.⁶³

Finally, some Catholic theorists embraced biodynamic agriculture. Rawe in particular was drawn to this approach, as articulated by Rudolf Steiner. Tactfully ignoring the latter's grounding in theosophy and spiritualism, Rawe emphasized Steiner's vision of "the wholeness, the oneness, the completeness of nature in the life ... of the farm." On the biodynamic farm, "the earthworm is recognized as a healthy visitor" for he "is a connoisseur of the better soils." More broadly, this form of agriculture recognized "the great life powers that lie hidden in land and its organisms."⁶⁴

The "heroic" phase of Catholic ruralism came to an end in 1941. At the most basic level, World War II—in David Shi's words—"shattered the hopes for a return to a society of small farms, small businesses, and small communities."⁶⁵ Decentralist yearnings were overwhelmed by the greatest centralizing event in human history. Important changes also took place among the Agrarians themselves. Virgil Michel died at a relatively young age in 1938. Two years later, illness forced James Byrnes to resign as executive secretary of the NCRLC; in early 1941, he also left his post as editor of the *Bulletin*. Then illness struck John C. Rawe as well, leading to his premature death in 1947.⁶⁶

Replacing Byrnes in both of his positions was Luigi Ligutti. *The Catholic Rural Life Bulletin* had reached a kind of perfection in late 1940 and early 1941, carrying provocative essays linking agrarian ideas to political and social solutions. In early 1942, Ligutti scrapped this format. Relabeling the periodical *Land and Home*, the philosophical essays largely disappeared, replaced by light fiction, human interest stories, and recipes.⁶⁷ Moreover, as the decade progressed, Ligutti turned his attentions ever more toward international food and agriculture questions. "Other Lands" became a regular feature in *Land and Home*. This work led eventually to Ligutti's launch of the International Rural Life Congress. The focus on rural America and—in practice—on the Midwest so gave way to global concerns.⁶⁸

By 1950, it was also clear that American agriculture had entered a seemingly irreversible new phase. Manpower shortages during the war sharply accelerated the turn from true horsepower to tractors. After the war, this larger scale, more mechanized production for markets retained its allure. As then commonly operated, the midwestern 160-acre farmstead lost economic viability. Promising political responses failed. The American farm population—still over 30 million in 1940—fell to 23 million in 1950, a form of rural depopulation that would continue through the 1980s. The Catholic rural philosophy developed during the interwar years now seemed irrelevant, a failure.[69]

In retrospect, though, the flowering of Catholic agrarianism left important legacies. To begin with, these midwestern writers succeeded brilliantly in translating neo-scholastic Thomism into American language, what one commentator has labelled "peddling Catholic ultramontanism in a specifically American idiom." Viewed more positively, "Thomas Jefferson and Thomas Aquinas spoke with one voice" for these agrarians, an impressive intellectual feat that contributed in important ways to the "normalization" of Roman Catholicism in American life.[70] They accomplished this without any hint of the "old" medievalism of Frederick Husslein or the "new" medievalism (featuring communal farms) introduced by Peter Maurin into the contemporaneous and initially Northeastern Catholic Workers Movement.[71] As Chesterton and Belloc had done in England, their midwestern American followers had succeeded in bringing Catholicism "out of private and into public life."[72]

Second, the Catholic Agrarians created an approach to social justice questions that differed in important ways from the better known work of John Ryan. Where the latter focused on heavy industry, urban issues, "the family living wage," and social security, the Agrarians emphasized property ownership, family autonomy, and decentralization: matters actually closer to the core Catholic concept of subsidiarity, which holds that larger entities should never take on tasks suitably performed by smaller ones. The Agrarian approach remains a solid "Third Way" model for future Catholic social action. Indeed, Jay P. Corrin suggests that Catholic distributist and agrarian ideas may have simply come several decades too early: that they actually have a "greater relevance to the problems of post-industrial than to industrial society." The recent expansion in the number of organic and biodynamic farms, the mounting interest in farmers' markets and "backyard chickens," the turn to decentralized and home-based work, and the "sheer boredom" of the contemporary welfare state support this contention.[73]

Third, historians Christopher Hamlin and John T. McGreevy persuasively argue that these ruralists crafted "a distinctly Catholic American environmental vision" that was also "an environmentalism ... of the Midwest," one worthy of much more historical and practical attention. Being "unapologetically anthropocentric," these agrarians did not see nature as sacred; rather, "work in nature was sacramental." This midwestern approach paid little attention to scenic places or wild spaces; rather, it focused on cycles, emphasizing "sky and soil, watching small parts of nature change through the seasons." Hamlin and McGreevy find particularly in John C. Rawe a neglected precursor to Wendell Berry.[74]

Finally, it appears that while the number of Americans on farms plummeted after 1940, the *relative share* of Catholics rose substantially—just as Edwin O'Hara had hoped. Looking specifically at "German Catholic islands" in the rural Midwest, Kathleen Neils Conzen has reported that when compared to 1880, second-generation Germans in 1950 were "overrepresented" in agriculture by fifty percent. A survey of twelve midwestern states in 1980 found that twenty-seven percent of the farm population identified themselves as of "purely German ancestry" and twenty-two percent as of "mixed German ancestry": forming nearly half of the population in the nation's farming core.[75] Paraphrasing both Scripture and the title of the leading biography of Fr. O'Hara, some Catholic Agrarian seed did fall on good ground.

## Notes

1. Peter A. Huff, *Allen Tate and the Catholic Revival: Trace of the Fugitive Gods* (New York and Mahnah, NJ: Paulist Press, 1996), 57.
2. From Andrew Denny Rodgers III, *Liberty Hyde Bailey: A Story of American Plant Sciences* (New York and London: Hafner Publishing Co., 1965 [1949]), 373.
3. Liberty Hyde Bailey, *The Holy Earth* (Ithaca, NY: New York State College of Agriculture, 1980 [1915]), 87; and L.H. Bailey, *What Is Democracy?* (Ithaca, NY: The Comstock Publishing Co., 1918), 95–96.
4. U.S. Congress. *Report of the Country Life Commission* (Senate Doc. 705, 60th Congress, 2nd Session, 1909).
5. See: William L. Bowers, *The Country Life Movement in America, 1900–1920* (Port Washington, NY: Kennikat Press, 1974); and David B. Danbom, *The Resisted Revolution: Urban America and the Industrialization of Agriculture* (Ames: The Iowa State University Press, 1979), 51–74.

6. This phrase came from the Catholic Land Movement in England; see: *Flee to the Fields* (London: Heath Cranton, 1934; new edition Norfolk, VA: IHS Press, 2003).
7. Huff, *Allen Tate and the Catholic Revival*, 9–10; and Arnold Sparr, *To Promote, Defend, and Redeem: The Catholic Literary Revival and the Cultural Transformation of American Catholicism, 1920–1960* (New York: Greenwood Press, 1990), 51–57.
8. Timothy Michael Dolan, *"Some Seed Fell on Good Ground": The Life of Edwin V. O'Hara* (Washington, DC: The Catholic University of America Press, 1992), 1, 5–8; and J.G. Shaw, *Edwin Vincent O'Hara: American Prelate* (New York: Farrar, Straus, and Cudahy, 1957), 2–7.
9. Dolan, *"Some Seed Fell on Good Ground,"* 11–13; Shaw, *Edwin Vincent O'Hara*, 10.
10. Dolan, *"Some Seed Fell on Good Ground,"* 13–15.
11. Ibid., 63–66.
12. Edwin O'Hara, *The Church and the Country Community* (New York: Macmillan, 1927), 7–11, 24–25, 33–34.
13. O'Hara, *The Church and the Country Community*, 8, 11, 21, 24–25; Shaw, *Edwin Vincent O'Hara*, 65–66.
14. Philip Gleason, *The Conservative Reformers: German-American Catholics and the Social Order* (Notre Dame, IN: University of Notre Dame Press, 1968), 90–108, 186–88; and August Brockland, "Rural Work of the Central Verein," *St. Isidore's Plow* 2 (December 1923), 3.
15. Michael W. Cuneo, *The Smoke of Satan: Conservative and Traditionalist Dissent in Contemporary American Catholicism* (New York: Oxford University Press, 1997), 49–52; and Jeffrey Marlett, *Saving the Heartland: Catholic Missionaries in Rural America* (DeKalb: Northern Illinois University Press, 2002), 19.
16. Huff, *Allen Tate and the Catholic Revival*, 60.
17. Peter McDonough, *Men Astutely Trained: A History of the Jesuits in the American Century* (New York: The Free Press, 1992), 51–57; and Sparr, *To Promote, Defend, and Redeem*, 67.
18. Marlett, *Saving the Heartland*, 15; and Christopher Hamlin and John T. McGreevy, "The Greening of America, Catholic Style, 1930–1950," *Environmental History* 11 (July 2006), 467.
19. David Bovée, *The Church & The Land: The National Catholic Rural Life Conference and American Society, 1923–2007* (Washington, DC: The Catholic University of America Press, 2010), 39–40; also Raymond Philip Witte, *Twenty-Five Years of Crusading: A History of the National Catholic Rural Life Conference*, 1948), 58–60.
20. Edwin V. O'Hara, "The Church and Rural Life," *St. Isidore's Plow* 1 (October 1922), 1.
21. "First National Rural Life Conference," *St. Isidore's Plow* 2 (November 1923), 1; and Henry Schuermann, "Catholic Rural Life Conference," *St.*

*Isidore's Plow* 2 (December 1923), 1. Also: "Joint Program, National Catholic Rural Life Conference and the American Country Life Association, St. Louis, MO, November 8-10, 1923" and "Announcement of First National Catholic Rural Life Conference," in National Rural Life Conferences (NRLC) collection, Marquette University Archives, Milwaukee, WI, Series 8, Box 1.
22. O'Hara, *The Church and the Country Community*, 59; and Dolan, "*Some Seed Fell on Good Ground,*" 75-76.
23. O'Hara, *The Church and the Country Community*, 72-109.
24. "Catholics Should Champion the Farmer's Cause. Press Bulletin of the Central Bureau of the Central Verein," *St. Isidore's Plow* 2 (February 1923), 3.
25. McDonough, *Men Astutely Trained*, 58-63.
26. Letters from Luigi Ligutti to the Editor, *Des Moines Register*, March 20, 1926; March 25, 1926; April 1, 1926; April 25, 1929; November 5, 1929; February 14, 1939; June 16, 1939; and December 30, 1939; in The Papers of Luigi Ligutti (LGL), Marquette University Archives, Milwaukee, WI, Series 1, Box 1; also "Italians Endorse Fascism," newspaper clipping from *Des Moines Register*, January 12, 1927, in LGL, Series 6, Box 1.
27. Russell Lord and Paul H. Johnstone, *A Place on Earth: A Critical Appraisal of Subsistence Homesteads* (Washington, DC: U.S. Department of Agriculture, Bureau of Agricultural Economics, 1942), 11-12.
28. A new group of midwestern-born "agrarian intellectuals" also emerged within the U.S. Department of Agriculture during the 1930s. See: Jess Gilbert, *Planning Democracy: Agrarian Intellectuals and the Intended New Deal* (New Haven, CT: Yale University Press, 2015), 25-59.
29. Bovée, *The Church & The Land*, 103.
30. Dolan, "*Some Seed Fell on Good Ground,*" 105; Hamlin and McGreevy, "The Greening of America," 466.
31. Sparr, *To Promote, Defend, and Redeem*, 59-62; Huff, *Allen Tate and the Catholic Revival*, 11-14; and Patrick Allitt, *Catholic Converts: British and American Intellectuals Turn to Rome* (Ithaca and London: Cornell University Press, 1997), 192, 197.
32. Pope Pius XI, *Quadragesimo Anno;* in *Two Basic Social Encyclicals* (Washington, DC: Catholic University of America Press, 1943).
33. Dolan, "*Some Seed Fell on Good Ground,*" 105.
34. John LaFarge, S.J., "The Groundwork of True American Culture." Address to the Annual Conference of the NCRLC, October 12, 1936, in NRLC, Series 8/1, Box 2.
35. Robert L. Dorman, *Revolt of the Provinces: The Regionalist Movement in America, 1920-1945* (Chapel Hill and London: University of North Carolina Press, 1993), 111-12. Their volume: Twelve Southerners, *I'll Take My Stand: The South and the Agrarian Tradition* (Baton Rouge: Louisiana State University Press, 1977 [1930]). A solid dissection of the intellectual

roots and legacy of the Southern Agrarians is found in: Paul V. Murphy, *The Southern Agrarians and American Conservative Thought* (Chapel Hill and London: University of North Carolina Press, 2001), especially 36–39, 62–91.
36. James A. Byrnes, "A Manifesto on Rural Life," *The American Catholic Sociological Review* 1 (March 1940), 30.
37. Hilaire Belloc, "The Mowing of a Field," *St. Isidore's Plow* 2 (February 1923), 3.
38. Vincent McNabb, "An Open Letter to the Honorary President of the Catholic Rural Life Conference" [1926], in NRLC, Series 8, Box 1.
39. Jay P. Corrin, *G.K. Chesterton and Hilaire Belloc: The Battle Against Modernity* (Athens: Ohio University Press, 1981), 9.
40. Quentin Lauer, S.J., *G.K. Chesterton: Philosopher Without Portfolio* (New York: Fordham University Press, 1988), 139.
41. Robert Hickson, "Belloc and Chesterton: Their Partial Reflections on The Revolution in France," unpublished paper, (1988), 4–5; and John P. McCarthy, *Hilaire Belloc: Edwardian Radical* (Indianapolis: Liberty Press, 1978), 314–16.
42. Herbert Agar, "A Great Democrat," *The Southern Review* 3 (1937–38), 96.
43. Corrin, *G.K. Chesterton and Hilaire Belloc*, 178.
44. Quotation in W. Howard Bishop, "Agrarianism: The Basis of the New Order." Keynote Address to the 1935 Meeting of the NCRLC, in *NRLC*, Series 8/1, Box 2, 2–3.
45. Corrin, *G.K. Chesterton and Hilaire Belloc*, 108, 110.
46. Paul K. Conkin, *Tomorrow a New World: The New Deal Community Program* (Ithaca, NY: Cornell University Press, 1959), 24.
47. Herbert Agar, *The People's Choice* (Boston and New York: Houghton Mifflin, 1933); and Herbert Agar, "The Task for Conservatism," *American Review* 3 (April 1934), 1–16.
48. Herbert Agar, *Land of the Free* (Boston: Houghton Mifflin, 1935), 274–78.
49. "Editorials," *Free America* 1 (January 1937), 3–4. On Agar's influence, see also Louis G. Miller, "Some Agrarian Beginnings," *The Catholic Rural Life Bulletin* 3 (November 1940), 23; and Corrin, *G.K. Chesterton and Hilaire Belloc*, 162.
50. Bovée, *The Church & The Land*, 131–32, 148; Dolan, "Some Seed Fell on Good Ground," 102–103, 106.
51. Bovée, *The Church & The Land*, 134–35, 143–45; Witte, *Twenty-Five Years of Crusading*, 163–65; and Vincent A. Ryan, "A Tribute to Father Byrnes," *The Catholic Rural Life Bulletin* 4 (February 1941), 14.
52. Paul Marx, *The Life and Work of Virgil Michel* (Washington, DC: The Catholic University of America Press, 1957), 3–5, 302–308, 320; Emerson Hynes, "The Social Thought of Virgil Michel," *The American Catholic Sociological Review* 1 (December 1940), 173–80; Gleason, *The Conservative*

Allan C. Carlson    205

*Reformers*, 190-91; and Hamlin and McGreevy, "The Greening of America," 472-73.
53. McDonough, *Men Astutely Trained*, 89.
54. See: Hamlin and McGreevy, "The Greening of America," 467. The first judgement they attribute to Jeffrey Marlett.
55. G.K. Chesterton, "The 'Green Rising,'" *St. Isidore's Plow* 2 (November 1923), 3.
56. Luigi G. Ligutti and John C. Rawe, *Rural Roads to Security: America's Third Struggle for Freedom* (Milwaukee, WI: Bruce Publishing Co., 1940), 3-6.
57. Michael Williams, "The Green Revolution," in James A. Byrnes, ed., *Catholic Rural Life Objectives. First Series* (St. Paul, MN: National Catholic Rural Life Conference, 1935), 35.
58. John C. Rawe, "Agriculture—An Airplane Survey," *The Catholic Rural Life Bulletin* 3 (February 1940), 1; James A. Byrnes, "The Conference Salutes the American Farmer," *The Catholic Rural Life Bulletin* 1 (November 1938), 12; Edgar Schmiedeler, *Catholic Rural Life* (Washington, DC: Rural Life Bureau, N.C.W.C., 1932), 17; "Flee to the Fields," *The Catholic Rural Life Bulletin* 3 (August 1940), 17; and Marlett, *Saving the Heartland*, 36.
59. *Manifesto on Rural Life* (St. Paul, MN: NCRLC, 1939), 3; John C. Rawe, "Agriculture and the Property State," in Herbert Agar and Allen Tate, eds., *Who Owns America?: A New Declaration of Independence* (Wilmington, DE: ISI Books, 1999 [1936]), 53; John C. Rawe, "The Home on the Land," *The Catholic Rural Life Bulletin* 2 (February 1939), 24-25; Rawe, "Agriculture—An Airplane Survey," 24; James A. Byrnes, "Foreword," *Catholic Rural Life Objectives, Second Series* (St. Paul: NCRLC, 1936), 3.
60. Dolan, "Some Seed Fell on Good Ground," 108; Rawe, "Agriculture and the Property State," 71; John C. Rawe, "Life, Liberty, and the Pursuit of Happiness in Agriculture," address to the 1936 meeting of the NCRLC, Fargo, North Dakota; in NRLC, series 8/1, Box 2; and Luigi Ligutti, "Agrarians, Cooperatives, and The Bishops' Statement," *The Catholic Rural Life Bulletin* 3 (May 1940), 4-5 [Michel quotation]. On the campaign against corporate farming after World War II, see: Jon Lauck, *American Agriculture and the Problem of Monopoly: The Political Economy of Grain Belt Farming, 1953-1980* (Lincoln and London: University of Nebraska Press, 2000), 19-38.
61. *Manifesto on Rural Life*, 11, 68; John C. Rawe, "Agrarianism: The Basis for a Better Life," *The American Review* 6 (December 1935), 188-91.
62. *Manifesto on Rural Life*, 63-64. On the origins of the "farm parity" campaign, see: Gilbert C. Fite, *George N. Peek and the Fight for Farm Parity* (Norman: University of Oklahoma Press, 1954), 21-37, 119-37, 192-202.
63. Byrnes, "A Manifesto on Rural Life," 32; Rawe, "Agrarianism," 182; LaFarge, "Decentralism and Rural Life," *The Catholic Rural Life Bulletin* 3 (August 1940), 1; Rawe, "Classics or Practical Subjects," *The Catholic Rural Life*

*Bulletin* 4 (November 1941), 114; and Rawe, "Agriculture—An Airplane Survey," 25.
64. Hamlin and McGreevy, "The Greening of America," 484; John C. Rawe, "Biotechnology on the Land," *The Catholic Rural Life Bulletin* 2 (August 1939), 21–22; and Rawe, "Agriculture—An Airplane Survey," 25.
65. David E. Shi, *Simple Life: Plain Living and High Thinking in American Culture* (New York: Oxford University Press, 1985), 245.
66. Bovée, *The Church & The Land*, 152–53.
67. *Land and Home* 5 (March 1942).
68. Bovée, *The Church & The Land*, 176–81.
69. Hamlin and McGreevy, "The Greening of America," 471.
70. Marlett, *Saving the Heartland*, 23, 41.
71. Allitt, *Catholic Converts*, 207.
72. Corrin, *G. K .Chesterton and Hilaire Belloc*, 208.
73. Ibid., 202–203.
74. Hamlin and McGreevy, "The Greening of America," 464–66, 484, 489.
75. Kathleen Neils Conzen, *Making Their Own America: Assimilation Theory and the German Peasant Pioneer* (New York: Berg, 1990), 2–5; also Sonya Salomon, *Prairie Patrimony: Family, Farming, and Community in the Middle West* (Chapel Hill: University of North Carolina Press, 1992).

Michael C. Steiner | The Midwestern Mind of Jane Addams

Cultural Pluralism and the Rural Roots of an Urban Idea

The Midwest was on the rise in the opening decades of the twentieth century. Observers as varied as Frederick Jackson Turner and Henry Louis Mencken recognized the Midwest's ascendency as a region rife with conflict and creativity. In 1901 Turner pointed out that six of the seven presidents elected between 1860 and 1900 had been Midwesterners, and he confidently declared the region "the economic and political center of the Republic" and asserted "the future of the Republic is with her." Sixteen years later, Mencken proclaimed Chicago "the literary capital of the United States," asserting that "all literary movements that have youth and a fresh point of view are products of Chicago ... the most civilized city in America."[1]

The immense power and potential that Walt Whitman, Louis Sullivan, and others had sensed in the sprawling prairies and great lakes in the 1870s seemed achieved by 1900. The Midwest had become, in Whitman's 1879 words, the "theater of our great future," and Hamlin Garland's 1893 prophecy that the region was destined to be the epicenter of American culture seemed fulfilled.[2] But the Midwest's new found dominance might have come at a steep price as it experienced ever-increasing ethnic, class, and racial turmoil in its burgeoning cities and expanding hinterlands. It was a region coming of age and coming to grips with massive immigration and the problems and promise of diversity.

The rising Midwest was a cultural maelstrom and a seedbed of thought between 1900 and 1920. During these decades it was the birthplace of the idea of cultural pluralism and the site of a far reaching debate about diversity and the meaning of an open versus a closed society. A significant number of Midwesterners praised the virtues of cultural diversity in reaction to the rampant fear of foreigners and the racist pressures of their times. Rejecting the doctrine of Anglo-Saxon supremacy, on the one hand, and the melting pot ideology of complete assimilation, on the other, they developed the expansive alternative of cultural pluralism. Broadly defined as "the general vision of a society made up of diverse groups all interacting harmoniously without losing their distinctiveness,"[3] cultural pluralism in several specific forms grew from a vigorous intellectual exchange in the rural and urban Midwest and still remains relevant. In tracing the evolution of this potent concept born in the Midwest, this chapter will briefly explore the historical circumstances that encouraged such thinking before focusing on the midwestern mind of Jane Addams (1860–1935), the first American to develop a comprehensive theory of cultural pluralism.

### The Rise of a Region and Background to an Idea

During the period from 1890 to 1920 that the nation's center of gravity shifted westward and the Midwest became our cultural, political, and economic heartland, the youthful region witnessed unprecedented ethnic, racial, and class conflict. Beginning with the Haymarket Massacre of 1886 and the Populist revolt a few years later and culminating in the virulent loyalty crusades of 1917 and the Chicago Race Riot of 1919, the Midwest was a cauldron of cultural turmoil and the epicenter of a far-reaching debate regarding the relationship between floodtides of immigrants and their host culture. An unprecedented influx of southern and eastern European immigrants and the beginning of the Great Migration of rural southern blacks to the Midwest precipitated deep-seated fear of the "other" and anxiety about the meaning of citizenship. Sprawling gateway cities as well as the region's farmlands and small towns, with their polyglot populations and anxious citizens, became catalysts for penetrating portrayals and discussions of personal and national identity in a shifting heterogeneous society.

The youthful Midwest was a flashpoint for such concerns. In many ways the cutting edge of American culture at the turn of the nineteenth century, the vast twelve-state region was a polyglot powerhouse, the antithesis of the homogeneous heartland stereotype that emerged generations later. The emergent Midwest, Jon Teaford has noted, "was not the calm center of American life but a cauldron of class conflict." It was a raucous cultural battleground, often surpassing New York and the East in the intensity of its conflict and creativity. Surveying this tumultuous landscape in 1896, Turner asserted, "the forces of reorganization are turbulent and the nation seems like a witches' kettle." Stressing the Midwest's sprawling diversity five years later, he noted, "At one edge is the Populism of the prairies; at the other, the capitalism that is typified in Pittsburgh," which was part of "a huge industrial organism ... created in the province—an organism of tremendous power, activity, and unity."[4]

Between 1890 and 1920, during an era of midwestern economic, political, and cultural dominance—or a Midwestern Moment, if you will—the region's population exploded from twenty-two million to thirty-five million, outstripping the population of the New England and Mid-Atlantic states combined and coming to constitute a third or more of the nation's inhabitants. Many of these new Midwesterners were fresh off the boat. For the waves of immigrants who came to settle the agrarian landscape, the region's spaciousness allowed them to refabricate Old World cultures, to re-root in a patchwork of ethnic pockets that persisted for generations. "The Middle West," Jon Gjerde has convincingly argued, "was a place where immigrant families recreated new Europes." It was, he continued, "an environment tailor-made for the formation of isolated ethnic communities.... Nowhere were the possibilities of the segregation of foreign cultures more viable."[5]

Cultural segmentation was even more pronounced in the urban Midwest, especially in Chicago. The broad-shouldered, bursting-at-the-seams metropolis was a spectacle of feverish growth and yawning inequities. Chicago expanded from roughly one million people in 1890 to nearly three million by 1920, making it arguably the fastest growing city in the western world and briefly the fifth or sixth largest city on the planet. A global flash point of cultural conflict and creativity, early twentieth-century Chicago was widely known and deeply studied. In the words of Chicagoan Richard Wright, Chicago was the *"known* city," where "more is known about it, how it runs, how it kills, how it loves, steals, helps, gives, cheats, and crushes than any other city in the world."[6]

Between 1890 and 1920, about seventy-five percent of all Chicagoans were either foreign born or the children of foreign born parents. And between those years Chicago's black population grew from

15,000 to over 100,000, with ninety percent of them—largely newly arrived from the Deep South—forced to live in the highly segregated Black Belt adjacent to the Union Stockyards.[7] With its vast divide between the native-born elite and newly arrived masses, Chicago was a mosaic of impoverished ethnic and racially divided neighborhoods. With its disturbing contrasts between palaces along Lake Shore Boulevard and hovels behind the Union Stockyards, between skyscrapers and slaughterhouses, between the opulent Gold Coast and the isolated Black Belt, Chicago was, in William Cronon's words, a great vortex both "glorious and abhorrent at the same time." In one multiethnic district alone—the Near West Side, which included Jane Addams's Hull House— crusading journalist Robert Hunter reported in 1904 that fully 50,000 working people were living in or on the brink of poverty and starvation.[8]

The region's explosive growth, multiethnic ferment, and rampant inequality went hand-in-hand with a flowering of thought and creativity, much of it exploring social tensions and inequities in Chicago and throughout the Midwest. From the brutal contrasts of urban wealth and squalor depicted in Theodore Dreiser's *Sister Carrie* (1900), Frank Norris's *The Pit* (1903), Upton Sinclair's *The Jungle* (1906), and Carl Sandberg's *Chicago Poems* (1913) to the grinding rural poverty and yawning cultural divides portrayed in Garland's *Main Travelled Roads* (1891), Edgar Lee Master's *Spoon River Anthology* (1915), Willa Cather's *My Ántonia* (1918), and Sinclair Lewis's *Main Street* (1920), midwestern writers vividly depicted the cultural transformation of the city and countryside.[9]

Amid this groundswell of creativity the Midwest experienced a probing debate regarding the nature of cultural pluralism, perhaps the most profound public discussion of diversity in the nation's history. The courageous politics of Illinois Governor John Peter Altgeld (1847–1902), the radical labor activism of Indiana native Eugene Debs (1855–1926), and the progressive legal advocacy of Ohio native Clarence Darrow (1857–1938) laid the groundwork for pluralistic thought and practice. University of Chicago philosophers Thorstein Veblen and John Dewey (who taught there from 1892 to 1906 and 1894 to 1904 respectively) deeply shaped theoretical and applied aspects of cultural diversity, and the subsequent work of the Chicago School of urban sociology, beginning with Robert Park's pioneering essay, "The City" (1915), and

W.I. Thomas and Florian Znaniecki's classic, *The Polish Peasant* (1918), contributed to a pluralistic climate of opinion. Altgeld, Debs, Darrow, Veblen, Dewey, Park, Thomas, and many other politicians, labor advocates, social scientists, philosophers, journalists, and social workers in the Midwest were at the forefront of American thought and practice regarding the relationship between working-class immigrants and their host society. All influenced the visions of cultural diversity that persist today. Yet several figures stand out for the power and prescience of their ideas, for their biting critiques of the melting pot concept and Anglo-centric notions of assimilation, and for consciously creating the concept of cultural pluralism. Looming above them all is Jane Addams, who profoundly influenced every aspect of pluralistic thought and practice in the era with her on-the-ground activism, influential publications, and firm faith in cultural reciprocity and the power of immigrant groups to create a richer, more vibrant national culture. Building upon Addams's insights published during the decade leading up to World War I, philosopher Horace Kallen (1882–1974) coined the term "cultural pluralism" in 1915 and amplified it as an ideology while teaching at the University of Wisconsin between 1911 and 1918.

Other midwestern-influenced intellectuals—including Randolph Bourne, Waldemar Ager, and Ole Rølvaag—contributed to this discussion, but Addams and Kallen made the earliest and most penetrating contributions, providing urban and rural visions of cultural pluralism that resonate a century later. Addams, the daughter of an abolitionist politician and friend of Lincoln in rural Illinois, and Kallen, the European-born son of an Orthodox rabbi in Boston, came from contrasting backgrounds and developed their pluralistic theories in settings dramatically different from the places of their childhood and youth. Kallen's introduction to the rural spaciousness of Wisconsin and Addams's immersion in the cultural maelstrom of Chicago's Near West Side indelibly shaped their visions of cultural pluralism. Inspired by settings strikingly different from their childhood landscapes, both pluralists relied, nevertheless, upon recollections of these earlier places. Addams in particular drew upon memories of her rural background in the Lincoln Republic to forge pluralist thought and practice in the heart of the city. Her pioneering theories of cultural pluralism and the cosmopolitan neighborhood evolved during the nearly two decades between the co-founding (with Ellen Gates Starr) of Hull House in 1889 and their full expression in her book *Newer Ideals of Peace* (1907). But these seminal ideas had even deeper, more subjective roots in Jane Addams's childhood in the emerging Midwest.

### Memories of a Midwestern Childhood

In February 1913, Jane Addams began four months of foreign travel to recuperate from a strenuous stretch of writing, publishing, and public advocacy. Fifty-three years old and at the height of her power, Addams had just finished an extraordinary year of accomplishment that helped make her, in the words of one of her biographers, "the best-known public woman in the world."[10]

1912 had been a whirlwind, halcyon year for Addams. In twelve months she had published two powerful books: her classic *Twenty Years at Hull-House* (1912) and her prescient analysis of prostitution, *A New Conscience and an Ancient Evil* (1912). In addition to her continuous organizing, committee work, and efforts at Hull House, Addams published at least twenty-six articles that year; she also testified before Congress for women's suffrage, promoted the NAACP, spoke out against lynching, seconded Theodore Roosevelt's nomination for President at the Progressive Party Convention in Chicago, and campaigned for Roosevelt and for women's rights by giving stump speeches across twelve states.[11]

Addams did this and more at a breakneck pace in the space of a year. She would go on to publish five more books and hundreds of articles, spearhead a courageous pacifist campaign during World War I, win the Nobel Peace Prize in 1931, and complete many other projects before her death in 1935. When she set sail for Egypt and the Mediterranean in early 1913, she was at the peak of a prolific career and at a retrospective moment at midlife. The trip sparked serious reflection about the course of her life, a sentiment explored in an article she published a year later entitled "Need a Woman over Fifty Feel Old?"[12] It also released a flood of deeper, unexpected emotions that reveal the regional foundation of her life and thought.

While visiting the Theban hills of Egypt, Addams had a sudden insight, an epiphany unlocking long-hidden childhood memories and uncovering a vision of human continuity across time and space that gave higher purpose to her life's work. Viewing 3000-year-old hieroglyphics on the wall of a royal tomb, Addams experienced a Proustian moment releasing a flood of forgotten events from her Cedarville childhood. "In the presence of these primitive attempts to defeat death" in Egypt, she recalled, "I found myself living over the emotions of a child of six years old" coming face-to-face with "the terrors of death" in Illinois.[13] Experiencing a sudden "revival of primitive and overpowering emotions" belonging "to a small person with whom I was no longer intimate," Addams recaptured memories of a revival meeting where she and other children "felt the hot breath of hell upon their cheeks." She instantly recalled two funerals for parents and the anguish of their grieving families, and she relived her childhood rebellion against Christian notions of reward, retribution, and afterlife.[14]

A final recovered memory brought resolution to these haunting images, allowing her to transcend her fear of death to a larger vision of human purpose. Addams would recall other childhood moments in other publications, but her 1913 revelation contains her deepest midwestern memory, and it deserves to be quoted at length:

> I saw myself a child of twelve standing stock-still on the bank of a broad-flowing river, with a little red house surrounded by low-growing willows on its opposite bank, striving to account to myself for a curious sense of familiarity, for a conviction that I had long ago known it all most intimately, although I had certainly never seen the Mississippi River before. I remember that, much puzzled and mystified, at last I gravely concluded that it was one of those intimations of immortality that Wordsworth had written about and ... the memory of the evening light shining through the blades of young corn growing in the field passed on the way has remained with me for more than forty years.[15]

Such "ghosts of reminiscence" indicating higher truths became, for Addams, powerful "manifestations of that new humanism which is perhaps the most precious possession of this generation." As a secular faith in human solidarity that motivated the settlement movement, new

Jane Addams, ca. 1890s.
JAMC_0000_0005_0494,
University of Illinois at
Chicago Library, Special
Collections.

humanism sustained Addams and other communitarian activists of her time. Her 1914 essay ends with an illustration of this reform-grounded faith through a sudden shift of perspective as Addams's memory of being a child beside a broad-flowing river is abruptly replaced by the sight of present-day Egyptians toiling to wrest a living from parched soil beside the Nile. Instantly recognizing a link between struggling fellaheen in Egypt and a fearful child in Illinois, and between striving immigrants in Chicago and common people everywhere, Addams's time transport provided, in her words, "an almost mystical sense of the life common to all centuries, and of the unceasing human endeavor to penetrate into the unseen world." Such transcendent moments and visions of solidarity, she concluded, offer "glimpses into a past so vast that the present generation seems to float upon its surface as thin as a sheet of light which momentarily covers the ocean and moves in response to the black waters beneath it."[16]

If Addams's Egyptian epiphany unlocked her deepest memories of the Midwest revealing a cosmic vision of a unifying over soul, other less mystical childhood recollections provided a more practical foundation for her theories of cultural pluralism and the cosmopolitan neighborhood. A number of social scientists have explored the vital relationship between childhood places and cognitive development. They have argued that preadolescent memories of place have a lasting impact, establishing a necessary bedrock and compass for the rest of one's life. Echoing Carl Jung's belief that the "little world of childhood with its familiar surroundings is a model of the greater world," Edith Cobb and Paul Shepard have described how memories of places experienced between the ages of six and twelve are lodged in our consciousness and shape our developing intellect. During these crucial years, Shepard argues, "the terrain and its natural things become a model of cognitive structure for the plastic, order-seeking juvenile" that last a lifetime. Cobb pushes this even deeper, tracing how creative thinkers throughout history have relied upon memories of childhood places to inspire intellectual breakthroughs and moments of creativity. Both authors describe, in Cobb's words, "universal links between mind and nature" and how recalling childhood places or actually returning to them is the source of our most significant ideas and inspirations, a key to renewing our power to create.[17]

Jane Addams depended upon such foundational memories throughout her life. Just as her midwestern contemporaries Frederick Jackson Turner, Frank Lloyd Wright, and Hamlin Garland used recollections of Portage, Spring Green, and West Salem, Wisconsin, respectively in the 1860s and 1870s to shape their mature regional expressions, Addams tapped childhood experiences in nearby Cedarville, Illinois, during the same period to forge her theories of pluralism and the cosmopolitan neighborhood. Rural childhood landscapes were embedded in their psyches, yet in various and seemingly paradoxical ways, Chicago precipitated their thought. While the city's Columbian Exposition helped inspire Turner, Wright, and Garland in 1893, the multiethnic tumult of Chicago's Nineteenth Ward deeply influenced Addams as she co-founded Hull House in 1889. A powerful country-city dynamic stirred each of these and many other midwestern writers and artists during these years, and Addams more than any member of this generation devoted her life to the city while drawing upon indelible memories of growing up in the country. And more than any of her contemporaries, she keenly understood the enduring impact of her childhood in the emerging Midwest.

Although Addams's life's work revolved around the dense multiethnic neighborhood in Chicago's Nineteenth Ward, her pluralist vision had its source in the rural Midwest. Recovered childhood memories of the sort that Cobb and Shepard documented served as the template for her pioneering work by the late 1880s. Growing up the 1860s and early 1870s in Cedarville, a small town of 500 people on the rolling prairie just south of the Wisconsin border, left an indelible mark and became the *genius loci* of her life, and she was keenly aware of this enduring impact. As one of her most perceptive biographers has noted, "Most social scientists do not take childhood to heart. Jane Addams did, and that helps account for the richness of her thought."[18]

Jane's parents, John and Sarah Addams, had migrated to northern Illinois from Pennsylvania in the 1840s, and after setting up a saw and a wheat mill in the wooded valley of Cedar Creek, her father prospered and became a prominent landowner and Republican politician by the 1850s and 1860s. During these decades, Cedarville and surrounding Stephenson County had a varied population of first- and second-generation Scottish, Irish, Dutch, Norwegian, Swedish, Alsatian, and German-Prussian settlers, and Jane recalled many of these groups and her father's warm relations with them. Such memories of ethnic diversity and interaction would serve as a rural microcosm of the denser, richer immigrant mix Addams would experience in the Hull House neighborhood where eighteen nationalities were crowded together.[19]

Addams lived a privileged yet death-haunted childhood that she recalled with unblinking realism. While growing up in a big house on the prairie, she witnessed a gamut of human experience and developed an expansive social conscience.[20] The eighth of nine children born to Sarah Addams, and one of only four siblings who survived to adulthood, one of Jane's earliest memories was her mother's death in childbirth in 1863. Death seemed ubiquitous. Living in "a household of children, whose mother is dead" imparted a lasting sense of empathy, and the first two chapters of *Twenty Years at Hull-House* offer vivid, unvarnished memories that shaped her later life. In this respect, Addams's memories are much closer to the dark vision of Michael Lesy's *Wisconsin Death Trip* (1973) than to the uplifting images of Laura Ingalls Wilder's *Little House on the Prairie* (1935).[21]

The opening pages of Addams's book are a quilt work of traumatic as well as bucolic memories. Jane's earliest recollections are of nights filled with fear of mortality and pangs of conscience: the "dread of death," fear of "fiery Hell," and a search for comforting words from her Quaker-influenced father. This is followed by her first glimpse of poverty. Travelling to the nearby city of Freeport with its 10,000 people with her father, six-year-old Jane was distressed by the poor section of town. Shocked by her "first sight of poverty which implies squalor," she asked her father why people lived on such ragged streets in tumbled down houses. After hearing his explanation, Addams recalled her six-year-old self declaring "with much firmness that when I grew up I should, of course, have a large house, but it would not be built among other large houses, but right in the midst of horrid little houses like these." Addams describes this event without comment, but it is clear that Hull House had an early childhood source, and she mentions some pages later that as an eight year old, "My mind was busy ... with the old question eternally suggested by the inequalities of the human lot."[22]

Cedarville's natural landscape also had an impact on Addams's mature thought. "The prairie around the village," she recalled, "was broken into hills, one of them crowned by pine woods, grown up from a bag full of Norway pine seeds sown by my father in 1844." She remembered exploring caves, woods, and the bluff-lined creek bed and creating hideaways and secret spots "as only free-ranging country children can do." She remembered her "favorite places and trees and birds and flowers" and "sudden joy over the soft radiance of the rainbow" and the elusive "companionship children have with nature." Such memories of the natural landscape helped shape her urban ideology, especially her sense of the requirements of life for children and youth growing up on city streets and the redemptive, revitalizing impact of nature and of youth on the nation as a whole.[23]

### The Influence of Lincoln and Uses of the Frontier and Small Town

Memories of Lincoln had an equally powerful impact on Addams's notions of the common good and cultural pluralism. Her father knew and worked with Lincoln, and both father and daughter admired the great man's humble background, his unflagging awareness of injustice, and his belief, in Addams's words, that "the people themselves were the greatest resource of the country."[24] Addams's affinity for Lincoln touched even deeper personal levels. Though coming from different social strata and generations, both experienced tragedy-filled prairie childhoods scarred by their mothers' deaths, both wrestled with dark periods of doubt and depression, and both drew upon their early lives to find meaning in public service and faith in the common folk.

Addams credited Lincoln as a sustaining force for Hull House, where from the onset she used his example to impart cultural pride and self worth. "We were often distressed by the children of immigrant parents," she recalled, "who were ashamed of ... and repudiated the language and customs of their elders, and counted themselves successful as they were able to ignore their past." Countering such self-destructive efforts to erase their culture, Addams upheld Lincoln, "the greatest American," for his steadfast pride in his humble midwestern past. Emphasizing that he "never forgot how the plain people of Sangamon County thought and felt" and stressing "that this habit was the foundation for his marvelous capacity for growth" in Washington during the depths of the Civil War, Addams urged the children of immigrants to draw upon their cultural heritage as Lincoln had to achieve full lives and successful careers in "our conglomerate America."[25]

In addition to using Lincoln's faith in the common folk of Sangamon County to inspire confidence in cultural diversity in Chicago's Nineteenth Ward, Addams also praised "the invigorating and clarifying power of his influence" as the final ingredient for the idea of Hull House, providing a deep *American* foundation for her project.[26] During the seven-year period of soul-searching leading up to the founding of Hull House in 1889, Addams, like many privileged American women of her generation, turned much of her attention away from her native ground and searched for higher meaning through several extensive tours of Europe. Two transformative experiences toward the end of her second Grand Tour in 1888 were crucial to finding her true vocation in Lincoln's Midwest.[27]

Addams's first European trip quickened her social conscience, inspiring her toward direct action rather than distant views of social problems. After watching a bull fight in Madrid in April 1888 and suddenly seeing herself as a willing spectator of such brutality, she felt "tried and condemned, not only by this disgusting experience but by the entire moral situation it revealed." It became clear that she had been "the dupe of a deferred purpose," wasting her life with indefinite study and travel abroad above the human fray. Realizing that she had been "lulling" her conscience "by a dreamer's scheme, that a mere paper reform had become a defense for continued idleness," Addams resolved to engage in direct, face-to-face efforts to improve the human condition back home.[28]

Visiting Oxford University two months later in June 1888 with the hazy idea in mind of establishing a settlement house in the United States modeled after one she had just visited in London's East Side, Addams sat for tea with Professor Edward Caird, who had written about the settlement movement. Troubled by the class-conscious British approach that seemed "artificial to a western American who had been born in a rural community where the early pioneer life had made social distinctions impossible," and fumbling "for a synthesis" to fit American circumstances, Addams instantly recalled a lecture Professor Caird had given two years earlier praising Lincoln. "The memory of Lincoln, the mention of his name," she recalled, "came like a refreshing breeze from off the prairie, blowing aside all the scholarly implications in which I had become so reluctantly involved." Until then, she had a vague notion of "the beginnings of a secular religion," and suddenly the simple sound of Lincoln's name in Oxford came as a bracing prairie breeze, an epiphany brushing away her doubts and putting everything in place in a truly American and midwestern context.[29]

If Lincoln's example affirmed Addams's faith in her native grounds and planted a seed for her theory of cultural pluralism, her sense of an affinity between rural and urban frontiers had an equally significant impact on her philosophy and the evolution of Hull House. She recalled how early "pioneer" inhabitants of the Nineteenth Ward who had moved to more desirable locations would return to their old community and complain about upstart "foreigners" destroying property values and "lowering the tone of the neighborhood." When she pointed out the similarity between their first years adrift in an unknown city and the loneliness of current "immigrants on a sea of new and strange impressions," the older settlers realized a "kinship between the pioneer and the immigrant, both 'buffeting the waves of new development'" and both finding strength in their cultural pasts to survive the urban wilderness.[30]

Perhaps the first American to develop what is now a common trope of pioneers in the urban wilderness, Addams visualized her frontier "settlement" at the corner of Halstead and Polk Streets as an outpost of cooperation and inclusiveness. Far from being a Turnerian melting pot, Addams's urban frontier would function as a quilt or mosaic, encouraging immigrants to proudly retain their cultures while interacting and reciprocating with others. Her frontier settlement was conceived as a seedbed of cultural self-esteem, and in Hull House's Labor Museum a spectrum of ethnic arts and crafts were nurtured to encourage intergenerational respect and to "lay a foundation for reverence of the past which Goethe declares to be the basis of all sound progress."[31]

Downplaying the restless, individualistic, hyper-masculine frontier that her contemporary Turner emphasized, Addams drew upon the less celebrated though equally significant feminine frontier as a guiding force behind Hull House and a central feature of her thought. She evoked the community-building side of the agrarian frontier with its house-raising parties and husking bees to inspire multiethnic solidarity in the city. "In time it came to seem natural," Addams recalled, "that the Settlement should be there. It is natural to feed the hungry and care for the sick ... to give pleasure to the young, comfort to the aged ... to wash the new-born babies, and to prepare the dead for burial." Hers is a hard-won collective vision based on "a philosophy whose foundation is the solidarity of the human race, a philosophy which will not waver when the race happens to be represented by a drunken woman or an idiot boy."[32]

Addams's urban vision of pluralism also drew upon personal memories of post-frontier, small-town life. As a child in Cedarville in Stephenson County and in neighboring Freeport in the 1860s and 1870s, young Addams experienced a range of ethnic groups, social classes, and personal challenges. As we have seen and as philosopher Jean Bethke Elshtain has convincingly argued, "Jane Addams absorbed lessons in paying attention to the concrete and particular person from growing up in the cauldron of small-town life." Her pragmatic focus on immediate needs and particular individuals in the human maelstrom near Hull House was inspired by "[t]he routine and seemingly spontaneous cooperation Addams saw around her while growing up—and later found in the poor who helped one another in their 'teeming quarters.'" This small-town experience, Elshtain concludes, "gave her a secure foundation of rough and ready social egalitarianism.... an encompassable universe in which she could sort out the complexities of human society."[33] Addams's rural childhood, with its gamut of experiences and emotions, supplied the groundwork for her urban vision. Her childhood world, to paraphrase Carl Jung, was the model for the wider world she would deeply influence throughout her life. That she chose to be buried in Cedarville rather than Chicago testifies to the lasting impact of her place of origin.

## Summing Up

Many factors shaped Addams's theories of cultural pluralism and the cosmopolitan neighborhood as they emerged during the years between the co-founding of Hull House in 1889 and the publication of *Newer Ideals of Peace* (1907). Hers was a deeply urban vision. While Cedarville provided an early template, Chicago had the most profound impact. Addams would have many life-changing experiences beyond the Midwest, including what she would call her "years of deferred purpose" from 1881 until 1888, which were filled with bouts of serious illness and depression, deep disillusionment as a medical student, two lengthy tours of Europe, and a series of awakenings there, as we've seen, to her life's purpose at Hull House.

Her capacious mind would reveal a true genius for absorbing a multitude of ideas. Addams knew and interacted with many of the most important public intellectuals and reformers of her time and brilliantly merged their ideas with her own. William James's pragmatism and vision of "a pluralistic universe," Leo Tolstoy's Christian socialism and radical pacifism, Peter Kropotkin's theory of mutual aid, W.E.B. Du Bois's notion of "double consciousness," the interracial ideals and efforts of Ida B. Wells-Barnett and Reverdy Ransom—Addams absorbed these and many other concepts while living in and appreciating the cauldron of cultures around Hull House.[34] A cosmopolitan in the deepest sense of the term, Addams fully embraced the wider world beyond her rural background by using memories of that simpler past as a touchstone to the more chaotic present. Like those of many other intellectuals and activists of her time and place, Addams's childhood in Cedarville and the emerging Midwest served as a foundation for her life and thought.

The cultural diversity that Jane Addams witnessed as a child was heightened in the city; the interactions that occurred between different types of people in Cedarville were intensified and writ large in the streets of Chicago, where, in Addams's words, "the crowded city quarters become focal points of progress" and immigrants from a multitude of cultures are "turned into kindly citizens of the world through the pressures of the cosmopolitan neighborhood." Addams's utopian hope that this urban mosaic of interacting cultures would be the seedbed for the peaceful "patriotism of a great cosmopolitan nation" remains beyond reach. Her pluralistic vision endures, nevertheless, as a beckoning ideal that had its beginnings in her childhood in the emerging Midwest.[35]

I express my gratitude to a number of colleagues and friends, especially Jon Lauck, Karen Lystra, Nicole Rehnberg, and Leila Zenderland, whose encouragement and advice strengthened this chapter.

## Notes

1. Frederick Jackson Turner, "The Middle West" (1901), in Turner, *The Frontier in American History* (New York: Henry Holt and Co., 1920), 127, 155; Henry Louis Mencken, "Civilized Chicago," *Chicago Tribune* (October 28, 1917), 5; Hamlin Garland, *Crumbling Idols: Twelve Essays on Art and Literature* (Chicago: Stone and Kimball, 1894), 177 and throughout. Turner mentions the 1860–1900 midwestern presidential streak on page 156 of his 1901 essay.
2. Walt Whitman, "America's Characteristic Landscape," in *The Works of Walt Whitman: The Collected Prose*, Malcolm Cowley, ed. (New York: Farrar, Straus & Giroux, 1969), 149; Hamlin Garland, "Literary Emancipation of the West," *The Forum* (October 1893): 56–66.
3. Philip Gleason, "Americans All," in Gleason, *Speaking of Diversity: Language and Ethnicity in Twentieth Century America* (Baltimore: The Johns Hopkins University Press, 1992), 177. Of the vast literature on the early history and meaning of cultural pluralism, a few of the most useful sources include: Arthur Mann, *The One and the Many: Reflections on the American Identity* (Chicago: University of Chicago Press, 1979); Werner Sollors, "A Critique of Pure Pluralism," in Sacvan Bercovitch, ed. *Reconstructing American Literary History* (Cambridge: Harvard University Press, 1986), 250–79; and David Hollinger, *Postethnic America: Beyond Multiculturalism* (New York: Basic Books, 2000).
4. Jon C. Teaford's *Cities of the Heartland: The Rise and Fall of the Industrial Midwest* (Bloomington: Indiana University Press, 1993), 71; Frederick Jackson Turner, "The Problem of the West" (1896) in Turner, *The Frontier*, 221, and Turner, "The Middle West" (1901), Ibid., 127, 149. James R. Shortridge's *The Middle West: Its Meaning in American Culture* (Lawrence: University Press of Kansas, 1989) is an indispensable study of the shift from regional powerhouse to bucolic backwater across the first half of the twentieth century. Steven Hahn's *A Nation Without Borders: The United States and Its World in an Age of Civil Wars, 1830–1910* (New York: Viking

Press, 2016) locates the beginnings of heartland dominance in the three decades leading to the Civil War, arguing that "the principal struggle of the period was not between the North and the South but rather between the Northeast and the Mississippi Valley for control of the continent, and, perhaps, the hemisphere," 9.

5. Jon Gjerde, *The Minds of the West: Ethnocultural Evolution in the Rural Middle West, 1830–1917* (Chapel Hill: University of North Carolina Press, 1997), 2, 18. Developing the theme of persistence and subtle change, Gjerde concludes, "immigrants and their children found it useful to reify, to reconstruct, and sometimes to reinvent multiple traditions and allegiances within the United States. The contours of American political and economic life, like the American landscape itself, remained segmented by culture" (247). Frank R. Kramer's *Voices in the Valley: Myth Making and Folk Belief in the Middle West* (Madison: University of Wisconsin Press, 1964) is a pioneering discussion of nineteenth-century rural settlement patterns.

6. Richard Wright, "Introduction" to St. Clair Drake and Horace R. Cayton, *Black Metropolis: A Study of Negro Life in a Northern City* (New York: Harcourt Brace and Co., 1945), xviii.

7. Ibid., 8–9, 53. Drake and Cayton's three opening chapters, pages 31–76, vividly trace the history of black Chicago from its French-speaking founder, Jean Baptiste Point du Sable, in 1790 to the Race Riots in 1919.

8. William Cronon, *Nature's Metropolis: Chicago and the Great West* (New York: W.W. Norton, 1991), 20; Robert Hunter, *Poverty* (New York: Macmillan, 1904), 324. Hunter, who lived at Hull House in the late 1890s, recalled of the surrounding district: "In this community, the saddest in which I have ever lived, fully fifty thousand men, women, and children were all the time either in poverty or on the verge of poverty. It would not be possible to describe how they worked and starved and ached to rise out of it" (324). William T. Steadman's sensational best seller, *If Christ Came to Chicago: A Plea for the Union of All Who Love in the Service of All Who Suffer* (Chicago: Laird & Lee, 1894), is a vivid account of rampant poverty and crime in the city during the 1893 World's Fair. Cronon's *Nature's Metropolis* is an indispensable, magisterial account of Chicago's feverish growth and power during the late nineteenth and early twentieth centuries.

9. Regarding the early twentieth-century flowering of midwestern literature, see Ronald Weber, *The Midwestern Ascendancy in American Writing* (Bloomington: Indiana University Press, 1992) and Timothy R. Spear, *Chicago Dreaming: Midwesterners and the City, 1871–1919* (Chicago, University of Chicago Press, 2005). Among the many accounts of Chicago's literary renaissance see: Dale Kramer, *Chicago Renaissance: The Literary Life in the Midwest, 1900–1930* (New York: Appleton-Century, 1966); Bernard L. Duffy, *The Chicago Renaissance in American Letters: A Critical History* (Westport, Conn.: Greenwood Press, 1977); and Carl S. Smith, *Chicago*

*and the American Literary Imagination* (Chicago: University of Chicago Press, 1984).
10. Katherine Joslin, *Jane Addams, A Writer's Life* (Urbana: University of Illinois Press, 2004), 132. Emphasizing Addams's long-standing celebrity, Joslin, echoing other biographers, points out that as early as the mid-1890s she had gained public veneration as "Saint Jane," Ibid., 10.
11. Jane Addams, *Twenty Years at Hull-House with Autobiographical Notes* (New York: Macmillan, 1912); Jane Addams, *A New Conscience and an Ancient Evil* (New York: Macmillan, 1912). For a complete list of Addams's published works, see "A Bibliography of the Printed Works of Jane Addams," in Jean Bethke Elshtain, ed., *The Jane Addams Reader* (New York: Basic Books, 2001), 449–74.
12. Jane Addams, "Need a Woman over Fifty Feel Old?" *Ladies Home Journal*, 31 (October 1914): 7.
13. Jane Addams, "A Personal Experience in Interpretative Memory," chapter six of Addams, *The Long Road of Woman's Memory* (1916); reprint (Urbana: University of Illinois Press, 2002), 70. Addams published her original account two years earlier as: "Unexpected Reactions of a Traveler in Egypt," *Atlantic Monthly*, 113 (February 1914): 178–86.
14. *The Long Road of Woman's Memory*, 68, 72.
15. Ibid., 78.
16. Ibid., 79. Described as a "secular religion" shared by a generation of settlement workers critical of notions of Anglo-Saxon conformity and sensitive to the cultural contributions of immigrants to the national whole, Addams's "new humanism" is strikingly different from the conservative movement in literary criticism of the same name founded by Ohio-native Irving Babbitt in 1908. See Addams, *Twenty Years at Hull-House*, 39, 41, for a brief discussion of the "wide humanitarianism" of this "secular religion." For a thoughtful discussion of the pluralistic and cosmopolitan dimensions of the "settlement workers' romantic-humanitarian ethic," see Eric P. Kaufmann, *The Rise and Fall of Anglo-America* (Cambridge, MA: Harvard University Press, 2014), pages 96–98. The quotation is on page 97.
17. Carl Jung cited in John A. Jakle, "Childhood on the Middle Border: Remembered Small Town America," *Journal of Geography*, 85 (July/August 1985): 159; Paul Shepard, "Place in American Culture," *North American Review*, 262 (Fall 1977): 23; Edith Cobb, *The Ecology of Imagination of Childhood* (New York: Columbia University Press, 1977), 87, 88. On the lasting imprint of childhood places and place in general, see: Harold F. Searles, *The Nonhuman Environment in Normal Development and in Schizophrenia* (New York, 1960), and Maurice Halbwachs, *On Collective Memory* (Chicago: University of Chicago Press, 1992). Paraphrasing Cobb, Shepard writes that "the home range for the eight year old is the prime, patterned concrete reality ... upon which his wavering and nubile powers of memory and logic cling and develop, like seals climbing onto the rocks to

give birth." 23. Also see Paul Shepard, *Man in the Landscape: A Historic View of the Esthetics of Nature* (New York; Knopf, 1967), pp. 28–37, for an earlier discussion of childhood, place, and *genius loci*.

18. Jean Bethke Elshtain, *Jane Addams and the Dream of American Democracy: A Life* (New York: Basic Books, 2002), 126.
19. Addams mentions several rural ethnic groups, including Germans, Norwegians, and Pennsylvania Dutch in *Twenty Years at Hull-House*. For a succinct discussion of the multi-cultural working class mosaic of Chicago's Nineteenth Ward, see Sarah Wilson, "Cosmopolitan Cordelia: Jane Addams's Industrial Parables," *Modern Language Quarterly* 75 (2014): 461 and throughout.
20. Addams's close contemporary Laura Ingalls Wilder (1867–1957) was born in Pepin, Wisconsin, in Hamlin Garland's wooded coulee country, 250 miles north of Cedarville. The decidedly conservative message of her *Little House on the Prairie* (1935) and subsequent novels is a vivid contrast to Addams's vision of social work and human solidarity inspired while growing up in a *big* house on the prairie.
21. Jane Addams, *Twenty Years at Hull-House*, 39. She explicitly mentions that "My mother had died when I was a baby and my father's second marriage did not occur until my eighth year" on page 11. Michael Lesy's *Wisconsin Death Trip* (New York: Pantheon, 1973), another unvarnished, death-haunted account of life in the emerging Midwest, is a grim portrait of life in the 1880s and 1890s in Black River Falls, Wisconsin.
22. *Twenty Years at Hull-House*, 3, 3–5, 14.
23. Ibid., 16, 17. The need for recreation, glimpses of nature in the city, and the vitalizing qualities of youth are vividly discussed in Addams's *The Spirit of Youth and the City Streets* (New York: Macmillan, 1909), with its program for nurturing "the mystic beauty, the redemptive joy, the civic pride which these multitudes of young people might supply to our dingy towns" (9). For a recent, more polemical and rigid version of this argument, see Richard Louv, *The Last Child in the Woods: Saving Our Children from Nature-Deficit Disorder* (Chapel Hill, NC: Algonquin Books, 2005).
24. *Twenty Years at Hull-House*, 35.
25. Ibid., 36–37.
26. Ibid., 37.
27. By a remarkable coincidence, when twenty-three-year-old Addams crossed the Atlantic in August 1883 on the *SS Servia* to begin her first European tour, she made note of a fellow American traveler, forty-year-old novelist Henry James. Observing the writer from afar, Addams described him in her journal as "very English in appearance but not especially keen or intellectual." It is unknown whether they directly interacted during the voyage, but the convergence of the middle-aged author of *Portrait of a Lady* (1881), with its analysis of Isabel Archer, a vibrant young American who stayed in Europe, and the youthful future founder of Hull House who would

reject expatriation and return to America is an extraordinary intersection of powerful minds and antithetical responses to Old World culture. See Joslin, *Jane Addams, A Writer's Life*, 19–20, and Victoria Bissell Brown, *The Education of Jane Addams* (Philadelphia: University of Pennsylvania Press, 2004), 130–31, 173–74 for discussions of the Addams-James encounter. Addams's journal entry is cited by Joslin, page 20.
28. *Twenty Years at Hull-House*, 86.
29. Ibid., 37, 38, 40, 39. There is telling parallel between Addams's 1888 experience while sipping tea in Oxford and her contemporary Marcel Proust's celebrated "epiphany in a teaspoon" described in *Swann's Way*, the first volume of his posthumously published *Memories of Things Past* (1922).
30. Ibid., 108–109.
31. Ibid., 237.
32. Ibid., 109, 126. See Charlene Haddock Seigfried, "The Role of Place in Jane Addams and Margaret Preston," *The Pluralist* 8 (Fall 2013): 1–16, for a perceptive discussion of how, among other things, "Addams often appealed to the pioneer spirit at the heart of American mythology of place," a perspective that "provided a useful alternative history evoking a more cooperative, inclusive vision of America" (7). Robert V. Hine's *Community on the American Frontier: Separate but Not Alone* (Norman: University of Oklahoma Press, 1980) is a brilliant analysis of the cooperative dimension of the frontier that inspired Addams. For a freewheeling discussion of the new urban frontier, see Neil Smith's *The New Urban Frontier: Gentrification and the Revanchist City* (New York: Routledge, 1996). Smith's examples, ranging from "new frontier" gentrification on the Lower East Side to frontier imagery in the film "Fort Apache, Bronx" (1981), offers a telling contrast to Addams's much earlier humanitarian vision of a beloved community in the urban frontier.
33. Elshtain, *Jane Addams and the Dream of American Democracy*, 125, 126. There is an avalanche of creative literature depicting the small towns in the Midwest, with Sinclair Lewis's powerful send up, *Main Street* (1920), the tip of the iceberg. Among the many historical studies, Lewis Atherton's *Main Street on the Middle Border* (Bloomington: Indiana University Press, 1954) remains a classic. Recent useful sources include: John E. Miller, *Small-Town Dreams: Midwestern Boys Who Shaped America* (Lawrence: University Press of Kansas, 2014), whose subtitle might trouble Addams, and Julianne Couch, *Small-Town Midwest: Resilience and Hope in the Twenty-First Century* (Iowa City: University of Iowa Press, 2016).
34. Addams personally knew and responded to the ideas of these and many other thinkers and social activists of her time. Du Bois, Kropotkin, and Wells-Barnett spoke at Hull House and had a direct impact on Addams's pluralist thought. Other Hull House guests and speakers—among them John Dewey, Eugene Debs, Henry George, H.G. Wells, and George Bernard

Shaw—also influenced her ideology in ways that will be discussed in future work.
35. Jane Addams, *Newer Ideals of Peace* (New York: Macmillan, 1907), 15, 18, 216. That Addams balanced hardheaded skepticism with idealistic utopianism is reflected in her general complaint that "All members of the community are equally stupid in throwing away the immigrant revelation of social customs and inherited energy. We continually allow this valuable human experience to go to waste" (*Newer Ideals*, 79).

| Philip A. Greasley | The Rise of the Midwest, the Chicago Renaissance, and the Quest for National Recognition |

America's story, like that of the Midwest, has always been one of movement and change. From the earliest days of European exploration on this continent to the present, migrants and immigrants have participated in large-scale population movements. Consideration of the colonial and early U.S. experience makes clear the differing power, prestige, and perceptions of the elite colonizers and those of the populations they "colonized"; the early dominance of the original thirteen colonies, later the first U.S. states; and the growing negative reaction this eastern ascendancy elicited from "colonized" midwestern populations.[1] From initial legal, financial, educational, and cultural subservience to elite European and later American East Coast norms and values, particularly those of the Northeast, midwestern populations increasingly came to assert their own regional perspectives.[2] The rise of the Midwest and its leading city, Chicago, was soon followed by Chicago's literary renaissance, which demonstrated the region's growing rejection of eastern hegemony and its assertion of midwestern values.[3]

The events that would later lead to the development of midwestern regionalism began when European colonists established communities along the eastern seaboard that became the United States. These European and later American East Coast colonizers governed for their own benefit and regularly considered immigrant and migrant populations inferior because they lacked financial resources, education, and social standing.[4] For those reasons, immigrants and migrants regularly saw life on the frontier as their best chance for improving their lives. As they cleared the wilderness, established farms and towns, and built commerce, they hoped to share in the social and economic gains but recognized that parity with the East would not come rapidly.[5] Their collective successes enhanced the effective size, control, and power of the United States but they also buttressed the East Coast's social, cultural, and legal hegemony. The Northwest Territory and the trans-Mississippi midwestern lands of the Louisiana Purchase began as political, economic, social, and cultural provinces of the East.[6] Eastern values and standards rapidly became the norms the growing nation aspired to,[7] and although the original thirteen states had adopted Enlightenment ideas for incorporating emerging territories, they had simultaneously worked to advance eastern interests and ensure continuing eastern hegemony as the country developed.[8]

The legal and political decisions having been made for them, territorial settlers were precluded from choosing their own political status, laws, and governing officials.[9] The East established laws for the territories, set governmental policies and practices without consideration of territorial conditions or needs, and brought in territorial governors from the existing U.S. states.[10] In dictating the structure and mechanisms leading to statehood as well as the number of states to emerge from the territories, the early states ensured a continuing national balance of power favoring the East.[11,12]

Early midwestern literature began to chronicle the region's initial experiences. Looking backward in "Godliness, Part One" from *Winesburg, Ohio* (1919), Sherwood Anderson (1876–1941) portrays the struggles of Ohio frontier life, as exemplified by the Bentley family, early nineteenth-century migrants from New York.[13] Felling virgin forests, building homes, and breaking soil took all the strength people could muster, yet the numbers of those moving westward from the relative safety and certainty of the eastern seaboard continued to rise. The subsequent travail of the Civil War added to the physical and emotional demands. To maintain hope, frontier families needed to believe in a divine plan and a loving God who would preserve, protect, and advance them. Relaxation and culture were rare commodities.

In 1839, Caroline Kirkland (1801–1864), a sophisticated former New Yorker and a migrant with her family to east-central Michigan, published *A New Home—Who'll Follow?* Her narrative of a slightly later period of midwestern settlement than depicted by Anderson juxtaposes the beauty of the landscape and wild-flowers with the privations of daily life, the uneducated people, and the quirks of local culture; references to the "Michigan mud-hole" recur, and eastern creature comforts are replaced by:

the awkward and tedious inconvenience of our temporary sojourn at this place, where every [sic] thing was so different from our ideas of comfort, or even decency.... That morning was the first and the last time I ever attempted to carry through the ordinary nursery routine, in a log hut, without a servant, and with a skillet for a wash basin.[14]

Early sections of *A New Home* rail at local customs, nonstandard dialect, and the difficulty in getting and retaining capable, respectful servants. Although in time Kirkland grew accustomed to daily life in the territories, her cultural roots and loyalties remained with the East.

Hamlin Garland (1860–1940) also recognized the East's many advantages. He remained personally committed to the advantages of eastern life, but he rejected the moneyed East's exploitation of the rural Midwest. In "Up the Coulé" from *Main-Travelled Roads* (1891) Garland makes the case against this exploitation through the differential impact of regional conditions on two brothers. Howard McLane, an affluent New York and Boston-based actor, has left his family's midwestern farm, been educated, and lived a pleasant, prosperous life. His younger brother, Grant, on the other hand, has remained on the family's midwestern land, assumed responsibility for the farm after his father's death, and lost that farm. He struggles on against the odds. Seeing the unfairness of his brother's plight, Howard offers to pay off the mortgage. But Grant refuses, saying, "[L]ife ain't worth very much to me. I'm too old to take a new start. I'm a dead failure.... [L]ife's a failure for ninety-nine per cent of us. You can't help me now. It's too late."[15] In just that way, eastern money and the Yankee-inspired American economic system victimized many rural Midwesterners.

*O Pioneers!* (1913) by Willa Cather (1873–1947) describes the similarly heroic struggles of those trying to survive and build farmsteads in pioneering Nebraska during the late 1800s. Alexandra Bergson understands that Nebraska's intellectual and cultural opportunities do not equal those experienced in the East. Yet, in contrast to Kirkland, she, like Cather, has faith in the land and is loyal to the West.[16] Looking back later, she prefers Nebraska's early communal struggles to Nebraska's later East Coast–inspired materialism. Her confidence, arising from Nebraska's achievements, leads Alexandra to reject eastern values and hierarchy.

Much changed between the difficult early "western" frontier experience and the later affirmations of midwestern democratic values. Midwestern writers increasingly took stands against eastern money and exploitation. Upton Sinclair (1878–1968) in *The Jungle* (1906) calls for revolution against the corrupt, unconstrained capitalist system. Later, F. Scott Fitzgerald (1896–1940), in *The Great Gatsby* (1925), asks Midwesterners to reject the East's siren-song and its misplaced material orientation.[17] Rising certainty in midwestern experience, life, and values increasingly led Midwesterners to reject eastern hegemony. Chicago's literary flowering, which came to be known as the Chicago Renaissance, and the milieu from which it sprung similarly reflected a growing commitment to midwestern literary values and rejection of eastern literary and cultural norms.

Early in the 1800s the Midwest—with Cincinnati, the Queen City, as its first economic and cultural capital—began to emerge.[18] According to U.S. census data, the population of the Northwest Territory, just over 50,000 in 1800, rose to almost 300,000 by 1810. Ohio achieved statehood in 1803, the first state emerging from the Northwest Territory. More important, in that same year the United States purchased the Louisiana Territory, doubling the nation's size, moving its geographic center into the Midwest, and heralding future shifts in the national economy and the balance of political power.

The 1860 census counted over 9,000,000 people in the Midwest. Railroads were overtaking rivers as the predominant mode of transportation. The Civil War made the Midwest, with its rising population, its massive production of grain and meat, and its growing railroad network, critical to the Union war effort.[19] Chicago, already the nation's leading railroad center,[20] had displaced Cincinnati as the Midwest's leading city,[21] and midwestern animal production and shipment continued to rise.[22] By 1880, with the Midwest's population now above 17,350,000, Chicago and the Midwest were major forces in American life. By the mid-1880s city, corporate, and civic leaders began planning to showcase the city's emergence as a national power. By 1890 the Midwest had over 22,400,000 people, its population approaching the then-current population of the thirteen original states. U.S. Census Table 12 showed that Chicago had become the nation's second most populous city. City leaders, with significant corporate support, won congressional approval to host the world's fair commemorating the 400th anniversary of Columbus's arrival in the New World, defeating Washington, DC, New York City, St. Louis, and others.[23]

The 1893 Columbian Exhibition marked a major turning point for Chicago and the Midwest. The fair displayed technological advances in many fields, including anthropology, electricity, manufacturing, transportation, and weaponry, but Chicago's political and corporate leaders, having long suffered under the city's reputation as a hog butcher and gritty, unregulated railroad and industrial city, focused primarily on showing the East, the nation, and Europe that Chicago could achieve eastern and European standards of culture and refinement. For that reason, its architects chose to emulate the monuments of classical culture, the Italian Renaissance, Greece, and Rome, as still reflected today by two still-extant remnants from the exposition, the Museum of Science and Industry (initially the Palace of the Fine Arts) and the Art Institute (the downtown site for many of the Exposition's congresses).[24] Further reflecting the city's consciousness of European and eastern cultural hegemony, exhibits in the Court of Honor were restricted to those of the United States, its states, and prestigious western European nations. The exhibits of less prestigious, non-western European, and non-Caucasian nations were relegated to the Midway Plaisance—with its carnival milieu, the Ferris Wheel, Little Egypt, and Buffalo Bill's Wild West show—and to adjoining areas.[25]

The Chicago Renaissance was the literary counterpart of events, activities, and initiatives arising from and reflecting rising Chicago and regional certainty, pride, and economic standing in the decades following Chicago's fire. This burst of energy saw corporate, civic, and governmental collaboration to create and fund many initiatives designed to take Chicago from being merely a functional city to being a more beautiful, cultivated, even ethical city.[26] The 1893 Columbian Exhibition itself was the dominant embodiment of this rising economic strength, civic pride, and confidence, but among the many others was the Field Museum, first envisioned in 1891 and initially designated the Columbian Museum of Chicago.[27] Similarly, the evolution of the Art Institute and the provision of significant funds with which to purchase art gave Chicago what is today the world's second best impressionist art collection. During the late 1800s Chicago's cultural push also resulted in

Exposition grounds, 1893 World's Columbian Exposition, Chicago. Library of Congress, Reproduction Number: LC-USZ62104795.

the creation of the Chicago Symphony Orchestra, the Auditorium—a huge mixed-use hotel, retail, and theatre building with a technically advanced theatre—and Orchestra Hall. During this period Chicago also became home to dozens of elite salons, clubs, and societies, and a wide range of literary and cultural magazines and journals, as well as to the University of Chicago (1890) and the Armour Institute (1890, now the Illinois Institute of Technology), as well as to the Crerar (1894), Newberry (1887), and Chicago Public (1873) libraries.[28] The Civic Federation was founded in 1894 as an entity dedicated to fighting corruption, improving taste, enhancing beauty, and advocating culture.[29] In 1889 Jane Addams (1860–1935) and Ellen Gates Starr (1859–1940) founded Hull House, America's first settlement house, to address the economic, health, social, intellectual, and cultural needs of the city's poor immigrant populations.[30]

Architectural advances—including the Columbian Exhibition architecture, some of the nation's earliest skyscrapers, and the Prairie School of architecture—also marked the city's metamorphosis. On a larger scale, Chicago's City Beautiful movement and its Burnham Plan proposed making the city more attractive, accessible, and functional for all. Daniel Burnham's 1909 *Plan of Chicago* laid the groundwork for keeping Chicago's Lake Michigan shoreline open and accessible to all, creating a citywide system of parks and forest preserves, designing and developing major city thoroughfares, and sharing use of railroad tracks and stations.[31]

Chicago's flourishing literary scene became a movement, an embodiment of rising regional confidence, and a challenger of established literary traditions, themes, and techniques. This movement's roots lay in the development of high literacy rates in the region and the founding and evolution of newspapers. In earlier times, particularly in rural areas, newspapers had helped aspiring hinterland writers see and describe the world realistically. Print shop apprenticeships and immersion in day-to-day life had also helped regional writers in introducing frontier and small-town America to curious eastern urban audiences. Initially, these eastern audiences had needed assurances that they were intellectually and culturally superior to the people of America's interior, but the resulting condescendingly amusing "local color" stories succeeded in widening the range of American literature and opening journalistic and literary careers to those from what was then the West.[32]

In time, serious writers moved American literature toward a realistic portrayal of life. William Dean Howells (1837–1920), a member of the East Coast literati with roots in Ohio newspapers, was among those theorizing on and supporting literary realism.[33] The emergence of big-city newspapers in Chicago and elsewhere during the late 1800s resulted in new journalistic roles. The first of these was the advent of columnists dedicated to attracting readers through their wit, humor, and colorful language. Another innovation was the use of writers who merged humor and social commentary.[34] Finally, investigative reporters increasingly reported on crime, corruption, and injustice and advocated for the public good. More broadly, journalistic efforts to curb the abuses of money and power set up a growing opposition between established political and corporate power and the press. This anti-establishment stance increasingly marked midwestern perspectives and literary realism.

Beyond journalists, the Chicago Renaissance's first generation was marked by wealth, eastern connections, and Chicago society credentials.[35] As a group, the writers of the first generation followed eastern genteel tradition and flourished from the mid-1880s into the first decade of the twentieth century. Their writings were transitional but emphasized traditional romantic themes and techniques. These first-generation writers actively tried to shape literary and cultural tastes through their pronouncements, literary works, and salons. Several participants exemplified first-generation approaches.

Henry Blake Fuller (1857–1929) was an upper-class Chicagoan with New England roots, traditional romantic literary and cultural tastes, and diminishing finances. He longed for the European literature and life of the past. His writings varied from traditional romantic narrative plaints, like his *The Chevalier of Pensieri-Vani* (1890), to his realistic urban novel *The Cliff-Dwellers* (1893). The latter described the Clifton, an early Chicago skyscraper, the lives of the people associated with it, and Chicago's vulgar, unrestrained business ethic. Though mixed in his literary loyalties, Fuller experimented with realistic forms and laid the groundwork for others who followed.[36]

Writer and editor Harriet Monroe (1860–1936) was another fixture of the Renaissance's first generation. Like Fuller, Monroe had society connections. She was a Chicago *Tribune* art critic and read her genteel romantic dedicatory poem at the opening of the 1893 Columbian Exhibition.[37] Monroe's poetry is traditional in subject matter and diction and generally unremarkable, but, later, as an editor and advocate, she significantly advanced regional poets and new poetic approaches.

Hamlin Garland joined Chicago's elite literary circles for a few years in the 1890s, producing several books, most successfully *Main-Travelled Roads* (1891), a work of social-critical realism recounting the exploitation of midwestern farmers by eastern money and power. Ironically, however, Garland, who grew up on a succession of westering family farms from Wisconsin, Iowa, and Minnesota, to Dakota, had, in seeking a better life for himself, moved to the East, where his literary ability was recognized and he lived a prosperous life. The growing vogue for stories about the "West," in conjunction with his midwestern upbringing, provided his most significant subjects. Seeking commissioned publications and significant income, Garland wrote on many subjects and adopted the viewpoints he was assigned. Although he spent time in Chicago and was among the early regionalist literary leaders, he had no long-term commitment to midwestern values or orientations.[38]

Theodore Dreiser (1871–1945), a writer whose literary productivity included the period of the Chicago Renaissance's first generation, more fully reflected the literary orientations and products of the second generation. Born in rural Indiana and forced by his immigrant family's poverty to move frequently, he held positions as a journalist in Chicago and elsewhere. Perhaps his greatest masterpiece is *Sister Carrie* (1900), a fictionalized retelling of his sister's affair with a married man, using Chicago as its major setting. The novel tells of a pretty young working-class woman leaving small-town Wisconsin for the big city in hopes of a better life. Carrie's sister and brother-in-law are not interested in safeguarding her but use her to defray their own cost of living. Carrie's illness and the financial pressure they exert lead Carrie to escape to the only haven she can find, becoming a kept woman. Dreiser tells Carrie's story not as a tale of moral failure but rather as a naturalistic story, an assertion of human inability to understand oneself or compete successfully against the larger, stronger, amoral social and universal orders in which only the strongest survive and moral scruples only increase one's vulnerability. In this environment Carrie has no control and few options.[39] She is a helpless moth to the flame, not understanding her world or even her own actions or motivations. Dreiser documents the powerful, amoral, naturalistic city, rejects traditional moral judgments, and recounts *Sister Carrie* with a strong social-critical message and even stronger naturalism.

The real flowering of the Chicago Renaissance occurred in its second generation; Bernard Duffey in his *The Chicago Renaissance in American Letters* (1954) refers to it as "the Liberation" and its participants as "liberated intellectual bohemians."[40] Its prose writers, like Dreiser, who began publishing a decade earlier, and Sherwood Anderson, typically emerged from working-class families and small-town backgrounds, and were ready to take social-critical positions against the elite, corporate greed, political corruption, unbridled capitalism, and class exploitation.[41] Liberation writing, in prose and poetry, adopted strikingly realistic approaches. If the Chicago Renaissance's first generation was losing strength by approximately 1905, the second was coming into place by 1912 or earlier.

A holdover from the first generation, Harriet Monroe came to the forefront with the Chicago Renaissance's second generation. Convincing 100 leading Chicago citizens to each pledge five-year subscriptions at fifty dollars per year, she started *Poetry: A Magazine of Verse* in 1912 and paid writers for their contributions. In doing so, she helped aspiring new poets, often Midwesterners, and those espousing themes and techniques antithetical to those of nineteenth-century genteel romanticism.[42]

In the nineteenth century, and particularly in America and its poetry, literature typically presumed an overarching moral romantic-coherent worldview in which humans were central to the divine plan and God ensured that the good prevailed and the bad were punished.⁴³ European literature came to reject this perspective and adopted romantic incoherence—the worldview asserting the dignity and importance of humans but without cosmic support for morality—or realism well before the mid-nineteenth century.

Prior to the arrival of Chicago's "Liberation," American and Chicago *prose* writers had significantly advanced realistic techniques and worldviews and broadened the range of subjects open to portrayal. American *poetry*, however, staunchly maintained its long-held romantic orientations, its moralizing, often sentimental stories of small-town life and innocent rural people, and its assertion of divine providence and poetic justice. It also clung to traditional literary techniques, including rhyme, syllabic verse, and elevated diction.⁴⁴

With Monroe's support, Chicago's Liberation prose writers and poets advanced realism while asserting romantic portrayals of common people struggling amid societal injustice or naturalistic situations. Liberation writers typically held working-class perspectives and rejected exploitative capitalism and domination by the elite. They connected urban Midwesterners to their rural and small-town roots. If the first generation imitated and sought acceptance from eastern society, second-generation Chicago Renaissance writers rejected the past, the elite, and the East while asserting their own values, experiences, and norms. They celebrated the Midwest, Chicago, and common people.

Under Monroe, *Poetry* became central to the poetic revolution earlier given impetus by St. Louis editor William Marion Reedy (1862–1920) and *Reedy's Mirror* starting in 1894.⁴⁵ Reedy had championed Dreiser after Doubleday suppressed *Sister Carrie* and also encouraged use of plain-speaking realistic poetic approaches to Edgar Lee Masters (1868–1950) and Carl Sandburg (1878–1967), leading to their breakthrough works, *Spoon River Anthology* (1915) and *Chicago Poems* (1916).⁴⁶ So, too, Harriet Monroe provided regular publication opportunities, editorial encouragement and defense, significant literary prizes, and a sense of community for those attempting to overturn established poetic norms.⁴⁷

Liberation poets like Sandburg rejected traditional verse, its genteel orientation, and its assertion of poetic justice. Thematically, Sandburg strongly asserted that dignity, worth, and heroism mark working-class people, yet he portrayed their exploitation and victimization by those with money and power. His stylistic break from American poetic tradition becomes evident beginning with the aggressively direct first line of "Chicago," the lead poem of *Chicago Poems*: "Hog butcher to the world."[48] Sandburg's poems recognize the romantic incoherence of the city's brutality and the victimization of its working class, yet they celebrate Chicago's strength and the joy and tenacity of its laboring people.[49] They portray Chicago in worker portraits like those of the anarchist "Dynamiter," the "Jew" "Fish Crier," and the "Dago" "Shovel Man."[50]

Sandburg's poems call for rebellion against elite society, as in "The Fence" surrounding the home of a wealthy family, with "iron bars and steel points that can stab the life out of any man," ready to "shut off the rabble and all vagabonds and hungry men and all wandering children looking for a place to play."[51] Despite the strength of the elite and their determination to maintain their privilege, Sandburg foretells societal change, asserting, "Passing through the bars and over the steel points will go nothing except Death and the Rain and To-morrow."[52] Sandburg's worker heroes regularly maintain romantic worldviews despite their travail, but his workers cannot count on God or society for help. The elite continue to command and control events. Sandburg's poetry calls for revolution.

Owing much to William Marion Reedy's mentorship, Masters's *Spoon River Anthology* (1915) turns away from his previous genteel romantic poetic subjects and techniques and asserts rising midwestern self-confidence and advancing poetic realism; Masters's iconoclastically direct language and his direct presentation of previously taboo poetic topics shocked the literary establishment.[53] His volume looks below the apparently placid surface of midwestern small-town life and uncovers human drives that shape people's thoughts, actions, and lives. Masters describes the controlling power of sexual urges, lust for money, power, prestige, and revenge, among others. The *Spoon River* poems parallel Dreiser's direct realistic fictional portrayal of previously taboo subjects in *Sister Carrie*, but Masters's poems are more shocking because they appear in American *poetry*, which had held resolutely for much of a century to the increasingly outmoded romantic coherent worldview, subject matter, and genteel stylistic elements, and because Masters's poems are associated with midwestern small towns, the presumed bastions of moral virtue.

Both Sandburg and Masters's breakthrough works reject traditional poetic norms and perspectives. Sandburg revered Walt Whitman's poetry and adopted his direct, hard-hitting language of the people.[54] Similarly, Masters's "Petit, the Poet," in *Spoon River Anthology* (1915), rejects traditional poetics and asserts iconoclastic common speech and Whitmanesque approaches.

> Seeds in a dry pod, tick, tick, tick,
> Tick, tick, tick, like mites in a quarrel—
> Faint iambics that the faint breeze wakens—
> But the pine tree makes a symphony thereof
>
> . . .
>
> Seeds in a dry pod, tick, tick,
> Tick, tick, tick, what little iambics
> While Homer and Whitman roared in the pines![55]

Sherwood Anderson's *Winesburg, Ohio* (1919), a novel composed of interrelated short stories, follows the pattern of Liberation writers in rejecting accepted literary forms and constraints and advancing literary realism.[56] *Winesburg* reflects advanced realism in filtering the stories through an elaborate narrative frame. The opening section, "The Book of the Grotesque," sets the frame, which renders its own perspectives and those of the stories that follow influential but unverifiable. Anderson's three closing stories, "Death," "Sophistication," and "Departure" provide companion closing elements to the narrative frame. "Death" describes the passing of George Willard's mother. "Sophistication" recounts George's first pre-sexual experience. These two stories signal George's maturation and shifting perception of everything experienced through that point. "Departure" closes the collection with George Willard, the volume's maturing recurring character-narrator, leaving his small town for Chicago while attempting to grasp the meaning of life, America, cities, and small towns. *Winesburg, Ohio* is a work of psychological realism that presents *life as perceived*. George, now a young man, leaves small-town Ohio to pursue his dreams in the big city. Many Winesburg residents depicted in these stories can be viewed as uncompetitive and bypassed by change, yet George, like Anderson, reveres the town and its people. They have made him who he is.

Like his fellow Liberation writers Dreiser, Masters, and Sandburg, Anderson advanced realism as he probed behind the veil of nineteenth-century respectability. *Winesburg* includes stories of homosexuality; of a voyeuristic minister whose moment of moral strength leads him to smash a stained glass image of Christ calling all the little children to come to him; of sexual needs in men and women; and of the need by all to escape their psychological isolation and achieve communication. Anderson's works are primarily expressions of psychological realism in which the author realistically portrays the ways events, interactions, and feelings are perceived in the mind of specific characters, often in an intense state of mind. On that basis, Anderson worked to portray feelings, the sense of life, not empirical realities.

H.L. Mencken (1880–1956), an eastern writer, journalist, and opinion leader, rejected eastern censorship. He was impressed by the strength and independence of second-generation Chicago Renaissance writers and called Chicago *"The Literary Capital of the United States,"* praising it:

> for the sort of art that is recognizably national in its themes and its idioms and combines a Yankee sharpness of observation with a homely simplicity—the sort of art that one finds in a novel by Dreiser or a poem by Sandburg— the only sort that stands free of imitation and is absolutely American.[57]

The impact of the Chicago Renaissance's influential second generation was largely spent by the early 1920s. Later Chicago writers, however, such as James T. Farrell (1904–1979) with his *Studs Lonigan* trilogy (1935) and Nelson Algren (1909–1981) with *The Man with the Golden Arm* (1949), built on the Liberation's rebellion against elite society and traditional literary norms and its confident assertion of local experience and realism. Both had the courage to make the deeper recesses of American life their subjects.

The writers of the Chicago Black Renaissance—as exemplified by the realism of Richard Wright (1908–1960) in prose fiction with his novel *Native Son* (1940) and Gwendolyn Brooks (1917–2000) in poetry with *A Street in Bronzeville* (1945)—further extended the Liberation's rejection of elite power while realistically portraying the destructiveness of racist white society to the Chicago black community.[58] They portrayed those at the persecuted bottom of the social scale. In *Native Son*, Wright's Bigger Thomas acts out black rage against the dominant white society[59] while Brooks's *Bronzeville* graphically depicts victimization by poverty and racism.[60] Both writers further advanced literary realism in depicting the midwestern experience of those on the bottom of the social ladder.

The Chicago Renaissance marked rising midwestern determination to live and write from distinctively regional and national experiences, values, and traditions, not those of the East. The coming-of-age of the Midwest and Chicago carried that same message. What began as working-class departure from privileged eastern enclaves led in time to affirmation of common life in Chicago, the "City of the Big Shoulders,"[61] a city of iconoclastic ideas and revolutionary forms. The Chicago Renaissance reflected rising midwestern strength and self confidence. Although its first generation mimicked outmoded genteel eastern literary modes, its second generation, the Liberation, and those that followed, created poetry and prose that capture the lives, language, values, and dignity of democratic America. As Mencken asserted, these literary products made Chicago the literary capital of the United States.

## Notes

1. Edward Watts, *An American Colony: Regionalism and the Roots of Midwestern Culture* (Athens, Ohio: Ohio University Press, 2002), 3ff.
2. Watts, *An American Colony*, xiii–xiv, 5.
3. Marilyn J. Atlas, "The Chicago Renaissance," in *The Dictionary of Midwestern Literature*, vol. 2, *Dimensions of the Midwestern Literary Imagination*, ed. Philip A. Greasley (Bloomington: Indiana University Press, 2016), 130–46.
4. Watts, *An American Colony*, xviii–xix.
5. Watts, *An American Colony*, 138.
6. Watts, *An American Colony*, xiii–xiv.
7. Jon K. Lauck, *The Lost Region: Toward a Revival of Midwestern History* (Iowa City: University of Iowa Press, 2013), 15.

8. Watts, *An American Colony*, xix.
9. Lauck, *The Lost Region*, 15.
10. Watts, *An American Colony*, xvi, 15, 23–24.
11. Watts, *An American Colony*, 11–15.
12. Watts, *An American Colony*, 6.
13. Sherwood Anderson, "Godliness," *Winesburg, Ohio* (New York: B.W. Huebsch, 1919), 55–69.
14. Marcia Noe, "Caroline Kirkland," in *The Dictionary of Midwestern Literature*, vol. 1, *The Authors*, ed. Philip A. Greasley (Bloomington: Indiana University Press, 2001), 299; Caroline Kirkland, *Home as Found, or Glimpses of Western Life*, 4th ed. (New York: C.S. Francis, 1850), 10, 61.
15. Hamlin Garland, "Up the Coulé," *Main-Travelled Roads* (Arena Publishing Company, 1891), 136.
16. Marcia Noe, "Willa Cather," in *The Dictionary of Midwestern Literature*, vol. 1, 101.
17. Michael Wentworth, "F. Scott Fitzgerald," in *The Dictionary of Midwestern Literature*, vol. 1, 200.
18. John D. Fairfield, "Cincinnati, Ohio," in *The American Midwest: An Interpretive Encyclopedia* (Bloomington: Indiana University Press, 2007), 1153.
19. Carl Smith, *Chicago and the American Literary Imagination, 1880–1920* (Chicago: University of Chicago Press, 1984), 152–53.
20. Fairfield, "Cincinnati, Ohio," 1154.
21. Watts, *An American Colony*, 158.
22. Smith, *Chicago and the American Literary Imagination*, 153.
23. Williams, *In the City of Men*, 141–46.
24. Williams, *In the City of Men*, 149–53.
25. "Exhibits on the Midway Plaisance," in *The Electronic Encyclopedia of Chicago* (Chicago: Chicago Historical Society, 2005), www.encyclopedia.chicagohistory.org/pages/11421.html; "Exhibits on the Midway Plaisance, 1893" (pamphlet), (Chicago: W.B. Conkey Company, 1893), as digitally replicated there; "Living History of Illinois and Chicago," http://livinghistoryofillinois.com/pdf_files/Worlds%20Columbian%20 Exposition,%20Chicago,%20Illinois,%201893,%20Short%20Summary.pdf, 6.
26. Bernard Duffey, *The Chicago Renaissance in American Letters: A Critical History* (East Lansing: Michigan State College Press, 1954), 29–35.
27. *The Field Museum*, https://www.fieldmuseum.org/about/history.
28. Duffey, *Chicago Renaissance*, 27, 31–33, 51, 127.
29. Smith, *Chicago and the American Literary Imagination*, 149–50.
30. Guy Szuberla, "Hull-House," in *The Dictionary of Midwestern Literature*, vol. 2, 299–301.
31. Duffey, *Chicago Renaissance*, 29.
32. Duffey, *Chicago Renaissance*, 93.

33. Duffey, *Chicago Renaissance*, 10.
34. Williams, *In the City of Men*, 84–85.
35. Duffey, *Chicago Renaissance*, 138.
36. Mary DeJong Obuchowski, "Henry Blake Fuller," in *The Dictionary of Midwestern Literature*, vol. 1, 207.
37. Duffey, *Chicago Renaissance*, 64–65.
38. Duffey, *Chicago Renaissance*, 83–85.
39. Philip Gerber, "Theodore Dreiser," in *The Dictionary of Midwestern Literature*, vol. 1, 155.
40. Duffey, *Chicago Renaissance*, 131.
41. Duffey, *Chicago Renaissance*, 139, 141.
42. "Harriet Monroe," *The Poetry Foundation* website, http://www.poetryfoundation.org/poems-and-poets/poets/detail/harriet-monroe.
43. Bernard Duffey, "Romantic Coherence and Incoherence in American Poetry," *Centennial Review* 7, no. 2 (spring 1963): 219–36; "Romantic Coherence and Incoherence in American Poetry, Part II," *Centennial Review* 8, no. 4 (fall 1964): 453–64.
44. Philip A. Greasley, "American Vernacular Poetry: Studies in Whitman, Sandburg, Anderson, Masters, and Lindsay" (PhD diss., Michigan State University, 1975), 1–3, 14–36.
45. Ashley Hopkins, "*Reedy's Mirror*," in *The Dictionary of Midwestern Literature*, vol. 2, 712–14.
46. Penelope Niven, *Carl Sandburg: A Biography* (New York: Scribner's, 1991), 245–47.
47. Williams, *In the City of Men*, 376–79.
48. Carl Sandburg, "Chicago," *Chicago Poems* (New York: Henry Holt and Company, 1916), 3.
49. Philip A. Greasley, "Carl Sandburg" in *The Dictionary of Midwestern Literature*, vol. 1, 447.
50. Sandburg, "Dynamiter," "Fish Crier," and "Shovel Man," *Chicago Poems*, 44, 18, 16.
51. Sandburg, "The Fence," *Chicago Poems*, 32.
52. Sandburg, "The Fence," *Chicago Poems*, 32.
53. Herbert K. Russell, "*Spoon River Anthology*," in *The Dictionary of Midwestern Literature*, vol. 2, 811.
54. Philip A. Greasley, "Carl Sandburg," in *The Dictionary of Midwestern Literature*, vol. 1, 447.
55. Edgar Lee Masters, "Petit, the Poet," *Spoon River Anthology* (New York: Macmillan, 1921), 89.
56. Robert Dunne, "Sherwood Anderson," in *The Dictionary of Midwestern Literature*, vol. 1, 42.
57. Henry L. Mencken, Chicago *Tribune*, 28 October 1917; reprinted as *The Literary Capital of the United States* (Chicago: *The Daily News*, 1920): n.p.

58. Darlene Clark Hine, "Chicago Black Renaissance," in *The Encyclopedia of Chicago*, 132.
59. Johnnie Wilcox and Marilyn J. Atlas, *"Native Son,"* in *The Dictionary of Midwestern Literature*, vol. 2, 571.
60. Philip A. Greasley, "A Street in Bronzeville," in *The Dictionary of Midwestern Literature*, vol. 2, 819–20.
61. Sandburg, "Chicago," *Chicago Poems*, 3.

Jon K. Lauck

Typecast Rebels

The Strange Careers of *Winesburg, Ohio* and *Main Street*

The flattened arc of territory known as the Midwest, stretching from Ohio toward the West under the elongated bulges of the Great Lakes out to a hazy border ending somewhere in the eastern Dakotas, Nebraska, and Kansas, does not figure very prominently in the American popular imagination. In the broader culture, the Midwest is often relegated to the role of "flyover country."[1] But it was not always thus. In the late nineteenth and early twentieth century the Midwest was considered the pacesetter region. In the wake of the Midwest's ascendance, a group of historians active in the early twentieth century brought some attention to the region.[2] At the same time, an impressive group of midwestern regionalist writers also gave life to the region.[3] But the mood sustained by that effort and its effects—that once energetic Midwestern Moment—has now been largely forgotten. The Midwest now does little to divert or disrupt the main currents of American culture.[4]

One of the reasons for the waning of the Midwest's presence in American life since the first quarter of the twentieth century has been its reputation as a boring and backward hinterland, a fate sealed by the critical reaction to two prominent works of fiction that were published just after World War I. *Winesburg, Ohio* (1919), by the Ohioan Sherwood Anderson, and *Main Street* (1920), by the Minnesotan Sinclair Lewis, became twin pillars in a new genre of works purportedly critical of the small-town Midwest and all it represented.[5] These authors, it came to be believed, represented a final rebellion against and overthrow of the old agrarian and bourgeois order in the Midwest, which was impeding modern American progress. The literary editor of *The Nation* lodged the notion of a "revolt from the village" genre in the minds of scholars.[6] Despite its deep flaws, the "village revolt" trope persisted for decades in the common trading of the American cultural scene, and variations on the theme of rural and small-town provincialism and backwardness remain a staple of contemporary popular culture.[7] Call it the Footloose Effect, or the conventional and formulaic retreat into common clichés and prosaicisms about small-town pettiness and moralizing and its ritualized portrayal in, to pluck one example from a forest of possibilities, the popular movie *Footloose* (1984), in which an insular small town bans dancing and rock music.

While the authority of the school of thought popularly associated with *Winesburg* and *Main Street* is still recognized, the texts themselves, after another look, are not capable of carrying the burdens of cultural significance and common stereotypes with which they have been saddled. They have been, in other words, badly typecast. They are much less than they were once thought to be and they do not represent what the critics claim, but their effect, despite its now amorphous origins, remains ubiquitous and unfortunate. To see these works differently and to understand their forgotten nuances and to scrape away the layers of barnacled meaning attached to them by decades of cultural criticism is another path toward finding the forgotten culture of the Midwest and recognizing the Midwestern Moment and even, perhaps, conjuring some small amount of solace in an anxious culture. Seeing even further, past these works and into a world of literature and cultural regionalism nearly erased by time, may provide entry into a world beyond solace, one where contentment and hope is not alien to the common rhythm of life, a midwestern world that the Iowan Ruth Suckow, who is the subject of a full chapter in this volume, tried to bring into view in novels such as *New Hope* (1942).

*Winesburg, Ohio* is a book of stories about a midwestern town that are mostly discrete but also interrelated by their setting and the frequent appearance of the local newspaper reporter, George Willard. The book begins with a short and strange tale of an old writer dreaming in his bed about a series of figures who are deemed "grotesques" even though some of them are beautiful. When these figures embraced certain truths imagined by the man—all beautiful truths—they became grotesques, or people somehow misshaped by the truths they tried to grasp. The old man in the story recorded all of this in "The Book of the Grotesques," which he rose from his bed to write but never published. This puzzling short story sets the stage for *Winesburg*.[8] Based on the

Jon K. Lauck    249

stories that followed and their placement anterior to an odd story laden with the idea of grotesqueness, the meaning of which Sherwood Anderson does not explain, it is not shocking that *Winesburg* was often categorized as a critique of small-town life.

The assorted stories in *Winesburg* are mostly dry and uninspiring and tend to focus on the vexations of various souls: the man with trembling hands who was falsely accused of touching a student and run out of a Pennsylvania town; the doctor who oddly collected random thoughts on loose bits of paper he placed in his pockets; the mother anxious about her son getting ahead in life; the doctor who was ashamed that his father had died in an asylum and was paranoid about people in town not liking him; the unlovely woman who had a liaison with George Willard; the slight but tenacious man whose three brothers were killed in the Civil War and who served as a Presbyterian minister and took over the family farm and eagerly sought a vision to guide his life; the "oversensitive" and "neurotic" young woman who alienated the girls she lived with by trying too hard in school (86); the man who had unexpected seizures; the woman whose loneliness finally caused her to inexplicably run naked down a street; the depot agent angry at his wife for infidelity who was relegated by a telegraph company to Winesburg; the young man known as the "deep one" who was inhibited by fears of others' talking about him; a broken man from Cleveland who had succumbed to drink but tried to empower a little girl to lead a better life; the earnest and devoted Presbyterian minister temporarily tempted to look on a woman who reads in her bed below the window of his study; the lonely teacher who thought she had become an old maid; the artist who had failed in New York City and returned to Winesburg; the woman who worked in the millinery shop and was awkwardly courted by a bartender and George Willard; the son of a farmer who opened a store in Winesburg that was disorganized and failed to sell much merchandise and who was angry about seeming "queer" and ran away to Cleveland; the farm hand who could not warn his co-worker about his anxiety about "getting stuck in the harness" of domestic life; the lazy young boy who wanted to get drunk only once so he could dream.

The doses of disappointment and loneliness in *Winesburg* are potent and mildly abase the reader—even though they are somewhat neutralized by the rather plodding and tedious unfolding of *Winesburg's* stories—but they also are put in the service of simple social recognition. They give some oxygen to the lives of the forgotten, not simply to spotlight pathos, but also to recognize their "sweetness." In the story about Dr. Reefy, the characters enjoy the "twisted little apples" that remain on the trees because the autumn apple pickers have rejected them and not shipped them to the "cities where they will be eaten in apartments that are filled with books, magazines, furniture, and people," or places of sophistication. "Only the few know the sweetness of the twisted apples" that remained in Winesburg, Sherwood Anderson explains. (36) They are different from the "round perfect fruit that is eaten in the city apartments." (38) They are different, but still sweet, still deserving of recognition and a place in collective memory. Anderson wants us to see all the people of Winesburg. In keeping with the midwestern historical school of his era, Anderson calls us to look beyond high diplomacy and finance and coastal culture and see the common life of the interior's towns too.

Part of the difficulty affecting some of *Winesburg*'s characters is disconnection and alienation, or a failure to fit in. The character Seth Richmond thinks himself an "outcast in his own town" and pities himself in comparison to the young reporter George Willard, who "belongs to this town" and is a part of its goings-on. (137) Seth seeks solitude, a refuge from common socializing and repartee, and is irritated by the chatter and bothersome small talk of people in the town. He thinks he will lose his love to "someone who talks a lot—someone like that George Willard." (142) But to be able to enter the community conversation and connect to the world, a rather simple matter that eludes Seth Richmond, could bring happiness. The at-times lonely artist Enoch Robinson, for example, felt much better when he became a "producing citizen of the world" and voted, paid taxes, read the newspaper, and became "a real part of things." (171) Sherwood Anderson wants us to see all of the souls in his little Ohio town who may go unrecognized, but he also calls them forth, urging them to transcend a self-imposed silence or marginalization, to find their roots and the sense of place that succors their fellows.

The most commonly occurring character in *Winesburg* is George Willard, the eager newspaper reporter at the *Winesburg Eagle*, who comes of age and naturally begins searching for his path to the future. After his mother dies when he is eighteen he decides to move to a larger city. George begins, along with most boys of his age, to take "a backward view of life" and to wonder how it will all turn out for him and to contemplate the "figure he will cut in the world." (234) He begins to ponder the "countless figures of men who before his time have come out of nothingness into the world, lived their lives and again disappeared into nothingness." (234) George realizes that "he must live and die in uncertainty, a thing blown by the winds, a thing destined like corn to wilt in the sun." (234) In other words, the "sadness of sophistication," as Anderson names the condition, or the common existential doubts of adolescence have settled in George and he begins to manage the psychic burdens of adulthood and finding a purpose. (234) When George visits the Winesburg fairground late at night—an open place of social and civic energy in a "Middle Western town" of the era, Anderson notes— he "shudders at the thought of the meaninglessness of life while *at the same instant*" he realizes that "if the people of the town are his people, one loves life so intensely that tears come into the eyes." (italics added, 241) At the fairground in the darkness George begins "to think of the people in the town where he had always lived with something like reverence." (241) A dozen people show up to wish George well as he boards the train to his future, and, as the train pulls away, he remembers his father's advice: "Don't let anyone think you're a greenhorn." (246) He looks out the window of the train and Winesburg is gone. It "had become but a background on which to paint the dreams of his manhood," but a place, Anderson intimates, worthy of reverence. (247)

Winesberg is not perfect, Anderson is saying. Some of its people struggle with loneliness and alienation and finding their place in the world, just like people everywhere. But that's not all Winesburg is, despite, to the contrary, the force of historical memory, which gives power to the notion of a literary "village revolt." George Willard, the central figure in *Winesburg*, becomes teary and sentimental about his little town as he sets off to make his way in the world. He recognizes its beauty. It is a place where the countryside is "splashed with yellows and reds" in the fall and where one could slip into the "woods to gather nuts, hunt rabbits, or just loaf about" and smoke a pipe. (204) Winesburg has a women's club for the study of poetry and the town's main event, the Winesburg County Fair, holds people's affections. And the common life of Winesburg is certainly preferable to Cincinnati's gangs and thievery and drunkenness and disorder (212) and, as Anderson makes clear elsewhere, to the darkness of Chicago. While the displays of the human condition in *Winesburg* could appear most places, the book maintains a midwestern flavor that does not appear often in popular culture. Some men in Winesburg argue about prominent Ohioans such as Mark Hanna and William McKinley; Winesburg has a Buckeye and a Maumee street; Winesburg exists in the orbit of Cleveland; for recreation, people go to Sandusky on Lake Erie. The Midwest has a presence in the book and, if the centrality of George Willard to *Winesburg* is properly seen, it serves as a source of roots and comfort and strength.

*Winesburg* contains its share of positive points about the Midwest, but it is ultimately ambiguous, as was common with the work of Anderson, who was known to be amorphous, dreamy, and vague. A second look at *Winesburg*'s companion volume in the "village revolt" tradition, however, shows it to be much less ambiguous. In *Main Street*, while Lewis takes some obvious jabs at small-town gossip and bucolic ways, the central thrust of the story is to unmask the cosmopolitan pretensions of Carol, the main character.[9] Sinclair Lewis has his fun with small-town norms, to be sure, but a twenty-first-century reading of *Main Street* exhausts a reader with Carol's absurdities and, in the process, spotlights much of the contemporary cultural angst that might be treated with a dose of the midwestern-ness that Lewis also chronicles.

Carol Milford grew up in Mankato, Minnesota, in the picturesque Minnesota River valley as the daughter of a prosperous and caring judge. "Carol was not," Lewis emphasizes, "an intimate of the prairie villages" of the rural Midwest. (22) After finishing college in Minneapolis and working in Chicago for a short time, Carol meets and marries Dr. Will Kennicott, a University of Minnesota–trained doctor practicing up north in Gopher Prairie, one of the Midwest's "prairie villages." Kennicott likes Gopher Prairie and finds it pleasant and sociable, but twenty-six-year-old Carol seeks to change the world and thinks she might begin by "getting her hands on" a prairie town and transforming it.[10] (21) Carol does become involved with local women's groups, serves on the town library board, promotes various reforms, and even conducts a play. But Carol's more ambitious and grandiose dreams are frustrated and she considers leaving Kennicott and Gopher Prairie. She flirts with the idea of having affairs with Guy Pollock, an artsy but timid lawyer in town, and Erik Valborg, a young and sensitive farm boy-turned-tailor.

Carol's frustrations are in full view in her discussions with Vida Sherwin, a college-educated teacher in Gopher Prairie who also seeks some civic reforms—although much more modest than Carol—such as the building of a new school, but Vida generally sees Gopher Prairie as a "comfy homey old town" where revolutionary change is unnecessary. (274) Carol agrees with some of Vida's small reform efforts—shade trees, gardens, better sewers, more mosquito control—but demands more "startling, exotic things" (289) and longs for the coming of a "thick, black-bearded, cynical Frenchman who would sit about and drink and sing opera and tell bawdy stories and laugh at our proprieties." (290) Carol goes through the motions of helping Vida but "all the while she saw herself running garlanded through the streets of Babylon." (292) Vida points out how others were helping to fix up the school and the train depot while Carol refuses to be a pragmatic and "sound reformer" and remains an "impossibilist." (290) To Vida, Carol comes "rushing in, and expect[ed] in one year to change the whole town into a lollypop paradise with everybody stopping everything else to grow tulips and drink tea." (274)

Dr. Will Kennicott is excessively patient with his young bride, but finally speaks his mind, airing his frustrations and defending his town. Carol complains about the rural and "provincial" "peasants" of Gopher Prairie and its environs in Northern Minnesota (37) and sees Gopher Prairie as "the end—the end of the world." (42) But Kennicott defends the farmers of his country, many of them Norwegian and German immigrants, as decent and hard-working folk: "Look here, Carrie. You want to get over your city idea that because a man's pants aren't pressed, he's a fool. These farmers are mighty keen and up-and-coming." (37) Kennicott says: "Bully people, these Scandinavian farmers," and "prosperous," and whose children "will be doctors and lawyers and governors of the state and any darn thing they want to." (72)[11] Kennicott also defends his old and good friend Sam Clark and prefers him to "all the poets and radicals in the entire world," a choice that Carol fails to comprehend. (167) Will tells Carol that in a "showdown you'd prefer Sam Clark to any damn long-haired artist." (217) When Carol is being "high and mighty," Will stands up for Sam, "best soul that ever lived, honest and loyal and damn good fellow" whom Carol dislikes because he occasionally chews tobacco or lights a cigar. (189) Will says Carol is scaring off his friend because "every time he speaks of the weather you jump him because he ain't talking about poetry or Gertie—Geothe?—or some highbrow junk." (189) Will wants Carol to stop acting so "superior to folks" and trying to change them—"why can't you take folks as they are?" (191) As the novel progresses, Will grows increasingly flustered with Carol and her complaining and narcissism and her "willingness to think the worst you possibly can of us poor dubs in Gopher Prairie"— "you don't make any effort to appreciate us. You're so damned superior, and think the city is such a hell of a lot finer place, and you want us to do what *you* want, all the time." (186, italics in original)

Sinclair Lewis, through the voice of Will and other characters, is pointing to the problem of human contentment. Will asks: "Carrie, what the devil is it you want, anyway?" (442) Carol tries to get Guy Pollock to explain the "discontent" of people like herself: "What do we want?" (219) Pollock responds that like other discontented people, they want a higher consciousness, a new "Utopia." "We want everything. We sha'n't get it. So we sha'n't ever be content." (220) But even the once-dreamy Pollock impresses upon Carol that he does not want to get "mixed up in all this orgy of meaningless discontent." (221) Vida makes the same point. She is a reformer and wants to improve certain things in Gopher Prairie, but she thinks Carol is a foolish "revolutionist" whereas Vida believes the essential ingredients of a good town are in place. (274) Vida thinks her suitor Raymie Wutherspoon feigns too much interest when Carol has "some crazy theory that we all ought to turn anarchists or live on figs and nuts." (278) Carol cannot abide Vida's counsel: "I'm not content to leave the sea and the ivory towers to others. I want them for me! Damn Vida!" (293) Others try to explain to Carol that her discontent is not the fault of Gopher Prairie. Percy Bresnahan, a Gopher Prairie native who found success in the car business in Boston and was loved and admired by all his mates back in Gopher Prairie, tells Carol that the "faults you find in this town are simply human nature, and never will be changed." (303) Bresnahan says, "you overshoot the mark ... the town can't be all wrong." (304)

Despite its common reputation—to the extent its details are remembered much at all—and familiar role as a prime exhibit in a broad indictment of midwestern small towns, Sinclair Lewis's *Main Street* is highly ambiguous at best and perhaps better seen as a brutal critique of small town critics.[12] Lewis keys on Carol's "frivolousness" (69) and "wonderlust" and "wanderlust" (73) and her tendency to be "flighty." (69) Lewis describes her wont to "shock" people and then turn "flighty" and "temperamental." (189–90) Will says to Carol: "Either you want to dance, or you bang the piano, or else you get moody as the devil and don't want to talk or anything else." (189–90) While Lewis does not leave Gopher Prairie unscathed and is at times sympathetic to Carol's discontents, some of which he suffered from in his own life, the overall force of *Main Street* leaves his audience exasperated with her badgering and disgruntlement.

In the end, Lewis slowly navigates Carol toward a different point of view. In this process, she recognizes at various times the errors of her longings. Even in her pre-marital days when Carol worked in Chicago after college, she recoiled from the Bohemian party she attended replete with drinking, smoking, and renditions of the Internationale, a scene that should have pleased her. (26) In Gopher Prairie she comes to notice, against her assumptions of provinciality, that the supposedly dull mill owner Lyman Cass reads "Gibbon, Hume, Grote, Prescott and the other thick historians." (250) At times she could admit she is a "fool" because of her "dream of Venice." (156) She also comes to see Kennicott's good work for the community. Carol tells Guy Pollock that, compared to the rigorous schedule of farm visits by Dr. Kennicott, which actually help people, "we're a pair of hypercritical loafers, you and I, while he quietly goes and does things." (199) Compared with her romantic dabbling in French and German novels, Carol notes how Will "speaks with a vulgar, common, incorrect German of life and death and birth and the soil" with the German farmers in the area. (210) Carol says she admires Will and his work: "one farmer he pulls through diphtheria is worth all my yammering for a castle in Spain. A castle with baths." (179) Before her final realization and while she is still seeking a grand plan for her life, Carol goes off to Washington to do clerical work during the war but also finds it monotonous and her office "as full of cliques and scandals as a Gopher Prairie." (445) The Outside World is not as glamorous as she imagined. After being away from Gopher Prairie her attitude toward the town becomes warmer and she becomes more tolerant of and open to life in the small-town Midwest. (463)

Carol moves closer to the view of life in Gopher Prairie embraced by Will Kennicott: "It's good country, and I'm proud of it. Let's make it all those old boys [the original settlers] dreamed about." (32) Will can see the town's advantages and understand how democratic it could be. He observes in Minneapolis that "you don't get to know folks here, way you do up home. I feel I've got something to say about running Gopher Prairie, but you take it in a big city of two–three hundred thousand, and I'm just one flea on the dog's back." (29) Unlike those who "take it" in an urban center and have little influence on the life of the city, people in Gopher Prairie are actively involved and give life to civic organizations such as the library and school boards. The social capital of Gopher Prairie could be measured by its thriving lodges and clubs: the Knights of Pythias, GAR, IOOF, Eastern Star, Ancient and Affiliated Order of Spartans, United and Fraternal Order of Beavers, Chautauqua, the Jolly Seventeen club, and the Thanatopsis study club. Will also appreciates his environs. He likes the "country driving" and the "hunting in the fall" (29) and even Carol loves the "summer cottages" on the lakes of Minnesota. (166) The efforts at promoting or "boosting" Gopher Prairie sit well with Will because he genuinely likes the town. Unlike Carol, who wants Gopher Prairie to be Venice and therefore groans at efforts to promote the town's amenities, Will finds boosting his town perfectly natural.

Against an early twenty-first-century culture ramifying in so many other directions, *Main Street* offers a genuine glimpse of a region and its traditions that have disappeared from the popular imagination. As a native son, Sinclair Lewis can elucidate in detail the shape of that big and "bewildered empire called the American Middlewest." (17) Even Carol sees the Midwest as the "newest empire of the world," a place filled with "dairy herds and exquisite lakes" and "silos like red towers" where she hopes things might turn out differently than for other empires which became encrusted by "ancient stale inequalities." (40) Before her later contentment when Carol is still attempting to revolutionize Gopher Prairie, some old-timers point out how much had already been done in the town that Carol cannot see because of her constricted view of the town's and the Midwest's history. One friendly older woman tells Carol she is "too tender-hearted" and does not understand that when the woman and her husband arrived in Gopher Prairie "there was nothing here but a stockade and a few soldiers and some log cabins." (152) In opposition to Carol's grand plans, she notes all the pioneers' hard work and the new trees and lawns and running hot-water and electric lights and dismisses Carol's efforts to turn the town into something from a "Dutch storybook." (153) Carol cannot see the Midwest and its history and the development of Gopher Prairie, another woman observes, and her plan to transform Gopher Prairie is grounded in the foreign vision and style of a "Boston architect." (155) In a related scene in *Winesburg* Helen White, the banker's daughter, returns home from college in Cleveland for a visit and brings along a cosmopolitan professor. The disconnected professor puts on the "airs of the city" and looks upon the people of Winesburg as a sociologist would, not as a living place in a vibrant region. (239)

Through such scenes *Main Street* and *Winesburg* can help us find a place and its rhythms and see it unobstructed by a high modernist urge to categorize it and reform it. Seeing a place is in part a matter of "sparing," as the geographer Edward Relph describes it, or allowing places to "be the way they are; it is a tolerance for them in their own essence; it is taking care of them through building or cultivating without trying to subordinate them to human will. Sparing is a willingness to leave places alone and not to change them casually or arbitrarily."[13] Relph is warning against the imposition of "general solutions according to the place-free dictates of current social science and planning," or, as in the mind of Carol, the demands for "other-directed architecture."[14] To find and see and appreciate a place such as the Midwest, the first step is to search for it, not a castle in Spain.

In the end, *Winesburg* and *Main Street* can speak to the odd agonies of modern discontentedness and offer solace. In addition to recognizing the decencies of his little town and its simple pleasures, Will Kennicott urges a midwestern level-headedness on his utopian spouse. Will says he wants to travel and see the world too, but he is "practical" about it and wants to earn some money to pay for it first. (193) Will's request is perfectly sensible—he is alert to the dangers of a "champagne taste and beer income." (186) Until he has more money, Will is happy to take short driving trips down to Des Moines or up to Winnipeg or over to Grand Marais on Lake Superior. While midwestern blizzards were fun for a youthful Carol in the city of Mankato because her father would stay home from court for the day, Will, when making his way through a winter storm, approaches them with the caution of an early settler: "Not much fun on the prairie. Get lost. Freeze to death. Take no chances." (211) Will favors "solid citizens" over unstable artists, enjoys the midwestern regionalist writings of James Whitcomb Riley, not the "highbrow art stuff," and generally prefers "uplifting" literature, not the kind "full of temptations."[15] (75–76, 138) Will's contentment and practicality—as against Carol's dreamy grandiosity, which is foreordained to yield a dreary discontentment and final disillusionment—can cut a path, not to perfection, but to happiness, a good and rooted place, one with a history, one that can save many from paralyzing angst and existential dread.

Finding this Midwest of Will Kennicott requires not only a deeper reading of the works of the supposed "village revolt," but a transcendence of this canon and a resurrection of a buried and forgotten corpus of midwestern voices and history, a counter-tradition represented by authors such as the Iowan Ruth Suckow, who was discovered by John T. Frederick and first published in Frederick's Iowa-based literary magazine, *The Midland*.[16] Suckow's German immigrant grandparents were natives of feudal Mecklenburg province and moved to Clayton County, Iowa, in 1869, and her father became a Congregational minister and took his first pastorate in Hawarden, Iowa, in 1889.[17] Suckow's literary works about Iowa focused on small towns, farming, hard work, thrift, threshing, fairs, weddings, picnics, Fourths of July, little school houses and churches, band and chorus concerts, public speeches, poetry readings, friendly socializing, the beauties of being placed, the pervasive "ruralism" of the early twentieth-century Midwest, and, along with its trials, the "deep stabilities of country life."[18] Suckow recognized that the communities of the Midwest certainly faced hardships and that they included "'characters,' queer ones, variety"—or some of the people in Sherwood Anderson's *Winesburg*—but her focus tended to the broad world of midwestern "folks," the people who worked the land, ran the stores, built schools and churches, and put on dances, feeds, and corn-husking bees, or the "people who do actually form the great mass basis of our particular civilization," not the peculiar and alienated, not the Seth Richmonds and Carol Kennicotts.[19]

In her literary work and her personal efforts, Suckow was pressing for more attention to the common life of the Midwest, but grew frustrated by her fellow artists' and intellectuals' dispersal to Paris, New York, San Francisco, and Taos—"running away from the folks to nowhere"—and their pursuit of the "primitive" and exotic and their rejection of the communal life of the Midwest as "completely out of keeping with any idea of culture."[20] She was also irritated by the "village rebel" types, those "rebellious children who have totally, explicitly revolted from the 'folks' practices of their own communities," the "prodigal sons and daughters" who behaved "like a bunch of frightened and lonely children trying to huddle together out of the way of authority" and "must hustle off to find themselves an art and a civilization that was ready-made for them somewhere else."[21] Against the sneering of New York and the alienation of disaffected rebels and the "bewilderment of variety" that caused "intellectual and aesthetic confusion," Suckow was asking her fellow artists to find and see the "folks spirit, with its directness, its simplicity, its intimacy, and its broad generosity" and its rooted inclusiveness.[22]

Suckow's energies yielded, for example, her 1942 novel *New Hope*, a lost counterpoint to the perceived rebuffs of the Midwest by village rebels and a book loosely based on her youth in Hawarden.[23] Her portrayal was not fiction to her, however, because she genuinely loved the town and saw it as a "real, acting democracy" and, in a not-so-subtle rebuff to those rebelling against their midwestern homes, she dedicated the novel to her parents.[24] *New Hope* focuses on the town of New Hope in northwestern Iowa, located a few miles from the Big Sioux River, which forms the boundary with South Dakota. New Hope took its name after a tornado destroyed the first settlement a few miles away (the townspeople rejected the railroad's choice of "Taylorsburg"—"just another burg!").[25] In the novel, the town welcomes a new minister, William Greenwood, who reads Aristotle, dwells on the hopefulness of the New Testament ("I don't care for all those Old Testament kings, don't care about kings anyway, all those wars and battles, and those superstitions"), enjoys the local talk of crops and weather and visiting farms, and generally projects a calm contentedness, an "unworldliness that yet was salted with good sense and good judgment."[26] Reverend Greenwood preaches about "light and hope," not a "stern theology," but one "diffused with the open prairie light."[27] The Miller family, who moved in from a farm in Illinois, welcomes the new minister and is proudly led by Dave Miller, who appreciates the "equality" of the town and its "natural comradeship," its absence of "layers of classes and customs" and "aristocratic tradition": "That's the way to keep it. That's the way things ought to be."[28] Dave

Miller thinks "that right here and right now we people have the chance to work out one of the greatest experiments in mankind's history," a recognition of pioneer aspirations that Will Kennicott seeks to embrace in Gopher Prairie.[29] The young Greenwood girl Delight and the young Miller boy Clarence grow close and form the main action in the novel and are disappointed when a reluctant Reverend Greenwood accepts the call of a new post in Oregon. The Methodist minister in New Hope dismisses his congregants early so they can hear Reverend Greenwood's final sermon from a pulpit bedecked with summer flowers and is welcomed by a soaring rendition of "Joy to the World," Greenwood's favorite hymn. He prays that his people will "continue in the faith grounded and settled, and be not moved away from the hope of the gospel."[30] A dozen families bid the Greenwoods farewell at the depot.

More important than *New Hope*'s underlying story is Suckow's projection of the foundational ingredients of existence in the early twentieth-century American Midwest: the social life of the town, the rises and falls of the seasons, farming, courtships, marriages, piano playing (under a picture of Mozart), baking, making fudge and ice cream, listening to Schubert in church, meals of chicken, biscuits, tomatoes, beets, corn, and cottage cheese, pitchers of lemonade, conclaves in kitchens, the editor of the local newspaper named the *Citizen* "sitting at a big untidy desk under flag-draped pictures of Washington, Lincoln, and Benjamin Franklin," the Grange, GAR, Christmas Eve cantata, the Harvest Dinner, Decoration Day, May Day, Washington's Birthday Bazaar, porches, parsonages, picnics, sewing bees, May baskets, Sunday School, baseball, "Yankee"-precise woodpiles, and "Swedishly bright" houses.[31] The vision of Suckow's books such as *New Hope* did not tend toward the utopian or exotic, but featured a focus on a "careful country minutiae," as she said, and in the background played a "certain monotonous music, like the tuneless tune of the windmill in the stillness of the country air."[32] Suckow helped readers see the essential elements of midwestern life and maintained that her books were "neither indictment nor celebration," but she also sought a recognition, in contrast to Carol Kennicott's wearying discontentedness, of Iowa's practical and grounded people.[33] The world's oceans were grand and exotic and exciting, one object of Carol's dreams, but in New Hope, young Clarence thinks that Iowa's Okoboji lakes are pretty good too.[34]

In the settings and scenes of *New Hope*, Suckow sought to capture the reality of her state but she also resisted attempts at categorization and the temptations of outside pressures and agendas of the period and any method that privileged "one strand" of "human life" and made it "bear too much burden."[35] She wanted her readers to see her Midwest, to "look down into the material as if into a well of water that was for the moment undisturbed."[36] She believed that the "effort to perceive, as far as possible without prejudice or partiality, has a value of its own."[37] The "deepest reason for a middle western literature," Suckow thought, was to capture what "we have here in the Middle West, the particular way, the fresh way, in which the ancient stream of life manifests itself, colored and shaped by local conditions."[38] Her desire was "to see some aspect of greater truth through a particular situation in a particular place with a particular people."[39] She was capable of seeing far beyond the trendy clichés of the imagined village revolt.[40] Suckow traced her ability to see to her early years in Hawarden and came to "understand the obligation and privilege" of that "early association" and worried about a growing ingratitude toward the past among others "born in the light" but who had their "eyes open too soon to comprehend what [they] saw."[41] Against the predilections of the village revolt school, Suckow sought, one critic noted in the 1920s, to distinguish between "factors which draw out and build up human capacities, and those whose effect is to confine and kill," or breed discontent, such as alienation and placelessness.[42] She wanted, foremost, for us to see the Midwest, to trace its contours and fix it on the map of our consciousness and extend to it the dignity of recognition and not be detained by imperfection and to draw us toward its warm center of rooted and practical contentment. She represents the rhythms and spirit of the regionalist upsurge of the Midwestern Moment and tells us much more about that era than the stereotypes seemingly purveyed by the popular and critical interpretations of *Winesburg* and *Main Street*.

## Notes

1. Anthony Harkins, "The Midwest and the Evolution of 'Flyover Country,'" *Middle West Review* 3.1 (Fall 2016), 97–121.
2. Jon K. Lauck, "The Prairie Historians and the Foundations of Midwestern History," *Annals of Iowa: A Quarterly Journal of History* 71.2 (Spring 2012), 137–73.

3. Jon K. Lauck, *From Warm Center to Ragged Edge: The Erosion of Midwestern Regionalism, 1915–1965* (Iowa City: University of Iowa Press, 2017).
4. Jon K. Lauck, *The Lost Region: Toward a Revival of Midwestern History* (Iowa City: University of Iowa Press, 2013).
5. References to *Winesburg, Ohio* and *Main Street* in this essay are taken from Sherwood Anderson, *Winesburg, Ohio: Text and Criticism*, edited by John H. Ferres (New York: The Viking Critical Library, Penguin Books, 1996 [1919]) and Sinclair Lewis, *Main Street* (New York: New American Library, Signet Classics, 2008 [1920]) and the page references to same will be noted in the text instead of individual footnotes.
6. Carl Van Doren, "Contemporary American Novelists X. The Revolt from the Village: 1920," *The Nation* 113.2936 (October 12, 1921) (Fall Book Supplement).
7. Jon K. Lauck, "The Myth of the Midwestern 'Revolt from the Village,'" *MidAmerica* 40 (2013), 39–85.
8. Anderson originally proposed "The Book of the Grotesque" as the title for his book, but his publisher, B.W. Huebsch, changed the title to "Winesburg, Ohio." "A Note on the Text," *Winesburg, Ohio*, 248.
9. For a parallel reading of Lewis's other famous work, see Jon K. Lauck, "Reading *Babbitt* in Cancun," *Old Northwest Review* (Fall 2015), 117–34.
10. Carol was based on Lewis's first wife, Grace Livingstone Hegger, an attractive "beauty editor at *Vogue*" who was from a once-wealthy family and was a "sophisticated and ultra-feminine Easterner." Although she lived in New York her entire life, she spoke with an English accent. Lewis imagined what Gopher Prairie seemed like to "Gracie" and imparted these sentiments to Carol. Brooke Allen, "Sinclair Lewis: The Bard of Discontents," *Hudson Review* (Spring 2003), 195–96.
11. According to his second wife, Lewis cared deeply for the "dirt farmers, 'Svenska' (Scandinavian) and 'Dutch' (German)," of Minnesota and, in a similar vein, he favored the small business man and entrepreneur and "hated the corporation empires." Dorothy Thompson, "The Boy and Man from Sauk Centre," *Atlantic Monthly* 206 (November 1960).
12. In 1993, John Updike wrote that Lewis was "at last fading from the bookshops." John Updike, "Exile on Main Street," *New Yorker* (May 17, 1993), 91. More than twenty years before, George Douglas argued that "Lewis is not a highly regarded writer today, and few critics are well disposed either to his art or to his subject matter." George H. Douglas, "*Main Street* after Fifty Years," *Prairie Schooner* 44.4 (Winter 1970/1971), 338. Both Updike and Douglas believed that *Main Street* had been wildly misunderstood.
13. Edward Relph, *Place and Placelessness* (London: Pion Limited, 1976), 38–39.
14. Relph, *Place and Placelessness*, 92–93.

15. On the popularity of Riley during this era, see John E. Miller, "The Funeral of Beloved Hoosier Poet, James Whitcomb Riley," *Studies in Midwestern History* 2.6 (July 2016), 70–78.
16. John T. Frederick to Ruth Suckow, April 27, 1920, John T. Frederick Papers, University of Iowa Archives; Leedice McAnelly Kissane, *Ruth Suckow* (New York: Twayne Publishers, Inc., 1969), 24.
17. Kissane, *Ruth Suckow*, 11; Margaret Stewart Omrcanin, *Ruth Suckow: A Critical Study of Her Fiction* (Philadelphia: Dorrance & Company, 1972), 19, 50.
18. Omrcanin, *Ruth Suckow*, 22–29, 55 (quotations on pages 26 and 29).
19. Suckow, "The Folk Idea in American Life," *Scribner's Magazine* 88 (September 1930), 246–49 (source of quotation); Suckow, "I Could Write, If Only—," *Outlook*, March 21, 1928.
20. Suckow, "The Folk Idea in American Life," 247, 252, 255. Suckow studied at Grinnell College in Iowa and then in Boston, but life in Boston "turned out to be a lonely and obscure existence," so she turned her focus back to Iowa. Kissane, *Ruth Suckow*, 20.
21. Suckow, "The Folk Idea in American Life," 251, 253.
22. Suckow, "The Folk Idea in American Life," 255.
23. Suckow, *New Hope* (New York: Farrar & Rinehart, Inc., 1942); Omrcanin, *Ruth Suckow*, 18, 48–49.
24. Suckow, *Some Others and Myself* (New York: Rinehart and Co., 1952), 176 (source of quotation); Omrcanin, *Ruth Suckow*, 51–52.
25. Suckow, *New Hope*, 25, 80.
26. Suckow, *New Hope*, 19, 42, 45.
27. Suckow, *New Hope*, 43, 46.
28. Suckow, *New Hope*, 27, 60.
29. Suckow, *New Hope*, 97.
30. Suckow, *New Hope*, 328.
31. Suckow, *New Hope*, 15, 22–23, 29, 31, 42, 48, 56–57, 67, 108–109, 120, 140, 145, 157, 161, 183, 311.
32. Suckow, "Comments and Addenda," *Carry-Over* (New York, Fararr & Rinehart, Inc., 1936), ix.
33. Suckow, "Comments and Addenda," vii (source of quotation); Kissane, *Ruth Suckow*, 52.
34. Suckow, *New Hope*, 304.
35. Ruth Suckow to John T. Frederick, September 29, 1925, John T. Frederick Papers, University of Iowa Archives. Although Suckow did not want her work to be too narrowly construed, it was strongly midwestern. Abigail Ann Hamblen, "'The Poetry of Place': The Early Work of Ruth Suckow," *The Husk* 40.3 (March 1961), 75.
36. Suckow, "Comments and Addenda," viii.
37. Suckow, "Comments and Addenda," viii.

38. Suckow, "Middle Western Literature," *English Journal* 21 (March 1932), 176.
39. Unpublished notes quoted in Omrcanin, *Ruth Suckow*, 93.
40. Hamblen, "'The Poetry of Place,'" 77.
41. Ruth Suckow to John T. Frederick, September 21, 1943, John T. Frederick Papers, University of Iowa Archives. An acquaintance from Suckow's time in Iowa City remembered that "She believed it is a help to others to be shown more than they can see." Kissane, *Ruth Suckow*, 161, quoting letter from Mrs. John M. Bridgham.
42. Omrcanin, *Ruth Suckow*, 95, quoting B.E. Boothe.

Tom Perrin

Edited for the Old Lady in Dubuque

The Middlebrow Literature of the Midwest

Despite the novel's setting on Long Island, Nick Carraway, the narrator of F. Scott Fitzgerald's *The Great Gatsby*, famously declares that the book has been "a story of the West, after all": the "Middle West," where both Nick and Fitzgerald originated.[1] Why? The solution to this conundrum exemplifies the argument of this essay: Nick's journey of upward mobility from hardware-wholesaler's son to New York financier—a journey we might describe as middlebrow—stands in tension with a midwestern regionalist worldview in which home is where the heart is, small-town life is best, and the big city is fraught with corruption and danger. After having studied at Yale and fought in World War I, for Nick, "the Middle West now seemed like the ragged edge of the universe," and he is "keenly aware of [New York's] superiority to the bored, sprawling, swollen towns beyond the Ohio."[2] Yet this mistaken belief in the city's superiority produces tragedy, not just for Nick, but for the other "Westerners" too: Gatsby (who attends college in Minnesota), Tom (from Lake Forest, Illinois), Daisy, and Jordan (both from Kentucky, here characterized as midwestern). All have, for Nick, "some deficiency [...] which made us subtly unadaptable to Eastern life."[3] At the end of the novel, Nick returns to "my Middle West," the place he is "a part of," "where dwellings are still called through decades by a family's name."[4]

To consider middlebrow literary culture from the early twentieth-century Midwest is typically to consider two different value systems that are related but in tension with one another. Midwestern literature has frequently been identified as inhabiting a regionalist paradigm that celebrates rural community.[5] By contrast, middlebrow literature is often engaged in smoothing out the anxieties of upward mobility and cosmopolitan, urban life.[6] Middlebrow and regionalist literatures, then, deal with similar problems and anxieties—the rise of urban and suburban life, and of industrial and knowledge economies, and the corresponding decline of rural, farming communities. Both genres are also fraught with ambivalence and anxiety: never merely bucolic, regionalist literature frequently paints farm life as both precarious and back-breaking, while middlebrow literature frets continually about the inauthenticity of white-collar existence. Yet, in the end, a defining feature of regionalist literature is its ambivalent celebration of the rural as distinct from the urban, the old ways as opposed to the new. By contrast, a defining feature of the middlebrow is its similarly ambivalent celebration of precisely the opposite. When midwestern authors write middlebrow literature, the result typically centers on managing this dialectic. Sometimes the farm wins, sometimes the office; sometimes the protagonist synthesizes the two paradigms. But in any case, the midwestern middlebrow often takes the form of a contest between the country and the city, with nothing other than the meaning of modern existence at stake.

This chapter examines this issue by means of four primary case studies: a magazine and three novels. The relatively short-lived magazine *The Chicagoan* constitutes a fascinating case study because of the tensions inherent in its very project. The novels are Booth Tarkington's *The Magnificent Ambersons* (1918), Sinclair Lewis's *Arrowsmith* (1925), and Edna Ferber's *So Big* (1924). Why these? These three novels were received in exemplarily middlebrow fashion, both selling in huge numbers and receiving significant critical acclaim. *So Big* and *Arrowsmith* climbed high on the *Publishers Weekly* bestseller list (Tarkington was also in general a perennial bestseller, but *The Magnificent Ambersons* was released before any national publication regularly published a list), and all three won the Pulitzer Prize (although Lewis declined it, disapproving of the Prize's middlebrow commitment to "wholesome [...] manners and manhood").[7] Lewis also won the Nobel Prize in 1930. Tarkington, in addition, received honorary doctorates from Princeton, Columbia, and a number of other institutions. All three novels were adapted into Hollywood feature films, *So Big* on three separate occasions. Orson Welles's celebrated adaptation of *The Magnificent Ambersons* has more than once been named as one of the best films of all time, and John Ford's adaptation of *Arrowsmith* was nominated for four Oscars. In addition, each novel is middlebrow in form. Each, for instance, self-consciously treats its protagonist's life as a *Bildung* narrative, a hallmark of middlebrow literature.⁸ Finally, Lewis, in particular, had a career-long interest in the unhealthy relationship between capitalism and culture that would, after 1945, spawn much U.S. periodical discourse on the middlebrow. Indeed, his 1922 novel *Babbitt*, with its talk of "capitaliz[ing] Culture" in order to make it into "an adornment and advertisement for a city," sometimes functioned as both a blueprint and a shorthand for theories of kitsch and the middlebrow.⁹

Each author was born in the Midwest: Lewis in Minnesota, Ferber in Michigan, and Tarkington in Indiana. Each also spent at least some of their adult life in the Midwest, and made the Midwest the setting of multiple novels—including each one under consideration here. Tarkington in particular maintained a house in Indiana throughout his life and considered his midwestern-ness a major part of his identity.

What do we gain by examining middlebrow culture in a specifically midwestern context? From a midwestern point of view, such an examination helps us to see how literature that clearly frames itself as geographically and culturally specific to the Midwest need not be considered solely through the lens of regionalism. From the point of view of middlebrow studies, focusing on the Midwest produces a different picture of the middlebrow than the characteristic focus on New York and its suburbs. Indeed, we might go as far as to say that middlebrow studies has overlooked a rich seam of middlebrow culture by failing to focus on the Midwest. For, as the title of this essay (taken from *The New Yorker*'s famous editorial quip) suggests, it was precisely by designating the Midwest as unhip, stodgy, and middlebrow, that the coastal cities were able to imagine themselves as havens of cosmopolitan sophistication. *The New Yorker* was *The New Yorker* because it was (unlike the old lady from Dubuque) neither midwestern nor middlebrow. That is to say, as Tad Friend wrote in the *New Republic* in 1992, the concept of the middlebrow might be "exemplified by a grandmother rocking on a porch somewhere near Decatur, Illinois."¹⁰ Finally, the synthesis of the regional and the middlebrow reveals a new set of artistic responses to the anxieties about modernity to which both paradigms were responding.

As is quite well known, so-called middlebrow culture emerged, in the United States, out of the self-culture of the rising nineteenth-century middle classes.¹¹ Middlebrow culture helped build cultural capital for families ascending from the working to the middle classes, and was as such exemplified by tastemaking projects such as the Book-of-the-Month Club, or ready-made sets of canonical texts such as Charles Eliot's Five-Foot Shelf of Classics. As the century wore on, middlebrow culture became the culture of a "professional-managerial class" working in burgeoning knowledge economies, such as advertising, whose members relied on the possession of cultural capital in order to succeed at their jobs.[12]

The circulation of the term itself was strongly linked with the ascendancy of modernism, whose own possession of cultural capital relied on the disavowal of its place in such an economy.[13] The term circulated most widely in the United Kingdom in the 1920s and in the United States during the 1950s. Its circulation was driven by intellectuals sympathetic to modernism, such as Virginia Woolf and Dwight Macdonald, who used it as a way of dismissively identifying modernism's Other. For example, Virginia Woolf famously argued that, while popular fiction concerned itself with executing tired novelistic clichés, the new, modernist breed of writers would depict the world as they truly experienced it: the modernist "could base his work upon his own feeling and not upon convention."[14] This was not true, of course—as the many satirical depictions of it that lined the pages of middlebrow magazines showed, modernism had an easily identifiable set of tics and moves. But the myth of modernist artistic purity could be upheld by the creation of another figure: the middlebrow—one whose affinity for art was purely conventional, and grounded not in aesthetics but in social climbing. If the modernist writer was hot "in pursuit of ... art itself [or] life itself," the middlebrow's art was "mixed indistinguishably, and rather nastily, with money, fame, power, or prestige"—everything modernism defined itself against.[15] "Middlebrow" was at the same time taken up by middlebrow magazines such as *Life* and *Harper's*, who gleefully took up the parlor game of dividing cultural artifacts according to their brow-height.[16]

For all these reasons, U.S. middlebrow culture has tended to be associated with cities and suburbs, New York City and its environs in particular—classic middlebrow novels, such as Sloan Wilson's *The Man in the Gray Flannel Suit* and Herman Wouk's *Marjorie Morningstar*, are set in New York and its suburbs. Both the rise of the middle classes and the displacement of farming and manufacturing by the knowledge economy involved the flow of populations from rural to urban areas, and the middlebrow culture that documented these movements reflected its urban focus. One of middlebrow culture's most famous Midwesterners, Stuart Pratt Sherman, editor of the influential *Books* supplement of the *New York Herald Tribune*, enacted this shift, leaving his professorship at the University of Illinois and moving to New York in order to take up the position that made his national reputation. In addition, the concept of the middlebrow was most fully theorized in the United States by critics associated with the leftist-modernist journal *Partisan Review*—Dwight Macdonald, Clement Greenberg, Phillip Rahv, and others—a group so centered on Manhattan that posterity labels them the "New York Intellectuals."[17]

By contrast, regional literatures—those of the Midwest and the South in particular—are often seen as having a somewhat different project. Instead of wrangling with readerly anxiety about modernity by ultimately, ambivalently, accepting it, as middlebrow literature tended to, regionalist literature disavowed modernity's claims. Wendy Griswold characterizes regionalist literature as "pastoral," in one of William Empson's well-known "versions," insofar as it is structured by what she calls a "retreat-refresh-return movement."[18] For a largely urban and suburban reading public, regionalist literature facilitated a vicarious holiday from modern life that would allow the reader to return to that life refreshed. In the conflicted-yet-ultimately-green world of regionalist literature, rural simplicity invariably trumps a resented middlebrow sophistication. For Griswold, the quintessential sentiment is encapsulated in a line from Leonardo Sciascia's regionalist crime novel *The Day of the Owl*: "I'm not a well-read man: but there's one or two things I do know, and they're enough for me."[19] In regionalism, rural characters, whose innate honesty and goodness are signaled by "a deep suspicion" of the middlebrow shibboleths of "reading, writing, and/or education," typically battle and prevail against phony urban incomers.[20]

Yet it is easy enough to see how the apparent opposition between regionalism and the middlebrow might be understood dialectically. If the cultural currency of the moment was anxiety about modernity, regionalism and the middlebrow might be seen as two sides of its same coin.

In *The Chicagoan*—which ran in its initial version from 1926 to 1935—we can clearly see how a text could play both sides of an opposition in the service of a single argument. *The Chicagoan* was a periodical shamelessly imitative of *The New Yorker*, but centered on the Midwest, as opposed to the Northeast. Yet, in *The New Yorker*'s economy of cultural capital, the magazine's success flowed from a New York sophistication imagined precisely in opposition to the Midwest: it was, famously, "not edited for the old lady in Dubuque."[21] The *Chicagoan*'s editorial strategy, exemplified by its direct engagement with *New Yorker* editor Harold Ross's pithy dismissal of the Midwest, provides a further instance of midwestern middlebrow culture resolving its inherent tensions.

Protesting its anti-regionalism a little too much, the magazine distanced itself from the rural Midwest in order to present Chicago as a national metropolis equal to New York. It mocked, for instance, the midwestern regional genre inaugurated by Ferber's *So Big*, "the novel of the Nordic farm community," as a mere "formula which is apparently good for a hundred thousand copies to any author able to put it over."[22] Yet in 1932 it included *So Big* in "Chicago's Five-Foot Shelf": a list of essential books featuring Chicago in clear imitation of Eliot's foundational middlebrow institution, the Harvard Five-Foot Shelf of Classics.[23]

The magazine treated *The New Yorker* in a similar fashion. The briefest glimpse of the magazine reveals *The New Yorker* as its obvious progenitor: its fonts, its illustrations, and its ironic tone are all almost identical—early issues even open with a Chicago-centric "Talk of the Town" column. Yet its pages were also filled with a ressentiment-driven mockery of Manhattan. A 1927 sketch skewered a provincial "New Yorker" incredulous at meeting a sophisticated Chicagoan who claims never to have witnessed either a hold-up or a murder.[24] Ross's quip about the old lady in Dubuque seems in particular to have stuck in the magazine's various editors' craws. Again taking aim at New York provincialism, a 1929 cartoon depicting "The New Yorker's Map of The United States" labels every city in America "Dubuque" (with the sardonic exceptions of "Hollywood," "Reno," "Atlantic City," and "Palm Beach").[25] In like fashion, a 1933 advert shouts that "The old lady from Dubuque reads THE CHICAGOAN!" informing any *New Yorker* reader snobbish enough to dismiss her that "You'd love her if you really knew her."[26] On the other hand, a 1930 item on subscribers outside Chicago notes that the editor has asked that "no envelopes postmarked Dubuque be brought to this desk."[27] Whether championing or mocking the Midwest, imitating or thumbing its nose at New York City, though, it is not difficult to see a common anxiety driving *The Chicagoan*: its worry about whether or not the Second City was truly Manhattan's equal.

Like *The Chicagoan*, Booth Tarkington's *The Magnificent Ambersons* has little nostalgia for the pastoral Midwest. Its antibucolic setting is one of "old dead bugg[ies]," "lonesome rail fences," "frozen barnyards," and "metallic earth."²⁸ Amid this sterile landscape the Amberson family runs its mini-metropolis, a fictionalized version of Indianapolis, as a fiefdom. Yet the family is so turned in upon itself that it fails to notice as it is supplanted by a modern industrial middle class whose labor transforms the city.

The novel's protagonist and reluctant *Bildungsheld* is George Amberson Minafer, pig-headed heir to what he assumes is a boundless family fortune. Central to his aristocratic creed is the belief that "being things is rather better than doing things."²⁹ His angry disdain for new-money industrialists leads him, in an act of hubris that leads to his downfall, to break up his widowed mother's relationship with her childhood sweetheart, automobile tycoon Eugene Morgan, on the grounds that Morgan is engaged in "trade."³⁰

Following the deaths of his grandfather and mother, George discovers that the family, which has mismanaged its money because of its mistrust of modern industry, is penniless. Not only that, but the Ambersons have, unnoticed by them, been completely forgotten by the city's new governing middle class. In one humiliating scene George discovers that the Ambersons do not appear in a new "Civic History" of the "500 Most Prominent Citizens and Families in the History of the City."³¹ George is forced into his hated trade, becoming an explosives technician in order to earn the danger money necessary to support both himself and his old-maid aunt, but subsequently becoming an invalid after being run down by (what else?) a motor car. The novel ends with George's imminent recovery and hinted marriage to his own longtime sweetheart, Eugene's daughter Lucy. Lucy can finally accept him now that he has given up his aristocratic airs and become a modern member of the middle classes, a "most practical young man."³²

The movement of the novel is one in which the middlebrow supplants the regional. Not only is Tarkington's Midwest arid and unattractive, but its "old stock" is composed of "provincial snobs."³³ By contrast, the middle class that displaces them are coded as middlebrow cultural capital–mongers. The town's new leaders are boosters (as they typically also are in Lewis's work); their "motto is 'Boost! Don't Knock!'"[34] Like Lewis's Babbitt, they fetishize culture and education as markers of the city's quality: they idealize "beauty." "They boasted of their libraries, of their monuments and statues," and "They boasted of their schools," because all these totems demonstrate how much "more prosperous [their] beloved city" has become.[35]

It is true that Tarkington exhibits a certain amount of ambivalence about the rise of the middlebrow. The new city is defined by the dirtiness of industry: "as the town grew, it grew dirty with an incredible completeness." Its buildings are "begrimed," its statues covered in "soot" and its schools and people "dirty." Its people are "hustlers" whose prosperity is mere "credit at the bank" rather than property. Their worship of the "god of their market-place" will, the narrator predicts, lead them ultimately to "serfdom."[36] Yet compared to the overwhelming prejudice and self-destructive idiocy of the Ambersons the middlebrows are heroes. Their serfdom beats a regionalist self-immolation too grounded in bigotry ever to resemble martyrdom.

By contrast, the most ostensibly straightforwardly regionalist of the novels under discussion is Lewis's *Arrowsmith*, and yet its use of regionalist tropes is also complex. The novel makes an argument about the value of pure, disinterested scholarship. The book is a picaresque *Bildungsroman* that tells the life story of MD Martin Arrowsmith. Born and raised in the fictional midwestern state of Winnemac, the setting for five of Lewis's novels, Martin attends college and medical school at the University of Winnemac, before working as a private practitioner, a public-health official, and a medical researcher in Zenith, Winnemac; Chicago; New York City; North Dakota; and ultimately a cabin in the Vermont woods.

Martin's life takes the form of a back-and-forth progress between, on the one hand, a phony path leading to personal enrichment and scientific reputation, and, on the other, the authentic path of honest science for its own sake, without concern for reward. Interestingly for the purposes of this chapter, the novel signifies inauthenticity with the tropes of middlebrow culture, while it strongly aligns truth and value with rural life.

Thus, the characters who tempt Martin away from the straight path of the intellectual anchorite are, in typical Lewis fashion, parodic avatars of middlebrow self-culture. Madeline Fox, the shallow girl Martin dates before marrying his true love, Leora, is a graduate student in English who values fiction only for the air of distinction it lends her: "She believed herself to be a connoisseur of literature; the fortunate to whom she gave her approval were Hardy, Meredith, Howells, and Thackeray, none of whom she had read for five years."[37] Angus Duer, a smooth go-getter with whom Martin attends medical school, and in whose deluxe private practice Martin later temporarily sells his soul, needles Martin about his lack of middlebrow sophistication: "How's your French verbs? How many big novels have you ever read? Who's the premier of Austro-Hungary?"[38] As far as Angus is concerned, Martin could do with Eliot's Five-Foot Shelf; and indeed, the memory of Angus's scorn drives Martin at one stage to "get educated" by reading history books, Conrad, and Henry James.[39]

By contrast, authentic experience tends to appear against a rural backdrop. As a student, Martin "experienced a miracle" during a summer job as a telephone lineman in Montana:

> He was atop a pole and suddenly, for no clear cause, his eyes opened and he saw; as though he had just awakened he saw that the prairie was vast, that the sun was kindly on rough pasture and ripening wheat, on the old horses, the easy, broad-beamed, friendly horses, and on his red-faced jocose companions; he saw that the meadow larks were jubilant, and blackbirds shining by little pools, and with the living sun all life was living. Suppose the Angus Duers and Irving Watterses were tight tradesmen. What of it? "I'm HERE!" he gloated.[40]

In the light of this epiphany of the miraculousness of the rural American landscape, Martin's status anxiety about Duer and his middlebrow classmates transforms into a "gloating" awareness of them as mere "tight tradesmen." Martin's struggle is to learn, over and over again, that he is, and ought to be, a "backwoods hick." As his beloved first wife, Leora, berates him: "Are you going on for the rest of your life, stumbling into respectability and having to be dug out again? Will you never learn you're a barbarian?"[41] At the end of the novel Martin leaves the political games and glad-handing of mainstream scientific research, as well as a private laboratory bankrolled by his socialite second wife, Joyce, in order to retreat to "Birdies' Rest," a remote laboratory in the Vermont woods, and work with his fellow scientist Terry Wickett. At the end of the novel, "Martin Arrowsmith and Terry Wickett lolled in a clumsy boat" on their lake, looking gleefully ahead to a future in which they can spend "two or three years" working on "quinine derivatives" related to a bacteria-eating compound, at the end of which they will "probably [...] fail."[42] But they will not have to pretend to anyone that they have succeeded. Pastoral retreat would seem to trump urban acquiescence.

Yet Lewis's regionalist pastoral sits strangely. Cutting-edge medical research, a field that is intrinsically contemporary and temperamentally urban, is an odd choice for Lewis's Thoreauvian utopia. Joyce's dismissal of Birdies' Rest as an "absurd" fantasy of "[t]he simple life," arising out of her bitterness at Martin's abandonment of her and their son, is surely supposed preemptively to defuse the reader's own similar criticism—and yet there is something to it.[43] Birdies' Rest reflects the novel's ultimate ambivalence about middlebrow institutions: it admires, for instance, universities as research centers, but disdains them as rehearsal rooms for the performance of middle-classness; it lionizes modern science for its power to cure, but disdains scientific institutions for their selfishness and corruption.

The novel may be more middlebrow than it at first appears. Lewis mostly writes off Martin's self-improvement project of reading the classics as a youthful misstep, yet at the same time, "in those long intense evenings of reading with Leora he advanced a step or two toward the tragic enchantments of [his mentor's] world."[44] At the University of Winnemac, Martin's fraternity brothers resent the fetishization of science through which Martin imagines himself superior to "us lowbrows." Yet at the same time he resentfully feels his inability to socialize with "those highbrows" with whom his later peers surround themselves, and he bristles when Joyce insults him as one of "these tired highbrows."[45] Ever betwixt and between, perhaps his ambivalence makes Martin a little middlebrow after all.

Lewis's gesture at synthesizing middlebrow and regionalist ideologies had found fuller expression the year before *Arrowsmith* was published, in Edna Ferber's *So Big*. *So Big* stages an opposition between farmer Selina DeJong and her financier son Dirk (the novel's titular "So Big"). Selina is honest but poor; farming is precarious and allows her little opportunity for the "self-expression" she craves.[46] Dirk has the wealth and freedom his mother has desired for him, but is shallow and materialistic. The opposition is resolved in the person of Dallas O'Mara, a graphic designer whose work allows her to combine authentic artistic expression with middlebrow financial comfort.

Selina is the daughter of a gambler whose winnings afford his daughter a middle-class education but no security. She is a voracious middlebrow reader of Jane Austen, Mrs. E.D.E.N. Southworth, *Godey's Lady's Book*, and the *Fireside Companion*, and her reading breeds in her the desire to become a writer and a fervent love of "beauty."[47] Following the death of her father, Selina is forced to relocate to High Prairie, a Dutch farming community a day's ride from Chicago. Selina's "beauty-loving eye," which finds pleasure in the prairie's "[m]ile after mile of cabbage fields, jade-green against the earth" makes her the butt of jokes among the farmers.[48] Distrusted by the locals, she works as a school teacher before marrying Pervus DeJong, a hard-luck farmer whose distrust of modern methods keeps him in poverty. The back-breaking work he and Selina are forced to perform in order to keep the farm alive quashes her dreams of the artistic pursuit of beauty.

Following Pervus's early death from pneumonia, Selina improves the farm enough to make money, but her work continues to be intolerably hard since she saves everything she makes in order to provide "[t]he best thing for Dirk," so he will never have to "go to the Haymarket" and sell vegetables.[49] She wants Dirk to have the life she could not: "Beauty! ... Rooms in candle-light. Leisure. Colour. Travel. Books. Music. People—all kinds of people. Work that you love. And growth—growth and watching people grow. Feeling very strongly about things and then developing that feeling to—to make something fine come of it."[50]

Delighted that Dirk wants to study "Languages and literature" instead of an "Agricultural course," Selina sends him to the University of Chicago, here named "Midwest University," which she imagines as a middlebrow ideal of scholarship: "Oxford. Cambridge. Dons. Ivy. Punting. Prints. Mullioned windows. Books. Discussion. Literary clubs."[51]

However, the ideal turns out to be a lie: earnest students who "ask only for bread—the bread of knowledge," receive instead a "stone."[52] As in *Arrowsmith*, college is really an upper-middle-class finishing school. It breeds snobbery in Dirk. He cuts out his closest friend, an Iowa farm girl, in order to gain entrance into a fraternity. After university he abandons an apprenticeship as an architect in order to become a financier and a member of the *"jeunesse dorée."*[53] Selina berates him for "desert[ing] ... Beauty!"—for having stopped reading and dreaming and for having become a shallow pursuer of wealth.[54]

However, Ferber imagines a specifically modern synthesis of the emptiness of middlebrow social climbing and the unending toil of regionalist rural life. The solution lies in Dallas O'Mara, a graphic artist who appears in the narrative's last act. So well-reputed that she can afford to charge Dirk's company 1500 dollars for producing a single advertisement, she also has the integrity to travel to Paris to study portraiture. Despite her commercial career, she is a prize-winning fine artist. Her work in life classes at the Art Institute is "insultingly superior to that of the men and women about her."[55] She "look[s] like Helen of Troy."[56] She adores Selina and her farm, and wants to paint her portrait, as someone who is "really distinguished looking—distinguishedly American" (though in true middlebrow fashion she notes that the portrait of Selina will "make me famous at one leap").[57] At the climax of the novel she turns down Dirk's suit in favor of Roelf Pool, a former High Prairie farm boy, once mentored by the young Selina, who has become a distinguished artist in Paris. Dirk concludes the novel dejectedly saying to himself "over and over, 'You're nothing but a rubber stamp.'"[58]

If *The Magnificent Ambersons* narrates modern industry's revitalization of tired provincial cities, and *Arrowsmith* lionizes modern scientific research by reframing it as a rural profession, then in the universe of *So Big*, modern, middlebrow knowledge fields such as graphic art allow one happily to make money while at the same time retaining one's soul. These case studies of the midwestern middlebrow, then, present a particular network of tropes. Their pages represent early twentieth-century anxieties about modernity by depicting the rise of industrial society, knowledge professions, research science, and the urban metropolis itself. But, notably, in each case, the seemingly uneasy pairing of middlebrow and regionalist values resolves an argument in which readers could assuage such anxieties for themselves.

Notes

1. F. Scott Fitzgerald, *The Great Gatsby* (New York: Scribner, 2004), 176; 3.
2. Ibid., 3.
3. Ibid., 3; 176.
4. Ibid., 176.
5. See, e.g., David Marion Holman, *A Certain Slant of Light: Regionalism and the Form of Southern and Midwestern Fiction* (Baton Rouge: Louisiana State University Press, 1995); Wendy Griswold, *Regionalism and the Reading Class* (Chicago: University of Chicago Press, 2008).
6. See, e.g., Joan Shelley Rubin, *The Making of Middlebrow Culture* (Chapel Hill: University of North Carolina Press, 1992); Janice A. Radway, *A Feeling for Books: The Book-of-the-Month Club, Literary Taste, and Middle-Class Desire* (Chapel Hill: University of North Carolina Press, 1997).
7. "Lewis Refuses Pulitzer Prize," *New York Times*, May 6, 1926, A1.
8. See Tom Perrin, "Rebuilding *Bildung*: The Middlebrow Novel of Aesthetic Education in the Mid-Twentieth-Century US," *Novel: A Forum on Fiction* 44.3 (Fall 2011): 382–401.
9. Sinclair Lewis, *Babbitt* (New York: Oxford University Press, 2010), 218. On *Babbitt* as a blueprint for theories of the middlebrow see, e.g., Rubin, *Making*, 30.
10. Tad Friend, "The Case for Middlebrow," in *Lost in Mongolia: Travels in Hollywood and Other Foreign Lands* (New York: AtRandom, 2001), 135. Thanks to Jon Lauck for this quotation and for his aid with this point generally.
11. On "self-culture," see Rubin, *Making*.
12. Also see Radway, *Feeling*, especially page 221.
13. See Perrin, *The Aesthetics of Middlebrow Fiction: Popular US Novels, Modernism, and Form, 1945–75* (New York: Palgrave Macmillan, 2015).
14. Virginia Woolf, "Modern Fiction," in *Theory of the Novel: A Historical Approach*, ed. Michael McKeon (Baltimore: The Johns Hopkins University Press, 2000), 741.
15. Woolf, "Middlebrow," in *The Death of the Moth, and Other Essays* (Adelaide: The University of Adelaide, 2015), https://ebooks.adelaide.edu.au/w/woolf/virginia/w91d/chapter22.html.
16. See Dwight Macdonald, "Masscult and Midcult," in *Against the American Grain* (New York: Random House, 1962), 3–75; "Everyday Tastes from High-Brow to Low-Brow Are Classified on Chart," *Life*, April 11, 1949, 100–101; Russell Lynes, "Highbrow, Lowbrow, Middlebrow," *Harper's Magazine* 198.1185 (1949): 19–28.

17. See, e.g., Macdonald, "Masscult"; Clement Greenberg, "Avant-Garde and Kitsch," in *Mass Culture: The Popular Arts in America*, edited by Bernard Rosenberg and David Manning White (Glencoe, IL: The Free Press, 1957), 98–107; John Berryman et al., "The State of American Writing: 1948: A Symposium," *Partisan Review* 15.8 (1948): 855–93.
18. Griswold, *Regionalism*, 28. See William Empson, *Some Versions of Pastoral* (New York: New Directions, 1974).
19. Quoted in Griswold, *Regionalism*, 25.
20. Ibid., 21.
21. "Of All Things," *The New Yorker*, February 21, 1925, 2.
22. Susan Wilbur, "Books: Stories Strung on Strings," *The Chicagoan* 5.7 (June 1928), 26.
23. Wilbur, "Chicago's Five Foot Shelf: Spring Cleaning Comes to the Library," *The Chicagoan* 12.8 (March 1932), 18.
24. R.G.B., "Conversation with Significance," *The Chicagoan* 4.3 (October 1927), 13.
25. "The New Yorker's Map of the United States," *The Chicagoan* 7.8 (June 1929), 10.
26. "The Old Lady from Dubuque Reads The CHICAGOAN!" *The Chicagoan* 13.9 (April 1933), 17.
27. "Melancholia," *The Chicagoan* 10.3 (October 1930), 9.
28. Booth Tarkington, *The Magnificent Ambersons* (Salt Lake City: Project Gutenberg, 2009), Kindle location 925.
29. Ibid., Kindle location 1825.
30. Ibid., Kindle location 2147.
31. Ibid., Kindle location 4006.
32. Ibid., Kindle location 3956.
33. Ibid., Kindle location 3288; 2149.
34. Ibid., Kindle location 3296.
35. Ibid., Kindle location 3301; 3307; 3300.
36. Ibid., Kindle location 3305; 3306; 3307; 3296; 3304; 3315; 3317.
37. Sinclair Lewis, *Arrowsmith* (Indooroopilly: Project Gutenberg Australia, 2002), Kindle location 367.
38. Ibid., Kindle location 457.
39. Ibid., Kindle location 2729.
40. Ibid., Kindle location 488.
41. Ibid., Kindle location 3280; 3472.
42. Ibid., Kindle location 7149; 7082; 7151.
43. Ibid., Kindle location 7049.
44. Ibid., Kindle location 2697.
45. Ibid., Kindle location 454; 3307; 7050.
46. Edna Ferber, *So Big* (New York: Harper Perennial, 2000), 146.
47. See ibid., 4; 9; 16.
48. Ibid., 16.

49. Ibid., 142; 145.
50. Ibid., 146.
51. Ibid., 156.
52. Ibid., 161.
53. Ibid., 205.
54. Ibid., 206.
55. Ibid., 235.
56. Ibid., 251.
57. Ibid., 250.
58. Ibid., 251.

| Contributors

**Jeremy Beer** is the editor of *America Moved: Booth Tarkington's Memoirs of Time and Place, 1869–1928* (Wipf and Stock, 2015), and the author of *The Philanthropic Revolution: An Alternative History of American Charity* (Penn Press, 2015). He is currently at work on a biography of the great midwestern baseball player Oscar Charleston. A native of Indiana, Beer is the president of the American Ideas Institute and a principal partner at American Philanthropic, LLC.

**Allan C. Carlson,** born and raised in Des Moines, Iowa, received a BA degree from Augustana College (Illinois) and a PhD in Modern European History from Ohio University. He has taught at Gettysburg College, the John Paul II Institute for Studies on Marriage and Family at the Catholic University of America, and Hillsdale College. He served as the president of several "think tanks," most recently at The Howard Center for Family, Religion & Society, from which he retired in 2015. In 1988, President Ronald Reagan appointed him to The National Commission on Children, on which he served until 1993. Carlson has contributed over 50 essays to published anthologies and is the author of fourteen books, including *The New Agrarian Mind: The Movement Toward Decentralist Thought in 20th Century America; The "American Way": Family and Community in the Shaping of the American Identity;* and most recently *Family Cycles: Strength, Decline & Renewal in American Domestic Life, 1630–2000.* He has also written for *The Washington Post (Outlook Section), The Wall Street Journal, Chicago Tribune, Detroit News, USA Today,* and many other newspapers and periodicals. He currently resides on his wife's family farm in northern Illinois, where they raise chickens and entertain the grandchildren.

**Harl A. Dalstrom,** Professor Emeritus of History, University of Nebraska at Omaha, received a BA degree (1958) and MA (1959) from the Municipal University of Omaha (now the University of

Nebraska-Omaha) and a PhD from the University of Nebraska (Lincoln), in 1965. He taught at the University of Omaha/University of Nebraska-Omaha for nearly forty years, specializing in the history of Nebraska and the Great Plains. Dalstrom has authored or co-authored works on diverse topics on the history of Plains and Midwest. He sees value in using fiction to teach history, and the present essay began as a paper presented at the Missouri Valley History Conference, Omaha, in March 1989. Other projects, including articles on Bess Streeter Aldrich, intervened before the current work was finished. This essay is presented in memory of his good friend and graduate school colleague, Dr. James T. King, a fine historian and distinguished alumnus of Hastings College.

**Cherie Dargan** grew up in Central Iowa before going to college in Springfield, Missouri, where she met and married a young minister. They spent a decade in Newport, Rhode Island, where they had two children and pastored a church before moving back to Iowa. After they divorced, she returned to college. She got her BA in English and Psychology from Buena Vista University, her MA in English from Iowa State, and a second MA in Educational Technology from the University of Northern Iowa. Cherie remarried in 2000: her husband Mike is a librarian and took her to a Ruth Suckow event while they were dating. Mike created the first Suckow website and Suckow's Wikipedia entry. They have two children and two grandsons. She retired from Hawkeye Community College as a professor in the Communications Department in August 2016. She is a writer, blogger, geek, and family historian working on several writing projects.

**Philip A. Greasley** is the General Editor of the *Dictionary of Midwestern Literature: Volume One, The Authors* (Indiana University Press, 2001) and *Volume Two, Dimensions of the Midwestern Literary Imagination* (Indiana University Press, 2016). He has written and presented extensively on midwestern literature, the Chicago Renaissance, and midwestern authors and poets. He is a past president of the Society for the Study of Midwestern Literature, a recipient of the Society's Gwendolyn Brooks Midwestern Heritage Prize for the outstanding article of the year, a recipient of the MidAmerica Award for contributions to the Study of Midwestern Literature, and a long-time continuing corporate

Contributors    283

board member of the Society. In 2013, he retired from the University of Kentucky, where he had served as Associate Professor of English, Dean, University Extension, and Associate Provost/Associate Vice President for University Engagement.

**John E. Hallwas** is Distinguished Professor Emeritus at Western Illinois University. An historian as well as a literary scholar, he has written or edited twenty-eight books related to the Midwest, including titles such as *Western Illinois Heritage* (1984), *Illinois Literature: The Nineteenth Century* (1986), *Spoon River Anthology: An Annotated Edition* (1992), *Cultures in Conflict: A Documentary History of the Mormon War in Illinois* (1996, with Roger Launius), *The Bootlegger: A Story of Small-Town America* (1998), *Keokuk and the Great Dam* (2001), and *Dime Novel Desperadoes: The Notorious Maxwell Brothers* (2008). He has also written dozens of scholarly articles on Illinois literature and history, as well as hundreds of newspaper and magazine articles, plus several history-focused plays. And he has won more than a dozen awards, such as the MidAmerica Award (1994), for literary scholarship, and the Midland Award for "Best Biography from the Midwest." Hallwas speaks widely on a variety of topics, including small-town culture, midwestern authors, and the writing of nonfiction. For more information on him and his books, see his website: www.johnhallwas.jimdo.com.

**Zachary Michael Jack** is the author or editor of many books on agrarian, conservation, environmental, and regional and rural histories, including those nominated for the Theodore Salutous Award and the Benjamin F. Shambaugh Award. An associate professor of English at North Central College, in Naperville, Illinois, Jack teaches courses in writing, leadership, and place studies. A board member of the Midwestern History Association and a past contributor to the *Middle West Review*, Jack has presented at the Newberry Library Seminar in Agriculture, the Northern Great Plains History Conference, and the annual meeting of the Agricultural History Society, among others. He is the seventh generation to make his home on the Iowa farm.

**Jon K. Lauck** received a PhD in economic history from the University of Iowa and a law degree from the University of Minnesota. Lauck is the author of *American Agriculture and the Problem of Monopoly: The Political Economy of Grain Belt Farming, 1953–1980* (University of Nebraska Press, 2000), *Daschle v. Thune: Anatomy of a High Plains Senate Race* (University of Oklahoma Press, 2007), *Prairie Republic: The Political Culture of Dakota Territory, 1879–1889* (University of Oklahoma Press, 2010), and *The Lost Region: Toward a Revival of Midwestern History* (University of Iowa Press, 2013) and co-author and co-editor of *The Plains Political Tradition: Essays on South Dakota Political Culture* (South Dakota State Historical Society Press, 2011) and *The Plains Political Tradition* vol. 2 (South Dakota State Historical Society Press, 2014). Lauck's newest book is *From Warm Center to Ragged Edge: The Erosion of Midwestern Regionalism, 1920–1965* (University of Iowa Press, 2017). Lauck has worked for several years as a full-time professor, a part-time professor, and a lawyer and is currently serving as an adjunct professor of history and political science at the University of South Dakota, as the Associate Editor and Book Review Editor of *Middle West Review*, and as the series editor of *Studies in Midwestern History*. He is the immediate past-president of the Midwestern History Association.

**Robert Loerzel** is a freelance journalist and photographer in Chicago. His historical nonfiction book *Alchemy of Bones: Chicago's Luetgert Murder Case of 1897* was published in 2003 by the University of Illinois Press. His reporting and writing have appeared in many publications, including the *Chicago Tribune, Chicago Sun-Times, Chicago Reader,* and *Chicago* magazine. He has also reported on-air for WBEZ Chicago Public Radio, including stories for the *Curious City* show. Loerzel has won more than 30 awards from press associations for his work, including three Peter Lisagor Awards from the Chicago Headline Club. He served as the president of the Society of Midland Authors from 2009 to 2013.

**John E. Miller** grew up in six midwestern small towns and one Chicago suburb, graduating from Monett (Mo.) High School in 1962. He received a BA degree from the University of Missouri and MA and PhD degrees in history from the University of Wisconsin. After being drafted in 1968, he spent thirteen months as an Army court reporter in Vietnam. He taught mostly twentieth-century American history courses for a year at the University of Tulsa and for twenty-nine years at South Dakota

State University before becoming a full-time writer in 2003. Among his eight books are *Looking for History on Highway 14*, a political biography of Wisconsin governor Philip F. La Follette, and a biography of and two volumes of essays on Laura Ingalls Wilder. His latest books, *Small-Town Dreams: Stories of Midwestern Boys Who Shaped America* and *First We Imagine: 22 Creative South Dakotans Speak on the Subject of Creativity*, were released in 2014. He is currently co-editing a third volume of *The Plains Political Tradition: Essays on South Dakota Political Culture*. He lives with his wife, Kathryn, in Brookings, five blocks west of the South Dakota Art Museum, which was built to house the paintings of Harvey Dunn.

**Tom Perrin** is an assistant professor of English at Huntingdon College. He is the author of *The Aesthetics of Middlebrow Fiction* (Palgrave, 2015). His essays have appeared in *American Literature*, *Novel*, the *Times Literary Supplement*, *Public Books*, and elsewhere.

**Michael J. Pfeifer** is Professor of History at the John Jay College of Criminal Justice and the Graduate Center, City University of New York. His books include *Rou gh Justice: Lynching and American Society, 1878–1947* (University of Illinois Press, 2004), *The Roots of Rough Justice: Origins of American Lynching* (University of Illinois Press, 2011) and, as editor, *Lynching Beyond Dixie: American Mob Violence Beyond the South* (University of Illinois Press, 2013), *Global Lynching and Collective Violence, Vol. 1: Asia, Africa, and the Middle East* (University of Illinois Press, 2017), and *Global Lynching and Collective Violence, Vol. 2: The Americas and Europe* (University of Illinois Press, 2017). He has published numerous articles, including several in the *Journal of American History*: "At the Hands of Parties Unknown?: The State of the Field of Lynching Studies" (December 2014) and "The Northern U.S and the Genesis of Racial Lynching: The Lynching of African-Americans in the Civil War Era" (December 2010). Professor Pfeifer's current research includes work on the cultural and social history of American orchestras and on the regional cultures of American Catholicism.

**Kimberly K. Porter** (PhD, University of Iowa, 1995) is a true Midwesterner, a fifth-generation Iowan. A professor at the University of

North Dakota, she focuses her attention on rural America, particularly the changes wrought by technology and urbanization. She also researches and publishes on subjects related to North Dakota. Her teaching centers on the United States, 1877–1945, as well as on public and oral history. She is the former editor of *The Oral History Review*. She is currently completing a biography of Henry Field, seedsman, politician, and radio broadcaster. When not in the classroom or the archives, Porter can be found on her family's century farm.

**Paul Emory Putz** is a doctoral candidate in history at Baylor University. Born and raised in Nebraska, he spent five years as a high school social studies teacher before beginning PhD work. He is an associate editor for *Studies in Midwestern History,* and his research has been published in *Nebraska History, Chronicles of Oklahoma, The Annals of Iowa* (forthcoming) and *The Journal of the Gilded Age and Progressive Era* (forthcoming). Broadly, his work focuses on themes of religion, print culture, and sports in the twentieth-century American Midwest.

**Elizabeth Raymond** is Professor and Grace A. Griffen Chair in History at the University of Nevada, Reno, where she studies the intersections of landscape, culture, and regional identity, particularly in the Great Basin and the Midwest. The origin, mechanics, and historical evolution of regional sense of place are abiding interests. With photographer Peter Goin, she has published *Changing Mines in America* and *Stopping Time: A Rephotographic Survey of Lake Tahoe*. Other works include *George Wingfield: Owner and Operator of Nevada* and *Comstock Women* (co-edited with Ronald James). She has long been intrigued by matters Midwestern.

**Michael C. Steiner** is Professor Emeritus of American Studies at California State University, Fullerton where he taught a wide range of courses on environmental history, folk culture, the built environment, regionalism, California, and the West from 1975 to 2015. He won a national teaching and advising award from the American Studies Association in 2006, and has twice been a Distinguished Fulbright Chair (in Hungary in 1998–99 and in Poland in 2004). Steiner has authored award-winning essays on Frederick Jackson Turner's sectional thesis and on Walt Disney's Frontierland, and his books include *Regionalists on the Left: Radical Voices from the American West* (Oklahoma, 2013), *Region and Regionalism in the United States* (written with Clarence Mondale, 1988); *Mapping American Culture* (ed. with Wayne Franklin, 1995); and *Many Wests: Place, Culture, and Regional Identity* (ed. with David Wrobel, 1997). He is currently at the beginning stages of a book-length project, tentatively titled *The Idea of the Midwest: An Intellectual and Grassroots History*.

www.ingramcontent.com/pod-product-compliance
Lightning Source LLC
Chambersburg PA
CBHW021429080526
44588CB00009B/478